MATERIAL MEMORY:

DOCUMENTS IN PRE-CONFEDERATION HISTORY

MATERIAL MEMORY:

DOCUMENTS IN PRE-CONFEDERATION HISTORY

Cornelius Jaenen
Department of History, University of Ottawa

Cecilia Morgan
*History Program, Department of Theory and Policy Studies,
OISE/University of Toronto*

Addison-Wesley

An imprint of Addison Wesley Longman Ltd.

Don Mills, Ontario • Reading, Massachusetts • Harlow, England
Melbourne, Australia • Amsterdam, The Netherlands • Bonn, Germany

Publisher:	Brian Henderson
Managing Editor:	Linda Scott
Editors:	Barbara Tessman, Muriel Fiona Napier, Madhu Ranadive
Production Coordinator:	Linda Allison
Manufacturing Coordinator:	Sharon Latta Paterson
Design:	Anthony Leung
Printing and binding:	Webcom Limited

Canadian Cataloguing in Publication Data

    Material memory : documents in pre-Confederation history
Includes bibliographical references.
ISBN 0-673-98479-6

1. Canada - History- To 1763 (New France) - Sources. 2. Canada - History -
1763-1867 - Sources. I. Jaenen, Cornelius J., 1927- . II. Morgan, Cecilia Louise, 1958- .

FC161.M37 1998   971   C98-930200-8
F1032.M37 1998

ISBN 0-673-98479-6

Printed and bound in Canada.

B C D E -WC- 02 01 00

Preface

Material Memory: Documents in Pre-Confederation History examines documents and themes from Canada's early history, beginning with Native societies prior to contact, and ending with the Confederation of the Canadas, Nova Scotia, and New Brunswick in 1867.

The documents suggest how different kinds of colonial societies, each with its own distinctive history, economy, and social structure, have experienced a number of historical events and processes. During the eighteenth and nineteenth centuries there were common themes that linked these societies—the growth of immigration, the rise of urban centres, the development of 'classes,' the formation of political and social reform movements, and the increase (albeit slow and uneven) of state institutions at both regional and local levels. The roles of First Nations societies, and the effects upon them of such political, social, and economic changes are also documented.

Historians must wrestle with using traditional chronological divisions that conform to political, diplomatic, and military events—the 'Conquest' of 1763 or the Rebellion of 1837—or the different kinds of time divisions suggested by research in social history, such as the rise of industrialization and the growth of urban centres. Must everything, for example, lead up to Confederation? Many scholars have questioned whether dividing Canadian history at Confederation is a logical strategy, since so many social, cultural, and economic processes began before 1867 and continued throughout the nineteenth century—immigration, industrialization, class formation, the founding of local and regional institutions, and, in particular, the colonization of Native peoples. Nor can 1867 be taken as a watershed date for all areas, since only a part of what we now think of as 'Canada' either chose to join Confederation or even existed as an administrative entity at the time.

Nevertheless, we have chosen to examine the Confederation of certain areas of British North America as a separate topic, since it was a turning point for some prominent and influential groups, and affected other groups and colonies in a number of legal and administrative ways. However, we hope that those who use this volume will recognize that many of the processes discussed in these documents did not end in 1867.

Keep in mind that historians make choices in determining what they will scrutinize and analyse—it is impossible to be truly comprehensive in studying the past. This collection of documents illustrates central problems and questions in Canadian colonial history; it also suggests how groups considered marginal to some of these events and processes might have experienced or understood them. Some of the themes might be classified as 'traditional'—the role of the state in New France and responsible government; others reflect more recent approaches developed by social historians. This work in social history has begun to alter our understanding of the colonial period, showing us that the experiences of workers, women of different classes, racial, and ethnic backgrounds, immigrants, African-Canadians, and First Nations peoples are essential to our perceptions of the time. It is also beginning to open our eyes to the significance of religious experiences and structures, going beyond the political relations of church and state to look at the impact of religious organization on colonists' daily lives and on colonial societies in general. Where possible, we have suggested how events such as the War of 1812 or the Rebellion of 1837-1838 were also shaped by the categories of race, ethnicity, class, and gender.

Each section of documents is divided into subsections in order to illustrate particular themes—but the past does not always neatly conform to set patterns. Some of these themes overlap, and may be found running through each subsection, or a subsection that examines one theme may also contain others. In discussing the Rebellion, for example, one subsection looks at women's experiences of and reaction to the events of 1837-1838—but it also contains information on British attitudes toward the French-speaking population of Lower Canada.

Historians have pointed out that there are always limits to every source and that, when possible, a range of material should be consulted. Included here are government documents and reports, newspaper articles, business records, letters, and diaries. In evaluating these different kinds of materials, we must ask what a document's purpose was. Who was the intended audience? Was a document produced in order to convince or coerce a wider audience—such as government propaganda during the War of 1812? Was it intended to win concessions from a more powerful body—such as a petition to the Governor asking for his mercy? Or was it meant to convey the experiences and thoughts of an individual to a circle of friends and family, as in the case of Nova Scotia Loyalist Rebecca Byles' letters to her Boston family?

We also present some visual records of colonial society, ones that were created at the time. As well as paintings by colonial artists—male and female, amateur and professional—these include examples of early 'people' photography, and photos of Native artifacts that have been preserved by museums. But just as we must read written material critically, we also cannot assume that paintings and photographs are literal descriptions of reality, or that they are somehow more 'truthful' than written evidence. Landscape painting, for example, often used particular genres and styles that followed European models of what was 'beautiful' and 'worthwhile.' Paintings of Native peoples might conform to European ideals of beauty, or myths of 'noble savages'; portraits of Lower Canadian *habitants* also might be influenced by British stereotypes of French culture or middle-class notions of peasant life. Photographers might persuade subjects to dress up and pose in ways that would appeal to a commercial audience in order to sell their photographs.

Many of the problems Canada faces in the 1990s were also present in the colonial period—the colonization of First Nations, tensions between French- and English-speaking peoples, struggles between employers and workers, discrimination against immigrants, ethnic and racial minorities, conflict over region and religion, and unequal power relations between men and women. Of course, the ways in which colonial societies understood these issues and dealt with them were often quite different from those of the present. We hope that these documents will alert students of Canadian history to the diversity that can be encountered in studying the colonial period—both colonial societies' own diversities and their distinctions from, as well as their similarities to, the modern era.

Introduction

Historians try to bring the past to life and to explain why events followed certain patterns. To do this, they turn to evidence—principally primary sources that were created during the period in question, and are not later-day interpretations by people not directly connected with events. There are many primary sources available, including newspapers, state and personal papers, oral testimony, popular music, photographs, paintings, furniture, architectural styles, costumes, statistical accounts, personal wills, court reports, and novels.

But potential pitfalls as well as possibilities accompany evidence—a fact that should prompt you never to blindly accept the work of another scholar. Always consider, for example, whether an author interpreted particular sources according to the previous, and not present-day, meaning of the language. Was the author's documentation written by someone capable of making authoritative claims on the issues being analysed? Did the creator of the evidence (or the historian currently using it) have an affiliation—political, class, ethnic, or some other—that might have affected a point of view? Was the documentation generated close in time to the matter under investigation, or was it possibly clouded by increasing distance from the event? Studies undertaken by the U.S. military during World War II found that, after only six days, soldiers forgot significant details of battles in which they had participated.

Before approaching primary source material, a researcher must acquire a solid understanding of the salient issues and major players at the time. It is also critical to cast a wide net when gathering source material, for with more documentation there comes an increased ability to discover dominant patterns, to recognize anomalies and minority positions, and, by comparing different types of evidence, to acquire a more accurate assessment of what the source is really saying or attempting to accomplish. While government records will sometimes reveal underlying agendas, only the well-informed researcher can determine those cases where state papers are deliberately obscuring the truth. Similarly, candid accounts might be found in personal correspondence, but here too, the desire to convince and thus, inadvertently, to misrepresent will sometimes emerge; in certain circumstances, a writer may attempt to hold back potentially upsetting information. Diaries can also be suspect. While usually revealing much about the daily life and the psychological makeup of the writer, they also frequently lean toward rationalization or even self-congratulation, especially if composed by well-known people apt to think that their observations will be consulted by later generations.

Even if it is possible to 'pin down' the factors that guided decision making by an influential individual, it does not necessarily follow that that person's ideas permeated the 'body politic'—and it is no easy feat to take the pulse of a population. Public opinion polls can provide a snapshot, but their reliability can be affected by many factors, including the particular wording or order of the questions asked. Newspapers, and what has become the mass media, are among the most widely used primary sources for gauging popular trends. Considerable information on a variety of issues and social trends can be gleaned from news columns and editorials, and even from comic strips and classified ads. Yet, we cannot just assume that what the press reported, or the ideas that it conveyed, corresponded to those things that citizens considered significant in their day-to-day lives. It is important to bear in mind that the press does not speak with a single voice, that it sometimes sensationalizes in order to attract business, and that, in certain situations such as wartime, its opinions are curtailed.

Novels, paintings, photographs, music, and movies also provide the essence of an era. In some cases, such sources have influenced the way later generations have come to view a particular time—F. Scott Fitzgerald and Ernest Hemingway, for example, are largely responsible for the still influential perception that the 1920s were the time of a disillusioned, live-for-the-day, 'Lost Generation.' But often the artist stands as an outsider in society, whose ideas must therefore be rigorously tested as to the degree they represent reality. In fact, documentation on a number of issues during the 1920s does not reflect what Fitzgerald cast as the 'death of all Gods,' but rather paints it as an era when social and political conservatism were prevalent.

To obtain evidence beyond the written record, some academics have sought out oral testimony. For those who work in the area of Native history, this has been of particular value in trying to retrieve information from First Nations cultures, whose traditions were originally oral, not written. Oral recollections are a way of obtaining specific information from both paupers and princes, but we must be wary of them, and use other types of evidence to try and identify those that might be tarnished by a defective memory. People have a tendency to embellish their exploits; it is also possible that later events helped create interpretations distorting what the subject actually thought and did at the time. It is hard, too, for an interviewer to avoid asking leading questions. Yet oral history can challenge our reliance on the authenticity of the written word, and remind us of the need to be sceptical of *all* sources.

Material evidence—which can include artifacts ranging from barnyard equipment to *haute couture* fashions—has also been utilized to resurrect past lives and communities, especially where written records are unavailable. However, because no specified parameters, or written guidelines, accompany such objects, some scholars view the use of (and especially the reliance upon) material evidence as dubious because, they claim, such objects are too vague and open to too many interpretations.

Statistical data are perhaps most widely accepted as being accurate and value-free—but even facts can sometimes obscure. Certainly, a great deal of valuable information can be found in census and tax rolls, church records, personal wills, and similar fact-laden documents. However, many such sources, particularly older ones, contain numerous inaccuracies. Coverage of the population, especially in outlying areas, was uneven due to poor communications and relatively few or incompetent government employees; people often lied about their wealth in order to escape levies; and the questions asked in different locales were often not standardized. The ways in which statistical data have been formulated must also be taken into account—what biases, perceptions, and assumptions underlie the questions asked? Factual evidence usually provides only a skeleton of the times—missing, for example, its emotional temper—and by no means is it value-free.

Language, too, has its limitations. The meaning of specific words or phrases changes over time. Much exciting recent work has brought techniques or methodologies used in other disciplines such as literature to examine the ways that specific elements of language—metaphors, for example—are used by people at any given time. Canadian historians also face the challenge of sources being generated in a variety of languages. Even a knowledge of both English and French can be limiting when faced with the myriad of First Nations' languages (especially those that existed during the period of contact), or the numerous languages brought to Canada by different groups of immigrants. For example, a knowledge of Chinese characters is necessary to read Vancouver's *Dahan Gongbao* which began publishing in 1907. Hence, a great deal of the non-English or French language press remains unexplored. For the purposes of this volume, all documents have been translated into English.

Clearly, the documents that follow barely scratch the surface of Canadian history. The topics selected reflect the *smorgasbord* of the themes and topics that you might encounter in a university-level survey course on Canadian history. A mixture of political, social, cultural, and economic themes gives a 'taste' of issues that interest historians and a chance to develop your own skills as a scholar.

Some distinctions exist both between and within the two volumes comprising *Material Memory: Documents in Canadian History*. These can be attributed to, first, the differences in backgrounds and research interests of the various authors involved. Second, there are different kinds of sources available for the pre- and post-Confederation periods—there are, for example, far more mass media as well as government departments and commissions for the twentieth century. For historians who work in the pre-Confederation period, particularly prior to the nineteenth century, newspapers may be quite skimpy, have published erratically, have not survived, or simply not exist. How, then, do we take a public opinion poll of seventeenth-century New France? These facts have obviously helped shape the ways in which we approached our respective themes.

Several criteria were used in creating both volumes of *Material Memory: Documents in Canadian History*. These were: to introduce students to some of the sources from traditional political history as well as from newer social/cultural history; to include material covering all regions of Canada and as many population sub-groups as possible; to achieve some form of chronological balance; and to furnish examples of contemporary debates.

Guides to Primary Documents in Canada, and the Use of Historical Evidence

Canadian Periodical Index
Canadian Index
Union List of Manuscripts
Joyce Appleby, Lynn Hunt, and Margaret Jacob, *Telling the Truth About History* (New York: W. W. Norton, 1994)

Jacques, Barzun and Henry F. Graff, *The Modern Researcher*, 3rd edition (New York: Harcourt, Brace, Jovanovich, 1977)

Norman F. Cantor and Richard I. Schneider, *How to Study History* (New York: Thomas Y. Crowell, 1967)

Kitson G. Clark, *The Critical Historian* (London: Heinemann, 1967)

James West Davidson, *After the Fact: The Art of Historical Detection* (New York: Knopf, 1982)

Louis Gottschalk, *Understanding History: A Primer of Historical Method* (New York: Knopf, 1950)

Marius Richard, *A Short Guide to Writing About History* (New York: Harper Collins, 1995)

Richard E. Sullivan, *Speaking for Clio* (Kirkesville, Missouri: Thomas Jefferson University Press, 1991)

John Tosh, *The Pursuit of History: Aims, Methods, and New Directions in the Study of Modern History*, 2nd edition (New York: Longman, 1991)

Robin Winks, ed., *The Historian as Detective: Essays on Evidence* (New York: Harper and Row, 1968)

Table of Contents

TABLE OF CONTENTS

First Nations' Territory and European Intrusion

When did Canadian history begin? Was it with Confederation in 1867, the capitulation of New France in 1760, or the arrival of the first Europeans around 1000 AD? We know that the First Nations, or Amerindians,[1] were the earliest inhabitants of this continent. On most occasions they welcomed the intruders from Europe, whether Norse adventurers, Breton and Norman fishermen, or Portuguese marine hunters, and, according to their traditional customs, shared their resources with them.

The Amerindians were the first 'Canadians,' although such a limiting designation would probably have astounded them. They were the first possessors of the vast land mass and its adjoining seas—Canada in an historic sense is First Nations' territory. The original inhabitants never ceded their rights or lands to the first European settlers either by purchase or by treaty of surrender following a war of conquest. In the course of time, much of their land was occupied by newcomers, and their rights and freedoms were greatly restricted by governments.

These First Nations kept track of time by observing the seasons as dictated by nature and recorded in the heavens. Their occupation of the continent, their cycles of subsistence, had originated with the Creator in the mists of the distant past. They assured newcomers that the Creator had placed them, along with the animals, birds, and fishes, on the lands they inhabited, and that they were to pass on this heritage to succeeding generations. The land, waters, and air were communal to all living creatures, and they saw no obstacle to sharing both space and resources with newcomers, if the latter required them.

[1] We employ the international designation *Amerindians* in place of the historic misnomer 'Indian,' which still appears in administrative and legal documents. We also use the term 'Native' or 'Aboriginal peoples,' implying they are the original inhabitants. The accurate translation of the French term *sauvages* in the sixteenth and seventeenth centuries meant 'native' or 'indigenous inhabitants.' By the mid-eighteenth century the French term began to take on some of the derogatory implications of the English term 'savages.'

The first European arrivals, therefore, did not 'discover' Canada—they found an inhabited land. The earliest intruders were Norsemen in search of timber and farmlands, followed by various marine hunters looking for cod, walrus, and whale, and eventually by explorers such as Cartier who sought precious metals and a route to the Orient. When settlers arrived they found that the Aboriginal peoples held deep spiritual beliefs without any apparent religious institutions, transmitted their cultures without need for schools, and maintained social order and community harmony without need for codified laws, police, or jails. Of course, they also noted their comparatively primitive technologies, their supposed cruelty in warfare and treatment of captives, and their general indifference to institutional organization.

The Europeans viewed the Amerindians as unsophisticated children of nature still at a primitive stage of social development. In time, and with European stimulation, it was believed they would become 'civilized,' progress from being nomadic hunters to become agriculturists, and eventually develop arts and technology like Europeans. In the meantime, they were valued producers of dressed furs for the hatters and costumiers of Europe, as well as candidates for religious conversion.

Were these Native nations indigenous to the continent or were they the first immigrants to have occupied the land? All of the Amerindian nations maintained that they had originated on this continent and were its rightful first occupants. The French quickly set aside theories of Jewish origins and of concurrent creations to adopt the Spanish view of Amerindian migration from Asia over the Behring Strait to North America. They also found it necessary to accept Amerindian claims of occupancy. When the Mi'kmaq insisted 'it is our land,' upon being informed their lands had been ceded to the British Crown by the Treaty of Utrecht (1713), Governor Saint-Ovide at Louisbourg conceded that he recognized that 'the land on which I tread you have possessed from all time.' Although the French would assert their sovereignty over a large expanse of the North American continent against the rival English and Spaniards, they found it necessary in the interests of trade and the security of their small settlements along the St. Lawrence valley (Canada) and the Bay of Fundy (Acadia) to respect Amerindian self-rule and independence. This included the exclusion of colonial agricultural settlement from most of the 'upper country' inhabited by the Amerindians, and the establishment of a system of parallel justice to deal with cross-cultural violence. The Beothuks of Newfoundland were not so fortunate because the English fishers cut off access to much of their coastal sources of food.

In addition to having to conciliate the Amerindians, the French were much concerned about the effects of colonization on their own society. A spirited debate arose about the effects of transplantation of plants, animals, and human beings to a North American environment. Some believed that contact with Native peoples was responsible for a supposed decline of traditional European social distinctions and increased disregard for constituted authority in the colonies. Amerindians, on the other hand, deplored the introduction of epidemics, alcohol, intensified warfare, and factionalism arising out of missionary work.

Section A
The Origin and Nature of the First Peoples

Europeans speculated wildly about the first inhabitants of North America that they encountered. Were Amerindians 'truly men' capable of being converted and civilized? Amerindians, on the other hand, had no doubts about their origins and rights of possession, but nevertheless were willing to be hospitable and share land and resources with the European intruders. The documents in this section demonstrate the wide gap in cultural perceptions.

Six Nations' Iroquois chiefs meeting with the governor-general at Quebec in 1748 recounted their version of European intrusion. Chief Cachouitimi's remarks have come down to us from a French source. To explain the origin of hitherto unknown populations in the Americas, the free-thinker Isaac de La Peyrère (1594-1676) advanced a thesis that challenged the accepted philosophical and theological view that all human beings were descendants of a common ancestor. It is not surprising that he was persecuted for these radical views by both Catholics and Protestants.

Missionary Joseph François Lafitau (1681-1746) adopted the theory that Amerindians had migrated from Asia, and thus also embraced the *figurist* thesis that suggested all people had once shared a common revelation of the divinity, but as they moved away from their time and place of origin (supposedly in the Middle East) they lost much of their original identity, retaining only a figure, or a shadow of one. François Marie Arouet de Voltaire (1694-1778), a harsh critic of French colonialism, was skeptical of all origin theories and oral traditions, whether European or foreign, and is remembered especially for his comment that there was no compelling reason to retain Canada, 'a few arpents of snow.' Michel de Montaigne's (1533-1592) idealized description of Amerindian cultures influenced subsequent French concepts.

The Amerindians consistently maintained their rights of possession to the land they said the Creator had assigned them. When the British planned a naval base at Halifax, the Mi'kmaq sent a strong protest to Governor Cornwallis in 1749, written in the hieroglyphics the French missionaries had taught them.

Cheveux-Relevez (Algonkins), after a drawing by Samuel de Champlain, c. 1570–1635. *[National Library of Canada, C113067]*

Chief Cachouitimi's Affirmation of Iroquoian Origins

At one time there were no whites in the whole continent. But about a hundred years ago some French as well as English had implanted themselves. [We] engaged in trade with one and the other to obtain guns, blankets and other commodities which hitherto were unknown to us, and we ever regarded with pleasure the settlement of traders in our neighbourhoods but we never ceded our lands to anyone, for we hold them from the Creator alone. He [Cachouitimi] terminated by saying that what he had said was in the name of all the nations there present in the persons of their Deputies, including the Tuscaroras.

[NAC, MG 5, B-1, Vol. 8, Speeches of the Six Nations delegates, 1748, pp. 297-298. Trans. CJJ]

The Thesis of Concurrent Creations

It is a natural suspicion that the beginning of the world is not to be received according to that common beginning which is attributed to Adam, inherent in all men, who have but an ordinary knowledge of things. For that beginning seems questionable, at a far greater distance and from times concluded long before; both by the most ancient accounts of the Chaldeans, as also by the most ancient records of the Egyptians, Ethiopians and Scythians, and by parts of the frame of the world newly discovered, as also from those unknown countries to which the Hollanders have sailed lately, the men of which, as is probable, did not descend from Adam.

I had this suspicion also as a child when I heard or read the story of Genesis: where Cain goes forth, kills his brother when they were in the field, doing it warily, like a thief, least it should be discovered by any; where he flees, where he fears punishment for the death of his brother. Lastly, where he married a wife far from his ancestors, and builds a city. Yet, although I had this doubt in my mind, yet dared I not speak anything about it, which did not support received opinion concerning Adam, first created of all men; until I met with verses 12, 13, and 14 of the 5th chapter of the Epistle of St. Paul to the Romans, which I have now in hand, and which I have considered now for twenty years, or thereabouts. And as someone who goes upon ice, goes warily where he cracks it, it being not well frozen or soft, but where he finds it frozen, and well hardened, walks boldly; so I dreaded at first, least this doubtful argument might either cut my soles or threw me headlong into some deep heresy, if I should insist upon it. But as soon as I knew by these verses of the apostle, that sin was in the world before it was imputed; and when I knew, and that for a certainty, that sin began to be imputed from Adam onwards, I took heart, and found all this argument so solid, that I passed through it with less fear...

Who will be surprised then that men being left by God, after their creation, in their own power, and subject to so many spirits, gods and lords, who set them to work, did appoint and worship so many different kinds of gods, under so many different shapes of things created.

[Isaac de La Peyrère, Praeadamitae (Amsterdam, 1655), pt. 2, pp. 1-3, 5, 31. Trans. CJJ]

The Figurist Thesis and Migration

This vast continent, divided, as most people think, into two great peninsulas to which the names of North and South America have been given, extends on both sides well towards the two poles. It forms, as it were, another world which may be called new because the two vast seas of the north and south surrounding it entirely or almost entirely, had, by their vast extent, kept the peoples of the Old World from knowing about it until recent times. Indeed, they do not yet know the limits even of that continent which they inhabit.

It was only towards the end of the fifteenth century that these immense regions were discovered by one of those events seemingly born of chance but really reserved by God in the treasures of his Providence for the happy moment marked by the grace of the Redeemer to enlighten, with the light of the faith, the innumerable nations held in slavery by the demon, buried in the darkness of error, in the shades of death and plunged in all the horrors always resulting from brutal ferocity and the errors of idolatry...

The discovery of America was so startling to the scholars themselves that the first question to which it gave rise was to find out whether the men who lived there were of the race of Adam. In the event that they were of the issue of our first fathers as faith gave us no occasion to doubt, the questions which followed were, at what time? how? and from whence had this part of the world begun to be peopled? had the ancients any knowledge of it? finally who were the peoples of the Old World who had passed into the New? These last questions were exceedingly problematical and gave the scholars occasion for a great display of erudition...

The view most universally accepted and most probable is that which makes all these nations come to America by way of Asia. There are very probable reasons to suppose that America joins the continent of eastern Tartary although, until now, we have supposed that there is a strait separating them. I believe that I ought not to try to prove by simple conjecture a thing upon which light can be cast only by exploration. Whether these lands join each other or are divided by little arms of the sea, it has been easy to make entrance [to America] at that point. I hope that, from a comparison of the customs of the Americans with those of the Asiatics and of the peoples included under the names of Thracians and Scythians, there will result, in the conclusion of this work, a kind of evidence, as it were, that America was peopled from the easternmost lands of Tartary...

God had shown himself too much to our first fathers for them to be able to fail to recognize him and to let him be unknown to their posterity. He had not been satisfied with painting himself in their eyes in the beauty of his works and in speaking to their hearts by the witness of their conscience; he showed himself again as clearly as God can make himself visible in the flesh, giving them instructions either himself or by the ministry of his angels, engaging in conversation with them as man to man as the Holy Scriptures represent him as doing, conversing with Adam and other patriarchs of the ancient law. It was by communication of that sort that he intended to serve them as master, teaching them not only everything concerning the dignity of his being and the honour which should be rendered to him, but also revealing himself to them on the essential mysteries of the faith...

At first, these men had as clear ideas of God as our condition of sojourners permitted...In spite of the depravity of the human heart God was known and honoured before and after the deluge. In the midst of pagan peoples even, he kept hearts faithful to him. Not only among the chosen people [Jews] did he have adorers in spirit and truth...

This religion, pure in its beginning, suffered great alterations in the course of time, fixed epochs of which it is difficult to mark. Ignorance and passion caused in it a confusion which intermingled everything, either in the object of religion, or its forms of worship, or its goal. The concept of God became obscured... But whatever alteration has taken place in this religion, the concept of God was not effaced in such a way that no trace of it remained; for, in whatever errors he plunged them [Amerindians], they are not so abandoned to their idols as to have lost the knowledge of a true and unique God, the author of all things.

> *[Joseph François Lafitau,* Moeurs des Sauvages amériquains comparées aux moeurs des premiers temps *(Paris: Saugrain, 1724), pp. 27-29, 34, 115-118. Trans. Elizabeth L. Moore]*

A Sceptical Ideological Interpretation

Present events ... are not the offspring of all past events, they have their direct lines, but with a thousand small collateral lines they have nothing to do. The cause of every event is contained in some preceding event; this no philosopher has ever called into question...

It follows, therefore, that there are some events which have consequences and others which have none. Their chain resembles a genealogical tree, some branches of which disappear at the first generation, whilst the race is continued by others. There are many events which pass away without ever generating others...

All the origins of nations are evidently fables. The reason is that men must have lived long in society, and have learned to make bread and clothing (which would be matters of some difficulty) before they acquired the art of transmitting all their thoughts to posterity (a matter of greater difficulty still)...

The history, therefore, of preceding periods, could be transmitted by memory alone; and we well know how the memory of past events changes from one generation to another. The first histories were written only from the imagination. Not only did every people invent its own origin, but it invented also the origin of the whole world.

> *[François Marie Arouet de Voltaire,* Oeuvres complètes *(Paris, 1877-85), Vol. II, pp. 125-127; Vol. XVI, p. 353. Trans. CJJ]*

An Early Definition of 'Savagery'

These people are wild (*sauvage*) in the sense in which we call wild the fruits that nature has produced by herself and in her normal course; whereas in truth it is those we have altered artificially and diverted from the common order, that we should rather call wild. In the first we still see, in full life and vigour, the genuine and most natural and useful virtues and properties, which we have bastardized in the latter, and only adapted to please our corrupt taste. And yet in some of the uncultivated fruits of those countries there is a delicacy of flavour that is excellent even to our taste, and rivals even our own. It is not unreasonable that art should gain the point of honour over our great and powerful mother Nature. We have so overburdened the beauty and richness of her works with our inventions, that we have quite smothered her. And yet, wherever she shines in her purity, she marvellously puts to shame our vain and trivial efforts...

Those nations, then, appear to me so far barbarous in this sense, that their minds have been formed to a very slight degree, and that they are still very close to their original simplicity. They are still ruled by the laws of Nature, and very little corrupted by ours...

I am afraid that we shall have greatly hastened the decline and ruin of this New World by our contagion, and that we will have sold it our opinions and our arts very dear. It was an infant world; yet we have not whipped it and subjected it to our discipline by the advantage of our natural valour and strength, nor won it over by our justice and goodness, nor subjugated it by our magnanimity. Most of the responses of these people and most of our dealings with them show that they were not at all behind us in natural brightness of mind and pertinence.

[Donald H. Frame, ed., Montaigne's Essays and Selected Writings *(New York: 1963), pp. 89-93]*

Mi'kmaq Declaration of Historic Possession

The place where you are, where you lodge, where you are building a fort, where you seem presently to want to entrench yourself, the place which you want by all means to control, that place belongs to me. I came out of this ground, just like the grass, me the native, I was born here, generation after generation from father to son, so this land is my land. I swear, it is the Creator who gave me this land to be my country in perpetuity...

My [French] King and your [British] King divided between themselves the lands; that is what brings peace between them today. But as for me, I can in no wise enter into an alliance with you. Where do you want me to retreat? You are chasing me away, so tell me where you want me to take refuge?

[NAC, MG 5, B-1, Vol. IX, Declaration of the Mi'kmaq, 24 September 1749, pp. 133-135. Trans. CJJ]

Section B
European Intrusion and Implantation

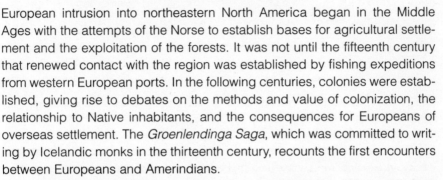

European intrusion into northeastern North America began in the Middle Ages with the attempts of the Norse to establish bases for agricultural settlement and the exploitation of the forests. It was not until the fifteenth century that renewed contact with the region was established by fishing expeditions from western European ports. In the following centuries, colonies were established, giving rise to debates on the methods and value of colonization, the relationship to Native inhabitants, and the consequences for Europeans of overseas settlement. The *Groenlendinga Saga*, which was committed to writing by Icelandic monks in the thirteenth century, recounts the first encounters between Europeans and Amerindians.

André Thévet, a French cosmographer, recorded some information from a personal interview with Jacques Cartier, who had just returned from his first voyage to New France in 1534. It offers some insight into the Laurentian Iroquoian view of the encounter with Cartier at Gaspé. Sieur de Combes, who is the alleged author of the positive (and possibly imaginary) account of Canada as a field for colonization and evangelization, remains unidentified.

The anonymous memorandum on colonizing New France appears to have been prepared for the guidance of royal officials charged with administering the colony when it came under the direct control of the Crown in 1663. In 1665, Louis XIV instructed Governor Rémy de Courcelles to follow a conciliatory and paternalistic policy that served both the French and Amerindians well until the end of the French régime

Although the French recognized Native possession of most of the continent, and respected the Amerindian' right to govern themselves, they extended their claims of sovereignty over a vast expanse of territory against other European powers. An example of a formal 'taking possession' is that of Daumont de Saint-Lusson, a deputy commissioner of the Intendant Jean Talon, who, in 1671, proclaimed France's sovereignty over the regions surrounding the upper Great Lakes on the Intendant's orders.

The Count de Buffon (1701-1788), a respected naturalist of international reputation, saw emigration resulting in colonists exposing themselves to a debilitating environment. His views on the effects of a North American environment on the Amerindians gave rise to some negative stereotyping. Cornelius de Pauw (1739-1799), an anti-colonialist philosopher, also wrote of what he considered 'colonial degeneracy.'

A royal memorandum issued at Versailles in 1716 restricted the area of French settlement to the St. Lawrence valley below the west end of the island of Montreal.

In New France two systems of justice operated: a French criminal justice system for the colonists based on the ordinances of 1498 and 1539 which were consolidated into the Grande Ordonnance of April 1670; and an Amerindian system of collective responsibility under military procedures approved by Versailles. It was by taking cognizance of such documentary evidence that the Supreme Court of Canada in 1996 overturned the myth that the French had never recognized aboriginal title and rights.

The First Recorded European Encounter with Amerindians

There was now much discussion of Leif's expedition to Vinland. His brother Thorvald considered that the land had been explored in too restricted a fashion. So Leif said to Thorvald, "If you want to, go you to Vinland, brother, in my ship; but first I want her to go for the timber which Thorir had [shipwrecked] on the reef." That was done, and now Thorvald made preparations for this voyage with thirty men... They brought the ship to where they could moor her, thrust out a gangway to the shore, and Thorvald walked ashore with his ship's company. "This is a lovely place," he said, "and here I should like to make my home." Then they made for the ship and saw three mounds on the sands up inside the headland. They walked up to them and could see three skin-boats there, and three men under each. So they divided forces and laid hands on them all, except for one who got away with his canoe. The other eight they killed, and afterwards walked back to the headland, where they had a good look around and could see various mounds on up the fjord which they judged to be human habitations. Then after this so great a drowsiness overcame them that they could not keep awake... With that there came from inside the fjord a countless fleet of skin-boats and attacked them. "We must rig up our war-roof," ordered Thorvald, "each side of the ship, and defend ourselves to the utmost, yet offer little by way of attack." Which they did. The Skraelings kept shooting at them for a while, but then fled away, each one as fast as he could... [Thorvald had been mortally wounded by an arrow and was buried with a cross at his head and another at his feet on the headland.]

There was the same talk [several years later] and to-do over the Vinland voyages as before.. people put strong pressure on Karlsefni [Leif's brother-in-law] to undertake an expedition. So his voyage was decided on, and he secured himself a ship's company of sixty men and five women. Karlsefni entered into this agreement with his shipmates, that they should reserve equal shares of everything they made by way of profit. They took with them all sorts of livestock, for their intention was to colonize the country [Leifsbudir] if they could manage it...

After the first winter came summer. It was now that they made acquaintance with the Skraelings, when a big body of men appeared out of the forest there. Their cattle were close by; the bull began to bellow and bawl his head off, which so frightened the Skraelings that they ran off with their packs, which were of grey furs and sables and skins of all kinds, and headed for Karlsefni's house, hoping to get inside there, but Karlsefni had the doors guarded. Neither party could understand the other's language. Then the Skraelings unslung their bales, untied them, and proffered their wares, and above all wanted weapons in exchange. Karlsefni, though, forbade them the sale of weapons. And now he hit on this idea; he told the women to carry out milk to them, and the moment they saw the milk that was the one thing they wanted to buy, nothing else. So that was what came of the Skraelings' trading: they carried away what they bought in their bellies, while Karlsefni and his comrades kept their bales and their furs. And with that they went away.

The next thing to report is how Karlsefni had a formidable stockade built around his house and they put everything in good order. At this time too his wife Gudrid gave birth to a boy whom they named Snorri. Early in the second winter the Skraelings came to visit them; they were much more numerous than last time, but had the same wares as before. "And now," Karlsefni ordered the women, "you must fetch out food similar to what made such a hit before, and not a thing besides." And once the Skraelings saw that they tossed their packs in over the palisade... one of the Skraelings was killed by a housecarle of Karlsefni's because he had tried to steal their weapons, and away they ran as fast as they could... "We had best lay our heads together now," said Karlsefni, "for I fancy they will be paying us a third and hostile visit in full force. So let us follow this plan, that ten move forward on to the ness here, letting themselves be seen, while the rest of our company go into the forest to clear a space there for our cattle, against the time when their host advances from the wood. Also we must take our bull and let him march at our head."

The ground where their clash was to take place was set out after this fashion, that there was lake on one side and forest on the other, so they followed Karlsefni's plan. The Skraelings advanced to the spot Karlsefni had fixed on for the battle, battle was joined, and many fell from among the Skraelings' host. There was one big, fine-looking man in the Skraeling host who Karlsefni imagined must be their chief. One of the Skraelings had picked up an axe, he stared at it for a while, then swung at a comrade of his and cut at him. He fell dead on the instant, whereupon the big man caught hold of the axe, stared at it for a while, then flung it as far out over the water as he could. After which they fled to the forest, each best as he might, and that was the end of their encounter.

[Gwyn Jones, "The Greenlanders' Saga," in The Norse Atlantic Saga, *Second edition (Oxford: Oxford University Press, 1986), pp. 195-196, 200-202]*

An Interview with Jacques Cartier

And the Christians [French] built a huge wooden cross to which they affixed a large *fleur-de-lis*, around which was written, Long live the King of France. When this cross was planted the savages who were present were greatly astonished as to why they were doing such a thing. And these brutes, noticing that certain Christians of the company were prostrating themselves to the ground before the said cross with joined hands, thought that these signs were intended to deceive them and that they charge upon them and trick them into coming near so as to kill them. Eight days following this there arrived a King from sixty leagues distance from the place where the Frenchmen were staying. This kinglet, all clothed in skins, accompanied by six score of savages (each of whom had bows and arrows, others armed with pieces of wood and clubs), was likewise irritated and interrogated our men and wanted to know by sign language why this cross had been set up, whether it was to trick them and put them to death, or whether they wanted to take hereditary possession of that region and make themselves master of it.

At this juncture there arrived another king, the most feared of all these regions, named Donnacona (accompanied by another king whom they called Agouhanna, no less prestigious and feared by his peoples as much as anyone), who came to see the Christians who had already fortified themselves in several places. This king then, accompanied by fourteen boats and some hundred savages to reconnoitre our vessels, at first attempted to frighten those who were inside, but his anger passed when he was informed by an interpreter that we wished only to be their friends and to establish a new colony in their country to support them and protect them from their enemies. This king then began to approach our men and to make an oration using certain ceremonies according to the barbarian custom. This lord was accosted by and followed by another character extremely dangerous who was named Taignoagny. Following a general reconciliation the barbarians as well as the Christians wound up good friends. They brought to them [the French] straightaway provisions from all sides, venison, as much or more cooked fish, so that there were more than sixty persons all loaded with meat, fish, and fruits.

[BN (Paris), Ms. fr. 15452, Le Grand Insulaire et pilotage d'André Thévet angoumoisin, *fols. 156r-156v. Trans. by Arthur B. Stabler*]

A Positive Literary Assessment of Canada, 1609

It is necessary to plough the land only once and then to seed it: and I can assure you that from one bushel of this Trine [hybrid of wheat and rye] one can harvest more than forty-five without any weeds being found or mixture which spoils it. I cannot describe for you the fertility of the country. There is so much wheat as well as other kinds of fruit and things necessary for the life of man, all sorts of merchandise, draperies, silk, wool. To tell you in a word, I believe it is some Promised Land, and that the simplicity of those who inhabit it brings down the blessings of Heaven, because without having the trouble of killing themselves with work, nor to work so much to make a living as one must do up in your Europe, they have all goods in abundance.

Now to describe the nature of those who inhabit it. You should know that they are a very handsome people, white as snow, who allow their hair to grow, men as well as women, with high-browed foreheads, eyes bright as stars, heavy set and well proportioned bodies. The women likewise are very beautiful and graceful, shapely and delicate, so that with their kind of dress, which is a little strange, one would say they are Nymphs, or some Goddesses, very mild and tractable. But aside from that, they would rather be massacred than consent to their own dishonour, or to the knowledge of any other man except their husband. As for the rest, in their manner of living, they are very brutish, but they are beginning to become civilized, and to take on our manners and deportment. They readily allow themselves to be instructed in the Christian faith, without showing themselves too opinionated in their Paganism. So much so, that if Preachers were to go down I believe that in short order the whole country would give itself to the Christian faith without being otherwise compelled. And even by that means, the way would be open in all the rest of America to accomplish the conquest of souls, which is greater than all the lands one could ever conquer.

Now, you should know that we hold a large expanse of land in the name of the French and have undertaken the conquest of the Atares [Atarea's Iroquoian nation?], which is one of the wealthiest countries of the land of Canada, and where there are mines of gold and silver in great abundance, which are very rich. And even all along the rivers one sometimes finds like little pebbles of fine gold, many precious stones, diamonds and other riches.

That nation is cruel and bellicose, so much so that they give us much trouble and we are in great need of succour from France. As I believe Monsieur du Dongeon has written to the King and promises you that if we are aided we will manage and will accomplish things whose fame will be memorable to all posterity and we will see that the glory of the French will live forever in all of America.

That succinctly is what I can write you at this time, as I have not been in the country sufficiently long to know all its particulars. I will beg you to content yourself with this bit, until time and experience will have given me the means of sending you more and describing for you at length the merit of such a fair conquest, for I assure you that outside of France, Canada is one of the most beautiful and pleasant countries one can see or desire.

[NAC, MG 1, J-1, Copie d'une Lettre envoyée de la Nouvelle France ou
Canada, par le Sieur de Côbes, Gentilhomme Poictevin, à un sien amy
(Lyon: Léon Savine, 1609), 13 February 1608, ff. 3-4, 12-15. Trans. CJJ]

Memorandum on Colonizing New France

The dispatch and establishment of colonies has always been one of the surest means of preserving conquests. The Romans made it one of the principal maxims of their policy and the advantages which they drew from it caused them to acknowledge that it was the strongest chain which they could grant conquered peoples, and the secret bond of their Empire. Other peoples imitated them with good fortune, especially during these last centuries—such as the Portuguese and the Dutch in the East Indies, the Spaniards in America and the French in New France. The latter alone have the advantage of having for motive only the glory of God and the conversion of the infidels.

These settlements have been very difficult in New France. The country is of great dimensions but it is full of rivers and lakes and is so covered with woods that the snow can melt and run off only very late, so that preserving the cold for a long time the earth cannot be warmed by the rays of the sun and it remains sterile. The first inhabitants contented themselves with what was produced naturally without cultivation, or with what hunting and fishing could furnish.

Experience has shown that work could give it fertility, and that by cutting down the woods and giving the sun a chance to penetrate it was capable of producing abundantly all that is necessary to live... It is not sufficient to have planted colonies. They are bodies which have their birth, their development and their end, like other bodies. They suffer from accidents and disease and have need of remedies. Those who are charged with their administration must continually see to their sustenance, their preservation and their increase.

To enable them to survive it is necessary to procure an abundance of things essential to life—to have those lands which are distributed carefully cultivated, to stir up individuals to lay up provisions, to establish public store-houses for the distribution of reserves in time of need, to prevent high prices, waste and laziness, to search out all kinds of ways of enriching the country either by the search for mines of all kinds, or the establishment of manufactures to promote trade with those of the country or of France.

Preservation depends on the government which has two functions: one which regards religion, and the other temporal matters. As for religion, either to keep it pure among the French and the newly converted or to preach it to the infidels, it was necessary to send here a bishop and some missionaries. The good behaviour, zeal and charity of the missionaries joined to that of the [women] religious already established here, and who so generously began conversions, gave hope that by working in concert and with Holy Emulation under the direction of a leader of exemplary probity on hand to give the necessary direction they would reap abundant harvests...

As for the governing of the native peoples, since the principal design of His Majesty is their conversion, the establishment and preservation of peace with the colonies is absolutely essential. Religion does not become persuasive by taking up arms. One must attract them through gentleness, benefits, self-interest and good example...

The Christian Religion which orders so absolutely submission and obedience to one's superiors, yet whose principles are all founded on charity, will soften the wild and libertine humours of these people. And it will not be difficult after their conversion to attract them into the colony and the French habitations in order to carry out more conveniently and advantageously the exercises of their religion, and to reduce them little by little to give up hunting and fishing to clear the land and render it capable of producing abundantly the things necessary for subsistence, and to consent that their children be raised in public institutions in order to be instructed and to learn trades as are practiced in our hospitals. By these means we will be able to separate them and transplant them, we will imperceptibly take away their children who will be so many hostages, and we will smother all grounds for revolts.

[NAC, MG 1, Series C11A, Vol. 2, Anonymous memorandum of 1663, pp. 44-49, 53-56. Trans. CJJ]

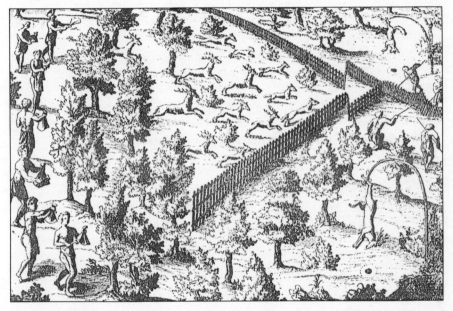

Huron Deer Hunt, after a drawing by Samuel de Champlain, c. 1570–1635. *[National Library of Canada, C113066]*

Introduction of Seventeenth-Century Paternalism

The King has two principal objectives with regard to the native Indians.

The first is to procure their conversion to the Christian and Catholic faith as quickly as possible, and to achieve this, in addition to the instruction that will be given them by the missionaries which His Majesty maintains to that end, under the direction of Mgr. de Petrée [Bishop Laval], it is His intention that the officers, soldiers and all other subjects treat the Indians with gentleness, justice and equi-ty, without ever causing them any hurt or violence; and that the lands which they inhabit never be usurped on the pretext that they are better and more suited for the French.

The second objective of His Majesty is eventually to make of these Indians His subjects, working for the growth of the commerce that will become estab-lished little by little in Canada, when it will have become well cultivated; but His intention is that all these measures be carried out with goodwill and that these Indians take it up out of their own proper interest.

His Majesty knows that the males among these peoples do not want to devote themselves to the cultivation of the soil, but only to hunting of animals whose hides they trade to the Europeans, in exchange for cloth and some small wares. But His Majesty also knows that the Indian women are very hard-working, espe-cially in the growing of maize, which is their staple food.

In order to conform to the inclinations of these people, and especially to those who inhabit the land of Acadia, it is appropriate that the French put them-selves in a position to be able to obtain through barter everything that the Indian hunters will bring them, giving them the same price as the English do.

[Législature de Québec, Collection de Manuscrits (Québec: Coté, 1883), Vol. I, Louis XIV à Rémy de Courcelles, 1665, p. 175. Trans. CJJ]

A Proclamation of French Sovereignty

Upon the orders which we received from Mgr. the Intendant of New France, on the 3rd of September last, signed and sealed, Talon, to betake ourselves forthwith to the country of the natives, Ottawas, Nez Percez, Illinois, and other nations dis-covered and to be discovered in North America, in the direction of Lake Superior or the Freshwater Sea, to search out and discover mines of all kinds, especially of copper; ordering us besides to take possession in the name of the King all the country inhabited and uninhabited where we should pass, planting the cross at the first important village in order to produce there the fruits of Christianity, and also the Coat of Arms of France, to ensure there the authority of His Majesty and French dominion; We, by virtue of our commission, having made our first land-ing at the village or straggling hamlet of Sainte-Marie du Sault, a place where the Reverend Jesuit Fathers carry on their missions, and the native nations called Achipoés, Malamechs, Noquets, and others have their present residence, we caused to be assembled, as much as was possible for us to do, the greater number of the other neighbouring nations, which numbered in all fourteen nations... we caused to be read our said commission and had it interpreted into their language by the sieur Nicolas Perrot, interpreter for His Majesty in this part, so that they should not be ignorant of it, having next raised a cross to produce the fruits of Christianity, and near to it a cedar post on which we posted the Arms of France, repeating three times in a loud voice and making public proclamation, that in the name of the most high, most powerful, and most revered monarch Louis, fourteenth of his name, Most Christian King of France and of Navarre, we were taking possession of the said place Sainte-Marie du Sault, as also of Lakes Huron and Superior, the island of Caientenon [Manitoulin] and of all other countries, rivers, lakes and streams contiguous and adjacent, discovered and apt to be discovered, bounded on the one side by the seas of the North and West and on the other side by the sea of the South in all their length and breadth, raising at each of the forementioned three times a clod of earth, crying out: Long live the King! and having the entire assembly shout it out, French as well as Natives, declaring thus to the said nations above mentioned that hereafter, and from the present time forward, they were answerable to His Majesty, subject to coming under his laws and following his customs, while promising them all protection and aid on his part against incursion or invasion by their enemies; declaring to all other potentates, princes, sovereigns, States as well as republics, they or their subjects, that they could or should not lay hold of nor settle in any place in the said country except at the good pleasure of His said Most Christian Majesty and the person who will govern the country in his stead, under pain of encountering his resentment and the weight of his arms.

[Pierre Margry, ed., Découvertes et Etablissements des Français dans l'ouest et dans le sud de l'Amérique septentrionale, 1614-1754 *(Paris: Maisonneuve, 1876), Vol. I, pp. 96-99. Trans. CJJ]*

Perils of a New World Environment

There is therefore in the combination of elements and other physical causes something contrary to the development of lively Nature in this New World. Transplanted peoples shrivel and grow smaller beneath this ungenerous sky and in this empty land, where the inhabitants, scarce in number were thinly spread, wanderers, and were far from making themselves masters of this territory as their own domain, ruling over nothing. Having neither subjugated the animals nor the elements, he was no more than an animal of the first order, existing within nature as a creature having little significance, a sort of helpless automaton, powerless to change nature or to assist her...

For although the native of the New World is of almost the same stature as the men of our world, that does not suffice for him to be an exception to the general rule of the reduction of living nature in the whole American continent. The native is feeble and small in his organs of generation; he has neither body hair nor beard, and no ardour for the female of his kind. Although lighter than the European, on account of his habit of running more, he is nevertheless less strong in body; he is also much less sensitive, and yet more fearful and more cowardly; he lacks vivacity, and is lifeless in his soul; the activity of his body is less an exercise or voluntary movement than an automatic reaction to his needs; take from him hunger and thirst, and you will destroy at the same time the active cause of all his movements he will remain either standing there stupidly or recumbent for days at a time.

[Georges Louis Leclerc, Count de Buffon, Histoire naturelle, générale et particulière *(Paris: Delangle, 1824-1828), Vol. IX, pp. 103-104, vol. XV, pp. 445-446. Trans. CJJ]*

Up to the present we have considered the peoples of America only according to their physical faculties, which being essentially corrupted had resulted in the loss of their moral faculties; degeneration had affected their senses and their organs; their soul had lost in proportion to their body. Nature, having taken away everything from one hemisphere of the globe to give it to the other, had placed in America only children whom it had not yet been possible to make into men. When Europeans reached the West Indies, in the fifteenth century, there was not a single American who could read or write; there is still not in our day an American who can think...

Superior to the animals, because they have the use of their hands and tongues, they are really inferior to the least of Europeans; being deprived at the same time of intelligence and perfectibility, they obey only the impulses of their instinct; no motive of glory can penetrate their heart; their unpardonable cowardice keeps them in the slavery in which they have been plunged, or in a savage way of life which they have not the courage to leave. It is nearly three centuries since America was discovered: they have not ceased since that time to bring Americans to Europe, and all manner of training was tried on them, but not a single person was able to make a name in the sciences, arts and trades...

As it is principally to the climate of the New World that we have attributed the cause for the corruption of the essential qualities of man and the degeneration of human nature, one is justified, no doubt, in asking if one has perceived any disruption in the faculties of the Créoles, that is to say of the Europeans born in America of parents coming from the other continent. All the animals brought from the Old World to the New have undergone without a single exception, a visible alteration, be it in their shape, be it in their instincts; this must first of all lead us to presume that men have felt some effect from the influences of the air, the earth, the water and the food. Finally, we have reached the point of affirming boldly that the Créoles of the fourth and the fifth generation have less genius, less capacity for the sciences, than real Europeans...

[Cornelius de Pauw, Recherches philosophiques sur les Américains *(London: n.p., 1770), Vol. II, pp. 153-154, 165. Trans. CJJ]*

Memorandum on Limitation of the French Settlement Area

4. As it is advantageous for the security of the inhabitants of Canada and of Isle Royale respectively that they be able to help each other against their enemies, it is necessary that in future the inhabitants of Canada who want to establish new settlements establish themselves along the St. Lawrence river opposite to Quebec down towards the mouth of the river in order to draw closer and closer to the said Isle Royale to facilitate and accommodate trade.

5. That it be prohibited in future to all French to settle above Montreal, in view of the length and difficulty of navigation and of commerce.

6. Past experience having taught us that war against the Natives can never be of any value, and that on the contrary it is always very ruinous and very disadvantageous, the Intention of His Majesty is that the Governor and the Intendant apply all their attention to maintaining at all times peace with all the Nations of the said natives, and that they regard this order as the principal objective of their consideration. His Majesty is well informed that a few of the preceding Governors of Canada in pursuing their own personal interests have given rise to previous wars. This is what obliges His Majesty to recommend to those in office not to fall into the same error, which would bring upon them his indignation and punishment.

[NAC, MG 1, Series C11A, Vol. 36, Mémoire instructif, 1716, pp. 38-39. Trans. CJJ]

Parallel Justice System

It would be attempting the impossible, even making matters worse rather than bringing about some solution, whoever would want to proceed with the Natives according to the justice of France which condemns to death a person convicted of murder. Every country has its own customs, adapted to the different native inhabitants of each nation. Now given the wisdom of the natives, their justice is no doubt very effective in preventing evil, although in France it may appear to be an injustice. For it is the public which makes satisfaction for the misdemeanours of individuals, whether the criminal be known or whether he remain hidden. In a word, it is the crime, not the criminal, that is punished.

[Relation de ce qui c'est passé en la Mission des Pères de la Compagnie de Iesus aux Hurons... (Paris: Sebastien Cramoisy & Gabriel Cramoisy, 1649), pp. 122-124. Trans. CJJ]

With regard to the pretension that the natives have that one cannot imprison them without their consent and that they are not subject to the laws of the country, this is a very delicate matter and must be treated carefully... One can hope to accustom them to submit to the laws, which must be done little by little with prudence and caution. One should begin by accustoming them to submit to military justice and then little by little one can get them used to the same justice as the French inhabitants.

[NAC, MG 1, Series B, Vol. 36(6), Memorandum of King to Vaudreuil and Bégon, 19 March 1714, pp. 28-29. Trans. CJJ]

...the murderer having been sent to you by his own nation he was condemned by the War Council to have his head broken, which was carried out in the very presence of the Natives who thanked you for the procedure the following day. His Royal Highness [Regent] has approved what you have done on this occasion and he hopes that you will proceed in the same way in similar cases, having the Natives consent. But if they were to refuse to do so [give consent] you must employ caution and never press matters to a conclusion.

[NAC, MG 1, Series B, Vol. 44, Conseil de la Marine to Vaudreuil, 14 June 1721, ff. 521-521v. Trans. CJJ]

Champlain's Second Victory on the Richelieu River, 1610, after a drawing by Samuel de Champlain, c. 1570–1635. *[National Library of Canada, Rare Books and Manuscripts Division, NL 15318]*

QUESTIONS

1. Might some of the apparent hostility that occurred during the Norse and Cartier encounters have predisposed Amerindians and Europeans to distrust each other? What common interests did they share?

2. To what degree did the French recognize aboriginal rights in New France? Could their claims of sovereignty be reconciled with Native rights?

3. What were seen as the advantages and disadvantages of colonization?

4. Did the colonial environment encourage settlers to develop self-reliance and independence? Did it present some formidable challenges and dangers?

5. How did French intrusion affect Amerindian values and lifestyle? How did the Amerindians influence the values and everyday lives of the colonists?

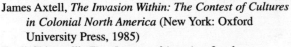

READINGS

James Axtell, *The Invasion Within: The Contest of Cultures in Colonial North America* (New York: Oxford University Press, 1985)

Fredi Chiappelli, *First Images of America*. 2 vols (Berkeley: University of California Press, 1976)

Denys Delâge, *Bitter Feast: Amerindians and Europeans in Northeastern North America, 1600-64* (Vancouver: University of British Columbia Press, 1993)

Olive P. Dickason, *The Myth of the Savage and the Beginnings of French Colonialism in the Americas* (Edmonton: University of Alberta Press, 1954)

Clarence J. Glacken, *Traces on the Rhodian Shore: Nature and Culture in Western Thought from Ancient Times to the End of the Eighteenth Century* (Berkeley: University of California Press, 1967)

L.C. Green and Olive P. Dickason, *The Law of Nations and the New World* (Edmonton: University of Alberta Press, 1989)

Bernard G. Hoffman, *Cabot to Cartier: Sources for a Historical Ethnography of Northeastern North America, 1497-1550* (Toronto: University of Toronto Press, 1961)

Cornelius J. Jaenen, *Friend and Foe: Aspects of French-Amerindian Cultural Contact in the Sixteenth and Seventeenth Centuries* (New York: Columbia University Press, 1976)

Ronald M. Meek, *Social Science and the Ignoble Savage* (Cambridge: Cambridge University Press, 1976)

Stanley H. Palmer and Denis Reinhartz, eds., *Essays on the History of North American Discovery and Exploration* (College Station: Texas A & M University, 1987)

Bruce G. Trigger, *Natives and Newcomers. Canada's 'Heroic Age' Reconsidered* (Montreal/Kingston: McGill-Queen's University Press, 1985)

Frederick Turner, *Beyond Geography: The Western Spirit Against the Wilderness* (New York: Viking Press, 1980)

Jack Weatherford, *Indian Givers: How the Indians of the Americas Transformed the World* (New York: Crown Publishers, 1988)

George H. Williams, *Wilderness and Paradise in Christian Thought* (New York: Harper & Brothers, 1962)

New France—State Intervention and Public Welfare

There is little doubt that the state intervened directly and frequently in all aspects of everyday life in New France. But was state intervention essential to colonial survival, and were the authorities more concerned about public order than about the welfare of the colonists because of the precarious nature of this colonial venture? The interests of both the colonial officials and of the community have to be considered.

Royal government introduced in the colony in 1663 could be taken to mean direct intervention by the Crown in the minutest details of local affairs. In theory, French society was characterized by a divine right absolutist monarchy, a national church that supported the monarch's preference for religious uniformity, and privileged orders of clergy and nobles. As well, a few wealthy members of the *grande bourgeoisie*, dominated the royal councils and bureaucracy that jealously guarded their offices, benefits, and exclusive rights. Although France had no parliament at the time, the same classes of individuals rose to power as in England under a parliamentary system. Just as parliament placed several limits on the exercise of extensive royal power in England, so in France the royal court, royal councils, *parlements*, or regional high courts, and a cumbersome bureaucracy in which offices were sold (venality of office) and collection of revenues was farmed out, placed important limits on the exercise of the King's power and initiatives. It would be wrong to equate absolutism with despotism and tyranny.

This seems to have been especially true of a distant colony like New France. The institutional framework consisted of a Governor General (a senior military officer of noble rank), an Intendant (a senior middle-class bureaucrat), a Bishop (appointed from the French nobility), and a Sovereign (later downgraded to Superior) Council composed of appointed, distinguished colonists. Government was carried on by correspondence between the Ministry of Marine and Colonies, especially the secretaries or *commis* who handled routine matters, in Versailles, and the Governor and Intendant in Quebec, and with their representatives in Louisbourg. Ideas and policies flowed in both directions.

The organizational principles relied on four power structures. At the administrative level there was the Ministry bureaucracy in France, and in Quebec and Louisbourg there was a smaller bureaucracy around the royal officials and the Sovereign Council. In terms of landholding, agricultural development, and rural organization, there was the seigneurial system. Although the colonial seigneurs enjoyed certain privileges and honours, they were not necessarily members of the noble or clerical class. The system was also not feudal inasmuch as the militia units were attached to the parish and not the seigneury. The ecclesiastical power structure governing the church and all its related educational and charitable institutions was headed by a Bishop nominated by the King from the upper class in the imperial country. The military power structure was commanded by the Governor General and his senior staff officers who directed the regular land troops sent from time to time from France, the Marine companies stationed in the colony that were increasingly commanded by Canadian-born officers from eighteen leading colonial families, and the citizen militia. This power structure existed to fulfill three fundamental objectives: to provide coherence and order in a distant colony; to promote social harmony and justice in an authoritarian framework; to promote within limits the interests of an elite, the ruling class.

In all cases, group interests were more revered than individual rights or interests. Prestige and rank were married, but this did not necessarily mean that the less privileged were to be oppressed, ruthlessly exploited, or ignored. In a colony far removed from the centre of control in Europe, administered by royal appointees who carried out their mandates through extensive consultation in the colony and time-consuming correspondence with the bureaucracy of the Ministry of Marine and Colonies, it was essential in the interests of 'peace, order and good government,' to maintain contentment among the populace.

Section A
Interventionist Measures

New France had few attractions for immigrants. State policies therefore were designed to retain those who did come by providing as attractive economic and social conditions as possible. Order, stability, and restraint were the order of the day. Colonists were aware of the relative freedom the New World offered in comparison to Europe. Three memoranda illustrate the accommodation that was deemed necessary to deal with the colonial independence of spirit and hatred of arbitrary and oppressive authoritarianism.

Louis XIV found it necessary to remind Governor Frontenac in 1680 that royal officials in the colony were to co-operate for the 'good of the King's service,' avoid bureaucratic quarrels, and concern themselves with the welfare of the colonists. Frontenac backed a number of fur traders, including some unlicensed traders or *coureurs de bois*, while excluding others who did not operate in his interest. *Congés*, or trading licenses, were issued as a control measure for the upper country trade, but the state was never able to eliminate the *coureurs de bois*, who were regarded by officials of church and state as a prime source of disorder.

Given the modest salaries they received, royal officials assumed that they were entitled to use their office for personal gain. The line between legitimate activities and illegal pursuits was not clearly drawn, and therefore some officials, such as Intendant Michel Bégon, were accused of overstepping the bounds of decency—a fact which rarely impeded their careers.

France, like other European colonizing nations, pursued an economic policy known now as mercantilism. Designed to protect home manufactures and create a favourable balance of trade, the policy envisaged colonies as suppliers of raw materials, and forbade them to engage in any extensive manufacturing of their own. Colonial living standards sometimes required a relaxation of the rules.

The living conditions of the common people are sometimes reflected in the type of legislation that the authorities feel compelled to enact. This was the case in Quebec early in the colonial period when urban space conducive to public order, safety, cleanliness, and tranquillity was regulated. Officials were concerned about such matters as scandalous and seditious behaviour, begging, garbage disposal, quality of air, fire hazards, and control of epidemics.

In the early seventeenth century the Jesuit missionaries and Bishop Laval wielded so much influence in the colony that there was a danger a theocracy would be established. Louis XIV would not tolerate church interference in temporal matters or challenges to his authority as 'eldest son of the church.' Colonial officials were often reminded of the need to keep the church subservient to the state.

Official Orders to Attenuate Absolutism in the Colony

Anonymous Memorandum of 1663

You must lean rather to mild means, it being very dangerous to employ arbitrary measures in dealing with transplanted peoples, who are distant from the majestic influence of their Prince, and to risk exercising an absolute power over them because once they have found a means of resisting they readily forget the respect and submission they owe...

[NAC, MG 1, Series C11A, Vol. 2, pp. 47-48 Trans. CJJ]

Louis XIV to Talon, 27 March 1665

The King considering all his Canadian subjects, from the highest to the lowliest, almost in the sense of his own children, and desiring to fulfill his obligation to make them sensitive, to the same degree as his subjects in France, of the mildness and delights of his reign, Sieur Talon [the Intendant] will study how to comfort them in all things, and encourage them to pursue industry and commerce which alone can procure abundance in the colony and render families comfortable. And inasmuch as nothing can contribute better to this objective than entering into the details of their daily affairs and household, it will not be misplaced if, after he is settled, he visit all their settlements, one after the other, to discover their true circumstances, and afterwards he provide as far as possible for the necessities he will have noticed there, so that in performing the duty of a good master of a household, he may expedite for them the means of realizing some gain and of undertaking the cultivation of the virgin lands lying nearest those already under cultivation.

[NAC, MG 1, Series C11A, Vol. 1, p. 53 Trans. CJJ]

Minister of Marine Pontchartrain to Governor Vaudreuil, 18 June 1712

I recommend that you appoint only persons acceptable to everyone [in the colony] to the positions which you are to fill. The reputation they have acquired should make them easy to identify and you can never exercise too much caution in choosing wisely, both for the good of our service and to avoid popular complaints. You must also strive to win the affection of those under your jurisdiction and the people you govern; and the surest way to achieve this goal is always to uphold justice, to maintain peace and good order among the households, to become involved in private disputes only to terminate them and never to meddle if you think yourself unable to bring about a reconciliation, never listen to the gossip of women, never allow anyone to speak badly of others in your presence, and avoid such talk yourself in order not to offend any feelings...

[NAC, MG 1, Series B, Vol. 34, fol. 28 Trans. CJJ]

Responsible Control of the Fur Trade
Louis XIV to Frontenac, 29 April 1680

Monsieur the Count de Frontenac, I was surprised to learn about all the new difficulties and all the new divisions that have taken place in my country of New France and about which you inform me in your letters of 6 October and 10 and 14 November of last year, especially as I had quite clearly and strongly informed you by your instructions and by all the letters I wrote you in these past few years, that your singular application was to see to the maintenance of unity and tranquillity of the minds of all my subjects who live in that country. But what surprises me even more is that in all the quarrels to which you have given rise there are few reasons that could authorize what you have pretended and my edicts, declarations and ordinances had so clearly informed you about my will so that I have much room to be surprised that you, who are supposed to see to it continually that no one ignores carrying out instructions, you should have formulated pretensions which are entirely contrary. I shall enter into details on the points contained in your despatches.

What is taking place with regards to the coureurs de bois being entirely contrary to the orders I gave you is again of the same nature. I cannot accept as an excuse for lack of application on your part to have them carried out the reasons that you allege that it is the Intendant that authorizes their activities by the trade he carried on. It seems clear to me that this deficiency comes only from you because you favour those who undertake this activity which is completely opposed to the welfare and the development of the Colony.

To carry out my orders on this matter you can and you must use the authority which I have granted you to be aware of all the inhabitants who leave their homes for a considerable period of time which serves as proof that they have gone to seek out the Natives in their dwellings in order to carry on trade, and you must urge my Sovereign Council to punish them severely, and in case they should fail to do so you can have them made prisoners on your authority and hold them for as long a time as you believe necessary to punish them and serve as an example...

All the public authorities and individuals who come from that country complain with such clear examples that I cannot doubt the many ill-usages that are completely contrary to the moderation that you must exercise towards all the inhabitants of that country to maintain them in the orderliness and concord that I recommended so much to you in my instructions and in my despatches. The farmers of my dues complain that trade is declining, and is being wiped out by the *coureurs de bois*, that they receive no protection whatever and that you will not allow the ships to depart when they can do so nor permit navigation on the rivers without your leave and passport. The Bishop and his clergy, the Jesuit Fathers and the Sovereign Council, in a word all the constituted authorities and individuals, complain. But I dare believe that you will change and that you will act with the moderation required to strengthen this Colony which runs the risk of being destroyed completely if you do not change your conduct and maxims.

*[Rapport de l'Archiviste de la Province de Québec pour 1926-27
(Québec, 1927), pp. 113-116. Trans. CJJ]*

Congé de Traite, 18 May 1747

We have permitted Sieur De La Vérendrye, captain of the [Marine] troops and commandant at the Mer de l'Ouest post, to send out from Montreal four canoes outfitted with six men each under Messrs. De Beaumois and Gonneville, whose names and addresses he has submitted to Mr. Debeaucour, to proceed to the Western posts.

To embark in the said Canoes the effects and merchandise proper for the trade at the said post along with the foodstuffs and provisions necessary for the subsistence of the said crews and of other *engagés*. During the voyage we expressly forbid the crew and hired servants to carry on any trade or commerce with the Natives or any other persons except at the said Western post and its dependencies, subject to the penalties stipulated in the King's ordinances.

We order the hired servants to each carry a gun going up country as well as returning but not to trade it to the Natives or any others, subject to three months imprisonment in case of disobedience...

We permit each hired servant to take on board four pots of brandy each for their own use only and not to be traded to the Natives under any pretext whatever. They are to return to the town of Montreal at the time stipulated in their contracts, subject to the penalties provided in His Majesty's ordinances against the *coureurs de bois* who rove about without license or permission.

*[Rapport de l'Archiviste de la Province de Québec pour 1922-23
(Québec, 1923), p. 233. Trans. CJJ]*

Limits on Private Gain from Public Office

Pontchartrain to Bégon, 13 July 1715

An infinite number of complaints against you have reached me from different sources; I am assured that you are making yourself the master of all the trade in Canada:

—that you have had three or four vessels built on the orders of Sieur Butler of La Rochelle and that he sends you from France a lot of merchandise;

—that you sent last year to the Islands [Antilles] two ships loaded with flour and that was the reason that made you forbid other ships from loading any, on the pretext that it was necessary to see if the harvest would be good;

—that the same reason caused you to issue your ordinance of 24 January 1714 forbidding the purchase of wheat and cancelling all the sales that might have been made by private individuals, while you had it all gathered up for your own account, which was the cause of the riot that took place in Québec last year, which you tried to pass off as a seditious action;

—that you had all sifting machines belonging to private individuals sealed up so that you alone through your accomplices could make flour;

—that you sold wheat for as much as fifteen and sixteen livres a bushel, not counting the finest flour of all this wheat to load the ships of Sieur Butler, your man of straw...

—that you had set aside the choicest flour from that destined for the making of bread which you had baked at the King's bakery for the public and which you ordered sold for far more than it cost, even though it was of poor quality because of the removal of the choicest flour;

—that you have purchased on your account, by different persons who are your secret agents, all the oxen and hogs that can be found and that you are operating a butcher-shop;

—that you commandeered all the barges at Montreal to transport your wheat to Quebec, while at the same time you prevented thereby private individuals from bringing theirs down for their business;

Briefly, it is affirmed that you are making yourself absolute master of everything and that the people of Canada are lost without recourse unless we bring some order into your avarice and your injustice.

I confess that, always having known you to have sentiments far removed from such conduct, I had a great deal of difficulty believing that you were capable of such a strange change, so contrary to religion, to the King's service, to your honour and duty. However, there is but one voice on the matter; everybody in general complains, and I ask you yourself if I should not believe them, it not being natural that all agree to speak ill of a man when he does what is right, I will be very pleased in the meantime if you can justify yourself, or if you have been able to forget yourself up to now, that you apply yourself as much as possible to repair all the wrong you have done and that in future you have such a conduct that it may be not only exempt from all reproach but also of all suspicion. I will not hide from you that this is absolutely necessary because, if after having warned you more such general complaints again reach me, I will be the first to inform the king and obtain his order to recall you from a country where it is affirmed you cause devastation and come to render account of your conduct here. I would be very satisfied if you would afford me the chance to submit a very different testimonial to His Majesty.

[NAC, MG 1, Series B, Vol. 37, fols. 204-205. Trans. CJJ]

An Exception to Mercantilist Enforcement

Pontchartrain to Governor Vaudreuil and Intendant Raudot, 9 June 1706

Since the settlers have been compelled by necessity to manufacture cloth, let us hope they will also find means to meet their other requirements. In general, it is not proper for manufacturing to establish itself in that country because that would only be done to the detriment of those manufactures in France; rather you must proceed so that the raw materials of Canada are shipped to France to be manufactured. That must be the general practice, nevertheless, one must not prevent some enterprises from becoming established in the colony, especially for the needs of the poor people.

[NAC, MG 1, Series B, Vol. 27, fol. 235]

Urban Regulations for the Town of Quebec, 1676

The court, after having reviewed the minutes of the [Sovereign] Council containing the decrees and ordinances for public order given in the days of Messieurs de Mezy, Courcelles, and Count Frontenac, governors of this country, and of Messieurs Talon and Bouteroue, intendants, has promulgated the following regulations to be enforced until it pleases His Majesty to confirm them.

1. —There shall be designated a most convenient location in the upper or lower town of Quebec for the establishment of a market, as soon as possible, which will be held twice weekly, Tuesdays and Fridays, at which all the inhabitants who will have any grain, poultry, game and other goods to sell can bring them.

2. —It is prohibited to all the inhabitants, either of this town or the countryside, to carry into individual houses poultry, game, eggs, butter and other small goods, without previously having displayed them for sale on market days, until eleven o'clock in the morning, without nevertheless preventing the townspeople from going to houses in the countryside to buy what they need.

3. —The same prohibition to all innkeepers of this town and its suburbs, and to all vendors and hucksters to go to buy at the market what they need before eight o'clock in summer, and nine o'clock in winter, have rung, to give the townspeople the time to buy what they need.

4. —All the weights and measures, such as bushel, half-bushel, peck, quart, pint, ell, half-ell, chain, steelyard, scales, balances, and generally all that is required for the sale and purchase of goods which are not stamped, will be stamped with the King's seal, in the presence of the Lieutenant-general of the provost court of this town, by his registrar, who will be paid five shillings for each seal, half of which will belong to him, and the other half payable to the town, all of which the registrar shall keep account of and report every six months.

5. —There shall be appointed a person who will have a standard chain with the King's mark to measure the cords of wood for fuel sold in future in this town, each cord to measure eight feet long and four feet high, and the said wood will measure three and one half feet in length between the two ends; the wood-cutters in the forests are ordered to cut it to the same length and height under penalty of losing their employment and a discretionary fine...

6. —All persons who will have houses constructed in future in this town are enjoined to have latrines and privies built, in order to avoid the infection and stink that these wastes bring when they are found in the streets; and that some will be made in the houses that are presently built if their situation permits...

7. —All proprietors or renters who occupy dwellings in this town will clean the streets in front of their lodgings and will carry away the garbage to a place which inconveniences nobody...

8. —It is prohibited to all to keep forage in their dwellings and other places liable to catch fire, especially in the lower town of Québec, or to feed animals over winter in the said lower town ...

9. —It is forbidden to the inhabitants of this town of Québec to throw, or have thrown, straw, manure, or all manner of materials into the streets liable to cause a fire, on penalty of a fine of ten pounds levied on those persons in front of whose dwellings these are found.

10. —Similar prohibition is made to all persons to smoke tobacco or carry fire through the streets of the said town on pain of corporal punishment.

11. —All proprietors of houses in the upper and lower town who will not have exits onto the roof to go to the top of their chimneys, will be required to install and maintain a ladder on the roof of their houses so that one can climb to the top of the house and break in if so required in case of a fire.

12. —At the first sound of the alarm bell each inhabitant, and the persons who will be at his place capable of rendering assistance, will leave his house and come to the place where the fire has caught carrying a pail or cauldron, on pain of punishment.

13. —All persons are required to keep their chimneys clean of soot, and for this purpose they will have them swept every two months...

15. —It is enjoined that all butchers when they slaughter animals in this town carry away immediately to the river the blood and entrails in order to avoid any infections that these could cause, on penalty of ten pounds fine.

17. —It is forbidden to all innkeepers of this country to make loans or give credit to sons of families, soldiers, domestic servants and others, nor to take from them any pawned articles, nor to serve drinks after nine o'clock at night...

21. —All bakers established or to become established in this town will always have their shops furnished with white and whole-meal bread for sale to the pub-

lic of the weight and at the price regulated by the authorities...

29. —It is forbidden to all persons of whatsoever rank and condition they may be, on any pretext or any occasion whatever, even the payment of debts owed them by the natives, to trade with the said natives their hooded cloaks and blankets, nor also their guns, powder and lead, on penalty of a fine of fifty pounds; also [forbidden] to the said natives, their wives and children to become drunk on pain of corporal punishment, or to the French to offer them drink to excess, on pain of the same penalties.

32. —It is forbidden to all persons to give refuge to or favour girls and women of ill repute, pimps and procuresses on pain of punishment in conformity with the ordinances, which said prostitutes, pimps and procuresses will be punished according to the rigours thereof.

33. —It is forbidden to all vagabonds of both sexes to stay and remain in this said town and its suburbs without previously having given notification of the reason for their coming and having obtained permission from the said lieutenant general and crown attorney, on pain of being chased out and a discretionary fine imposed, even corporal punishment if the case so warrants...

36. —It is expressly forbidden all the King's subjects of whatever state or condition they be to blaspheme, swear, and take in vain the name of God, or utter any words against the honour of the most holy Virgin his mother, and of the saints...

37. —It is forbidden to persons of the alleged reformed religion [Protestants] to assemble for the exercise of their religion throughout this said country, on pain of the rigorous punishment stipulated in the ordinances, who will not be permitted to winter over in future in this country without permission, and if some do winter over for legitimate cause they will enjoy no public exercise of their religion, but will live as Catholics without causing scandal.

38. —It is forbidden to all foreign merchants to retail any drinks, nor any tobacco under a pound weight, or to trade with the natives, directly or indirectly, under penalty of five hundred pounds fine and confiscation of goods...

42. —Every year the lieutenant general shall call two meetings for general order, one the fifteenth of November and the other the fifteenth of April, to which the principal inhabitants of this town will be called at which the price of bread shall be decreed, and he will be advised of the means to increase and enrich the Colony...

[Archives de la Province de Québec, Ordonnances, Commissions, etc. etc. des Gouverneurs et Intendants de la Nouvelle-France, 1639-1706 (Beauceville: l'Eclaireur, 1924), Vol. I, pp. 190-204. Trans. CJJ]

Limitation of Church Influence in the Colony

Instructions to Talon, 25 March 1665

It is absolutely necessary to hold in just balance the temporal authority, which resides in the person of the King and in those who represent him, and the spiritual authority, which resides there in the person of the said Bishop and the Jesuits, in such a manner nevertheless that the latter always be inferior to the former. The first thing which Sieur Talon will have to observe, and about which it would be good for him to have firm convictions before leaving here [France], is to know perfectly well the state in which these two powers are at present in the colony, and the relationship in which they normally ought to stand.

[NAC, MG 1, Series C11A, Vol. 1, pp. 50-51. Trans. CJJ]

Section B
Public Welfare Concerns

Those in authority tended to associate civil disturbances, violence, and crime with the lower classes of society. However, there is evidence that disorderly conduct took place at all social levels. In New France, the authorities had from time to time to deal with popular protests, youth unemployment, profiteering, abuses in slavery, poverty, rural dislocation, and widespread lack of education.

In 1691, Bishop La Croix de Saint-Vallier issued a *mandement*, or episcopal order, to be read in all parish churches, on the matter of popular indifference to the practice and teachings of the church. This document reveals some of the popular beliefs and practices of the colonists, and tends to undermine a long-held interpretation that the colonists were oppressed by their clergy. Governor Denonville attributed some of the antics of upper-class youths to the influence of Amerindian behaviour.

In times of crop failure, famine, and war, the state intervened to regulate retail prices and protect the common people from profiteering. The town of Quebec was reported in 1741 to have an over-abundance of merchants. The following year, the Superior Council at Quebec found it necessary to impose price controls and rationing. Bishop Pontbriand came to the support of the state authorities by issuing an ecclesiastical order reaffirming the church's traditional teaching on 'just price.'

In 1685, the Crown issued regulations known as the *Code Noir* for the conduct of slave-holders in all the French colonies. There were no plantations in New France so the slaves were domestics who served in the households of colonial administrators, merchants, military officers, and in religious institutions. When slaves were bought or sold the transaction was registered by a notary public. The *Code Noir* was designed to protect the property rights of the owner, while defining the personal rights of the slave.

When natural disasters, crippling disease, accidents, misfortune, and unemployment struck, townspeople were helpless and rural dwellers sought aid in the towns. The royal administration at Quebec assumed responsibility for caring for these unfortunates as the edict setting up a *Bureau des Pauvres* attests.

French governors and intendants often deplored the pioneering conditions, local initiatives, relaxed standards, and anti-intellectual sentiments of the colonial population. Intendant Gilles Hocquart, the probable author of the unsigned report on popular culture, spent 20 years in the colony and came to know it well.

Rural *habitants*, labourers, soldiers, *coureurs de bois*, lower-class women, and children do not usually produce the documents that are grist for the historian's mill. Court records and church monitories reveal only the problems of an unfortunate minority, but correspondence and travel accounts often tell us much about the lives of ordinary people. However, these must be read with caution to filter out the biases and prejudices of the eighteenth century, and of the authors themselves. The documents portraying immigrants, commoners—both men and women—*habitants*, soldiers, militiamen, and secular nuns describe the quality of life in the colony, and make it clearer why the state felt obliged to intervene in many aspects of everyday life.

Condemnation of Popular Practices

2. As we have been informed that some persons present themselves at the Sacrament of Matrimony without intentions of piety, modesty and the other required conditions, We enjoin all persons intending to marry to prepare for it through instructions in the matters which are necessary in order to receive this sacrament, and especially to approach it with piety and devotion, setting aside all the levity and other irreverent acts which sometimes are committed in church, as experience has shown...

5. We have been deeply grieved during the visits We made in the rural parishes to learn of the abuse which has slipped in among many to leave during the homily and the announcements of the parish mass on Feast Days and Sundays without valid reason to go and gossip in houses during the sermon...

7. And because we have been informed that in diverse gatherings dances and other entertainments were held on Feast Days and Sundays, and sometimes even during the hours of Divine Service, which are prohibited by the Ordinances of the King and by the Laws of the Secular Power, We exhort and adjure, in the love of Our Lord and the honour of Religion, all the Faithful of our Diocese to abstain in future from these kinds of practices...

8. We have also learned with much sorrow that a great number of persons, especially the young men and boys, take the liberty to utter in all their gatherings unseemly discourse with double meanings, which causes in their behaviour a corruption which cannot be sufficiently deplored...

9. Having noticed that notwithstanding the precision with which we made known to the people the obligation they have to pay their Tithes, many persons nevertheless dispense with doing so...

13. We cannot conclude this present Ordinance in a better fashion than by reminding fathers and mothers the obligation they have not to permit children of the opposite sex to sleep together, or with them, when they reach the age of knowing naughtiness. Although this may derive from poverty it is nevertheless true that if parents were moved by a true love for the salvation of their children they would often find expedients to prevent such disorders.

That is why we enjoin all Curates to be exercised about these matters and others who hear confessions to question frequently their penitents on this matter in order to learn from them if they are performing their duties.

[H. Têtu & C.O. Gagnon, eds., Mandements, lettres pastorales et circulaires des Evêques de Québec *(Québec: Coté, 1888), Vol. I, pp. 275-281. Trans. CJJ]*

Governor Denonville to Minister of Marine and Colonies, 13 November 1685

Mr. de la Barre has suppressed a certain gang called the Chevaliers, but he has not taken away its manners or disorders. A way of dressing up like savages, stark naked, not only on carnival days but also on all days of feasting and debauchery, has been treated as a clever action and a joke. These manners tend only to maintain the young people in the spirit of living like savages and to communicate with them and to be eternally profligate like them. I cannot express sufficiently to you, Monseigneur, the attraction of this savage life of doing nothing, of being restrained by nothing, of following every whim and being beyond correction, has for the young men.

[NAC, MG 1, Series C11A, Vol. VII, p. 46. Trans. CJJ]

Profiteering and Urban Distress

Report of Pierre Desauniers, 1741

A matter which requires reform is the large number of merchants established in the towns. In the town of Quebec there are more than one hundred retail stores where all kinds of goods are sold. Fifty stores would be sufficient. Having more than that makes them overly competitive. The surplus stores have no utility and those operating them would be better occupied working the land.

[NAC, MG 1, Series C11A, Vol. LXXV, pp. 11-12. Trans. CJJ]

Bishop's Appeal

Our dearly beloved Children, the Superior Council of this colony being duly informed of the odious cupidity of some of our rural inhabitants who profit from the shortages in which our towns find themselves by selling wheat and flour at an exorbitant price, found it necessary to issue a regulation on this matter... We believe, Our dearly beloved Children, that we must warn you that those who would contravene the Council's regulation would render themselves guilty before God and man, that it is not permitted to go beyond the limits prescribed by a legitimate authority...

The towns, Our dearly beloved Children, are like the core or heart of this colony. Would you become unjust members who would refuse the heart under stress the blood it requires? It is in the towns that you will find what is lacking in your countryside; it is in the towns that many of your children receive a Christian education. Would you be so ungrateful as to violate the laws of perfect gratitude which heaven will reward a hundredfold? It is in the towns that the hospitals are open to receive you in your infirmities; grant to these houses which will ever be the august monuments of the piety of your parents, the help which they await with impatience. It is in the towns that justice settles your quarrels and renders to each what is rightfully his; it is there that resides in a special way royal authority and where His Majesty maintains a large number of troops for the defence of this Colony, the maintenance of public tranquillity and your repose. Finally, it is in the towns that the poor of the countryside take refuge and come to burden the town-dwellers...

[H. Têtu & C.O. Gagnon, eds., Mandements, lettres pastorales et circulaires des Evêques de Québec *(Québec: Coté, 1888), Vol. II, pp. 22-24. Trans. CJJ]*

Regulating Slavery in the Colony

In the presence of the royal notary of the Provost Court at Quebec, resident thereof, before witnesses named below, there appeared Charles Reaume, merchant residing ordinarily in the seigneury of Isle Jesus, near Montreal, and at present in this town, having sold by these presents with guarantee to bear all subsequent difficulties and claims whatever to Louis Curieux commonly known as Saint-Germain, burgher of this town, here present and accepting for himself and his future beneficiaries, five Negro slaves consisting of two men and three women or girls whom the purchaserer declares to have seen at Madame Cachelievre's, and whom the said vendor promises to deliver immediately to the purchaserer in return for the sum of three thousand pounds that the purchaserer promises to secure and pay to the said vendor at the time of the delivery of the said slaves. Done at the aforesaid Quebec, in the study of the notary, in the forenoon of the twenty-fifth of September one thousand seven hundred and forty-three, before the witnesses Louis Lambert and Nicolas Bellevue of this town who have signed this document after reading it.

*[Rapport de l'Archiviste de la Province de Québec pour l'année 1921-22
(Québec, 1922), p. 113. Trans. CJJ]*

The Code Noir

2. All the slaves who are in our said province shall be instructed in the Catholic, Apostolic and Roman Religion, and be baptized; We do order the inhabitants who purchase Negroes newly arrived to have them instructed and baptized in reasonable time on pain of a discretionary fine...

3. We forbid the exercise of any other religion than the Catholic Apostolic Roman. We wish that those who contravene this order be punished as rebels and disobedients to our commands; We forbid all assemblies of this nature which we declare to be conventicle, illicit and seditious and subject to like penalties which will apply even to their masters who will permit or suffer them with regard to their slaves.

4. No overseers of Negroes shall be appointed who do not profess the Catholic, Apostolic and Roman Religion...

5. We enjoin all our subjects of whatever rank and condition they be to observe regularly Sundays and feast days; we forbid them to work and make their slaves work on such days between the hours of midnight to the following midnight in fieldwork or other labour, on penalty of a fine and discretionary punishment of the master...

6. We forbid our white subjects of both sexes to contract marriage with the blacks on penalty of punishment and a discretionary fine; and to all our curates, priests or secular and regular missionaries, and even chaplains of vessels, to marry them. We forbid also our black subjects, even blacks emancipated or born free, to live in concubinage with slaves...

8. We expressly forbid curates to proceed with the marriage of slaves unless they have obtained the consent of their masters; we also forbid masters to employ any constraints on their slaves to marry against their will.

9. The children born of marriages between slaves remain slaves, and will belong to the masters of the women slaves and not to the masters of their husbands, if the husbands and wives belong to different owners.

10. We wish that if a slave has married a free woman that the children, male and female, follow their mother's condition and be free like her, in spite of the servitude of their father; and that if the father is free and the mother a slave, the children also be slaves.

11. Masters are required to bury their baptized slaves in consecrated ground in cemeteries destined to this effect; and with regard to those who die without having received baptism, they will have them buried at night in some field close to the place where they died.

12. We forbid slaves to carry any offensive weapons, or large sticks, on penalty of the whip and confiscation of the arms to the profit of whoever seizes them, with the exception of those sent to hunt by their masters or who are messengers for them.

13. We also forbid slaves belonging to different masters to gather together during the day or night on pretexts such as a wedding, either at their master's or elsewhere, and especially along the roads or isolated places, on penalty of corporal punishment which shall consist of no less than a whipping and branding with a fleur-de-lys...

15. We forbid slaves to set up stalls at the market nor to take into individual houses goods for sale, including all kinds of merchandise, even fruit, vegetables, wood, hay or forage for animals, any kinds of cereals, herbs or old clothes without the permission of their masters in writing or other known consent...

20. Slaves who are not fed, clothed and cared for by their masters may advise the Attorney-General of the said [Superior] Council, or the subordinate court officers and hand them their complaints; upon which and in virtue of their office, if they obtain collaborating evidence, the masters will be pursued by the said attorney-general without costs, which we desire to see observed in cases of crimes and of barbaric and inhuman treatment of slaves by their masters.

24. Slaves may not be invested with office or commissions having a public function, nor act as agents for any other person except their masters in managing or administering any negotiations, nor be arbitrators or appraisers; also they may not act as witnesses in either civil or criminal cases, unless they be essential witnesses and then only in the absence of suitable white witnesses; in no case may they serve as witnesses for or against their masters.

27. A slave who will have struck his master, his mistress, the husband of his mistress, or their children, causing bruises or flowing of blood, or a blow to the face, shall be punished by death.

29. Aggravated theft, even of horses, mules, oxen and cows, perpetrated by slaves

or emancipated slaves, shall be subject to corporal punishment, even death if the case so merits.

32. A fugitive slave who will have been at large for a month, from the day that his master will have denounced him to the justice authorities, will have his ears cropped and will be branded with a fleur-de-lys on one shoulder; if he relapses for another month, counting from the day he is denounced, he will be hamstrung and branded on the other shoulder with the fleur-de-lys; a third time he will be put to death.

40. We order that slaves be reputed to be moveable property and as such be part of the community of goods...

43. We order nevertheless that the husband, wife and young children may not be seized or sold separately if they all belong to the same master...

Le Code Noir ou Recueil des Règlemens rendus jusqu'à présent
(Paris: Prault, 1767), pp. 284-306. Trans. CJJ]

Dealing with Poverty
A Bureau des Pauvres

Thursday 8th April 1688

Upon what has been presented to Council by the King's attorney-general that, notwithstanding prohibitions issued in the past forbidding all persons claiming to be poor and in need to beg and ask for alms unless they have a certificate of poverty signed by the parish priest or the local judge, these sorts of persons have not kept within these rules, have continued as before, and have maintained themselves, their wives and children in idleness and sloth instead of working to earn their living and upkeep. This being contrary to the good of the colony and a burden on the public, it appeared necessary by some new regulation to put a stop to this idleness by preventing fathers and mothers from continuing this kind of life and raising their children therein by obliging one and the other to serve usefully; also that the matter be resolved in such a manner that the shameful poor, elderly, truly needy, invalids could be identified in order that they might be helped and not have to beg for any reason whatever, which would relieve both the colony and those who are truly poor.

The matter was opened to discussion.

The Council to provide support to the poor of Quebec, Trois Rivières and Ville Marie [Montreal] orders and does order hereby that there be established in each of aforementioned towns a *bureau des pauvres* composed of: The Curate [parish priest] who will take care to inform the shameful poor and needy whom he knows... A Director of the poor who will take care to become informed about the poor who need assistance, and to whom those who wish to be admitted to receive public assistance will apply... Another Director who will have the charge and office of treasurer to manage all the sums of money donated for the poor at public collections, in church offering boxes, or in any other manner... and another Director to act as Secretary who will keep a Register of all the deliberations and an exact tally of the poor who will have been admitted to the roll together with the date on which they were received...

Meetings will be held at least once a month, at the discretion of the directors, at the place, date and time they choose. The presence of two directors will be sufficient to settle urgent business if all are not present at the meeting.

The secretary will see to having two women alternate each month, or more often if it is thought appropriate, to take up a collection from each individual in the parish. And in this kind of levy one must be very circumspect and not press anyone beyond measure to contribute, leaving everyone free to practice charity according to his zeal... The said Directors will draw a distinction between the different categories of the poor. To some they will give only a little money to purchase tools and materials for working, and for others the Directors will purchase these things themselves lest the money be spent inappropriately by the poor or employed for some other purpose... To some others the directors will give half a living allowance and will consult together on what is fitting work for each one according to what each is capable of doing. The Directors may have the poor punished, according to the circumstances, either by imprisonment, in a cell on bread and water, or by depriving them of their provisions for a certain time at their discretion. The Council grants at His Majesty's good pleasure the power to act as required.

It is prohibited to all the poor and needy to solicit alms or beg under any pretext whatever on the pain of such corporal punishment as this Council may order. When an extraordinary misfortune strikes a family it will be permissible to obtain leave from the Curate and directors of the region to solicit alms in the parish... The said Directors will enroll no poor for assistance unless they have been residents of the locality for at least three months... In the countryside, each parish or seigneury will look after its poor without being able to seek help from other parishes or seigneuries. The parish priest and two persons chosen by the inhabitants after high mass will serve as directors...

[Jugements et délibérations du Conseil souverain de la Nouvelle-France (Québec: Coté, 1887), Vol. III, pp. 219-223. Trans. CJJ]

Memorandum of Intendant Gilles Hocquart, 1738

I cannot describe, Monseigneur, the misery caused by the famine currently hitting all the villages. The majority of the inhabitants, especially those on the south shore, have been without bread for a long time. Many people walked all winter along the north shore begging for handouts or for a little wheat to sow in the spring. Others survived on a little maize, oats and fish. All winter the towns were full of these miserable itinerants who came seeking assistance in the form of bread or money. Town dwellers, particularly labourers and craftsmen, are in just as dire straits with no work to be found. They continue to be a drain on the public treasury, and an expense to the Bishop, myself and ultimately the King. I have been and still am required to supply bread regularly as well as meat and vegetables to these paupers and the disabled poor...

[NAC, MG 1, Series C11A, Vol. LIX, p. 192. Trans. CJJ]

Ordinance of François Bigot, 20 April 1749

The account that was given us to the effect that the considerable works that have been undertaken on the King's account during the past years have attracted to this town a number of married inhabitants from the countryside who have abandoned their land, either to become carters, or to become day labourers, or even to become tavern keepers, which results in considerable harm to the colony, lands not being cultivated nor expanded as they ought to be; that the said inhabitants thus established, there are seasons of the year when they cannot provide for their families, and it is to be feared that in future, as public works become less extensive, they be reduced to begging, which could expose a number of them to unfortunate circumstances and becoming a public charge.

It being of the utmost consequence for the general welfare of the colony to increase the cultivation of the land, we hereby expressly prohibit and forbid all inhabitants who have land in the countryside to come to live in this town, under whatever pretext, without our permission in writing, on penalty imposed on those who contravene this order to be driven out of the town and sent back to their farmsteads, having their furniture and effects confiscated, and in addition a fifty pounds fine payable on the spot, the whole to be applied to the accounts of the hospitals.

And in order to find out who of the said inhabitants came faultily to take up residence in town, we order that as of the first of May next all individuals in the said town and suburbs who in future will rent houses or rooms to people whose condition is not known, or whom they may suspect of being inhabitants from the countryside, will be required to go to declare to the lieutenant general of police, three days after they will have rented, the names, surnames and profession of those to whom they have rented the said houses or rooms on penalty against those who contravene this order of a fine of one hundred *livres* payable on the spot and applied as provided above.

We order the officials for maintaining public order to carry out exactly the present ordinance, which will be read, proclaimed and posted everywhere were required, so that none may plead ignorance thereof. Done at Quebec this 20 April 1749.

[NAC, MG 1, Series C11A, Vol. 19, pp. 152-154. Trans. CJJ]

A Report on Popular Culture, 1737

The Colony of New France may contain about forty thousand persons, of all ages and both sexes, among whom are found ten thousand men capable of bearing arms.

The Canadians are naturally tall, well proportioned, of a vigorous constitution. As trades are not regulated by guilds, and that at the beginnings of the establishment of the colony workers were scarce, necessity has rendered them industrious generation after generation. The inhabitants of the countryside handle the axe very adroitly; they make most of their tools and equipment for farming themselves, build their houses, their storehouses. A number of them are also weavers, making canvas, and a cloth called *droguet* which they use to clothe themselves and their families.

They love honours and flattery, pride themselves on their bravery, are extremely sensitive to scorn and the least punishment. They are selfish, vindictive, given to drunkenness, make great use of brandy, and are considered untruthful. This image fits a large number of them, especially the people in the rural areas; those in the towns are less depraved. All are religious: there are few villains to be found; they are fickle; have too high an opinion of themselves; all of which impedes them from succeeding as they might in the arts, agriculture and commerce. Add to this the idleness occasioned by the long and rigorous winters. They like hunting, boating, travelling and do not have that crude and rustic air about them of our peasants in France. They are often quite amenable when they are put on their mettle, and when they are controlled with fairness, but they are naturally lazy. It is necessary to strengthen more and more the correct subordination which must be present in all discipline, especially among the country people. This aspect of administration has been at all times the most important and the most difficult to implement. One of the means to attain thereto is to choose as officers in the rural communities the inhabitants who are the wisest and best able to command, and for the government to pay all requisite attention to maintaining them in their authority. One dares to observe that the lack of firmness in past administrations has greatly harmed subordination. For the past few years crimes have been punished, disorders have been repressed by appropriate punishment. Public order with respect to public roads, cabarets, etc. has been better observed, and in general the inhabitants have been more content than they were before...

For some years now *coureurs de bois* have appeared, principally in the region of Michilimackinac. They have the same life-style as the natives, and not only trade with foreigners but take on ideas from the English that are very pernicious for the colony.

The authorities cannot, for the time being, bring any remedy to this disorder apart from granting amnesty to the *coureurs de bois*, as was done previously. It appears they will all take advantage of it but to avoid falling into the same circumstance later on, it is important not to allow any but the voyageurs, on whose faithfulness and good conduct we can count, to go up to the upper country...

All the education which most of the children of officers and gentlemen receive amounts to very little; scarcely can they read and write; they are ignorant of the basic elements of geography and history; it is highly desirable that they be better educated. The teacher of hydrography at Quebec is so busy with his duties as principal of the college, even the functions of a missionary, that he cannot attend as much as is necessary to his work as a teacher.

At Montreal the youth are deprived of all education. The children go to public schools which are held at the seminary of St-Sulpice and the Charron Brothers, where they learn only the first elements of grammar. Young people who have no other opportunities can never become useful persons. It is reckoned that if, in each of the towns of Quebec and Montreal, His Majesty would be willing to support a schoolmaster to teach geometry, fortification, geography to the cadets in the [Marine] troops and that these cadets were made to be hard working at the lessons being taught, that would form persons capable later on of rendering useful service. Canadians generally are intelligent and it is believed that the proposed establishments would enjoy the success hoped for.

*[NAC, MG 1, Series C11A, Vol, 67, "Canada: Details of the Colony,"
(1737), pp. 40-45, 60-62]*

Discovering the Common People
Luc-François Nau to Jesuit Superior, 1734

On 28 May 1734 we embarked on the Rubis... The fourth bishop of Quebec, Mgr Dosquet, who had missed his departure at La Rochelle, was on board with us. He had as travelling companions a dozen protégés whom he had gathered up on the streets of Paris and at the doors of churches. Most of them were ignorant and misbehaved, taking on themselves the right to insult everybody and to quarrel continually among themselves. They even dared to raise a hand against the ship's officers. Had it not been for the Bishop they would have been put in irons... Moreover these beggars were covered with vermin and infectious sores. There were also on board a hundred or so soldiers from Picardy, poorly stripped of their uncouth ways, dirty and carriers of vermin. In less than a week these starving Picards had invaded the whole boat. As soon as we left the between-decks we were covered with vermin; I even found some in my shoes. Other carriers of lice and parasites were found among the twenty-four salt smugglers who had just spent a year in prison. These poor unfortunates [forced immigrants] would have elicited the pity of the most barbaric Turks. They were half-naked, covered with ulcers and some had worms.

*[L'Hôtel-Dieu de Montréal, 1642-1973 (Montréal: Hurtubise HMH, 1973),
pp. 248-249. Trans. CJJ]*

Report to the Duke of Orleans, 12 December 1715

It is commonly conceded that the French in Canada are well-built, agile, sturdy, very healthy, capable of standing up to exhausting work, and are warlike. It is for these reasons that the French shipowners during the last war [Spanish Succession] always gave the Canadian French one-quarter more pay than that given the European French. All these favourable physical traits of the Canadians are the result of having been raised in a country with pure air, of eating wholesome and plentiful food, and of being free since their childhood to hunt, fish and canoe which stimulates their development.

[Rapport de l'Archiviste de la Province de Québec pour 1922-23 *(Québec, 1923), p. 59. Trans. CJJ]*

Memorandum of Intendant Hocquart, 8 November 1739

Since the various trades are not regulated by guilds and since skilled workers were scarce in the early days of colonization, Canadians necessarily became industrious over time. The habitants in the countryside are handy with an axe and they make most of their implements and farm tools themselves. They also build their own barns and houses. Several of them have taken up weaving and make a coarse cloth they call *droguet*, with which they clothe themselves and their families.

They adore honours, flatteries, and take pride in their bravery. They are extremely sensitive to scorn and to the slightest reprimand. They are selfish, revengeful and given to drunkenness. They not only consume large quantities of brandy but also they have the reputation of being untrustworthy. This description fits the majority, especially those in the rural areas.

City dwellers have fewer faults. They all follow the religious rituals with devotion and there are few real villains. But they are moody and have too high an opinion of themselves, which prevents them from improving themselves in crafts, agriculture and commerce.

[NAC, MG 1, Series C11A, Vol. LXVII, p. 40. Trans CJJ]

Pehr Kalm's View of Women

The women in general are handsome here; they are well bred and virtuous, with an innocent and becoming freedom. They dress up fine on Sundays; about the same as our Swedish women, and though on the other days they do not take much pains with other parts of their dress, yet they are very fond of adorning their heads. Their hair is always curled, powdered and ornamented with glittering bodkins and aigrettes...In their domestic duties they greatly surpass the English women in the plantations [New York/Pennsylvania]...The women in Canada do not spare themselves, especially among the common people, where they are always in the fields, meadows, stables, etc. and do not dislike any work whatsoever. However, they seem rather remiss in regard to the cleaning of the utensils, and apartment; for oftentimes the floors, both in town and country, were hardly cleaned once in six months...

[John Reinhold Forster, ed., Travels into North America by Peter Kalm *(London: William Eyres, 1770), Vol. II, pp. 224-225]*

Chaussegros de Léry to Council of Marine, 29 October 1719

I ask the Council of Marine to consider that whereas in the past the troops in Canada were strong and well in all parts of the colony, which kept the colonists and Indians quiet, today they are quite different, insubordinate even. In the past, men sent out from France were well trained and able to serve upon their arrival here, but now young men and boys are sent, most of them undrilled. It is impossible to form a solid body of soldiers with this kind of recruits, as experience has demonstrated. In some cases some of the boys have grown up as puny disabled men, weak and unfit for soldiering. The troops are in bad shape because not all the men are fit for service.

[P.G. Roy, ed., Inventaire des Papiers de Léry *(Québec, 1940), Vol. I, pp. 51-52. Trans. CJJ]*

Instructions to Intendant Dupuy, 1 May 1726

The Bishop of Quebec is aware of the fact that the multiplication of taverns in Canada is the cause of great disorders. Young men in the colony drink excessively at the entrance of the churches causing great scandal. In order to pay for their debauchery they steal from their parents. Finally, the success that the tavern keepers enjoy encourages others to take up the same business. It is to be feared that eagerness to reap the same profits will persuade several habitants to abandon agriculture...

[NAC, MG 1, Series B, Vol. XLIX, p. 305. Trans. CJJ]

Secular Nuns

These sisters [of the Congregation of Notre-Dame] are eighty in number, thirty of them in the towns and the remainder scattered throughout the rural areas far distant from the [St. Lawrence] river and the gulf on the seigneuries. They are attracted there to educate the girls. Their usefulness seems obvious, but the harm they do acts like a slow poison that leads to a depopulation of the countryside. An educated girl acts up, puts on air, wants to settle in town, get a merchant for a husband and considers the social status of her birth beneath her dignity.

[Louis Franquet, Voyages et mémoires sur le Canada *(Québec: Coté, 1889), pp. 31-32. Trans. CJJ]*

Memorandum of 4 October 1718

The education now being proposed for the boys in this colony is only a pretext because there are already schools for them run by the Jesuits in Quebec and the [Sulpician] Seminary in Montreal. In addition, in remote areas located along both shores of the St. Lawrence River and the Gulf of St. Lawrence, the inhabitants are not clustered in villages, but are spread out instead in a line according to their farmlands. Therefore, the itinerant schoolmasters will not be able to carry on the education of the boys. This education can consist only of catechism classes held by the priests on Sundays and holy days.

[NAC, MG 1, Series C11A, Vol. XXXIX, pp. 8-9. Trans. CJJ]

1. Were the statements of paternal concern genuine expressions of responsibility for the welfare of the King's subjects in New France, or were they merely advantageous concessions?

2. Were the Catholics of New France any less religious than their neighbours, the English Puritans, who imbibed liberally, burned witches, courted in their meeting-houses, fought Indians, and discussed what should be done with illegitimate children?

3. Is there a moral responsibility for the state to care for 'sturdy beggars' and the unemployable, and is there a right to work? Do the measures of 1688 for dealing with different categories of poverty seem satisfactory?

4. Were the urban regulations of 1676 adequate and innovative at the time?

5. Was there some balance in this colonial society between authority and freedom, between social control and social justice?

READINGS

Charles Balesi, *The Time of the French in the Heart of America* (Chicago: Alliance Française, 1992)

Louise Dêchene, *Habitants and Merchants in Montreal in Seventeenth Century Montreal* (Montreal/Kingston: McGill-Queen's University Press, 1992)

W.J. Eccles, *Canada under Louis XIV* (Toronto: McClelland & Stewart, 1964)

_____, *Essays on New France* (Toronto: Oxford University Press, 1988)

_____, *France in America* (Toronto: Fitzhenry & Whiteside, 1990)

_____, *The Canadian Frontier, 1534-1760* (Albuquerque: University of New Mexico Press, 1974)

Cornelius J. Jaenen, *The Role of the Church in New France* (Toronto: McGraw-Hill Ryerson, 1976)

_____, *The French Regime in the Upper Country of Canada in the Seventeenth Century* (Toronto: The Champlain Society, 1996)

Louis Knafla, *Crime and Criminal Justice in Europe and Canada* (Waterloo: Wilfrid Laurier University Press, 1981)

Roger Magnusson, *A Brief History of Quebec Education* (Montreal: Harvest House, 1980)

Dale Miquelon, *New France, 1701-1744: A Supplement to Europe* (Toronto: McClelland & Stewart, 1987)

Joseph L. Peyser, *Letters from New France: The Upper Country, 1686-1783* (Urbana: University of Illinois Press, 1992)

Marcel Trudel, *The Beginnings of New France, 1524-1663* (Toronto: McClelland & Stewart, 1973)

_____, *L'Esclavage au Canada français* (Québec: Presses de l'Université Laval, 1960)

Yves Zoltvay, *The Government of New France: Royal, Clerical, or Class Rule?* (Scarborough: Prentice- Hall, 1971)

The Acadians— A Neglected or Persecuted People?

A cadia was the first area of New France to be visited, exploited, and settled by Europeans. Documentary evidence of the annual expeditions of Breton, Norman, and Basque fishers dates from 1504, but they most likely visited the Grand Banks earlier, in the mid-fifteenth century. The first fort was erected at Port Royal in 1605, and by 1680 a small settlement of about 1000 settlers had been established among 3000 to 4000 Mi'kmaq and Malecite. The charter granted to De Monts in 1603 laid claim to a vast expanse of the Atlantic region from Florida to the Arctic Circle, without clearly defining the boundaries of the colony. Matters were complicated in 1621, when James VI of Scotland (James I of England) granted Sir William Alexander the peninsula to be known as Nova Scotia. As a result of rival claims, the area now comprising Nova Scotia and eastern New Brunswick changed hands several times in the seventeenth century.

The numerous changes in official authority were accepted as a fact of life by the Acadians. They were francophone, Catholic, and deeply attached to their region; European sovereignty was not a major concern so long as they were left to pursue their marshland farming, fishing, hunting, and trading. As historian Naomi Griffiths has demonstrated, by the 1680s there was a recognizable strategically important Acadian community. Its farms were generally far apart in the self-sufficient communities of Beaubassin, Minas, and other small scattered settlements. Port Royal was the chief town. There were no prosperous seigneuries or imposing stone churches—only a few wooden churches and the individual farmsteads of large families who ate well from their flocks, herds, gardens, orchards, fields, and streams.

Two early eighteenth century events radically altered the course of Acadian history—the capture of Port Royal (renamed Annapolis Royal) by New England invaders in 1710, followed by the cession of Acadia 'within its ancient boundaries' to the British Crown by the Treaty of Utrecht three years later. The Acadians became British subjects and were permitted to retain their property and practise their Catholic religion 'as far as the laws of Great Britain allow the same,' or, if they chose, they could remove themselves within a year, 'together with their moveable effects,' to French territory—by this time restricted to the area constituting present day Cape Breton and Prince Edward Island.

Despite efforts of the French authorities to convince them to resettle on Ile Royale (Cape Breton) in particular, where the imposing fortress of Louisbourg was later constructed, most chose to remain on their farmsteads and continue their traditional self-sufficient lifestyle. The French missionaries that served both the settlers and the Mi'kmaq were also permitted to remain.

It was not long before efforts to integrate the Acadians into a British ideological blueprint for a colonial society aroused stubborn resistance. The Acadians refused to take any oath of allegiance, for example, that might compromise their Catholic beliefs or oblige them to take up arms against France. Of the two options that had been presented, either become British subjects with all that implied or remove themselves at considerable sacrifice to remaining French territory, the majority chose neither. Instead, they opted for a third situation which neither power had envisaged—to remain on their land, continuing to pursue their traditional lifestyle, and to remain staunchly Acadian in language, religion, and customs.

Their decision brought them into increasing conflict with their new rulers. The British had only a small garrison in Nova Scotia and virtually no English settlers—therefore there was no question of assimilating the Acadian 'new subjects.' The missionaries acted as diplomatic agents for the French administration at Louisbourg, and they succeeded in keeping the Mi'kmaq, Malecites, and Abenakis attached to Catholicism and the French alliance. As settlers from Massachusetts moved northwards onto Abenaki land, and as British fishers and the garrison intruded on Mi'kmaq and Malecite fishing and hunting grounds, open conflict broke out.

The long period of peace between France and Britain that followed the Treaty of Utrecht in 1713 came to an end in 1744 with the outbreak of war in Europe. In 1745, Louisbourg fell to a New England force, but by the Treaty of Aix-la Chapelle in 1748, Ile Royale and the fortified town of Louisbourg were returned to French control. After the founding in 1749 of the naval station of Halifax, an event resented by the Mi'kmaq, the perception grew that within Nova Scotia there were two dangerous elements of resistance to British dominion—the Acadians and their Amerindian friends.

The almost desperate solution was to defeat the Native bands and impose treaties of peace and friendship on them and so clear the way for European settlers. Deportation seemed the best remedy for dealing with the Acadians. As dispersed minorities in a number of Anglo-American colonies, they were cut off from their traditional sources of support, leaving them more vulnerable to conversion and to assimilation by anglophone Protestants.

Section A
French and English on the Atlantic Seaboard

Fishing fleets from both England and France frequented the waters off Newfoundland, the Gulf of St. Lawrence, and the Grand Banks long before the establishment of permanent settlements. Although their approaches differed, both nations realized that lower mortality rates and much higher average crew densities on fishing vessels than on royal vessels presented an opportunity to order youths to be apprenticed as sailors for the navy on the fishing vessels. The fishery was the 'nursery of seamen.'

As well as taking home the cod that became such a valuable staple, fishing vessels returned to Europe with furs bartered from the Amerindians, and exotic products much in demand by museums, botanical gardens, and private collectors. By the eighteenth century, there were numerous expeditions whose primary objective was scientific investigation.

Although the French were less involved in inshore fishing than the English, they too soon found it advantageous to establish settlements to assert their sovereignty and protect their interests. Placentia in southern Newfoundland became a principal base.

Many of the immigrants who settled on the marshlands bordering the Bay of Fundy had come from similar terrain in Poitou in southwestern France and were acquainted with methods of dyking and building of clappervalve gates, called *aboiteaux*, to drain the fresh water and exclude the salt. During the first two or three years of waiting for the rain to wash away the salt after dyking, the land was used for hay and pasture. As desalinization progressed, different crops were introduced—to the amazement of an artillery captain who left the report included here.

The Acadian missions are especially interesting because of the identification of many Mi'kmaq with the Catholic religion, dating from the first decades of the seventeenth century—without extensive missionary work or economic pressures. The Mi'kmaq always affirmed they were 'brothers' of the Acadians because they had accepted baptism into the King's religion. The Jesuit Relations record the beliefs of both the missionaries and the people they sought to convert.

The Sieur de Dièreville was a French surgeon with botanical interests, who in 1699 spent a year in Acadia collecting plants and gathering information on everything from the customs of the Mi'kmaq, Acadian farming practices, local pastimes, and colonial survival skills, to Amerindian and Acadian cuisine. He left a very comprehensive, although often superficial, description of the Acadian colony.

When Port Royal fell into British hands in 1710, Samuel Vetch, who had engaged in illicit trade between New York and Canada, became commander of the garrison and interim governor of Nova Scotia. In 1713, when he was recalled to Britain as an advisor to the Board of Trade on matters relating to North America, he submitted his opinions regarding the 'new subjects.'

Although the Acadians in Nova Scotia were since 1713 officially British subjects, they maintained close emotional and commercial ties with their compatriots in Ile Royale. The illicit trade carried on in violation of both French and British mercantilist regulations seemed to benefit the French garrison in Louisbourg, but not the British garrisons in Nova Scotia. The productivity of Acadian farms, while perhaps exaggerated in the report in this section of documents, was nevertheless impressive.

Just as the French administration in Acadia had had to deal with family feuds and frequent litigation, so the British administration found itself drawn into the quarrels and contentions of the Acadian population. In Louisbourg it was the overwhelming presence of undisciplined troops and overcrowding in the town that gave rise to domestic problems.

Interest in New World Products

Monsieur De Monts having returned in 31 days from the country of Acadia in New France, showed us a live female moose, about six months old at most and the height of a middle-sized horse, which had very small legs for the size of the animal, much like those of a deer. The head was very long for its size, and the ears very large; the tail was so short it could scarcely be seen. Its hair was three or four inches long and a burnt red and quite dark, speckled with small white and red hairs. Its shape in fact was not unlike that of a deer, except that it was much huskier.

We also saw a little bird that was no larger, even with its feathers, than an almond in its shell and that flies about like the butterflies and lives only on flowers like the honey bees. Its feathers are greyish, most of them enriched by a glowing green like those of the peacock. The inhabitants of the place call it Nirido

[Micmac: Niledow]. It has feet and claws like the sparrows, only no larger than a hair. Its beak is black, a half-inch long and very pointed.

But the crayfish [horseshoe crab] seemed to me the most marvellous of all because of its large shell which covers its head and body, larger than a foot in diameter and an inch thick, and full of very delicate flesh....

Of elk horns there were some of such massive size that it was all a man could do to carry one of them; and among them there were two that were still attached to the skull of the animal...

We saw, last of all, several bows larger then the height of a man and a mass of arm-length weapons made of the wood of the plane-tree [maple], fashioned in a strange manner with little pieces of bone and shells.

And finally a bark thirty feet long, four or five wide, and the same height, all made of mouldings intertwined about two inches large and ribbing of wood similar to that used for making baskets in Marseilles, then covered on the outside by large pieces of bark of a tree called the birch, sewn together, pitched completely with resin and painted red...

[NAC, MG 6, B 10, Bibliothèque de Carpentras, Peiresc Papers, Ms 1821, fols. 125-126. Trans. CJJ]

From Fishing to Settlement

In the year 1662 a ship sent out from France put into Placentia Bay and landed several soldiers with men and women to settle there under a Governor, who having a commission to command the whole country of Newfoundland, fortified that harbour with eighteen pieces of ordnance. After which in 1666 the French dispatched another Governor thither with two great ships of war, who carried with him several great guns, 150 soldiers, small arms, and other materials to fortify more harbours with 60 families of men, women and children of divers trades to settle there... In the Bay of Fortune there are some inhabitants—a great store of cattle of all sorts, and to all these places are brought yearly by the fishing ships considerable supplies of men, women and children who settle there, and catch fish in the like manner as the English inhabitants do in their harbours, and with equal privileges and accommodation with the fishermen. The places where the French fishing ships do most frequent are St. Mary's, Carbonear, Placentia, St. Peter's, Three Islands, Petty North, and several other harbours to the westward of Placentia...

The French send hither yearly about a hundred sail of ships from Honfleur, Dieppe, Boulogne, Calais and the region of Aunis. These ships carry from 80 to 120 tonnes, and from eight to fourteen guns, and are manned 1/8 part of men to their burdens, and make sometimes two voyages in a year. The fish is caught in the ships, there cured and salted, and is called green cod or wet fish for distinction from that which is taken on the coast which is white cod or dry fish. The smallest ships catch from twenty to twenty-five thousand, and the largest from thirty to forty thousand fish, which is carried directly to market, and consumed for the most part at Paris.

[Newfoundland Archives, C.O. 195/2, An Account of the French Colony and Trade of Newfoundland, 1676, pp. 25-28]

Marshland Farming

Their tillage is performed with such ease being entirely free from stones that two yoke of cattle is sufficient to plow up their stubble which is usually done in the fall of the year. It is plowed up in ridges about five feet wide for the sake of draining off the water into trenches which are cut in the meadow and enclose about four or five acres. These trenches drain off the water into channels which were formerly creeks in the meadow, and thus in the ebb of the tide all the fresh water is drained into the sea which without these trenches and this manner of plowing would rest upon the land and render it unfit for tillage. The land thus plowed up lays open to the winter frosts and in the spring, in the beginning of April, they have no further trouble but to sow their seed and harrow it in and from thence good crops are produced from year to year. That part of the marsh that is exposed to the inundation of the tides produces their hay which supports their cattle in the winter season. This salt grass is the first and natural produce of all their marshes, and by means of them they have been enabled to extend their settlements over the Bay of Fundy. The upland is made use of for the production of all sorts of roots and garden stuffs but very little is used by them either for grass or grain. Some particularly rich spots do produce good wheat and other grain, but that is not general... They have hitherto much neglected the improvement of their uplands, which require a good deal of labour to clear and which afterwards must be fenced in to prevent their cattle that have not been turned loose in the woods all the summer season destroying it.

[NAC, MG 18, F1O, Charles Morris, "A Breif (sic) Survey of Nova Scotia," Unpublished mss., cap. 5, pp. 6-7. Text modernized]

The Acadian Missions

Here is a third letter that I am writing to Your Reverence to inform you what has happened in the Acadian Mission where three of our fathers are working for the conversion of the Natives of this coast, and for the salvation of the French who live here.

Acadia is that part of New France that borders on the sea, stretching from New England to Gaspé where the entrance to the great St. Lawrence river properly begins. All this country, which extends for at least three hundred leagues, has but one name and [the natives] speak but one language.

The English have usurped all the Eastern coast from Canso to New England, and left to the French that which stretches toward the north...

A certain fellow called Capisto, a former captain of Cape Breton and much attached to his superstitions, one day fell into violent convulsions during which the Natives decided to apply to his body some images, rosaries and crosses in which they place great faith, using them to ward off the haunting of the Demons. This man, at the height of his attack, imagined that a number of Devils were throwing themselves on him, dragging him from one side to another as they strove to carry him off. In this anguish he laid hold of a large cross erected at the entrance to the river to which he clung so firmly that it was impossible for the devils to dislodge him. This vision touched him, and although he still continues in infidelity, he does value the Faith and this gives us hope that finally after so many favours God has shown him, aided by the example and urgings of his brother who was baptized this spring, he will break the ties that hold him so firmly bound to his wretchedness...

One day [an Eskimo captive] appeared as if possessed; she ran about screeching in a horrible voice and making strange gestures as do persons possessed of the devil. The French ran to her and tried to calm her, but all in vain; her torments increased to the point that she was in danger of suffocating. They finally decided to have recourse to divine remedies, so they begged the chaplain who then ministered to the settlement to help her. He had no sooner sprinkled her with holy water than she suddenly stopped and became as calm as if awakening from sleep... The interpreter, who was a heretic [Protestant], was seized with astonishment and admiration for the power of the holy water, renounced heresy, and publicized the wonder whereof he had been a spectator by his abjuration. If demons serve to convert Natives, and Natives to bring down heretics, what must we not hope to obtain through the help of the guardian angels of this region? Especially since these blessed spirits have brought us an Angelic Man, I mean Monseigneur the Bishop of Petraea, who while crossing the border into our Acadia, in the Gaspé region, administered the sacrament of confirmation to 140 persons, who perhaps would never have received that blessing if this worthy Prelate had not come to seek them out in the end of the world...

Kebec, this 16th day of October 1659.

[Lettres envoiées de la Nouvelle France (Paris: Sebastien Cramoisy, 1660), fols. 34-35, 39-40, 47-50. Trans CJJ]

A Surgeon's View of Colonial Conditions, 1700

Port Royal is no more than half a league in both directions. The houses are built on the higher ground and are quite far apart from each other. They are no more than badly built cottages with chimneys of clay...

I asked for the church which I could not perceive. It was in no way distinguishable from the other buildings, being more like a barn than anything else...

As to the Acadians, they have never been taught their trades, but they are good enough workers. They set themselves to all the tasks which life requires. From their wool they make their clothes, hats and stockings. They do not follow the fashion and always wear flat shoes which they make themselves from the skins of seals and moose. Cloth they weave from flax, and cover their nudity by their industry. Each has a country roof above him, and keeps himself warm during the cold...

All live as they can, without envy or ambition and await the reward of their labours. If blind fortune has made them equal she has also kept jealousy from them...

The work they do not tire themselves with is breeding vast quantities of children. Two neighbouring couples had respectively eighteen and twenty-two children. Even a girl from good family does not let snobbery stand in her way. If the only husband she can find is beneath her socially, nevertheless she prefers him to virginity. The love of children triumphs over the difficulties of social inequality.

[Sieur de Dièreville, Relation du voyage du Port Roval de l'Acadie ou de la Nouvelle France (Amsterdam: Pierre Humbert, 1710), pp. 60-61, 71, 72, 78]

Colonel Vetch's Report on the Conquered Peoples

London, Novr, 24th, 1714.

My Lords, —

In answer to Your Lordships Queries, delivered to me by Mr. Secretary Popple upon the 23rd of this instant, my most humble opinion is as follows:

As to the number of familys of French Inhabitants in the countrys of L'Accady and Nova Scotia, by the best account I ever could get during the space of three years and more I had the honor to command there, they were computed to be about five hundred familys at the rate of five persons to a family; which makes two thousand five hundred souls.

As to the next how many of them it is supposed will remove; by the last advices from thence, they had obliged themselves under their hands all to remove save two familys viz. one Mr. Allen and one Mr. Gouirday both of which had liv'd in New England formerly.

As to the 3rd Querie, how many family's may be upon Cape Breton is what I can't pretend to be so exact in. But according to the best advices, I could learn they are said to be now about five hundred familys besides the Garrison, which I consider, consists of 7 companys already. The French King to encourage them to settle the place gives them eighteen months provisions, and assists them with ships, and salt, to carry on the Fishery:

As to the 4th what may be the consequence of the French moving from Nova Scotia to Cape Bretton; They are evidently these, First their leaving that country intirely destitute of inhabitants; There being none but French, and Indians (except the Garrison) settled in those parts; and as they have intermarried, with the Indians, by which and their being of one Religion, they have a mighty influence upon them. So it is not to be doubted, but they will carry along with them to Cape Bretton both the Indians and their trade, Which is very considerable. And as the accession of such a number of Inhabitants to Cape Bretton, will make it at once a very populous Colony; (in which the strength of all the Country's consists) So it is to be considered, that one hundred of the French, who were born upon that continent, and are perfectly known in the woods; can march upon snow shoes; and understand the use of Birch Canoes are of more value and service than five times their number of raw men, newly come from Europe. So their skill in the Fishery, as well as the cultivating of the soil, must inevitably make that Island, by such an accession of people, and French, at once the most powerful colony, the French have in America. And of the greatest danger and damage to all the British Colony's as well as the universal trade of Great Britain...

[Public Archives of Nova Scotia, MS documents, Vol. V, Vetch to Lords of Trade, 24 November 1714]

Acadian Contacts with Louisbourg

They [Acadians] in a clandestine manner supply the French at Louisbourg and St. Johns [Prince Edward Island] with 6 to 700 head of cattle and about 2000 sheep in a year. In short, Louisbourg in my opinion would starve if it was not for them, though at the same time they do this our garrisons at Annapolis Royal and Canso, which are in their neighbourhood, are in great want, and can get neither beef nor mutton but at great expense from New England. The Acadians before mentioned have their woollen and linens and most of the necessities they want from Louisbourg, and are in a manner dependent on the French though they live in Nova Scotia.

[Adam Shortt et al., Documents Relating to Currency, Exchange and Finance in Nova Scotia. with Prefatory, Documents 1675-1758 (Ottawa: King's Printer, 1933), pp. 223-224. Text modernized]

Resolving Problems of Family Life
Minutes of 20 April, and 30 June 1726

Then was read a petition from Mary D'Aigre, wife to James Gonsile, against Beausoleil (alias Joseph Brosard) for committing fornication with her daughter Mary who being brought to bed of a daughter had laid the same to the said Brosard, and he refusing the child maintenance and denying himself to be the father prayed relief.

The said Brosard being come to answer in his own defence, replied that he was very innocent and not the father having never had any carnal dealings with her.

The midwife being put to her oath declared that the said Mary daughter to the said Mary D'Aigre did declare when she was in her most violent pains that the said Joseph Brosard was the real father of the said child.

The Governor with the advice of the board ordered that the said Brosard should pay to the mother of the said child for its maintenance three shillings and ninepence every week until that the child arrive at the age of eight years old, and that he shall immediately give some good security for his performing the same, or go to prison until that he shall find such security.

Abraham Bourg one of the deputies and William Bourgeway inhabitant engaged themselves each in an hundred pounds security for the said Joseph Brosard's punctual compliance and due observation. Said orders to be by them punctually paid upon the first complaint of his the said Joseph Brosard's not obeying or his refusing to pay the above ordered weekly allowance of three shillings and ninepence for the said child's maintenance as aforesaid.

...

The Honourable President acquainted the board that he had received a petition from the widow Brosard in behalf of her son Joseph praying relief in relation to the bastard child as per the minute of Council Wednesday the 20th April last.

Which being taken into consideration and the said widow and those concerned in both parties, being called and their arguments heard, the board judged it reasonable that the mother of the child should keep and maintain the said child at as cheap a rate as other nurses in the country would...

Then Charles Landry one of the deputies said (in order to finish all disputes, if the mother of the child and those with her concerned were willing) that he would take the child and be answerable for its nursing and all other necessaries and that he would also maintain the mother at his house for a year.

To which proposition all parties agreed. Then Jacques Gousile complaining that some part of the allowance formerly ordered by the Council was not paid; the board ordered immediate payment, which Abraham Bourg and Guillaume Boureway did accordingly.

[Archibald M. MacMechan, ed., Original Minutes of His Majesty's Council at Annapolis Royal, 1720-1739 *(Halifax: Nova Scotia Archives, 1908), pp. 112-113, 1212-123. Text modernized]*

Marriage Contract of Jean-Baptiste Lascoret and Anne Richard, 6 July 1739

Jean Richard and Anne Samson promised to feed & lodge with them free of charge the said future husband & wife for a period of three years & moreover also promised to give to the said Anne Richard [their daughter] in advance settlement of the said future inheritance a fully furnished room consisting of a bed complete with bedding, six chairs, an arm chair, six pairs of sheets, 4 dozen napkins, an armoire, 4 table cloths, a table, two silver table settings, a mirror, two dozen pewter plates, two pewter serving platters, a large pewter platter, a pair of andirons, a shovel, a pair of tongs, a pair of copper candlestick holders with their snuffers which are also made of copper. the said furnishings will then belong to the community of goods of the said future bride & groom.

[Kenneth Donavon, in "Communities and Families: Family Life and Living Conditions in Eighteenth Century Louisbourg," Material History Bulletin, 15 (1982), p. 41]

Section B
The Mi'kmaq Presence

In contrast to the Acadians who had adjusted to the presence of Mi'kmaq to the extent of intermarrying with them, the British remained aloof and suspicious of the Native population. During the first three decades of British rule in Nova Scotia, the chief concern was the influence of the French missionaries. The British faced open hostility from the original inhabitants as a result of the decision after the war of 1744-48 to establish a major naval base and encourage immigration. The Mi'kmaq felt their traditional way of life was threatened through the possible loss of their hunting and fishing territories.

Following the cession of Acadia to the British Crown, efforts were made to encourage the Mi'kmaq and Malecite to abandon their trade with the Acadians, to renounce the Catholic religion, and to consider intermarrying with the English. The Mi'kmaq in general seemed unwilling to abandon neither their new religion nor their alliance with the French, but were not unwilling to consider some benefits to be gained from the presence of British garrisons on what they deemed to be their land. The English account is more graphic than the French version of events.

In April 1725, Major Paul Mascarene investigated rumours of an impending plot. The British had appointed Acadian 'deputies' in the principal settlements to act as liaison officers between the authorities and the 'new subjects.' There remained much uncertainty about their loyalty and about the existing relations with Mi'kmaq bands.

The founding of Halifax was followed by a change in British policy toward the Native peoples. Immigrants would require lands that were held as hunting grounds. The Mi'kmaq who gathered at Port Toulouse in Cape Breton for the annual distribution of Louis XV's 'presents' in September 1749 had the missionary abbé Pierre Maillard draw up a formal declaration demanding the abandonment of Halifax.

Major Jean-Baptiste Cope, styled by the British as 'chief sachem of the tribe of Mick Mack Indians,' was the first band leader to sign a renewal of the earlier treaties of peace and friendship designed to drive a wedge between the majority who sympathized with the French and those who believed an accommodation with the British was necessary. The treaty has since given rise to problems of interpretation because the Mi'kmaq did not have a tribal organization as such, being made up of small independent bands, and therefore the delegates only bound themselves. During the ensuing decade, several other bands adhered to the treaty although it made no mention of any underlying aboriginal title and gave no entitlement to reserve lands.

Appeals for Mi'kmaq Co-operation
Ramsay to Governor, 16 September 1715

Three British officers visited the missions with three proposals: 1. to proclaim their new king [George I] in their riverine settlements; 2. to take the oath of allegiance to him; 3. to permit the English to settle amongst them and to become but one people...

The Natives after holding a council meeting replied to the first article that they would proclaim no foreign king in their country and that they did not want any king to be able to say that he had taken possession of their land. On the second article, they did not want to swear an oath of allegiance to any person because they had their natural king and that Onontio, the Marquis de Vaudreuil, was their chief and that the King of France was his Father because he obtained missionaries to instruct them...

[NAC, MG1, Series C11A, Vol. XXXV, p. 120. Trans CJJ]

Lieutenant-Governor Doucette to Governor Philipps, 11 March 1718

Likewise use your endeavours to obtain presents for the Indians. The Chief of them having been here with me stated that if I expected them to be our friends they expected presents as was every year made to them by the French Kings. And if they had such they should not only be good subjects to King George but would esteem him as their father. I told him I would not answer for any presents this Spring but hoped by the next to receive some for them and that in the meantime

I would take care to represent it to His Majesty. I gave them some few trifles and dismissed them and expect in the Spring the Chief of them from the St. John River.... Now if I may give you my opinion which is the same with all the English here, that if at your arrival you bring them presents with you they will be easily brought over to our Interests and not offer to molest you in case you should raise any new Forts on the coast or in the making of any new settlements.

[NAC, MG 11, A-10, pp. 39-40]

De La Varenne to a Friend in La Rochelle, 8 May 1756

One instance may serve to show you the temper of these. Some years ago the English officers being assembled at the Mines [Minas], in order to take a solemn recognition from them of the King of Great Britain, when a savage, a new convert, called Simon, in spite of all dissuasion, went himself to the English commander, and told him that all his endeavours to get the King of England acknowledged would be to no purpose; that, for his part, he should never pay any allegiance but to the King of France, and drawing a knife said, 'This indeed is all the arms I have, and with this weapon alone, I will stand by the King of France till death'.

[Ken Donavon, ed., "A Letter from Louisbourg, 1756," Acadiensis X,
1 (1980), p. 125]

Fears of Collusion Between Acadians and Mi'kmaq

Major Paul Mascarene acquainted the board that the Honourable Lt. Governor being out of order and not able to attend the board, that he was therefore directed by him to inform the board that the deputies [of the Acadians], Charles Landry excepted, being come according to his orders, concerning the behaviour of their young men and insolence of some others of the inhabitants since the time that the Indians were here, and that he was directed to ask them some questions about the same.

Whereupon the deputies being called, the Major accordingly asked them from whence such rude actions of their youth and other of the inhabitants since the Indians were here last year proceeded, and said that by several particular marks of misbehaviour amongst them, it seemed that there was something a hatching as if they depended upon the Indians return, and as if they designed by such practices to occasion some pretence for a revolt, whereby thinking to annoy this His Majesty's Government and so to force their way out of the country.

Upon which Major Mascarene also told them that he was ordered by the Honourable Lt. Governor to acquaint them they needed not by such pretences to promote a war, seeing those who have aimed to go may only apply themselves to the Governor and have liberty to depart this Province as soon as they pleased...

The deputies made answer that they were heartily sorry that either their young people (who perhaps through ignorance) or any of riper years amongst them should after so much leniency and goodness shown them from this government, behave themselves in the least disrespectfully towards it, or to any of the Gentlemen or others thereunto belonging, and that such people richly deserved such punishments as the government should cause to be inflicted for such offences.

That for their own parts according to their duty and promises, they would carefully admonish the inhabitants to a peaceable and respectful obedience and that they should respectively correct their children upon all appearances of affronts and of unbecoming deportment.

That they had no reason to wish the Indian's return, and that they knew of none who had any such dependance upon it, or any design thereby either to revolt, or to leave the country, but if that there is any such evil designing people amongst them they no ways deserved the least protection of the government; and that they would according to the Governor's desire present him with their answer in writing.

April 8th Mr. Landry who was absent the 6th instant came and made his excuse and submission for his absence occasioned through his want of health and declared as the others did as above.

[Archibald M. MacMechan, ed., Original Minutes of His Maiesty's Council at Annapolis Royal, 1720-1739 (Halifax: Nova Scotia Archives, 1908), pp. 94-96. Text modernized]

A Mi'kmaq Declaration of War, 1749

The ground where you stand, where you build houses, where you build a fort, where you wish as it were to enthrone yourself, this land of which you now wish to make yourselves absolute masters, this same land belongs to me. I have grown up on it like the grass, and it is the very place of my birth and my residence. It is my land, me a native. Yes, I swear, God gave it to me to be my country forever...

Show me where I, a native, will lodge? You chase me away, and where do you want me to take refuge? You have seized nearly all this land in all its vastness. All that is left to me is Kchibouktouk [Chebouctou]. You begrudge me even this bit... Your settlement at Port Royal does not trouble me because as you see for a long time I leave you in peace there. But at the present time you force me to speak out because of the considerable theft you inflict upon me.

[Archives du Séminaire de Québec, Lettres P, No. 66, abbé Maillard to abbé Du Fau, 18 October 1749. Trans. CJJ]

Treaty of Peace and Friendship, 1752

1. It is agreed that the Articles of Submission & Agreement, made at Boston in New England by the Delegates of the Penobscot Norridwolk & St. John's Indians, in the Year 1725 Ratified & Confirmed by all the Nova Scotia Tribes, at Annapolis Royal, in the Month of June 1726, & lately renewed with Governor Cornwallis at Halifax and Ratified at St. Johns River, now read over, Explained and Interpreted, shall be and are hereby from this time forward Renewed, Reiterated, and forever Confirmed by them and their Tribe; and the said Indian for themselves and their Tribe and their Heirs aforesaid Do make & Renew the same Solemn Submissions and promises for the Strickt observance of all the Articles therein contained as at time heretofore hath been done.

2. That all Transactions during the late War shall on both sides be buried in Oblivion with the Hatchet, and that the said Indians shall have all favour, Friendship & Protection shewn them from this His Majesty's Government.

3. That the said Tribe shall use their utmost endeavours to bring in the other Indians to Renew and Ratify this Peace, and shall discover and make known any attempts or designs of any other Indians or any Enemy whatever against his Majestys Subjects within this Province as soon as they shall know thereof and shall also hinder and Obstruct the same to utmost of their power, and on the other hand if any of the Indians refusing to ratify this Peace, shall make War upon the Tribe who have now confirmed the same; they shall upon Application have such aid and Assistance from the Government for their Defence, as the case may require.

4. It is agreed that the said Tribe of Indians shall not be hindered from, but have free liberty of Hunting and Fishing as usual: and that if they shall think a Truckhouse needfull at the River Chibenaccadie or any other place of their resort, they shall have the same built and proper Merchandize lodged therein, to be Exchanged for what the Indians shall have to dispose of, and that in the meantime the said Indians shall have free liberty to bring for Sale to Halifax or any other Settlement within this Province, Skins, feathers, fowl, fish or any other thing they shall have to sell, where they shall have liberty to dispose thereof to the best Advantage.

5. That a Quantity of Bread, Flour, & such other Provisions as can be procured, necessary for the Familys, and proportionable to the number of the said Indians, shall be given them half yearly for the time to come; and the same regard shall be had to the other Tribes that shall hereafter agree to renew and Ratify the Peace upon the Terms and Conditions now Stipulated.

6. That to Cherish a good harmony & mutual Correspondence between the said Indians & this Government, His Excellency Peregrine Thomas Hopson Esqr... hereby promises on the part of His Majesty, that the said Indians shall upon the first day of October Yearly, so long as they shall Continue in Friendship, receive

Presents of Blankets, Tobacco, some Powder & Shott; and the said Indians promise once every Year, upon the said first of October, to come by themselves or their Delegates and Receive the said Presents and Renew their Friendship and Submission.

7. That the Indians shall use their best Endeavours to save the lives and goods of any People Shipwrecked on this Coast, where they resort, and shall Conduct the People saved to Halifax with their Goods, & a reward adequate to the Salvage shall be given them.

8. That all Disputes whatsoever that may happen to arise between the Indians now at Peace, and others His Majesty's Subjects in this Province shall be tryed in His Majesty's Court of Civil Judicature, where the Indians shall have the same benefit, Advantage and Priviledges, as any others of His Majesty's Subjects.

In Faith & Testimony wherof, the Great Seal of the Province is hereunto Appended, and the partys to these presents have hereunto, interchangeably Set their Hands in the Council Chamber at Halifax this 22nd day of Nov. 1752, in the twenty-sixth year of His Majesty's Reign.

> [W. E. Daugherty, Maritime Indian Treaties in Historical Perspective
> (Ottawa: Indian and Northern Affairs Canada, 1981), pp. 76-77]

Section C
Expulsion of the Acadians

Old rivalries and deep-seated antagonism surfaced in the British and French seaboard colonies, giving rise to numerous acts of hostility in the seventeenth and eighteenth centuries. As Professor Andrew Hill Clark observed three decades ago, there is no simple explanation for the ultimate decision to uproot the Acadians, destroy their homes, confiscate their lands and livestock, and deport them. Wounded pride, prejudice, and self-interest all played a role, yet frustration and fear on the part of the British colonial officials cannot be discounted.

The ill treatment of the inhabitants of Louisbourg by the New England occupation force in 1745 and the dispersion of the Acadians 10 years later should be considered in the light of the long-standing acts of hostility that characterized French-British relations. One such action—the devastation of Newfoundland by Iberville's expedition in 1697—illustrates the degree of hatred and fear that colonists had when attacked by a Mi'kmaq and French force.

Jean-Paul Mascarene, a francophone of Huguenot descent, was appointed in 1720 to act as an intermediary between the British authorities and the Acadians, also to make a report on the state of defence works at Annapolis Royal and Canso. His 'Description of Nova Scotia' was written at a time when he witnessed the pitiful state of the British garrison and the dismal failure to extract an unqualified oath of allegiance from the Acadians.

The Acadians steadfastly refused to take the standard British oath of allegiance which might compromise their Catholic faith and oblige them to bear arms against the French in the eventuality of war. They were also conscious of Mi'kmaq pressure not to compromise with the British.

When some Acadians were found among the defenders of French forts on the Nova Scotian border in 1755, Governor Lawrence summoned a number of delegates from their settlements before the Council at Halifax, and informed them that they would have to swear allegiance without a proviso that they would not have to bear arms. Their refusal to do so seemed to justify the decision to clear the area of its French-origin population to make way for a British population that would guarantee the future security of this part of the empire.

The parishioners of Grand Pré, summoned to meet in the church to hear the latest orders from the Governor, appear to have been taken by surprise by the severity of his orders. Some escaped, but most were forcibly boarded on waiting vessels and shipped off to unknown destinations in the Anglo-American colonies. This traumatic experience has remained imbedded in Acadian consciousness and folklore and has become an issue in Canadian history.

French Raids on Newfoundland, 1697

I have none of yours unanswered, and am sorry that I have so sad a subject to write at present. This is to give you an account of a ship that put in here [Dartmouth] this day at Nones in 26 days from St. John's with 230 men, women and children, that place and all other harbours in Newfoundland having been taken by the French, so that what debts and goods we had there is utterly lost...

Passengers give this following account, more than is in the affidavit, viz. that they were informed by the French who had been in the Bay of Conception that Bonavista, Carbonear, and Harbor Grace were destroyed by four hundred Indians and one hundred French who came into the bay overland. That all at Bonavista were put to the sword, which was the treatment they intended to give to those at St. John's, could they have come on them before they had put themselves in a posture of defence; that the inhabitants of Harbor Grace and Carbonear were retired to two small islands off each harbour, which they would keep having provisions and ammunition wherewith to defend [themselves]. It will become everyone to do their utmost to regain this so profitable trade to the kingdom, which may be done by our sending four or five men-of-war thither, with all convenient speed. We do by the next post intend to petition the King to that end, which we hope will be backed with one from the tradery of your city, and all other western ports. Now is the time if ever to recover that country, and the season being so far advanced, I hope the King will take it into his consideration, and order a speedy force thither.

[Archives of Newfoundland, C.O. 195/2, John Likes to Simon Cole, 14 January 1696/7. Text modernized]

Mascarene's Report on British Vulnerability

There are four considerable settlements on the south side of the Bay of Fundy, Annapolis Royal, Minas, Chignecto, and Cobequid, which shall be treated on separately. Several families are scattered along the Eastern Coast which shall be also mentioned in their turn.

The Inhabitants of these Settlements are still all French and Indians; the former have been tolerated in the possession of the lands they possessed, under the French Government, and have had still from time to time longer time allowed them either to take the Oaths to the Crown of Great Britain, or to withdraw, which they have always found some pretence or other to delay, and to ask for longer time for consideration. They being in general of the Romish persuasion, cannot be easily drawn from the French Interest, to which they seem to be entirely wedded, tho' they find a great deal more sweetness under the English Government. They use all the means they can to keep the Indians from dealing with the British subjects, and by their mediation spreading among the Savages several false Notions tending to make them diffident, and frighten them from a free intercourse with them, and prompting them now and then to some mischief which may increase that diffidence, and oblige them to keep more at a distance.

There are but two reasons which may plead for the keeping of those French Inhabitants in this country. 1st. The depriving the French of the addition of such a strength, which might render them too powerful neighbours, especially if these people on their withdrawing hence are received and settled at Cape Breton; and secondly, the use that may be made of them in providing necessaries for erecting fortifications, and for English Settlements and keeping on the stock of cattle, and the lands tilled, till the English are powerful enough of themselves to go on, which two last will sensibly decay if they withdraw before any considerable number of British subjects be settled in their stead, and it is also certain that they having the conveniency of saw mills (which it will not be in our power to hinder being destroyed by them, at their going away) may furnish sooner and cheaper the plank boards &c, requisite for building.

[NAC, MG 11, Nova Scotia A, Vol. 4, "Description of Nova Scotia" pp. 215-216]

Negotiating the Oath of Allegiance

At a Council held as aforesaid in His Majesty's Town of Annapolis Royal on Sunday the 25th of September 1726... The Honourable Lt. Governor of the Province acquainted [them] that he this day expected the deputies and the inhabitants with their answer conform to the appointment on Wednesday last and therefore desired the advice of the board what he should [do] in case they refused signing and taking the oaths of His Majesty.

The board thought that the only method to be used, was to demonstrate to them first the necessity of their so doing, and invite them thereunto by laying before them the many advantages and privileges of English subjects to which they by taking the oath of fidelity to His Majesty King George were as fully and freely entitled to as if they were the natural born subjects of Great Britain, as also the free exercise of their religion, estates and fortunes, otherwise they must of necessity retire immediately out of the province conform to His Majesty's directions for if arguments and promises of kind usage did not prevail, it would be to no purpose to pretend compelling them by force further than telling them what they might expect; and if thereby those who have plenty and good estates should be once engaged, the others would be either the more easily wrought upon or forced to be gone...

His Honour the Lieutenant Governor of the Province with the Honourable Lt. Governor of His Majesty's Town and Garrison of Annapolis Royal with the other members of the Council met at the Flag Bastion according to adjournment where the deputies [of the Acadians] with a number of the inhabitants being also present.

The Honourable Lt. Governor of the Province told them that he was glad to see them and that he hoped they had so far considered their own and children's future advantages, that they were come with a full resolution to take the oath of fidelity like good subjects...

Whereupon at the request of some of the inhabitants a French translation of the oath required to be taken was read unto them. Upon which some of them desiring that a clause whereby they might not be obliged to carry arms might be inserted.

The Governor told them that they had no reason to fear any such thing as that it being contrary to the laws of Great Britain that a Roman Catholic should serve in the army, His Majesty having so many faithful Protestant subjects first to provide for, and that all that His Majesty required of them was to be faithful subjects, not to join with any enemy, but for their own interest to discover all traiterous and evil designs, plots and conspiracies any ways formed against His Majesty's subjects and government and so peaceably and quietly to enjoy and improve their estates.

But they upon that motion made as aforesaid still refusing and desiring the said clause.

The Governor with the advice of the Council granted the same to be written upon the margin of the French translation in order to get them over by degrees. Whereupon they took and subscribed the same both in French and English.

[Archibald M. MacMechan, ed., Original Minutes of His Majesty's Council at Annapolis Royal, 1720-1739 *(Halifax: Nova Scotia Archives, 1908), Minutes of 25 September 1726, pp. 128-130. Text modernized]*

Confidential Resolution on the Expulsion of the Acadians, 1755

Resolution of Council, at Halifax, July 28, 1755.

The Deputy's of the French Inhabitants of the Districts of Annapolis, Mines and Piziquid have been called before the Council, and have refused to take the Oath of Allegiance to His Majesty; and have also declared this to be the Sentiments of the whole People; Whereupon the Council advised and it is accordingly determined that they shall be removed out of the Country, as soon as possible. And as to those about the Isthmus, all of whom were in arms and therefore entitled to no favour from the Government, It is determined to begin with them first; And for this purpose, orders are given for a sufficient number of Transports to be sent up the Bays with all possible dispatch for taking them on board; by whom you will receive particular Instructions as to the manner of their being disposed of, the places of their destination and every other thing necessary for that purpose.

In the mean time it will be proper to keep this measure as secret as possible, as well to prevent their attempting to Escape as to carry off their Cattle &ca: and the better to Effect this you will endeavour to fall upon some stratagem to get the Men, both young & old especially the Heads of Families into your power & detain them till the Transports shall arrive so as that they may be ready to be shipped off; for when this is done, it is not so much to be feared that the Women & Children will attempt to go away and carry off the Cattle: But least they should, it will not only be very proper to secure all their Shalops, Boats, Canoes, and every other vessel you can lay your hands upon; But also to send out party's to all Suspected Roads & places from time to time that they may be thereby intercepted.

As their whole Stock of Cattle and Corn is forfeited to the Crown by their Rebellion, and must be secured and applied towards a Reimbursement of the Expence the Government will be at in Transporting them out of the Country; care must be had that nobody make any Bargain for the purchasing of them under any colour or pretence whatsoever, if they do, the sale will be void; for the Inhabitants have now (since the Order of Council) no property in them, nor will they be allowed to carry away the least thing, but their ready Money & Household Furniture.

[NAC, MG 18, Series 1, Robert Monckton Papers, p. 81]

Summons at Grand Pré, 5 September 1755

At three in the afternoon the French inhabitants appeared agreeable to their citation at the church in Grand Pré amounting to 418 of their best men upon which I ordered a table to be set in the centre of the church and being attended with those of my officers who were off guard duty delivered them through interpreters the King's orders in the following words:

Gentlemen: I have received from his Excellency Governor Lawrence, the King's commission which I have in my hand and by whose orders you are convened together to manifest to you his Majesty's final resolution to the French inhabitants of this his province of Nova Scotia, who for almost half a century have had more indulgence granted them than any other subjects in any part of his Dominions. What use you have made of them, you yourself best know.

The part of my duty I am now upon is what is thought necessary, is very disagreeable to my nature and temperament as I know must be grievous to you who are of the same species... That your lands and tenaments, cattle of all kinds and livestock of all sorts are forfeited to the Crown with all other effects, except your money and household goods and you yourselves to be removed from this Province. This is pre-emptorily his Majesty's orders that the whole French inhabitants of these districts be removed...

I shall do everything in my power that all those goods be secured to you and that you are not molested in carrying them off, and also that whole families shall go in the same vessel, and make this removal which I sense must give you a great deal of trouble as easy as his Majesty's service will permit and hope that in whatever part of the world you may fall you may be faithful subjects, a peaceable and happy people.

I must also inform you that it is his Majesty's pleasure that you remain in security under the inspection and direction of the troops I have the honour to command.

And then declared them to be the King's prisoners.

[Winslow's Journal, 5 September 1755, Report of the Public Archives of Canada for 1905 *(Ottawa: King's Printer, 1906-1909), Vol. II, pp. 19-29. Text modernized]*

1. Were the Acadians a backward and degenerated fragment of French metropolitan society, or a self-sufficient, independent and progressive, albeit isolated, colonial society?

2. What bound the Mi'kmaq to the French, and why were the British never able to undermine this alliance?

3. How do you respond to three important issues raised by the Treaty of Utrecht (1713): what were the 'ancient boundaries' of Acadia? how far did the laws of Great Britain allow Catholics to practise their religion and what restrictions remained on their civil liberties? what would happen to the farmsteads of the Acadians who chose to leave for French territory?

4. In what ways can military occupation and cession be traumatic for both the conquered and the conquerors? What did the Acadians hope for when they pleaded for 'longer time for consideration'?

5. Was the deportation of the Acadians necessary, legal, and/or well executed?

John Bartlett Brebner, *New England's Outpost: Acadia before the Conquest of Canada* (New York: Lennox Hill, 1973)

Jean Daigle, ed., *The Acadians of the Maritimes: Thematic Studies* (Moncton: University of Moncton Press, 1982)

Olive P. Dickason, *Louisbourg and the Indians: A Study in Imperial Relations, 1713-1760* (Ottawa: National Historic Parks, 1976)

Naomi E.S. Griffiths, *The Acadian Deportation: Deliberate Perfidy or Cruel Necessity?* (Toronto: Copp Clark, 1969)

_____, *The Acadians: Creation of a People* (Toronto: McGraw-Hill Ryerson, 1973)

_____, *The Contexts of Acadian History, 1686-1784* (Montreal-Kingston: McGill-Queen's University Press, 1992)

Douglas Edward Leach, *The Northern Colonial Frontier, 1697-1763* (New York: Holt Rinehart & Winston, 1966)

_____, *Aims for Empire: A Military History of British Colonies in North America, 1607-1763* (Toronto: Collier-Macmillan, 1973)

W.S. MacNutt, *The Atlantic Provinces: The Emergence of Colonial Society, 1712-1857* (Toronto: McClelland & Stewart, 1972)

Kenneth M. Morrison, *The Embattled Northeast* (Berkeley: University of California Press, 1984)

John G. Reid, *Acadia, Maine, and New Scotland: Marginal Colonies in the Seventeenth Century* (Toronto: University of Toronto Press, 1981)

L.F.S. Upton, *Micmacs and Colonists: Indian-White Relations in the Maritimes, 1713-1867* (Vancouver: University of British Columbia Press, 1979)

Staples Economy and Public Enterprise

The evolution of New France raises the question of whether public enterprise is essential to the growth of a sparsely populated, geographically overextended, and financially limited colony. It has been suggested that state intervention was necessary to assist private entrepreneurs, to stimulate local trade and commerce, and to ensure a stable social community in a challenging northern environment.

The colony was demographically weak. From 1600 to 1760, only about 12 000 immigrants came to Canada and remained to settle permanently. By 1760, the population of Canada was only about 70 000. Neighbouring Acadia may have had another 12 000 inhabitants when their deportation began in 1755. There were few pressures in France impelling people toward emigration. France was not overpopulated and it enjoyed comparatively diversified agricultural production. Unlike England, religious dissidents were discouraged from leaving (although significant numbers fled to surrounding states) and, after 1627, were not permitted officially to take up residence in New France. Thus, two important sources of immigrants in the seventeenth century—landless peasants and persecuted religious minorities—were not available to populate New France. Population growth in the colony may be attributed to natural increase, stimulated by relatively high fertility rates and comparatively low mortality rates. In the mid-seventeenth century there were few European women in the colony, but by the mid-eighteenth century a balance had been achieved and soon women outnumbered men.

The geography of New France was also an important element. It was in many respects an overextended colony, stretching eventually from Placentia in Newfoundland to the foothills of the Rockies, from the Gulf of Mexico in the south to Hudson Bay in the north. The upper country, which held out prospects of untapped sources of furs, mines to be discovered, and Native peoples to be evangelized, was viewed as the natural and logical dependency of the riverine establishment, hence its simple designation as the *pays d'en haut*, the upper Canada region.

The resources, both human and material, which France was willing and able to commit to any extensive expansion into the heart of the continent were limited. Therefore, it was soon decreed that boundaries should be set to the area of intensive agricultural settlement in order to create a structured space and a compact colony. The upper region represented colonization without settlement, as the French presence there was limited to a few military garrisons, some trading posts, and a restricted number of mission stations. In 1701, Louis XIV adopted a more aggressive strategy to counter and frighten off Anglo-American expansion beyond the Appalachian highlands into the Ohio and Mississippi valleys, a policy that brought France into inevitable conflict with Britain in North America.

Limited resources were available in the colony itself. It was soon realized that, unlike New Spain, this northern colony yielded little immediately in 'riches in gold and glory,' but was instead a source of only the less attractive primary products—staples such as codfish, furs, lumber, wheat and, from 1747 to 1754, wild ginseng.

The western European powers engaged in colonial ventures—France, England, Spain, and Portugal operated closed mercantile trading systems excluding foreign competition and limiting colonial enterprise. This economic theory or concept has been called *mercantilism*. It meant that a colony such as Canada was deemed to fit into such a system by supplying raw materials for metropolitan manufacture and providing a market for the finished products. Canada was considered to possess great potential for the development of agriculture, mining, and forestry. But few French entrepreneurs were willing to invest the large sums of capital necessary to launch such enterprises in a distant colony known to have long, severe winters, and still believed by many to be infested with cannibalistic savages, venomous snakes, and putrid forests exhaling noxious vapours. There was never a great flow of immigrants to the colony.

Section A
State Controls and Initiatives

The economy remained in a 'state of infancy' according to one Minister of Marine and Colonies. This situation has sometimes been attributed by historians entirely to French policy, notably mercantilist restrictions which encouraged metropolitan self-sufficiency at the expense of colonial initiatives. But a small, scattered population meant a small pool of producers, a restricted market for finished products, and few individuals with sufficient capital to invest in new enterprises. Not until the end of the French régime did regional service centres emerge, and a royal road linking Montreal to Quebec complement river transport. Wheat and lumber were added to the list of staples, but rich, productive mines were never discovered. There was limited intercolonial trade with the Antilles and Ile Royale in the eighteenth century. Local sawmills, grist mills, tanneries, tar works, and small shipyards for constructing fishing vessels for the offshore fishery made up local initiative.

Between 1736 and 1741, the Intendant Hocquart was able to obtain Crown investments in the colony for construction of a Lachine canal, support of the St. Maurice ironworks, founding a royal shipyard near Quebec, subsidizing La Vérendrye's exploration on the Western prairies, upgrading the port of Quebec, and constructing royal roads from Quebec to Montreal and from Montreal to Lake Champlain. Two of these state enterprises are of particular interest—the St. Maurice ironworks (which began as a private enterprise, was heavily subsidized, and eventually taken over by the Crown), and the St. Charles shipyards. Workers' shacks huddled around the belching smoke and roaring fires of the bloomery furnaces at the St. Maurice works to form the first company town. All supplies were bought at the company store, everyone attended mass at the company chapel, and no one could leave the compound without the manager's permission. At the St. Charles shipyards, the metropolitan workers were confined to barracks, and were in addition subject to military regulations. Little wonder they envied their free-wheeling unskilled colonial co-workers.

Louis XIV and his minister for colonial affairs, Jean-Baptiste Colbert, warned the overly ambitious Intendant Jean Talon not to make unwarranted commitments of metropolitan resources in order to expand Canada beyond a restricted Laurentian valley colony.

Marie de l'Incarnation, superior of the Ursuline convent in Quebec, was able to keep abreast of colonial affairs in spite of being cloistered. In addition to her theological writings, she maintained a large correspondence which revealed her insight into political and economic affairs. She was

La Pesche des Morues, 1698, vignette taken from map of North and South America, Nicolas de Fer, Paris. *[NAC, National Maps of Canada, NMC 26825]* impressed by the state initiatives under the first Intendant's direction to develop the colonial economy.

The fur trade as a principal source of revenue in Canada also gave rise to rivalry between merchant associations, sometimes backed by one or more colonial officials. The fort and trading post at Cataraqui [Kingston] had originally been operated by Robert Cavelier de La Salle, serving the interests of Governor Frontenac. There ensued a debate over whether the post should be maintained in the interests of the state.

When a glut of furs developed in France, the authorities were ordered to suppress the granting of *congés*, or trading licences, for the upper country of Canada. This administrative measure resulted in some serious consequences in the colony.

Commanders at the western posts had enjoyed exclusive trading rights, but in 1742 Louis XV and Minister Maurepas ordered that, with the exception of the forts at Michilimackinac and Detroit, trade would be farmed out to colonial merchants and *voyageurs*.

Pehr Kalm, a botanist and naturalist of Finnish origin who studied under such celebrities as Anders Celsius and Carl Linnaeus at the University of Uppsala in Sweden, spent the entire summer and autumn of 1749, a high point of French scientific interest in the colony, studying the fauna and flora of New France and collecting specimens for the Swedish Academy of Sciences. His visit to the Forges du Saint-Maurice was a side-trip, but its description retains a certain interest for students of colonial technology and the origins of a company town.

The unskilled workers at the St. Charles shipyards were hired in the colony by the day at a relatively high wage, while the skilled workers recruited in France worked by contract with the naval authorities. When the metropolitan workers called a work stoppage, complaining that they had to work in inclement weather and were provided with poor housing and food, official reaction was swift and severe.

Wild ginseng growing in the Canadian woods, first identified by the Jesuit missionaries, was shipped to France for the China trade beginning in 1721. The Company of the Indies made enormous profits from this exotic product from 1747 until 1753, when the Canton merchants refused to accept Canadian ginseng because it had become of poor quality, consisting of many immature or improperly cured roots.

Warning Against Colonial Over-Expansion, 1666

His Majesty cannot agree with all the arguments you make on the means of making of Canada a great and mighty state, finding therein diverse obstacles which could be overcome only after a long lapse of time because even if he had no other matters of state and he could apply both his attention and his power thereto, it would not be prudent to depopulate his Realm, which would be required in order to have Canada populated. Besides this consideration which you will recognize as essential, there is another matter which is that if His Majesty caused a larger number of people to go over there than what the country presently under cultivation could feed, it appears certain that if they did not all perish at the outset at least they would suffer great hardships which by reducing them to continuous listlessness would weaken them little by little... You will understand sufficiently from this discourse that the true means of strengthening this Colony is to make Justice reign there, to establish a sound civil administration, to take good care of the inhabitants, to procure for them peace, repose, and abundance, and to inure them to all sorts of enemies, because all these matters which are the basis and foundation of all colonies being carefully observed, the country will become populated by slow degrees and with the passing of a reasonable period of time it could become quite important...

You must always keep in mind the plan that I outlined in a few words, which is in line with what is contained in greater detail in your [royal] Instructions, as well as to the conversations I had with you here. And never depart therefrom because it is notoriously impossible that all those ideas about forming great and mighty states can succeed if one does not have unprofitable People to send over to the places one wishes to colonize.

[*Rapport de l'Archiviste de la Province de Ouébec. 1922-1923 (Québec: L.-Amable Proulx, 1923), Colbert to Talon, 5 January 1666, p. 41*]

Testimonial to Talon's Talents

Marie de l'Incarnation to Her Son, 27 August 1670

Monsieur Talon has at last arrived at Quebec...the King is making great expenditures here, He has sent five hundred more girls this year and a great many soldiers and officers—as well as horses, sheep, and goats to breed. Monsieur Talon has the King's orders precisely respected. He has commanded that hemp, linen cloth, and serge be made; work at this has begun and it will increase little by little. He has had a market built at Quebec, a brewery, and, because of the prodigious number of beasts in the country, a tannery. Such manufacturing has never been practised in the past in Canada, and if it succeeds, this will very much lessen the great expense required to bring everything from France. The women and girls are urged as strongly as possible to learn to spin. It is desired that we should teach our seminarians, both French and Savage, and we are offered material for the purpose.

As well, a threefold commerce is being introduced between France, the West Indies, and Quebec. Three vessels, laden with pine boards, peas, and Indian corn, are about to set sail for the islands: there they will unload their merchandise and take on a cargo of sugar for France, whence they will bring back the things necessary to supply the whole country. And this threefold commerce is completed in a year.

In addition there is cod-fishing a hundred leagues from here, which if properly undertaken will produce immense revenues. All this is to build with time a great country that will enrich the merchants.

As for us, our fortune is made; we are the portion of Jesus Christ and Jesus Christ is our portion, and our profit is to try to possess him by practicing our Rules and doing his will. Pray to divine Majesty that he will bestow this grace upon us.

> *[Joyce Marshall, ed.,* Word from New France: The Selected Letters of Marie de l'Incarnation *(Toronto: Oxford University Press, 1967), pp. 359, 361-362]*

Mercantilist Directives, 1704-1706

Pontchartrain to Vaudreuil and Beauharnois, 14 June 1704

His Majesty has been very pleased to learn that the growing of hemp has met with the success that we had hoped for. But he must explain that he never intended to allow cloth to be manufactured in Canada so that the settlers might do without that of France. Thus, no weavers will be sent to the colony. The settlers must forward their hemp to France to be sold there either to the state for the servicing of the royal navy, or else to private parties to dispense them from buying this product from foreigners. Generally, they must observe that whatever can compete with the manufactories of France must never be produced in the colonies. Colonies must act as suppliers of raw materials to enable the manufactories of the kingdom to do without imports from foreign states. They must consider this as one of the principal purposes of colonies which are established solely for the benefit of the mother countries and never to permit them to do without those metropoles.

King to Raudot, 17 June 1705

...since colonies must be conceived only in relation to the Kingdom, they must be scrupulously prevented from supplying each other with the merchandise which they are accustomed to import from France. It would not be proper, for example, for Canada to supply wheat to the islands [Antilles] in return for refined sugar because this would be prejudicial to the interests of the cities of La Rochelle, Bordeaux, Nantes and others which send their vessels to the colonies and which bear all the charges of the state.

It is equally important to prohibit every type of exchange between the inhabitants of Canada and the English, since the latter would only supply them with goods they would otherwise obtain from France...

Pontchartrain to Raudot, 9 June 1706

In general, it is not proper for manufacturing to establish itself in that country because that would only be done to the detriment of those in France; rather you must proceed so that the raw materials of Canada pass to France to be manufactured. That must be the general policy, nevertheless, one must not prevent some enterprises from becoming established, especially for the poor people.

[NAC, MG 1, Series B, Vol. 27, (i) Pontchartrain to Vaudreuil &
Beauharnois, 14 June 1704, fols. 117-118; (ii) King to Raudot, 17 June
1705, fol. 56; (iii) Pontchartrain to Raudot, 9 June 1706, fol. 235]

Debate on the Value of the Fort at Cataraqui

Reasons justifying how useless and expensive it is:

This trade will not be considerable in peacetime because the Iroquois as much as possible will take their furs to the English who pay more than the French. This trade is in itself contrary to the principles according to which the colony is to be administered...the fur trade can only be good inasmuch as the Natives bring the furs into the colony and there take their necessities in exchange.

It is necessary to go 30 to 40 leagues off the direct route to go to this fort through enemy country and we could not supply foodstuffs to a large group because there is too much difficulty transporting goods from Montreal just for the garrison... How could Cataraqui serve as a refuge for the French and the Natives when it is 50 leagues from the nearest village of our enemies [Iroquois] and separated by a large lake which is nearly always stormy?...

Reasons that can be cited to indicate its utility:

In peacetime we will be able to trade there with the Iroquois who hunt nearby and obtain from them some furs. By posting there a blacksmith to repair their axes and arms, the revenue could be attributed to the creditors of Mr. de La Salle, formerly the owner of this post, to whom considerable sums are owed.

In time of war, our Native allies will make this their base and obtain their supplies there.

It will serve as a supply base for foodstuffs and munitions necessary for any expeditions we wish to undertake, and serve as a retreat for the French and Natives going to or returning from raids on the Iroquois, and a place to shelter the sick and wounded.

[NAC, MG 1, Series C11A, Vol. 14, Memorandum concerning the fort at
Cataraqui, 6 November 1695, fol. 30. Trans. CJJ]

Suppression of the Fur Trade, 1696

The cancellation of the granting of congés [trading licences], which after mature consideration was found to be an indispensable necessity, has aroused the principal inhabitants of Canada—some out of love for their country, predicting it would reduce the number of beaver pelts brought in and consequently the wealth of the colony, others out of self interest in the trade. They say that the Natives our allies not being able to trade with us will go to the English who will supply them to our detriment. That in war time the English will oblige them to join them to make war on us, while others add that the Iroquois will fall on them and carry off their children to raise them...It was with these facts in mind that a letter was sent last year saying that the King found it good to keep open the posts at Michilimackinac and St. Joseph among the Miamis, but that he did not want the officers and soldiers posted there to carry on any trade. We wrote in reply that the officers and soldiers could not survive otherwise and so he would have to recall them... It is certain that these officers and soldiers will find it hard to spend their lives in a wild country with only their salaries.

[NAC, MG1, Series C11A, Vol. 14, Memorandum on the Affairs of Canada, 1696, fols. 413-415. Trans CJJ]

Orders to Reorganize Upper Country Trade
Louis XV to Governor Beauharnois and Intendant Hocquart, 30 April 1742

When His Majesty allowed posts to be established in the upper country for trading furs with the Native nations which were discovered there, His Majesty's intention was always that their exploitation be reserved to the merchants and voyageurs living in Canada. However, in order to afford the officers of the troops serving in the colony the opportunity to develop their affairs, he has for some years desired the exploitation of these posts to be granted on occasion to those officers under whose command they have been placed.

But in addition to the fact that such exploitations could create in these officers a state of mind hardly conducive to His service it appears also that, taking into account the present state of the trade of the colony, it is not appropriate that it be deprived any further of the benefits these activities could afford.

Therefore with the objective of having these taken advantage of, and at the same time getting some help from them in defraying the expenses of the colony, it has become necessary to make arrangements to place these matters on a sound basis. There seems to be no better means for His Majesty to proceed than by leasing the posts suitable to the advantage of our trade and of the King's service itself to the merchants and voyageurs... With this objective in mind, His Majesty has ordered that the posts of St. Joseph River, Green Bay, Lake Nipigon, Kaministiquia, Michipicotin, Temiscamingue, as well as the posts established among the Miami and Ouyatanons, and which are operated by the officers, be leased as of next year to the colony's merchants and voyageurs. Although at several of these posts we would not need to send commanding officers, His Majesty is nevertheless willing to retain these positions for them and to grant extra pay to those whom the Marquis de Beauharnois thinks appropriate for this distinction, and in whose appointment he can continue to have confidence.

So to persuade these officers to contribute to the success of the trade of these posts, there appears to be no surer means than interesting them by calculating their extra pay on a method of prorating it to the revenues from the trade carried on there. It is on such a basis that His Majesty desires their pay to be made...In order to benefit the most from the leases to be given out for the posts in question, it is appropriate to put them up at public auctions, it being necessary nevertheless to allot them only to merchants and voyageurs who by their conduct give no reason for concern, either in terms of the success of the trade or with regard to the disposition in which the Natives of the various posts must be maintained. That is a choice which demands particular attention on the part of Sieurs Beauharnois and Hocquart.

[NAC, MG 1, Series B, Vol. 74, fols. 503v- 511]

Pehr Kalm's Visit to the St. Maurice Ironworks

While my companions were taking some rest, I got on horseback and went to see the Forges [ironworks], passing through a fairly high, sandy and generally flat countryside. No mountains, not even any stones.

The plant, which is the only one of its kind in the country, is located three miles west of Trois-Rivières. There are there two large forges, besides two smaller ones at the back of each of these under the same roof. The bellows are made of wood as is everything else, like in the forges of Sweden. The melting-furnaces are close to the forges and resemble ours. The mine is two and one-half leagues from the foundry and the ore is hauled there on sleighs in the winter. It consists of a kind of moor ore which is found in veins lying six inches or a foot below the surface of the ground. Each vein is from six to eighteen inches in depth with white sand underneath. The veins are surrounded by sand on both sides and covered by thin earth on the top. The ore is quite rich and sits in the veins in loose lumps the size of a couple [of] fists, although a few are almost eighteen inches thick. These lumps are riddled with holes which are filled with red ochre. The ore is so soft that it can be crushed between one's fingers. Use is made of a grey limestone that is quarried in the vicinity for assisting in the smelting of the ore. For this purpose they also use a clay marle that is found nearby.

The country being covered with forests which are never cut down, it is easy to make charcoal in great quantities. The fuel coming from evergreen trees, such as fir, for example, is preferred for the forge, but the fuel of the deciduous trees is best for the bloomery process. The iron that is made in this plant is, I am told, soft, pliable and tough, and rust does not attack it as readily as ordinary iron. And on this point, it appears that a great difference is made between Spanish iron and iron from here in shipbuilding. The smelter was founded in 1737 by private individuals who afterwards ceded it to the king. They cast cannon and mortars of different sizes here, iron stoves which are common all over Canada, cauldrons, etc. not to mention iron bars. They tried to make steel here but they were unable to bring it to the required degree of perfection because of being unacquainted with the best way to harden it.

The smelter is under the surveillance of many officials and inspectors, who live in very lovely homes built expressly for them. Everyone is agreed that it does not pay its way and that in order to keep it operating the king each year must pay off its deficit. This fact is attributed to insufficient population, and the colonists have enough to do cultivating their fields, it is only by spending money and with great difficulty that one can obtain workers elsewhere. This explanation may appear plausible, yet this smelter ought to be a profitable enterprise for several reasons: the mine is easy to work, it is next door to the foundry, and the iron extracted is very fusible. The iron is of good quality and can be transported easily throughout the country. Besides, as it is the only enterprise of this kind in Canada, it faces no competition, and it is from there that all the iron tools and all other iron things one may need have to be bought. Moreover, a river which comes down from the smelter to the St. Lawrence river offers an easy and cheap transportation route for the metal to all points in the country. The personnel of the establishment, from the officials down to the servants, seem to live in opulence. In the evening I was back at Trois-Rivières.

[Louis-Wilfrid Marchand. éd., Voyage de Kalm en Amérique *(Montréal: Société historique de Montréal, 1880), Vol.2, excerpts from pp. 52-85]*

Royal Shipyards Strike of 1731

Beauharnois and Hocquart to Minister, 2 October 1731

The carpenters sent from Rochefort did their duty well. M. Hocquart meanwhile found it necessary to repress their mutiny, in the beginning and on one occasion only, by imprisonment and putting them in irons. It went to the point of resisting the orders of their Commandant and not accepting whatever to work in one of the King's hangars, although they are hired on a monthly contract, at a time when the Canadians had been given leave because of the bad weather. They recognized their mistake and became very submissive. They could become accustomed to the country. One of them has already married here...

The King's works are not without bringing some retardation in the enterprises undertaken by individuals and hindering them somewhat in their refitting. In the meantime we try to help them as much as possible. For their part, they ask permission to assign work on Sundays and feast days when they are pressed for time. We are much aware of the difficulty in obtaining workers from France. There are already several [Canadians] who have been trained here at the King's shipyards and we hope that a few will be able to come from Acadia...

[NAC, MG 1, Series C11A, Vol. 75, pp. 356-357]

A Short-Lived Exotic Staple—The Ginseng Boom

Ginseng is the current French name in Canada of a plant, the root of which has a very great value in China. It has been growing since time immemorial in the Chinese Tartary and in Korea, where it is annually collected and brought to China. Father Du Halde says it is the most precious and the most useful of all the plants in eastern Tartary, and attracts every year a number of people into the deserts of that country. The Mantchou-Tartars called it Orhota, that is, the most noble or queen of plants. The Tartars and Chinese praise it very much, and ascribe to it the power of curing several dangerous diseases and that of restoring to the body new strength and supplying the loss caused by the exertion of the mental and physical faculties. An ounce of ginseng brings the surprising price of seven or eight ounces of silver at Peking. When the French botanists in Canada first saw a picture of it, they remembered to have seen a similar plant in this country. They were confirmed in their conjecture by considering that several settlements in Canada lie in the same latitude as those parts of the Chinese Tartary, and China where the true ginseng grows wild. They succeeded in their attempt and found the same plant wild and abundant in several parts of North America, both in the French and English plantations, in level parts of the woods...

The French use this root for curing asthma, as a stomachic, and promoting fertility in women. The trade which is carried on with it here is very brisk, for they gather great quantities of it and send them to France, whence they are brought to China and sold there to great advantage. It is said that the merchants in France met with amazing success in this trade at the outset, but by continuing to send the ginseng over to China its price has fallen considerably there and consequently in France and in Canada; however, they still find some profit in it. In the summer of 1748 a pound of ginseng was sold for six francs or livres at Quebec; but its common price here is one hundred sols or five livres. During my stay in Canada all the merchants at Quebec and Montreal received orders from their correspondents in France to send over a quantity of ginseng, there being an uncommon demand for it this summer. The roots were accordingly collected in Canada with all possible haste. The Indians especially travelled about the country in order to collect as much as they could and to sell it to the merchants at Montreal. The Indians in the neighbourhood of this town [Quebec] were likewise so much taken up with this business that the French farmers were not able during that time to hire a single Indian, as they commonly do to help them in the harvest.

Many people feared lest by continuing for several successive years to collect these plants without leaving one or two in each place to propogate their species, there would soon be very few of them left, which I think is very likely to happen, for by all accounts they formerly grew in abundance round Montreal, but at present there is not a single plant of it to be found, so effectually have they been rooted out. This obliged the Indians this summer to go far within the English boundaries to collect these roots. From the merchants of Montreal one received 40 francs a minot of these fresh roots. After the Indians have sold the fresh product to the merchants, the latter must take a great deal of pains with them. They are spread on the floor to dry, which commonly requires two months or more, according as the season is wet or dry. During that time they must be turned once or twice every day, lest they should spoil or moulder. Ginseng has never been found far north of Montreal. The father superior of the clergy here and several other people assured me that the Chinese value Canadian ginseng as much as the Tartarian and that no one ever had been entirely acquainted with the Chinese method of preparing it. However, it is thought that amongst other preparations they dip the roots in a decoction of the leaves of ginseng. The roots prepared by the Chinese are almost transparent and look like horn inside, and the roots which are fit for use must be heavy, solid or compact inside.

[*Adolph B. Benson, ed.,* Peter Kalm's Travels in North America. The English version of 1770 *(New York: Dover Publications, 1964), Vol. II, pp. 435-437]*

Section B
Assessing Colonial Progress

Although there is no doubt that state intervention in the colonial economy was generally beneficial, the rate of progress was often judged unsatisfactory. New France's economy, considered in the imperial framework, was assessed in comparison to the value placed on the production of plantation colonies such as Guadeloupe, Martinique, and St.-Domingue [Haiti]. Scholars today often make comparisons with development in the Anglo-American colonies, failing to underscore the differences in climate and topography as well as incentives for emigration between the two situations. The mercantilist restrictions so often cited as having retarded economic development in New France were also enforced by the British in their colonies.

In comparison to prices in France, all merchandise in the colony was extremely expensive. The suppliers in Europe bore the costs of insurance and trans-Atlantic transport, and ran the risk of losing their vessels in storms, through piracy, and by seizure in wartime. Labour costs in the colony reflected the scarcity of skilled workers.

Both the Intendant and the Governor were required to give their assessment of the colonial situation in order that Versailles could draw up an *état du roi* listing financial allocations for the year. The absence of a real budget showing a yearly balance between revenues and expenditures suggests that heavy debts could be incurred, and that the administration could readily be defrauded not only by contractors but also by its officials. From time to time, colonial officials found it necessary, or convenient, to disregard the orders they received from Versailles.

The growth in population in New France was the result of natural increase, there being but a trickle of involuntary immigrants consisting of more brides and some prisoners—salt smugglers, counterfeiters, and poachers who were quickly rehabilitated in the colony as enterprising individuals. As more land was brought into cultivation, production increased, but there remained the threat of crop failure and widespread shortages.

Gilles Hocquart, who served as financial commissary in New France from 1729 to 1731 and as Intendant from 1731 to 1748, observed that very few Canadians possessed the requisite managerial skills and capital to invest, and that metropolitan firms skimmed off the major profits of colonial business. He became convinced that the state would have to intervene to protect the colonial entrepreneurs and help them gain a larger share of the colony's commerce. The control of trade in the Great Lakes basin was in the hands of the military officers commanding at each post.

The figures for total income in Canada are based on annual allocations from the royal treasury, reported in the *état du roi*, and from the war chest, reported as *recettes extraordinaires* in some years. There were some additional revenues from the royal domain surrounding Tadoussac to pay the salaries of colonial officials and bureaucrats. Expenditures greatly exceeded income as the colony experienced a new period of warfare after 1744.

Fiscal abuse in the colony under Intendant Bigot, and the increasing costs of keeping the Amerindian allies satisfied, made the Minister of the Marine, Antoine-Louis Rouillé, despair of being able to reduce the expenditures on Canada. Growing anti-colonialist sentiments in France, nourished by the writings of *philosophes* such as Voltaire, brought into question the advisability of continuing to spend large sums to retain a comparatively unprofitable colony.

The British conquest may have continued and even accentuated some of the characteristics of the colonial economy and its mercantilist policies. The British administrators, although very critical of the French régime and obsessed with their own concept of freedom, were also aware of some of the problems and weaknesses that had bedevilled the French administration, and they offered few different solutions.

Schedule of Prices in New France, 1652

Schedule of prices of merchandize coming from France in this year 1652 for which the merchants are paid seventy-five percent above cost;

Cask of flour weighing six hundred pounds	142#	10s	10d
Barrel of French wine	420#		
Barrel of brandy	872#		
Barrel of salt pork weighing about 200 l.	105#	18s	
Ell of linen worth 15 sols		28s	
Pair of shoes worth 50s. in France	4#	10s	
Shirts worth 35s in France	3#	5s	

In previous years the passage for a man coming from France cost twenty-five, thirty and thirty-five livres at most, but this year by way of ships from Normandy it cost fifty livres, also by way of ships from La Rochelle.

Price of goods produced in the country of New France:		
Bushel of peas, Parisian standard	8#	
Bushel of Indian corn [maize]	8#	
Bushel of wheat	8#	
Barrel of five hundred eels	26# to 30#	
Hundred planks ten ft. long, 10 in. wide and 1 in, thick	50#	
Pound of butter	12 - 15#	
Good slaughtering ox, 7 to 8 years	200#	
A good cow	70#	
An ordinary sow	30#	
A good slaughtering hog	46# to 50#	
Daily wages of a mason		40s
of a master carpenter		40s
of a master cabinetmaker		40s
Daily wage of a carter with two oxen during the winter season	3#	
during the summer	4#	
Daily wage of a good labourer		30s

Indentured servants after their contract time is fulfilled, according to their contracts for three, four, or five years drawn up in France, hire out at thirty, thirty-five and forty écus a year in spite of the fact that their board costs more than two hundred livres. This year we will do well to pay no more than three hundred livres each.

[NAC, MG 18, Bibliothèque du Louvre, H-27, Estat du prix des marchandises, 1652, pp. 161-162. Trans. CJJ]

Report on Economic Matters

Governor Frontenac and Intendant Champigny to Their Minister, 9 November 1694

Sieur de Frontenac is uncertain if accurate memoranda were sent off how His Majesty can regard the enclosure of the chateau at Quebec as an unnecessary matter, since it was the first work that was to be undertaken not only to enclose within this wall the powder magazine which was outside the old one and thereby exposed to all the attacks that the least of all hostile Natives or English prisoners dispersed throughout the town might proffer, but also to ensure the safety of the governor and the most distinguished people of the country who had no refuge in a town that was wide open and without fortifications. When we began this work we did not plan to make the fortifications enclosing the town all at once, but the information we have since received about the plans of the English against Quebec have obliged us to do so. This expense was taken from the 20 000 livres destined for fortifications, not wishing to overrun and with the thought of continuing year after year the other most essential projects of which sieur de Frontenac thought he was the judge. And His Majesty is most humbly begged to consider that when his orders not to proceed with this work were sent by the vessels which arrived the 20th of July last year, the said enclosing wall was almost finished since it was perfectly completed by the month of August.

We have been content to have work done on the most essential fortifications and the expenditure for that taken from the funds for the present year... We still have to have completed the terreplein of the enclosure at Quebec, for which we will employ the inhabitants next year. We have had stakes cut and transported to build the new wall along the river front at Montreal which will be put up in part at the expense of the inhabitants, and have taken measures to have a new guardhouse in the same town, having allocated the present one to be used as a storehouse and bakery following a few alterations. The expense for the new guardhouse will be of little consequence and will avoid paying 900 livres rent which we pay every year for the place that serves as a storehouse.

Although the inhabitants are employed at and contribute to the works that we plan to have carried out, as we have just said, it will nevertheless be necessary that His Majesty have the benignancy, as we very humbly beg him, to allocate funds... for the war it may be necessary to wage next year, more vigorously than in the past, and for the presents to be given our allied Natives to involve them too, not forgetting those in Acadia who rendered a very great service this year by taking the war to the gates of Boston and discouraging campaigns [against us] on whom we were obliged to bestow presents and to receive graciously those who came to Quebec and Montreal to give us account thereof. The relations which we are sending you, Monseigneur, will give you all the details; but we think it necessary here to underscore the effect of the presents that His Majesty was willing to grant them but also to find means to get merchandise and ammunition sent to their regions to be traded for their furs, so that they will meet their needs in trading with us and remove from them any occasion for entertaining any relations with the English...

As the projects completed this year have not been as considerable as last year, be it for fortifications, or war, or even the presents to the Natives, we hope that the 100 000 livres allocated by His Majesty for these expenses will suffice this year, although there was a loss of 19 372 1. 19s 6d of His Majesty's goods on the supply ship *St-Joseph*, which was captured in the St. Lawrence eighty leagues below Quebec by an English brigantine which cruised the area with another vessel the better part of the summer. They also captured a small vessel outfitted by one of our merchants to begin fishing...

We very humbly beg Your Majesty to have the goodness to grant us funds next year for the replacement of losses suffered at sea in past years, and to pay off the outstanding expenditures which are still due for the year 1693, for which Mr. de Lubert has advanced the largest part. We have no way of recouping this from the inhabitants of the colony whom we can only ask to make some contribution to public works, some in money, others in labour, as we have done heretofor. If we dared, we would ask you also, Monseigneur, replacements for the loss on the King's account on board the *St-Joseph*, which causes us great inconvenience.

If it appeared to you that the labourers worked a lot from November 1692 to May 1693, it can only be because of the expenses that were paid during that period which no doubt were owed for work done before winter set in and after the beginning of April because it is clear that during a good part of the winter no labourers can work because of the extreme cold, and those who work the land or in masonry can undertake nothing during the six or seven months that winter lasts, as we had the honour to inform you. And although it appears to you that they earn a great deal, we nevertheless pay them less when working for the King than when they work for private individuals, which we might be able to reduce still further by lowering the price of goods instead of by other means... You informed us that you were sending munitions and utensils without charge to our account. However we see only the cannon which was not put on our account. Part of the goods that we received are overcharged and of such poor quality that we will be far from making any profit on their sale and will not even obtain the purchase price.

Sieur de Champigny has made comments on all this, of which he informs you, Monseigneur, in the accounting he is sending you along with his personal letter. All this constrains us to beg you to have the goodness to employ business-like persons to make these kinds of purchases, otherwise it would be of more advantage to receive payment in specie, except what is required for the magazines and the presents for the Natives who consume a good part of these deliveries, which are still made up of a considerable quantity of back-fat the price of which is deducted from the wages of the soldiers without any increase in the price over its cost in France...

The vessels that came this year having only enough supplies to get to Quebec loaded here the flour they needed for the return trip. *L'Industrie* loaded a part to be taken to the islands [Antilles] and we allowed the *Pontchartrain* to take on wheat for France, in order to bring some small aid in the famine that we learned existed there, and to wait till the present time, which it would have been unable to do as it was destined to fish off the banks [Grand Banks] on its return from Quebec.

The crops seemed to be even more abundant than last year's, but the continual rains damaged them greatly. However, we have sufficient grain. The principal reason we had for authorizing the transport of grain and flour was the fear of reducing too greatly the price of grain and so dissuade the farmers from planting a great deal, but instead they are going to be mightily encouraged seeing that they find a market and consumption...

Sieur de Champigny judged it necessary to have drawn letters of exchange in the amount of 200 000 livres by the secretary of the Marine treasury for the payment of the troops and the extraordinary expenses next year until the arrival of the vessels...

We will obey for the present that order His Majesty gives us to cease paying the Christian Natives ten écus for every enemy warrior killed and twenty for every prisoner taken and half that amount for the women as long as we do not apprehend a falling away on the part of our Natives... So we beg, Monseigneur to consider these reasons and to pardon us if we do not fully comply with what His Majesty desires in this matter, believing that we are obliged by the zeal we have for his service to proceed in this manner, until he has made known to us, after having known our reasons, what he absolutely wishes. In the meantime we will try to find some pretexts to pay as little as possible.

[Rapport de l'Archiviste de la Province de Québec pour 1927-1928
(Québec: L.-Amable Proulx, 1928), pp. 196-202]

Statistics on Population and Agriculture, 1706-1739

Year	Population	Cultivated Arpents	Wheat (Minots)	Cattle
1706	16 706	43 671	211 634	14 191
1716	20 890	57 240	252 304	18 227
1726	29 859	96 202	411 070	24 298
1736	39 496	164 741	669 744	36 870
1739	43 382	188 105	634 605	38 821

[NAC, Series G 1, Vol. 461, Canadian Censuses, pp. 9-32]

Memorandum of 1737 on Colonial Progress

The chief crop is wheat. The country supplies enough not only for the needs of the inhabitants but also for trade with Isle Royale and the [West Indian] islands. In good years, 80 thousand bushels of wheat flour and biscuits leave the colony. Little will be exported in 1737, the crop having been very poor last year. The soils of Canada are not all of the same quality or productivity. Those in the district of Quebec are a mixture of uplands and lowlands, which means that rainy years are favourable for the former and the dry years for the latter...

The other kinds of seeds which are cultivated are oats, peas, little barley and still less rye; the other crops consist of flax, hemp and tobacco. There are a few orchards. It is proposed to improve the growing of tobacco. The general farmers estimate that, according to the samples taken from the tobaccos grown in Canada sent to them, that they will be appropriate for consumption in France, if care is taken to follow the instructions which they have given for this farming. The inhabitants will not fail to take it up as soon as they are paid a profitable price for it; but it is not convenient that it be too high for fear that this farming replace wheat growing...

There is little doubt that the investigation of the iron mines in the vicinity of Trois Rivières will prove as successful as we had hoped; the installation will be perfected this year...

For several years now the construction of ocean-going sailing vessels has been gaining favour; the subsidy which His Majesty grants for these building operations contributed much. The growing and marketing of tobacco will stimulate considerable building in future...

During the past few years we have conceded many plots on the shores of Lake Champlain, but they can be settled only one at a time, and little by little. We believe it would be desirable to have a windmill or a water-mill built at a convenient location, near to the fort at Pointe à la Chevelure [Crown Point], in order to have the lands settled there more quickly. The King will find another advantage in doing so in that we will be able to sustain the garrison more cheaply once the lands in the vicinity of the fort can furnish grain and other things essential to life. This settlement, which is close to the English, will attract eventually a number of inhabitants which will hinder our neighbours from penetrating to the heart of the colony.

[NAC, MG 1, Series C11A, Vol. 67, Memorandum of 1737, Extracts from pp. 40-62]

Compilation of Colonial Revenues and Expenditures

Year	Income	Expenditures
1713	442 348#	445 455#
1715	548 246	548 243
1720	381 499	381 499
1725	393 577	393 594
1730	496 253	494 217
1735	485 852	520 484
1740	417 968	503 766
1745	500 038	1 337 722
1750	904 722	2 774 715

[NAC, MG 1, Series C11A, Recettes et dépenses Vol. 113, fols. 286-305; Vol. 115, fols. 119-133, 316-327; Vol. 116, fols, 134-135, 214-217; Vol. 119, fols. 333, 406-408]

A Threat to Abandon Canada

Rouillé to Governor Duquesne and Intendant Bigot, 31 May 1754

I communicated to His Majesty the different observations that you wrote about to me in yours of the 26th and 27th October concerning the posts established in Canada; His Majesty was pleased with the attention you appear to be giving to the way for you to decrease the expenses for the posts. It is certain that the statements that the post commanders were accustomed to submit for presents given to the Natives on the King's account were among the most common and abusive excesses that characterized the expenditures for the past few years. You could do nothing more productive than to eliminate these statements by ruling that all presents that are to be given will be borne by the proprietors of the post. It was the sole method of avoiding the abuse which was such a heavy drain on the royal treasury. It also prevented the unnecessary distribution of presents to the Natives; and it is thought from another perspective that the proprietors will distribute only such presents as are necessary to satisfy the Natives because they will have a personal stake in so doing.

But the elimination of these certified statements would not be sufficient to meet the reductions that must be made in the expenditures for the posts. It is still necessary, as I point out in a despatch addressed to you and Monsieur Bigot to eliminate all the posts themselves that are not necessary for the security and tranquillity of the colony; and in those whose retention seems indispensable to you, it is necessary to make all the reductions and all the retrenchments that can be made. You have already eliminated posts at La Prairie, Lake of the Two

Mountains, and Sault St. Louis, and you have ordered cut-backs in those at Detroit, Chambly, and at Fort St. John; and His Majesty has been very pleased with these adjustments. But he is convinced there are still more substantial cuts to be made and he is counting on you making as many as possible...

I have not failed to inform His Majesty about the other measures you informed me you had taken to decrease the expenditures regarding the Natives, and His Majesty is grateful to you for that. Never has it been so necessary as at the present time to work effectively in order to reduce all expenses. You know the financial difficulties we were in when you left for Canada. You must have some realization how much the situation has deteriorated due to the immense drafts which have been drawn on the treasury by that colony since you have been posted there. It has become necessary to implement all these measures in order to be able to cope with the situation. But all resources are now so depleted that if matters cannot be restored to the condition they were found in before the advent of these immense fiscal excesses which we have been experiencing for a number of years, we shall be strongly obliged to consider abandoning the colony. You will notice that I am writing jointly to you and Monsieur Bigot on this matter. I am convinced that you will contribute in every domain for which you are responsible in carrying out the wishes of His Majesty on this heading. That is the most satisfying service you can render.

[NAC, MG 1, Series B, Vol. 99, fols. 199-200]

A British Assessment of the Colonial Economy
Memorandum of 1 May 1765

Given the colony's present capacity new resources are impossible to find, and after all is said and done it must be admitted that its survival depends on outside assistance that is all the more necessary as it must founder without it. And from whom is this assistance to be expected if not Old England, today its protector?

But, it will be said, the other North American colonies have not required the aid sought by the Province of Quebec; and moreover any colony unable to support itself is a burden to the state on which it depends. This is true. These two objections are undeniable... It is a fact that the other colonies of this northern continent have not required the aid sought by this province, but if one cares to look at the difference in its and its neighbours' situations he cannot avoid noting that the mildness of the climate and the heavy population from New England to Florida give the inhabitants a capacity for exporting to the Leeward and Windward Islands and to Europe which this colony does not yet possess...

The harshness of our climate in the north and the want of population in the south are insurmountable obstacles for us. This same want of population also makes labour extremely expensive, and prevents us from using the resources we could tap in the fishery.

[This colony] is still in its infancy, and this may be the consequence of the bad policies of the French before its surrender, who would never allow freedom here and yet who feared nothing more than the depopulation of their own Kingdom. The neighbouring colonies have never felt this want, on the contrary, devotion to the common good has always prevailed over ill-considered measures among the British, particularly when it was a matter of increasing their colonies. It is felt and even confidently anticipated that the same devotion will be showered on this province, but though freedom be admitted to it, [building up] the population is not something to be accomplished overnight...

No one must be surprised that after 170 years or thereabouts of existence the country is incapable of supporting itself, but it will be able to do so when, under the freedom already allowed, a large population in the southern part will supply enough grain, hemp and salted foodstuffs to overcome and more than overcome its present state of powerlessness...

[Dale Miquelon, ed., Society and Conquest *(Toronto: Copp Clark Publishing, 1977), pp. 200-201]*

1. To what degree did Canada fit a mercantilist model? Did French policy retard colonial development, or did it provide some benefits to the colony?

2. Can the support the state extended to the Forges St-Maurice be justified in terms of the welfare of the colonial community?

3. Was the illicit trade carried on between Montreal and Albany, and Louisbourg and New England, an 'underground economy' which profited or harmed New France? What are the differences between privateering and piracy?

4. It is sometimes asserted that France did not spend considerable sums to establish the colony, stimulate its economy, and protect it. Is this the case? Does it pay to have colonies?

5. Of the staples produced in New France—cod, furs, wheat, lumber, ginseng—which had the greatest impact on colonial development? Are there problems inherent in a staples economy?

READINGS

B.A. Balcom, *The Cod Fishery of Isle Royale, 1713-58* (Ottawa: Environment Canada, 1984)

J.F. Bosher, *Business and Religion in the Age of New France, 1600-1760* (Toronto: Canadian Scholars' Press, 1994)

_____, "The Imperial Environment of French Trade with Canada, 1660-1685," in *English Historical Review*, cviii (1993): 50-82.

Charles W. Cole, *French Mercantilism, 1683-1700* (New York: Columbia University Press, 1943)

Louise Dechêne, *Habitants and Merchants in Seventeenth-Century Montreal* (Montreal-Kingston: McGill-Queen's University Press, 1992)

Carl Ekberg, *Colonial Ste. Genevieve: An Adventure on the Mississippi Frontier* (Gerald: Patrice Press, 1985)

Brian Evans, "Ginseng: Root of Chinese-Canadian Relations," in *Canadian Historical Review*, 61, 1 (1985): 1-26.

Jean Hamelin, *Economie et société en Nouvelle-France* (Québec: Presses de l'Université Laval, 1960)

Harold A. Innis, *Problems of Staple Production in Canada* (Toronto: University of Toronto Press, 1961)

Louis P. Kellogg, *The French Regime in Wisconsin and the Northwest* (Madison: State Historical Society of Wisconsin, 1925)

Alice Jean Lunn, *Développement économique de la Nouvelle France, 1713-1760* (Montréal: Presses de l'Université de Montréal, 1986)

Jacques Mathieu, *La construction navale royale à Québec, 1739-1759* (Québec: Presses de l'Université Laval, 1971)

Christopher Moore, "The Other Louisbourg: Trade and Merchant Enterprise in Ile Royale, 1713-58," in *Histoire sociale/Social History* 12, 23 (1979): 79-96.

Thomas J. Schaeper, *The French Council of Commerce, 1700-1715: An Administrative Study of French Mercantilism after Colbert* (Columbia: Ohio State University Press, 1983)

Robert Stern, *The French Slave Trade in the Eighteenth Century* (Madison: University of Wisconsin Press, 1979)

Immanuel Wallerstein, *The Modern World System* (New York: Academic Press, 1976)

Yves Zoltvany, *The French Tradition in America* (Toronto: Fitzhenry & Whiteside, 1969)

_____, *Phillippe de Rigaud de Vaudreuil, Governor of New France, 1703-1735* (Toronto: University of Toronto Press, 1974)

Wars, Conquest, and Conciliation

Canada in the past was a region which experienced cruel warfare, attempted invasions, pitched battles and sieges usually associated with the European scene, conquest, military occupation, and a strict military régime. The colony of New France was governed by a high-ranking military officer, the network of empire was marked by military forts with small garrisons, a military ethos pervaded colonial affairs, and in times of invasion the colonists quickly transformed into a formidable militia force.

The military forces of the colony fell into four categories. First, the garrison troops belonged to companies of *Troupes de la Marine*, units recruited in France for service in metropolitan ports and overseas territories. Beginning in 1684, they were increasingly commanded by Canadian-born officers, sons of the local nobility. Second, after 1669, every able-bodied male between the ages of 16 and 60 (clergy excepted) was required to report regularly for arms drill to a militia captain appointed for each parish. The colonial militia provided the required manpower for raids into enemy territory, the defence of the colony, and aid to the civil power. This service was unpaid, but arms and provisions were generously provided. Third, in times of anticipated invasion, notably in the closing decades of the French régime, regular regiments of metropolitan troops dispatched by the Ministry of War, and known as *Troupes de terre*, confronted enemy naval and land forces. Finally, there were the bands of Amerindian warriors, allies who were consulted about over-all strategies—but once engaged in battle resorted to their guerrilla tactics, suffered no European command, and upon obtaining the desired loot and prisoners might decide to disengage.

Together these forces faced numerous external threats. An Anglo-Huguenot expedition controlled Quebec from 1629 to 1632, but larger scale invasion attempts directed against Canada—the Phips expedition in 1690 and the Walker expedition in 1711—were quite unsuccessful and discouraged British intervention. Acadia fared less well and was ceded to the British Crown in 1713. The French also enjoyed some success in overrunning areas under British sovereignty—notably the Hudson Bay region from 1686 to 1713, and some populated regions of Newfoundland. More importantly, a French military presence began asserting itself in the vast interior, reaching down to the Gulf of Mexico by 1701, driving back Spanish advances from Mexico at Santa Fe in 1720, and moving onto the western prairies in the 1730s. The Iroquois, who had posed a threat throughout the seventeenth century, finally made peace with the French and their Amerindian allies at Montreal in 1701. Around the upper Great Lakes, the dominant allies and trading partners formed the Three Fires Confederacy, while in the settled areas the 'domiciled' were united as the Seven Nations of Canada.

The final invasion began in 1754 before any official declaration of war, when George Washington and his Virginian force violated the rules of war by slaughtering a small French troop under a flag of truce. The British-led forces managed to co-ordinate a naval attack and land expeditions, which resulted in the capture of Louisbourg in 1758, and of Quebec in September 1759.

The surrender of the colony was not unconditional. Canada was occupied by a British army, and military rule was imposed until the signing of a definitive treaty of peace in Paris in 1763. Canada became the British colony of Quebec, its boundaries were fixed by a Royal Proclamation, and the following year a civilian government was installed.

In the interior of the continent, scattered French traders and many Amerindians hoped for a return of French rule in the event of a future war. After a number of secret council meetings, the interior tribes were influenced by the Ottawa war chief Pontiac, and the Delaware prophet Neolin, to take up arms in the spring of 1763 against the British garrisons and traders who ruthlessly exploited them. They hoped to persuade the Canadians to rebel, and France to reopen hostilities and come to their relief. The only reaction in France was the view that, because of the growing unrest in some Anglo-American colonies, Quebec colony might act as a kind of Trojan horse within the British empire and help bring about its collapse.

When thirteen of the sixteen British colonies in North America rebelled, France came to their assistance, but the Anglo-Americans were not anxious to see a return of a French presence on their northern frontier. In 1789, when France itself underwent a bloody revolution which brought down the monarchy and abolished the privileges of the nobility and the state church, Quebec was cut off ideologically from the old metropole. It would have to survive on its own inner strength under anglophone Protestant domination. But not all had changed since under British rule there was a continuation of much that characterized the *ancien régime*— monarchy, government by the elite, co-operation between church and state, a strong military tradition, seigneurial land tenure, civil code law, a communal view of society, and the everyday life of the common people. It was France and the new United States which had changed and broken with traditional forms and concepts.

Section A
Preparations for Conflict

New France enjoyed only one period of relative peace from 1713 to 1744. At other times it remained prepared psychologically and militarily to repel any invasion. Good relations with the hinterland Native nations, who were both trading partners and allies, were maintained by placing the trade of the upper country under military supervision. The Anglo-American colonies were subjected to sporadic bloody raids to keep them on the defensive. Regular troops were billeted with the settlers, and medical and hospital care were provided free at Quebec, Montreal, and Louisbourg.

When the colony was faced with foreign invasion, the bishop used the occasion to stir up patriotic resistance, while at the same time thundering that such a calamitous event was a form of divine punishment for immorality and lack of religious devotion.

In the eighteenth century the fur trade became closely tied to the military posts of the upper country, commerce to geopolitics, and bartering to the pattern of alliances. A military post in the interior was a centre of commercial as well as official transactions with the Native peoples and local traders, and its commandant, usually a Canadian-born officer belonging to one of the eighteen leading families, tended to replace the missionaries as diplomat and interpreter.

There were *casernes* to house the regular troops only at Louisbourg and Quebec. Elsewhere they were billeted with the colonists, an arrangement which appears to have been advantageous to both parties. Besides the financial advantages, the poorly paid soldier was assured of wholesome food and a convivial relationship with the *habitants*. Many married and remained in the colony as a result. Officers, such as the Baron de Lahontan who was stationed at Montreal, did not enjoy the same occasions to fraternize with the colonists.

The hospitals in the chief towns were established originally to provide free medical services for the navy and army. This care was extended to all colonists at the Hôtel-Dieu in Quebec, also to prisoners of war.

An important element in French strategy for maintaining its sovereignty over the vast hinterland, and in restricting Anglo-American settlement to the Atlantic seaboard, was the retention of the friendship and co-operation of numerous Amerindian nations. The secular intermediaries in Montreal who hosted the annual Amerindian delegations, when the governor came to meet with them, had to be remunerated as well as the Native delegations.

Church Attempts to Arouse Patriotism

You are sufficiently informed of the strange calamity with which we are all menaced by the approach of the English, enemies not only of us French but also of our faith and our holy religion. Is it possible that loving you tenderly and carrying you in my heart, I do not tremble at the sole thought of the ravages that heresy could cause among you, if divine justice should permit that fire should be lit in the hearts of your children. Let us lift up our eyes higher, My Very Dear Children, and let us look at God holding thunder and lightning in his hand which he is ready to rain down on us; he lets it rumble in order to withdraw you from the slumber of sin that has aroused his anger. All he wants is that you turn again to him and that through your penitence you have him retract the decree of condemnation that he may have issued against you. Do not be deaf to such a terrible voice; let the merchants no longer flatter themselves in their sly transactions and no longer put pillows over their heads in order to sleep untroubled by their conscience, let the usurer stop abusing by hurrying under different pretexts to make interest on his money, since God regards this commerce as an abomination, let the vindictive person renounce his desire to obtain vengeance and be not only disposed to meet his enemy but to love him cordially and do him good, let the lustful no longer continue in their disorderly conduct; but especially let the sacrilegious sinners cease to offend God through repeated profanities concerning everything that is saintly and the most sacred in religion. You understand quite well what I mean, My Very Dear Children. This reproach is only too well founded in a country where people take the Sacraments so often and where one sees so little amendment in behaviour...

But I apprehend that there are new dissensions among you, that certain individuals are not afraid to trouble public peace for their domestic interests, which would result in your downfall and discouragement, were it not that I promised on your piety and your loyalty to your country and your King that you would take all the measures possible to rebuff your enemies and to keep yourselves in peace with God through casting off all that offends him. Walk therefore, My Very Dear Children, as is proper for those whom God by his mighty power has brought out of the darkness and translated them into the Kingdom of His Son, walk in the light of the day in times of affliction as children of light, as children who abide in an inaccessible light, stave off his anger, prostrate yourselves before him in spirit, acknowledge that your crimes do merit a general desolation.

But having recourse to his mercy and offering him a contrite and humble heart, be assured that it will not be rejected, that it will rise to his throne as a sweet smelling savour, and prevent from falling on our heads the punishment of his greatest fury.

I invite you to guard well our coasts, to be careful in defending the entrances to our towns; but as you will guard it in vain unless the Lord keeps it, take as your best and surest measure of safety penitence and the amendment of your ways. Before terminating, let me recommend to you obedience to the established superior powers, as to God himself, the relief of the poor whose numbers increase every day, a truly modest Christian virtue to the women and girls, and an ardent devotion to the Holy Family; what would you have to fear having such a powerful protection, providing that in honouring him with your lips you honour him with your actions, and that you do not oblige him to leave you on account of your sins. These are the wishes of a father whose affection for you increases each day, and who carries you in his heart in order to bring you to the heart of Our Saviour Jesus-Christ, to whom be glory, honour and praise, world without end; may all who do not love him be anathema.

[H. Têtu & C. -O. Casgrain, eds., Mandements, Lettres pastorales et Circulaires des Evêques de Québec *(Québec: Coté, 1887), Vol. I, Pastoral letter for defence against the English, (1690), pp. 265-267. Trans. CJJ]*

An Elite Officer Corps

As I have already stated, the choice of officers to command these posts has not up until now been according to rank or seniority, at least as long as I have been in Canada up to the present, but it has been by favouritism with the appointments offering the richest returns going almost without exception to the same individuals and families. These are now solidly controlled by the De Ramesay and La Corne families, the elder and the younger Marin (the father himself is the son of an army officer), the De Repentignys, Villiers, Beaujeus and Demuys, Célerons and Laperrières, with the Péans and Merciers who now have the whole Illinois valley and the first post at the Pointe with Luc La Corne, plus a half share in numerous other posts. Many other families and French officers, though having offered satisfactory proof of their knowledge, application, zeal, and sacrifice on frequent occasions, are thus excluded. Yet these officers too work only for the promotion of the King's interests, and they have never been awarded the commands that would make it possible for them to maintain their social status, so they languish in poverty, unable to properly support their families. As for the French and Canadian unmarried officers, are their captains' salaries, which amount to only 1062 livres, sufficient to meet living costs of 1200 livres without a servant, or 1600 livres if they have one? Everyone knows their situation is on that footing. Where can they obtain the extra money to meet these expenses? How can they support themselves when they have no other resources in a country where everything, even the bare essentials, has become unaffordable? What must they do to feed and clothe themselves? The basest creature can assuredly be given no less than that. Yet persons of rank, splendid old officers, do not have it. Must they steal to obtain it? No. Then how are they to come to terms with this harsh reality? They borrow from businessmen who nearly always lose what they lend to these officers who die insolvent. This would never occur if, instead of all the patronage going to favourites and everything being monopolized in league with them, attention were paid to giving each officer a turn in these commands. Unfortunately, this is not being done.

> [Rapport de l'Archiviste de la Province de Ouébec, 1927-28 *(Québec, 1938), Chevalier de Raymond to Le Courtois de Surlaville, serving officers in New France, Memorandum of 1754, pp. 334-335. Trans. CJJ]*

Billeting of Troops with the Habitants

The troops are usually quartered with the habitants of the *côtes* or seigneuries of Canada from the month of October to May. The habitant provides only the tools to his soldier and employs him ordinarily to cut down trees, uproot stumps, clear land, or thresh wheat in the barn during the winter, at a wage of tens sols daily plus board. The Captain also profits from this arrangement because in order to ensure that the soldiers give him half of this pay, he orders them to report three times a week for drill. Since the houses are four or five arpents apart and a *côte* is two or three leagues wide in frontage, the soldiers prefer to come to an agreement with him rather than having to travel such distances in snow and mud. So, good will does not injure anyone is the Captain's reasoning. As for those soldiers who have good trades, he is assured of their entire wage when he gives them permission to work in the towns or elsewhere. Moreover, nearly all the Officers in general maintain themselves in this country, but God knows the lovely marriages they contract by taking girls who bring in dowry eleven écus, a rooster, a hen, an ox, a cow, and sometimes a calf too. I have seen several whose lovers, after have denied the fact, and after having proved before Judge the bad conduct of their mistress, were forced in spite of all their resistance through the persuasion of the clergy to swallow the bitter pill and marry the girl in question. There are a few who have found good partners, but they are scarce. Now, what makes for ready marriages in this country is that it is difficult to converse with persons of the opposite sex. One must declare one's intentions to the father and mother after four visits with their daughters; one must speak of marriage or cut off the relationship, otherwise scandalous talk is directed against both parties.

[Baron de Lahontan, Mémoires de l'Amerique septentrionale *(Amsterdam: François L'Honoré, 1705), pp. 79-80. Trans. CJJ]*

Provision for Medical Care

The hospital, as I have said before, forms part of the convent. It consists of two large halls, and some smaller rooms next to the apothecary's shop. In the great halls are two rows of beds, one on each side. The beds next to the wall are furnished with curtains, the ones on the outside have none. In each bed are fine bed linen with clean double sheets. As soon as a sick person vacates his bed, it is made up again in order to keep the hospital clean and orderly. The beds are two or three yards apart, and there is a small table near each bed. There are good iron stoves and good windows in this hall. The sisters look after the sick and bring them their meals and look after their needs. Besides them there are some male nurses and a surgeon. The royal physician is required to visit the hospital once or twice a day; he goes from bed to bed and orders his prescriptions. Sick soldiers are normally brought to this hospital; they are quite numerous in July and August, when the ships arrive, and also in time of war. But at other periods, when there are not many sick soldiers, other patients can take their place because the beds are free. The hospital is well provided with everything that is needed to care for the sick: food, medicines, fuel, etc. Those who are extremely ill are put into separate rooms so that they are not disturbed by the noise.

[L. W. Marchand, ed., Voyage de Kalm en Amérique *(Montréal: 1880), Vol. 2, p. 102. Trans. CJJ]*

Assuring the Amerindian Alliances, 1730
Beauharnois and Hocquart to Minister, 15 October 1730

My Lord,
We have received the letter which you had the honour to write us on 28th March last and we have the one addressing the detailed account of the presents which were made to the Natives of the different nations in 1729 amounting all told to the sum of 24662£. 19s. 4d. that could not be less because of the number who came down to Montreal and Quebec last year.

You are informed, Sir, that all the nations of Canada regard the Governor General as their father, who consequently in this capacity and according to their idea as always should give them what is necessary to eat, dress and hunt, and they have had reason to call the Governor General by this name up to now because of the goodness and kindness that he has shown them. One can say too that they have been treated as spoiled children and they will not mend their ways until such time as we are able to inspire them with more fear and more respect.

It is only the presents that attach them to us. The Natives would have become more useful to the colony if it had been possible to subjugate them little by little. They would now be good citizens and apparently the greater part would have embraced the Christian Religion to which, with the exception of a few domiciled natives, the other natives are only attached through pretence and through self-interest.

The requirement to give presents especially in rations to the domiciled Natives, must, Sir, must appear to you to be all the greater since their idleness and indifference for cultivating the land remain the same and that their resources from hunting are diminishing each day.

The time has not come yet, Sir, when all these nations will be one with the French. That will come when the colony will have become more powerful or when His Majesty will predispose it through an augmentation of the forces that can force it upon the natives to have no other will than that of the King.

We have never impeded the natives in their delegations. They settle in their councils the number and quality of deputies that they send and nothing would be more capable of moving them away from the King's service than to prevent them from coming to see their father in as great numbers as they think appropriate. As unsophisticated as they may be, they would soon probe the motives for such a reform and attribute it to a lack of generosity, the reasons for the savings that would cause M. the Marquis de Beauharnois to act, and that is what is good to avoid. We have informed the Baron de Longueuil of the continuation of the annual subsidy of 200f that His Majesty has granted him in consideration of the lodging he provides for the Iroquois when they come down to Montreal and of the expenses he is obliged to make during their stay. He will proceed with them as did his late father and their lodging will cost nothing.

We had employed last year for the projected expenses a similar sum of two hundred livres for the lodging of the domiciled Algonkians and Iroquois who are received and lodged with Sr. Morisseau and Lady La Chavignerie. This expense is indispensable and cannot be reduced, we beg you, Sir, to agree to continue it.

We are with profound respect, Sir, your very humble and very obedient servants. Beauharnois Hocquart

[NAC, MG 1, Series C11A, Vol. 52, pp. 30-33. Trans. CJJ]

Section B
The Nature of the Conflict

British and French commanders tried by all possible means to keep the Amerindians either as allies or as neutrals. The sieges of Louisbourg and Quebec were typical European-style battles, in which the militia and the Amerindian allies were prevented from playing a decisive role. In 1760, three armies began their approach to Montreal, which had no strong fortifications. The militiamen started leaving in order to tend to the harvest and to avoid the reprisals with which the British threatened them, and then the Amerindians, seeing the collapse of French resistance, came to terms with the invaders. So, Governor Vaudreuil had no alternative but to capitulate.

In the autumn of 1732, the French commandant at the Miami post, Jean-Charles Arnaud, reported that three hundred Miamis and neighbouring natives died in strange circumstances, apparently from a poisonous substance in the brandy obtained at Oswego. The French were able to use this incident in their propaganda campaign against the British.

News of the outbreak of war in March 1744 reached the French in Louisbourg before it did the British at Annapolis Royal, and so the French launched a surprise attack on Canso. Soon New England raised an army, and with the support of the British fleet in the West Indies there ensued a lengthy siege of Louisbourg, inflicting terrible destruction. When the relief expedition from France met with disaster, Governor Duchambon capitulated. The realities of a siege are recounted by Gilles Lacroix-Girard, who was drafted into the local militia while transporting provisions from Quebec to Louisbourg in the late autumn of 1744. He was taken prisoner of war, managed to escape, and wrote his journal after he returned to Quebec based on notes taken during the defence of the fortress.

The sad events following the surrender of the British garrison at Fort William Henry illustrate the differences between the type of 'organized warfare' carried on by European regulars, and the objectives, tactics, and behaviour of the Amerindian allies of European armies. Europeans in general viewed the events reported here by the chaplain of the Abenaki warriors as 'atrocities,' but many colonists had come to expect that their Native allies had a right to loot and take prisoners as their just reward for participating in a campaign. European armies could be equally cruel in warfare.

In the psychological warfare that accompanied armed action, General James Wolfe sought to capitalize on the fears and disaffections of the Canadian militia by threatening their families and property if they did not lay down their arms. To do so, however, meant they would be treated as deserters by the French.

The campaigns of the Seven Years' War were marked by growing hatred and fear, alleged atrocities, and apparent breaches of the protocols of war. A diary kept by the abbé Jean-Félix Récher, teacher at the Seminary of Quebec and curate of the cathedral parish, provides some insight into the autumn campaign and siege of Quebec, and of the physical and psychological effects of wartime conditions—destruction, starvation, and fear.

Faced with the retreat of the French on all fronts in the summer of 1760, the Seven Nations of Canada reached an agreement with the British invaders at Oswegatchie in late August whereby they abandoned the French alliance. The Hurons of Lorette, driven from their village near Quebec, then entered into an agreement with General James Murray, military governor of their region, at Longueil three days before the capitulation of Montreal.

The surrender of the colony was conditional, the outcome of the war in other theatres of operations not yet having been decided or peace negotiations concluded. In the Articles of Capitulation reproduced here, the French request is followed, in quotation marks, by the British conditions granted in each case. These conditions of capitulation were a binding agreement in terms of international conventions.

The allegation that France did little to defend Canada needs to be considered in the light of the enormous expenditures incurred during the last 15 years of the French régime. The normal annual allocation for Canada in the eighteenth century was about 500 000 livres, but during the war years expenditures skyrocketed into the millions, at a time when such large sums were virtually unknown. This huge debt did not save Canada, but it did contribute to the financial crisis in France before the Revolution.

A Case of Suspected Chemical Warfare
D'Arnaud to Beauharnois, 25 October 1732

The day after I arrived at my post fifteen or sixteen Miami canoes arrived from Oswego loaded with four hundred casks of brandy. Five or six days later they knocked one in, in which there was the complete skin of a man's hand. This news spread through the village and surprised them immensely. However, it did not put a stop to their drunkenness; after three days two individuals who were fine in the evening were buried the next day at eight in the morning. Then for more than three weeks, at least four died each day. My statements to them that they had no decent food whatever in their village, and that by dispersing in the woods they would find meat which would give them strength to fight off the ailment combined with the foul air (which the great number of bodies which surrounded them created) persuaded them to go off to their winter quarters from which I have heard that several were dying from time to time but not in as great numbers as in their village. (The number of dead is presently one hundred fifty persons).

The first did not astonish me at all; I attributed it to the excessive drinking. But the rest astonished me more. I had the dead stripped and examined, and the conclusion for me was that it was a poison as subtle as it was crafty, only taking effect after a rather considerable time. I wanted to have more certain proof of this: a war chief of this nation who had become particularly attached to me and who deserved to be saved was attacked by the sickness. I gave him a strong dose of orvietan which saved his life. In the same way I saved several with this medicine, but not having any more, those who were deprived of this help all died, and not one of those who used it perished.

The Miamis are not the only victims of this poison. The Ouiatonons came one hundred thirty strong to perform the dance of the peace pipe. The brandy was not held back from them, but after their return home, the same sickness overtook them and several letters from that location informed me that almost all of them had died.

[Joseph F. Peyser, ed., Letters from New France: The Upper Country, 1686-1783 *(Urbana: University of Illinois Press, 1992), p. 137]*

Siege of Louisbourg, 1745

28 May

The whole chapel of the fort was riddled with cannon shot and the barracks too. Several of M. Dacarrette's people came in the evening to enter the bastions. The English followed close behind them, but the fort and the bastions fired several rounds of grapeshot and several gunshots which killed seven English.

29 May

Our people came in during the morning who informed us that the English were dragging cannon during the night to the Francoeur battery. We saw the English erecting a battery near the Dauphine gate. This battery was set up on the Francoeur gravel beach with a retrenchment which they made during two days of fog. We did not fire much. They dug a trench which is more than four feet high. Their battery being sheltered by a mound, we could only see their cannon when fired. They gave us a hot time. They had five cannon and a mortar at this battery with which they bombarded us...

30 May

The Francoeur battery damaged the roofs of town houses. The bombs fell onto the houses, one on M. Fautoux's crushing it, two others on Carerot's house along with balls from the grand battery, another on Fisel's, one in Gibbert's, another on M.'s house which completely demolished it and several other houses. They killed nobody with the exception of a Basque who was running in the street and a pregnant woman who was at the door of the casemates and who was cut in half. The chapel of the fort was abandoned because it was all uncovered and broken up. The Recollet friars say mass at the hospital. The benediction of the Holy Sacrament was given every day during the siege. Every day the English dislodged some cannon. Once they dislodged 15 in a single volley, they broke the bell of the fort with a cannon shot but they did not harm the belltower...

25 June

An emissary came to Louisbourg around 11 o'clock in the morning. Mr. de Lopinot went to get him outside the town. He came in by the Queen gate and was taken to Mr. Thiery's house, where he complained that the natives were killing their people and were inflicting untold cruelties on them. Mr. Duchambon answered him that he was not the master of the natives.

The emissary said to Mr. Duchambon and the other officers who were with him that if they were thinking of surrendering they should do so to the regular troops, that is to say to those of the King of England rather than to the Bostonians, because in surrendering to the latter the town would be given up to pillage but in surrendering to the King of England's troops there would be none. At the meeting were present Messrs. Duchambon, Bigot, Le Perelle, Provost, Loppinot, de la Ronde, and Delort.

The emissary left the town around 3 o'clock in the afternoon. This emissary gone, council met and it was decided that a proposal should be made to the English to leave the town with arms and baggage, two mortars and 4 or 6 cannons on condition there be no looting and that the troops not be taken prisoners of war.

Mr. de La Perelle went out around five o'clock to find the English commander who was at Barachois. Some officers came up to meet him in front of the glacis. They sat down and talked together until such time as they went to speak to the commander. They then came to take the said Sieur La Perelle to go to Barachois where he found the English officer in command in the absence of Mr. Warren. He returned around 10 or 11 o'clock at night, and gave an account of his mission.

26 June

Council met from 9 o'clock in the morning until two o'clock in the afternoon. At the close of this council it was forbidden to fire. Mr. de Loppinot told me that the town was going to surrender and that they were on the point of capitulating, which took place. They drew up the capitulation and Messrs. Dailleboust and La Ronde went on board to the admiral in the afternoon to deliver this capitulation which was accepted. Around eleven in the evening the English fired two cannon shots as agreed indicating that the capitulation was accepted on the terms that had been proposed. That done, six English came as hostages in the city in place of Messrs. Dailleboust and La Ronde who were on board the English admiral's vessel. Word was sent to the battery of l'Islet immediately that the town had surrendered.

[NAC, MG 1, 24, Dépôt des fortifications des colonies, No. 216, Report of Girard-Lacroix, 26 June 1745, fols. 20-23, 39-41. Trans. CJJ]

Massacre at Fort William Henry, 1757

We are near the surrender of the fort and the bloody catastrophe which followed. Doubtless every corner of Europe has resounded with this sad occurrence, as with a crime the odium of which perhaps falls back on the Nation and disgraces it. Your fairness will at once judge if such a glaring imputation rests on any other basis than on ignorance or on malignity. I shall relate only facts of such incontestable publicity and authenticity that I could, without fear of being contradicted, support them by the testimony of even Messieurs the English Officers, who were the witnesses and victims of them.

Monsieur the Marquis de Montcalm thought that he ought, before consenting to any terms, to take the opinion of all the Savage Tribes, in order to appease them by this condescension, and to render the treaty inviolable by their assent. He assembled all the chiefs to whom he communicated the conditions of the capitulation, which granted to the enemy the right of going out of the fort with all the honors of war...

Accordingly the French army, in order of battle, advanced to the fort to take possession of it in the name of His Most Christian Majesty; while the English troops, ranged in good order, went out to take refuge until the next day in the intrenchments. Their march was not marked by any contravention of the law of nations; but the Savages lost no time in violating it. During the military ceremonial which accompanied taking possession, crowds of them had penetrated into the fort through the gun-embrasures, that they might proceed to pillage what we had agreed to give up to them, but they were not content with pillaging. A few sick soldiers had remained in the casemates, their condition not permitting them to follow their fellow countrymen in the honorable retreat accorded to their valor. These were the victims upon whom they pitilessly rushed, and whom they sacrificed to their cruelty. I was a witness of this spectacle. I saw one of these barbarians come out of the casemates into which nothing less than an insatiable avidity for blood could make any one enter, so insupportable was the stench which exaled from them. He carried in his hand a human head, from which trickled streams of blood, and which he displayed as the most splendid prize he could have secured.

This was only a very faint prelude to the cruel tragedy of the next day. At the very dawn of day, the Savages reassembled about the intrenchments. They began by asking the English for goods, provisions,—in a word, for all the riches that their greedy eyes could see; but these demands were made in a tone that foretold a blow with a spear as the price of a refusal. The English dispossessed and despoiled themselves, and reduced themselves to nothing, that they might buy at least life by this general renunciation. Such complaisance ought to soften any heart; but the heart of the Savage does not seem to be made like that of other men: you would say that it is, by its nature, the seat of inhumanity. They were not on this account less inclined to proceed to the harshest extremes. The body of four hundred men of the French troops, selected to protect the retreat of the enemy, arrived, and drew up in a line on both sides. The English began to defile. Woe to all those who brought up the rear, or to stragglers whom indisposition or any other cause separated however little from the troop. They were so many dead whose bodies very soon strewed the ground and covered the inclosure of the intrench-ments. This butchery, which in the beginning was the work of only a few Savages, was the signal which made nearly all of them so many ferocious beasts. They struck, right and left, heavy blows of the hatchet on those who fell into their hands. However, the massacre was not of long continuance, or so great as such fury gave us cause to fear; the number of men killed was hardly more than forty or fifty. The patience of the English, who were content to bend the head under the sword of their executioners, suddenly appeased the weapon, but did not bring the tormentors to reason and equity. Continually uttering loud cries, these began to take them prisoners...

Monsieur the Chevalier de Levis was running wherever the tumult appeared the most violent, endeavoring to stop it... The French Officers and the Canadians imitated his example, with a zeal worthy of the humanity which has always char-acterized the Nation; but the main part of our troops, occupied in guarding our batteries and the fort, was, on account of the distance, unable to give them aid... In the meantime, the tumult was continually increasing, when happily someone thought of calling out to the English, who formed a large body, to hasten their march. This forced march had its effect; the Savages—partly through the futility of their pursuit, partly satisfied with their captures—retired; the few who remained were easily dispersed. The English continued their way in peace to fort Lydis, where they arrived—numbering, at first, only three or four hundred. I do not know the number of those who, having gained the woods, were fortunate enough to reach the fort by the help of a cannon which our people took care to fire, for several days, in order to guide them.

[Reuben Gold Thwaites, ed., The Jesuit Relations and Allied Documents *(New York: Pageant Book Company, 1959), Vol. 70, pp. 175-181]*

Wolfe's Manifesto of June 1759

The formidable sea and land armament, which the people of Canada now behold in the heart of their country, is intended by the king, my master, to check the inso-lence of France, to revenge the insults offered to the British colonies, and totally to deprive the French of their most valuable settlement in North America. For these purposes is the formidable army under my command intended. The King of Great Britain wages no war with the industrious peasant, the sacred orders of reli-gion, or the defenceless women and children; to these, in their distressful cir-cumstances, his royal clemency offers protection. The people may remain unmo-lested on their lands, inhabit their houses and enjoy their religion in security; for these inestimable blessings, I expect the Canadians will take no part in the great contest between the two crowns. But, if by a vain obstinacy and misguided valour, they presume to appear in arms, they must expect the most fatal consequences; their habitations destroyed, their sacred temples exposed to an exasperated soldiery, their harvest utterly ruined and the only passage for relief stopped up by a most formidable fleet. In this most unhappy situation, and closely attacked by another great army, what can the wretched natives expect from opposition? The unparalleled barbarities exerted by the French against our settlements in America might justify the bitterest revenge in the army under my command. But Britons breathe higher sentiments of humanity, and listen to the merciful dictates of the Christian religion...

In this great dilemma, let the wisdom of the people of Canada shew itself; Britain stretches out a powerful yet merciful hand, faithful to her engagements, and ready to secure her in her most valuable rights and possessions; France, unable to support Canada, deserts her cause at this important crisis, and, during the whole war has assisted her with troops who have been maintained only by making the natives [Canadians] feel all the weight of grievous and lawless oppression.

[Brian Connell, ed., The Siege of Quebec and the Campaigns in North America, 1757-1760 by Captain John Knox *(Mississauga: Pendragon House, 1980), pp. 135-136]*

Siege of Quebec, 1759

[August] 19. — I learned that the English burned on the south shore, besides the parish of St-Antoine, that of St-Nicolas, part of that of Ste-Croix; on the island on Orleans, the houses of the parish of St-François, half of those of Ste-Famille; moreover, those of Baie St-Paul; and that they sent 600 men to the lower south shore to burn down the houses and destroy the crops...

20. — News that the English landed at Deschambault and reembarked as soon as they saw a detachment commanded by M. de Bouganville coming towards them, after having remained on land about six hours, we are told, and having burned down a house belonging to Perrault and two others, in which were the most valuable possessions, even silverware and the money of the troops belonging to both officers and soldiers. Someone said there was there eighteen thousand pounds in cash. They had gathered up about a hundred head of cattle in the church, and had even slaughtered part of them there; but they did not have time to carry them off and load them....

Note. The natives from upstream as well as downstream are a plague for all the inhabitants of the parishes neighbouring Quebec, by the liberty they take to kill with impunity and seize their goods of all kinds even in their homes, their animals, especially their oxen, cows, sheep, chickens, horses. They killed up to thirteen sheep at once belonging to M. de la Gorgendière, and so it was with others, and that often in the presence of the owners and in broad daylight. And this disaster has been going on since the beginning of the siege without the authorities daring to reprimand them, for fear of the consequences.

On the other hand, thieves continue to loot the houses in the town, breaking down the doors to vaults, even tearing down the masonry of doors to vaults that have been bricked up...

27. —A sergeant, an English deserter, who came to us yesterday reported that the English have many sick with flux and fevers, that Wolfe himself was so sick he feared for his life... that a detachment of English having gone up to the fourth church above Beauport had found there twelve men, among them a priest, who being no doubt too weak threw themselves on their knees and asked quarter, and that without any regard for their entreaties the English had shot and killed the priest with a few others; that makes us fear for the safety of M. de Portneuf, curate of St-Joachim. It is he in fact that they seized with 8 habitants, after having lured them from the woods by pretending to flee and then surrounding them. They lifted his scalp and split his head open. There is reason to believe they did not kill him by shooting him, but with sword blows, as with 7 habitants whose corpses were found in the house along with that of M. de Portneuf. The English were angry with our people who insulted them from afar....

30. — Since three or four days the people of the town have been reduced to a quarter [a fourth part of a hundred] of bread; and the soldiers and other warriors to 3 quarters of bread with a half-pound of pork fat and a swig of brandy. And the people of the town who have the means to buy flour are advised to make provision now, in view of the fact that the authorities will not furnish any after the siege.

[September] 3.— Monday morning... They burned all the houses from the Sault up to Cap Tourmente. They spared only the churches. Although they burned the one at Saint-Joachim. They burned the fishing equipment of the inhabitants and they tried to burn their crops, especially the wheat; but they were unable to do so because the crops were still too green.

3. — All morning, a landing at the town is expected. The general alarm is sounded, but needlessly: no landing...

9. — The Natives from the upper country file by returning to their country. There are some, it is said, who have 7 to 800 leagues to travel to reach home...

10.— A master gunner and little 17 year old sailor from the ramparts battery were hanged in town for having stolen at Mr. Mann's. It was M. Beaudoin and M. Parent, priest of Sainte-Anne who attended them...

12. — Wednesday, order given by M. de Montcalm, and then revoked by M. de Vaudreuil saying that we will see about that tomorrow, to the Guyenne battalion to go camp at le Foulon [Wolfe's Cove].

13. — The English land a little below the Foulon at three o'clock after midnight, take M. de Vergor prisoner, and at 10:30 rout our army...

[November] 7. — At 11 o'clock at night I am robbed and left wounded [by an English soldier].

[abbé Jean-Félix Récher, Journal du Siège de Québec en 1759 (Québec: Société historique de Québec, 1959), pp. 35-45. Trans. CJJ]

Collapse of the Support of the Seven Nations of Canada

These are to certify that the Chief of the Huron tribe of Indians, having come to me in the name of His Nation, to submit to His Britannick Majesty, and make Peace, has been received under my Protection, with his whole Tribe; and henceforth no English Officer or party is to molestt, or interrupt them in returning to their Settlement at Lorette; and they are received upon the same terms with the Canadians, being allowed the free Exercise of their Religion, their Customs, and Liberty of trading with the English: — recommending it to the Officers commanding the Posts, to treat them kindly.

Given under my hand at Longueil, this 5th day of September, 1760.

By the Genl's Command,

John Cosnan, Ajut. Genl. Ja. Murray

[Supreme Court of Canada, Arrêt Sioui, No. 20628]

Articles of Capitulation of Montreal, 1760

Between their Excellencies Major-General Amherst, Commander-in-Chief of His Britannic Majesty's troops and forces in North America, on the one part, and the Marquis de Vaudreuil, etc. Governor and Lieutenant-General for the King in Canada, on the other.

Article I

Twenty-four hours after the signing of the present capitulation, the British General shall cause the troops of His Britannic Majesty to take possession of the gates of the town of Montreal; and the British garrison shall not enter the place until the French troops shall have evacuated it. "The whole garrison of Montreal must lay down their arms, and shall not serve during the present war. Immediately after the signing of the present capitulation, the King's troops shall take possession of the gates, and shall post the guards necessary to preserve good order in the town."

Article II

The troops and the militia, who are in the garrison in the town of Montreal, shall go out by the gate of Quebec, with all the honours of war... "Referred to the next article..."

Article IV

The militia, after evacuating the above towns, forts and posts, shall return to their habitations, without being molested on any pretence whatever, on account of their having carried arms. "Granted."

Article V

The troops who keep the field, shall raise their camp, drums beating, with their arms, baggage and artillery, to join the garrison of Montreal, and shall be treated in every respect the same. "These troops, as well as all others, must lay down their arms."

Article VI

The subjects of His Britannic Majesty, and of His Most Christian Majesty, soldiers, militia or seamen, who shall have deserted...shall be, on both sides, pardoned for their crime... "Refused."

Article VIII

The officers, soldiers, militia, seamen, and even the Indians, detained on account of their wounds or sickness, as well as in the hospital, as in private houses, shall enjoy the privileges of the cartel, and be treated accordingly. "The sick and wounded shall be treated the same as our own people."

Article XII

The most convenient vessel that can be found shall be appointed to carry the Marquis de Vaudreuil, M. de Rigaud, the Governor of Montreal, and the suite of this General, by the straitest passage to the first seaport in France... "Granted, except the archives which shall be necessary for the Government of the country."

Article XXI

The British General shall also provide ships for carrying to France the officers of the Supreme Council, of justice, police, admiralty, and all other officers having commissions or brevets from His Most Christian Majesty, for them, their families, servants and equipages...They shall, however, be at liberty to stay in the colony, if they think proper to settle their affairs, or to withdraw to France whenever they think fit. "Granted; but if they have papers relating to the Government of the country, they are to be delivered up to us."

Article XXVII

The free exercise of the Catholic, Apostolic, and Roman religion, shall subsist entire... "Granted as to the free exercise of their religion; the obligation of paying tithes to the priests will depend on the King's pleasure."

Article XXVIII
The Chapter, Priests, Curates and Missionaries shall continue, with an entire liberty, their exercise and functions of curés, in the parishes of the towns and country. "Granted."

Article XXX
If by the treaty of peace, Canada should remain in the power of His Britannic Majesty, his Most Christian Majesty shall continue to name the Bishop of the colony, who shall always be of the Roman communion, and under whose authority the people shall exercise the Roman religion. "Refused."

Article XXXII
The communities of nuns shall be preserved in their constitutions and privileges; they shall continue to observe their rules, they shall be exempted from lodging any military, and it shall be forbid to molest them in their religious exercises, or to enter their monasteries: safe-guards shall even be given them, if they desire them. "Granted."

Article XXXVI
If by the treaty of peace, Canada remains to His Britannic Majesty, all the French, Canadians, Acadians, merchants and other persons who chuse to retire to France, shall have leave to do so from the British General... "Granted."

Article XL
The savages or Indian allies of his most Christian Majesty, shall be maintained in the lands they inhabit, if they chuse to remain there; they shall not be molested on any pretence whatsoever, for having carried arms, and served his most Christian Majesty; they shall have, as well as the French, liberty of religion and shall keep their missionaries. The actual Vicars General, and the Bishop, when the Episcopal See shall be filled, shall have leave to send to them new missionaries when they shall judge it necessary. "Granted, except the last article, which has been already refused."

Article XLVII
The negroes and panis of both sexes shall remain, in their quality of slaves, in the possession of the French and Canadians to whom they belong; they shall be at liberty to keep them in their service in the colony, or to sell them; and they may also continue to bring them up in the Roman religion. "Granted, except those who shall have been made prisoners."

[Adam Shortt & Arthur G. Doughty, eds., Documents Relating to the Constitutional History of Canada, 1759-1791 *(Ottawa: King's Printer, 1921), pp. 5-22]*

The Enormous Cost of War

Year	Etat du Roi	
1745	1 337 722	livres
1746	2 943 421	
1747	2 908 106	
1748	2 065 695	
1749	2 031 990	
1750	2 774 715	
1751	3 503 123	
1752	4 099 128	
1753	5 513 424	
1754	4 466 021	
1755	6 101 837	
1756	11 343 019	
1757	19 269 966	
1758	27 945 774	
1759	30 168 429	
1760	20 727 739	

[NAC, MG 5, B-1, Tableau des dépenses faites au Canada, p. 121]

Section C
Attempted Conciliation of 'New Subjects'

Military defeat and occupation were undoubtedly traumatic for the francophone Catholic 'new subjects' and their former Amerindian allies. British policy was to assimilate them ultimately, but in the meantime it seemed necessary to reconcile them to British rule, and as much as possible to British institutions and customs. Since some of the leading members of the nobility and merchant class had chosen to leave Quebec colony, the clergy and the seigneurs appeared to the authorities to be the best instruments to employ in conciliating the inhabitants.

The cession of New France to the British Crown required an 'instrument of the royal prerogative' to institute civil government in the new British colony of Quebec, to define the boundaries of the colony, and to restrict settlement upon and alienation of Amerindian territory. But the process envisaged for limiting the transfer of title from the native inhabitants to the Crown also provided the means of vacating lands for occupation by European settlers.

The institution of civil government in 1764 was expected to be followed by the replacement of Canadian civil law with English common law, the calling of an elected assembly on the basis of a restricted franchise, a limitation of the privileges of the Catholic Church, the abolition of seigneurial tenure, and the imposition of the English language in all official and public transactions. Murray's response to the Lords of Trade and Plantations, the equivalent to the French Ministry of Marine and Colonies, indicated that he would pursue a policy of seeking to accommodate the francophone Catholic majority, and reconcile them to a gentle form of British rule.

Governor Guy Carleton quickly came to the conclusion that the high birth rate in Canada and the lack of large-scale British immigration ensured the numerical and cultural survival of the French Canadian 'new subjects.' On his recommendation, the British parliament passed a statute giving the colony of Quebec a new constitution that reflected Lord Mansfield's judgment rendered in 1774, reaffirming that articles of capitulation 'are sacred and inviolate, according to their true intent and meaning,' and that 'the laws of a conquered country continue in force until they are altered by the conqueror.' The Quebec Act reflected the policy of conciliation that appeared to recognize Quebec as a 'distinct society' in the British Empire.

The Chief Justice of Quebec, William Hey, expressed the surprise of British officials at the general indifference of the French Canadians to both the appeals of the Americans to join in the revolution against British rule, and the favourable terms of the Quebec Act. The British had hoped to control the 'new subjects' through the influence of the clergy and seigneurs. They discovered that they were no more influential leaders in 1775 than they had been under French rule.

Lord Haldimand was also in a position to assess whether the Quebec Act had succeeded in winning the loyalty of the Canadian 'new subjects' in the face of American revolt and invasion and of French attempts to stir up rebellion in Quebec. There was some opposition to the policy of conciliation, and demand for the imposition of a policy of Anglicization.

Royal Proclamation of October 1763

Whereas We have taken into Our Royal Consideration the extensive and valuable Acquisitions in America, secured to our Crown by the late Definitive Treaty of Peace, concluded at Paris, the 10th Day of February last...

We have thought fit, with the Advice of our Privy Council, to issue this Royal Proclamation...to erect...First, The Government of Quebec bounded on the Labrador Coast by the River St. John, and from thence by a Line drawn from the Head of that River through the Lake St. John, to the South end of the Lake Nipissing...

And whereas it is just and reasonable, and essential to our Interest, and the Security of our Colonies, that the several Nations or Tribes of Indians with whom We are connected, and who live under our Protection, should not be molested or disturbed in the Possession of such Parts of our Dominions and Territories as, not having been ceded to or purchased by Us, are reserved to them, or any of them, as their Hunting Grounds...We do further declare it to be our Royal Will and Pleasure, for the present as aforesaid, to reserve under our Sovereignty, Protection and Dominion, for the use of the said Indians, all the Lands and Territories not included within the Limits of our said Three new Governments, or within the Limits of the Territory granted to the Hudson's Bay Company, as also all the Lands and territories lying to the Westward of the Sources of the Rivers which fall into the Sea from the West and North West as aforesaid.

And We do hereby strictly forbid, on Pain of our Displeasure, all our loving Subjects from making any Purchases or Settlements whatever, and taking Possession of any of the Lands above reserved, without our especial leave and Licence for that Purpose first obtained...

We do with the advice of our Privy Council strictly enjoin and require, that no private Person do presume to make any Purchase from the said Indians of any lands reserved to the said Indians, within those parts of our Colonies where, We have thought proper to allow Settlement; but that, if at any Time any of the said Indians should be inclined to dispose of the said Lands, the same shall be Purchased only by Us, in our Name, at some public Meeting or Assembly of the said Indians, to be held for that Purpose...

[Adam Shortt & Arthur G. Doughty, eds., Documents Relating to the Constitutional History of Canada, 1759-1791 *(Ottawa: King's Printer, 1921), pp. 136-141]*

Governor Murray's Colonial Policy
To the Lords of Trade, 19 October 1764

Little, very little, will content the New Subjects but nothing will satisfy the Licentious Fanaticks Trading here, but the expulsion of the Canadians who are perhaps the bravest and best race upon the Globe, a Race who could they be indulged with a few priveledges which the Laws of England deny to Roman Catholicks at home, wou'd soon get the better of every National Antipathy to their Conquerors and become the most faithful and useful set of Men in this American Empire, I flatter myself there will be some Remedy found out even in the Laws for the Relief of this People, if so, I am positive the popular clamours in England will not prevent the Humane Heart of the King from following its own Dictates. I am confident too my Royal Master will not blame the unanimous opinion of his Council here for the Ordonnance establishing the Courts of Justice, as nothing less could be done to prevent great numbers from emigrating directly, and certain I am, unless the Canadians are admitted on Jurys, and are allowed Judges and Lawyers who understand their Language his Majesty will lose the greatest part of this Valuable people.

To the Lords of Trade, 14 April 1766

My Lords, it is evident that Two very principal sources of the Disorders in the province have been: 1st The attempt to carry on the Administration of Justice without the aid of the natives [Canadians], not merely in new forms, but totally in an unknown tongue, by which means the partys Understood Nothing of what was pleaded or determined having neither Canadian Advocates or Solicitors to Conduct their Causes, nor Canadian jurors to give Verdicts, even in Causes between Canadians only, nor Judges conversant in the French Language to declare the Law, and to pronounce Judgment; This must cause the Real Mischiefs of Ignorance, oppression and Corruption, or else what is almost equal in Government to the mischiefs themselves, the suspicion and Imputation of them.

The second and great source of disorders was the Alarm taken at the Construction put upon His Majesty's Proclamation of October 7th, 1763. As if it were His Royal Intentions by his Judges and Officers in that Country, at once to abolish all the usages and Customs of Canada, with the rough hand of a Conqueror rather than with the true Spirit of a Lawful Sovereign, and not so much to extend the protection and Benefit of His English Laws to His new subjects, by securing their Lives, Liberty's and properties with more certainty than in former times, as to impose new, unnecessary and arbitrary Rules, especially in the Titles to Land, and in the modes of Descent, Alienation and Settlement, which tend to confound and subvert rights, instead of supporting them.

[W. P. M. Kennedy, ed., Documents of the Canadian Constitution, 1759-1915 (Toronto: Oxford University Press, 1918), pp. 40-41, 44-45]

Survival of French Canadians

The new subjects could send into the Field about eighteen thousand Men, well able to carry Arms; of which Number, above one half have already served, with as much Valor, with more Zeal, and more military Knowledge of America, than the regular Troops of France, that were joined with them...

But while this severe Climate, and the Poverty of the Country discourages all but the Natives, its Healthfulness is such, that these multiply daily, so that, barring Catastrophe shocking to think of, this Country must, to the end of Time, be peopled by the Canadian Race, who already have taken such firm Root, and got to so great a Height, that any new Stock transplanted will be totally hid, and imperceptible amongst them, except in the Towns of Quebec and Montreal.

[Adam Shortt & Arthur G. Doughty, eds., Documents Relating to the Constitutional History of Canada, 1759-1791 (Ottawa: King's Printer, 1921), pp. 282-284]

The Quebec Act, 1774

An Act for making more effectual Provision for the Government of the Province of Quebec in North America.

V. And for the more perfect Security and Ease of the Minds of the Inhabitants of the said Province, it is hereby declared, That His Majesty's Subjects, professing the Religion of the Church of Rome of and in the said Province of Quebec, may have, hold, and enjoy, the free Exercise of the Religion of the Church of Rome, subject to the King's Supremacy...and that the Clergy of the said Church may hold, receive, and enjoy, their accustomed Dues and Rights, with respect to such Persons only as shall profess the said Religion.

VII. Provided always, and be it enacted, That no Person, professing the Religion of the Church of Rome, and residing in the said Province, shall be obliged to take the Oath required by the said Statute passed in the First Year of the Reign of Queen Elizabeth, or any other Oaths substituted by any other Act in Place thereof...

VIII. And be it further enacted by the Authority aforesaid, That all His Majesty's Canadian Subjects, within the Province of Quebec, the religious Orders and Communities only excepted, may also hold and enjoy their Property and Possessions, together with all Customs and Usages relative thereto, and all other their Civil Rights, in as large, ample, and beneficial Manner, as if the said Proclamation, Commissions, Ordinances, and other Acts and Instruments, had not been made...and that in all Matters of Controversy, relative to Property and Civil Rights, Resort shall be had to the Laws of Canada, as the Rule for the Decision in the same...

XII. And whereas it may be necessary to ordain many regulations for the future Welfare and good Government of the Province of Quebec...and whereas it is at present inexpedient to call an Assembly; be it therefore enacted by the Authority aforesaid, That it shall and may be lawful for His Majesty, His Heirs and Successors, by Warrant under His or Their Signet and Sign Manual, and with the advice of the Privy Council, to constitute and appoint a Council for the Affairs of the Province of Quebec...

[W. P. M. Kennedy, ed., Documents of the Canadian Constitution, 1759-1915 (Toronto: Oxford University Press, 1918), pp. 132-136]

Indifference to British Policy

...it may be truly said that Gen. Carleton had taken an ill measure of the influence of the seigneurs & Clergy over the lower order of people whose Principle of conduct founded in fear & the sharpness of authority over them now no longer exercised, is unrestrained, & breaks out in every shape of contempt or detestation of those whom they used to behold with terror & who gave them I believe too many occasions to express it. And they [the seigneurs and clergy] on their parts have been and are too much elated with the advantages they supposed they should derive from the restoration of their old Priviledges & customs, & indulged themselves in a way of thinking & talking that gave just offense, as well to their own People as to the English merchants.

[Adam Shortt & Arthur G. Doughty, eds., Documents Relating to the Constitutional History of Canada, 1759-1791 *(Ottawa: King's Printer, 1921), pp. 670-671]*

Governor Haldimand's Assessment of the Situation
Haldimand to Germain, 25 October 1780

As it is my Duty, it has been my Business to inform myself of the State of the Country & I coincide with the Majority of the Legislative Council in Considering the Canadians as the People of the Country, and think that in making Laws and Regulations for the Administration of these Laws, Regard is to be paid to the Sentiments and Manner of thinking of 60,000 rather than the 2,000—three fourths of whom are Traders & Cannot with Propriety be considered as residents of the Province. — In this point of view the Quebec Act, was both just and Politic, tho' unfortunately for the British Empire, it was enacted Ten Years too late—It requires but Little Penetration to Discover that had the System of Government Solicited by the Old Subjects been adopted in Canada, this Colony would in 1775 have become one of the United States of America. Whoever Considers the Number of Old Subjects who in that year corresponded with and Joined the Rebels, of those who abandoned the defence of Quebec in virtue of Sir Guy Carleton's Proclamation in the fall of the same Year, & of the many others who are now the avowed well wishers of the Revolted Colonies, must feel this Truth however national or Religious Prejudices will not allow him to declare it.

[W. P. M. Kennedy, ed., Documents of the Canadian Constitution, 1759-1915 *(Toronto: Oxford University Press, 1918), Vol. II, p. 166]*

1. How important was the participation of Amerindians in colonial warfare? Did Europeans share some common views and perceptions of Native warriors?

2. Did Canadians come to believe Wolfe's assertion that France 'deserted' her colony, failed to support it properly, and had imposed an oppressive rule? What do you think of that perception?

3. What have you learned about the prejudices, fears, and conduct of the British and French respectively in the War of the Conquest? Do you think accounts of such wars should be 'sanitized' and students not be exposed to some of the gruesome details of warfare?

4. Was there more continuity than change in colonial government and everyday life following the British conquest?

5. To what extent can the Royal Proclamation of 1763 be viewed as a charter of Amerindian rights, and the Quebec Act of 1774 as a charter of French Canadian rights?

READINGS

Jeremy Black, *Natural and Necessary Enemies: Anglo-French Relations in the Eighteenth Century* (London: Duckworth, 1986)

René Chartrand, *Canadian Military Heritage. Volume I: 1000-1754* (Montreal: Art Global, 1993)

Guy Fregault, *The War of the Conquest* (Toronto: Oxford University Press, 1969)

Brian Given, *A Most Pernicious Thing: Gun Trading and Native Warfare* (Ottawa: Carleton University Press, 1994)

Julian Gwyn, "French and British Naval Power at the Two Sieges of Louisbourg, 1745 and 1758," in *Nova Scotia Historical Review* 10, 2 (1990): 63-93.

Francis Jennings, *Empire of Fortune: Crowns, Colonies & Tribes in the Seven Years' War in America* (New York: Columbia University Press, 1988)

Lee Kennett, *The French Armies in the Seven Years' War* (Durham: Duke University Press, 1969)

Peter MacLeod, *The Canadian Iroquois and the Seven Years' War* (Toronto: Dundurn Press, 1996)

Dale Miquelon, *Society and Conquest: The Debate on the Bourgeoisie and Social Change in French Canada* (Toronto: Copp Clark Pitman, 1977)

Hilda Neatby, *Quebec: The Revolutionary Age, 1760-1791* (Toronto: McClelland & Stewart, 1966)

_____, *The Quebec Act: Protest and Policy* (Scarborough: Prentice-Hall, 1972)

James Pritchard, *Anatomy of a Naval Disaster: The 1746 French Expedition to North America* (Montreal-Kingston: McGill-Queen's University Press, 1995)

G.F.G. Stanley, *New France: The Last Phase, 1744-1760* (Toronto: McClelland & Stewart, 1969)

Ian K. Steele, *Guerrillas and Grenadiers: The Struggle for Canada, 1689-1760* (Toronto: Ryerson Press, 1969)

_____, *Betrayals: Fort William Henry and the "Massacre"* Revised edition (New York: Oxford University Press, 1993)

_____, *Warpaths: Invasions of North America* (New York: Oxford University Press, 1994)

Immigrants and Refugees—The American Revolution and the Coming of the Loyalists

The American Revolution had an impact not only on relations between England and its former Thirteen Colonies, it also triggered the formation of new colonies, such as Upper Canada, and precipitated an influx of refugees and immigrants to Upper and Lower Canada as well as the Maritimes. It is difficult to estimate the exact numbers involved, but approximately 40 000 immigrants were given land grants and aid by the British government. The majority of these new arrivals settled in Nova Scotia (part of which became New Brunswick in 1784) and the rest went to the Island of St. John (later Prince Edward Island), Cape Breton, and the Canadas. Those who migrated to Nova Scotia joined the community of New England 'Planters,' who had arrived in the 1760s, attracted by the British government's offer of free land, tax-exempt for ten years. The initial influx of Loyalists to the Canadas in the 1780s was followed by the so-called 'late Loyalists' who appear to have come for land.

A number of reasons have been suggested for the Atlantic colonies' and Quebec's motives for not joining the Revolution and deciding to remain 'loyal.' Each colony, of course, was influenced by its own specific economic, political, and social situations. Newfoundland, for example, was heavily dependent on British-dominated trade and did not have its own political institutions that could have initiated a break from colonial rule. Similarly, St. John's Island was at such an early stage of colonial settlement that there were no community structures to form local political organizations that might question imperial relations. In Nova Scotia, the presence of British troops and colonial economic ties and, possibly, the influence of religious leader Henry Alline's 'Great Awakening' resulted in the colonists remaining aloof from active support of the Thirteen Colonies. Yet, despite its neutrality, the Atlantic region was directly affected by the war—British soldiers brought trade into Halifax, while at the same time New England privateers caused much hardship with their raids on outport settlements from the southern tip of Nova Scotia to Labrador.

Perhaps the Americans were not as interested in gaining control of the Atlantic colonies, since a successful invasion of Nova Scotia would have required a large-scale naval campaign. The situation in Quebec, however, was quite different. Believing that the Canadians would seize the opportunity to rid themselves of the English and that support would be forthcoming from a number of English-speaking merchants, American propagandists sent broadsides to the colonists encouraging them to join in the Revolution. American troops then invaded and occupied Quebec in the winter of 1775-1776, but were forced to retreat in the late spring when 10 000 British troops arrived in the colony. The seigneurs and clergy decided to support the British; the habitants, for the most part, preferred to remain neutral, since they saw little reason to support either faction, were tired of fighting, and observed that those suspected of supporting the Americans were severely punished by the colonial government.

Those who came as refugees or immigrants to British North America were mainly farmers, artisans, merchants, and labourers; 10 percent were recent immigrants from Europe, such as Huguenots, Germans, and Scots. Half of the refugee population consisted of women and children who came as members of families. A Loyalist identity was not only European; there were approximately 5 000 free black Loyalists and Native Loyalists, while other blacks had arrived as slaves in the Atlantic colonies and the Canadas. However, after being given poorer-quality land to farm and experiencing hostility and violence from their neighbours, in 1792 almost 1 200 black Loyalists left Nova Scotia when offered free passage by the British-based Sierra Leone Company, led by prominent abolitionists, to Sierra Leone, in Africa.

The Loyalist influx affected the areas in which they settled in a number of ways. Loyalist merchants in Quebec, while comprising only 10 percent of the population, were highly vocal critics of the Quebec Act and French laws and customs, and they pressured the colonial government for an elected assembly and the introduction of British common law. In the Maritimes, members of the Loyalist elite settled in the growing cities of Halifax, Saint John, and Fredericton, occupying many political offices in Nova Scotia and New Brunswick as well as providing the impetus for the founding of educational institutions. Outside of urban areas, however, in both the Maritime colonies and in the Canadas, the Loyalist experience of farming generally resembled that of other pioneers. In Upper Canada, the arrival of Loyalist settlers created a number of problems for the Ojibwa who had lived in the southern part of the colony since the early 1700s: disease, increased availability of alcohol, and, in particular, Loyalist encroachment upon and appropriation of Native land.

Section A
Revolution and the Ordinary People

The following are excerpts from, first, the diary of Jonathan Scott (1744-1793?), a New England-born fisherman and minister who, at the time of writing, was living in Yarmouth, Nova Scotia. Scott's diary is followed by Rebecca Byles' letters to her paternal aunt, Catherine Byles, of Boston. Rebecca (1762-1853) was the daughter of a prominent Loyalist family from Boston who fled to Nova Scotia during the American Revolution. These documents suggest how the American Revolution altered the lives of so-called 'ordinary folk,' those who did not play leading military and political roles but were forced to cope and, at times, struggle with the intrusion into their lives brought about by the clash of imperial powers.

Privateers and Press-Gangs

Nov 29 1775

By Orders from Governor Legge, Colonel Gould came to Yarmouth last Summer, and Commissioned Officers for, and constituted a Company of Light Infantry, gathered out of Yarmouth and Argyle, consisting of 50 Men, always to be ready for the Government's Service, and to be paid by the Government. These men were draughted by Colonel Gould of Halifax, the Men being nominated by Capt. Allen of Yarmouth, and no previous notice at all given to the men nor any offer to enlist, but they were enrolled in the manner above. The Officers of this new Establishment were Capt. Eleazar Hibbard, and Lieutenants Benjamin Brown and David Scott, the Clerk, Nehemiah Porter.

Things being thus disposed, the men were warned to appear and answer to their names and receive further orders and Instructions; the place where they were warned to meet was Esquire Durkee's at Cape Fourchu, and this was the day appointed; and I am informed that some of the men appeared at the Time and Place and appointed a Speaker who in person went to Capt. Hibbard and requested, in behalf of the Company, to know what Demands he had on them; upon which Capt. Hibbard produced his Commission and read it, and likewise his Orders which came from the Governor. When he had thus done, the Speaker (Benjamin Brown) declared that they would not submit to, nor pay any regard to him or his Orders; and then the men went about their business. Soon after, some of the Company went on board two vessels that had just come into the Harbour, and in about an Hour there came a number of Armed Men from the Vessels, headed by Nathan Brown, and entered into Esq. Durkee's house, and took from thence

Capt. Jeremiah Allen, Capt. Hibbard, Lieut. Brown, and Nehemiah Porter, Clerk, and carried them all on board the vessels, without any resistance, there being no power sufficient to relieve those who were apprehended; that happened about 3 O'clock P.M.

In the evening following, a number of men from the same vessels came to Jebogue and took my brother David Scott, a Lieutenant in the Infantry Company who did not meet with the Officers at Esq. Durkees because he had been sick and was not recovered so as to be able to go so far, and took him and carried him on board the same Night.

Upon enquiry into this sudden and alarming affair, it was made to appear that the two vessels were from New England, Armed Schooners, mounting eight carriage Guns each, and a number of Swivels, and fully manned; and came out with a design to oppose all that they took to be their enemies; and having been into Barrington, and there got intelligence (from some of our own People who were there) that there was this new Establishment, and that this was the day when they were to be embodied, they made all possible speed and got here at the Nick of Time when the Officers were met, and took them without any previous Notice.

The unfortunate Sufferers were not allowed to come ashore to see their Families, though the vessels tarried till Friday towards night; but what appeared most unnatural and barbarous was, that most People seemed Glad at the calamity of the Sufferers; and looked upon it as a good Providence, because thereby the Infantry Company was like to be broken up.

But I am afraid that this is but the Beginning of Sorrow, and that those who are now Rejoicing, and appear to be glad at the Calamity of others, will not go unpunished, but will hereby prepare themselves for, and bring on calamity and Distress upon themselves. May a gracious God prevent the Evil which I fear is coming upon us.

Friday Dec 1 1775

This day I went over to see the poor Men that were taken Prisoners last Wednesday, and see if there was no way to get them Released; but by conversing with the Masters of the Vessels I soon found that they were fully determined to carry them away, and therefore I left off entreating for them and was obliged to take my leave of them. Capt. Allen appeared much cast down; and though he had spoken lightly of me without cause (as I think) yet I felt my heart ache for him; and were it in my power, I would gladly help him and set him at liberty.

My poor brother David has treated me with more ill Words and Indignity than Capt. Allen has; but yet I could not refrain from Weeping at his Calamity, and that in his Presence too. He committed to me the care of his little children, desiring that I would not let them suffer, and I willingly promised him that I would do what I could for them. All the parting Consolation that I could give my brother was that he must go to God for Relief and Help in time of trouble. I returned home in company with Deacon Crocker, exceedingly cast down and filled with Sorrow, both for the Poor Men carried away Prisoners and their distressed Families which are left among us. I did not feel a Spirit of Revenge working in me, but I was Grieved and could not but Weep sure for the Calamities of others.

Monday Dec 4 1775

This day, being desired, I went over to Mr Amos Hilton's, where were Assembled the Officers of Militia and two Justices of the Peace to consult what Report should be sent to the Governor concerning the Hostility committed last week by the Privateers from New England in carrying away the Men; the Conclusion of this meeting was to send an Exact Narrative of the Proceedings of the Privateers to the Governor and Council and desire their advice and Protection. After the Meeting was over, I went to see my Brother David's Wife and advise with her about the concerns of her family, and to see whether she stood in need of the Comforts of life.

Saturday Dec 16 1775

Yesterday, the unfortunate men that were carried away on 29th Novr. all arrived safe to their families, having been absent about three weeks. I did not expect they would have got home so soon, if ever.

> *[Charles Bruce Fergusson, ed.,* The Life of Jonathan Scott *(Bulletin of the Public Archives of Nova Scotia, No.15, 1960), pp. 52-54]*

In This Time of Universal Confusion: The Letters of Rebecca Byles

8 November 1777

I received your agreable Letter very safe. It gives me great pleasure to hear that you are alive, and well, which is all I can know in the present state of affairs; we are impatient to get Letters from our Friends, and when we do, we know very little more than we did before. I hope with you that the unhappy Barrier will soon be removed, and we shall meet again, but we must not Repine. I know it will give you pleasure to hear how happily we are situated in this Time of Universal confusion. We enjoy a large share of the Comforts of Life, and the gratest uneasiness is the Situation of our Country. Mrs. Cottnam is in Town at the Head of a Female Academy. My sisters and myself go to her; they to plain sewing and Reading, and I to Writing, learning French (parley vous Francais Mademoiselle) and Dancing, which employs a good Part of my Time. We have enjoyed our Health better since we came down here than ever we did before in our Lifes, and have a great deal to be Thankful for. My Brother and Sisters join me in Duty to Grandpappa Aunt Polly and you...

27 December 1779

Tho' we had but about half an Hour's notice of a Cartel's sailing for Boston, my Pappa had taken up his Pen to write to you a few lines, when he was call'd off to a perticular friend. Dying of an Apoplexy, on whom he was oblig'd to attend directly. He therefore disired me to take his Place, and inform you that we are all well and that there has been no material Alteration amongst us since we last wrote, which was in September by Mr Tidmarsh who took Charge of a Packet consisting of seven Letters for you, my Grandmamma & Miss Patten, which we suppose you recei'd & which we impatiently wait the return of the Flag to have them acknowledged. When, my Dear Aunt will this stupid intercourse of saying nothing be put a stop to; for my part I am heartily tired of it, & I am sometimes determin'd I will not write again, till I can write and speak with freedom. But upon second thoughts, that is an imprudent determination; we will therefore go on in the same track and mutually pray that it may be put a speedy end to. I thought much of you and Sally Patten on Christmas Day when we used to be generally together. Louisa is to be enoculated for the Small Pox this week, which I wish was well over. Your friends the Miss Cumming's are well. Our Family all join me in tenderest Affection and Duty to our ever Dear Grandpappa and you, whose situation I sincerely Sympathize with, and heartily wish it was in my power to alleviate. But how ever my Dear Aunts keep up your Spirits and follow the old Maxim, 'that whatever is is right.' I will now put me close to Letter, with sending you compliments of the Season.

16 August 1780

Tho' you are, let me see, one, two, three, and four & I believe five Letters in my Debt, & I have rack'd my invention in vain to find something to write about, I cannot forbear indulging the scribbling Humour I find myself in, and the disire I have of assureing you of my unalterable Duty & Affection, which believe me Time has not diminish'd: how much, how earnestly do I long to see you, to do every Thing in my Power to soften and alleviate all your Distresses, & divide with you all my Pleasures. But since the divine disposer of all Things has seen fit to separate us, it becomes us cheerfully to submit, nor even allow ourselves in one anxious wish, one murmurring Thought.

We, I think, seem to settled here. We have bought a large, convenient House, with a very good Garden, Yard & every other convenience, & what I exceedingly value, live exactly opposite our Friends Mrs. and Miss Cottnam, with whom I spend a good deal of my Time very happily. They both disire to be remember'd. The Widow Taylor this Spring married her second Daughter to a Captain Ross, & her third, my Namesake, is soon, I hear, to follow her example, so that she will have but one left with her. Mr. Domett & Wife went from New York to England some time ago, and I hear has return'd to the same Place with an employment under Government. Mrs. Lovell & her Daughters are well & often speak of you.

Her two Youngest Daughters are soon to be married to a couple of Hessian Officers. The Miss Cuming's are well. You see my Dear Aunt I write you an account of all your Friends, pray do the same by me, particularly of my Grandmamma Walter, my Aunt Otis, my Cousins Abbot & Hesilrige to whom present my duty and best Regards. Tell my Grandmamma that I have wrote her three times, & would have wrote now, if I had had Time. Let me know also whether Sally Patten is Dead or Alive. Your Packet by the way of Penobscot has not reach'd us, nor do I think it ever will: I therefore beg you will send Duplicates by the return of the Flag, as we are all impatient, especially Nancy, who is quite discourag'd at waiting so long for an answer to the first Letter that ever she wrote. Louisa desires me to tell her Aunts she loves them Dearly. My Brother & Sisters beg leave to present with mine their Duty to our much esteem'd Grandpappa, Aunt Polly and you, but I fancy I hear you say, I am very sorry Becca your Scribling Humor, as you call it, came on when you were writeing to me. Have Patience, my Dear Aunt & I will conclude with assuring you, etc...

[Margaret Conrad, Toni Laidlaw, and Donna Smyth, eds., No Place Like Home: Diaries and Letters of Nova Scotia Women, 1771-1938 *(Halifax: Formac Publishing Co., 1988), pp. 48-57]*

Governor's House and Mather's Meeting House on Hollis Street, Also Looking Up George St., Halifax, 1765, Dominique Serres, after a drawing by Richard Short. *[Art Gallery of Nova Scotia, 82.41]*

Section B
Immigrants' Experiences and Goals

This section considers the different goals of the new groups of immigrants and refugees; it also contrasts the experiences of Anglo-American and black Loyalists. The correspondence between Sir John Johnson, British Superintendent of Indians for the Northern Department, General Frederick Haldimand, Governor of Quebec, and Joseph Brant, a member of an influential Mohawk family and a British ally during the Seven Years' War and the American Revolution, depicts negotiations between the British and their Six Nations allies, and suggests the potential consequences of these negotiations for the Ojibwa residents of the territory under discussion.

Joseph Brant visited Quebec and informed General Haldimand that although the band of Mohawks led by Captain John and other chiefs had decided to settle at the bay of Quinté, the remainder wished to obtain a tract of land which he described as lying in the valley of the Grand River, and was recognized as being the property of the Mississagas. This application resulted in the agreement included here.

The Montreal merchants' petition outlines this group's desire to see British institutions established in the colony. We can contrast their experiences with those of Boston King, the residents of Preston, Nova Scotia, and Richard Pierpoint, black men and women who came to Nova Scotia and Upper Canada as a result of the Revolutionary War. While they managed to escape slavery, they were faced with great economic hardship and received little help from the colonial government. Pierpoint's petition was refused and, instead of returning to his birthplace, he was given a land grant of 100 acres (40.5 hectares) along the Grand River, Garafraxa Township.

The final document in this section is an excerpt from the diary of Anne Powell, a member of a prominent Loyalist family from Boston who emigrated to Upper Canada; it describes the happier fate of a former family servant who settled in Quebec on the shores of the St. Lawrence.

From Sir John Johnson to General Haldimand

Montreal 11th August 1783.

Sir

I have the honor to transmit herewith the Proceedings of the Several Meetings held with the Six Nations, &c., at Niagara, and with the Messasagas at Carleton Island, by the latter your Excellency will observe that some uneasiness has arisen among them in consequence of a Report prevailing that a Number of the Six Nations intended Settling in the Neighbourhood of Cataraqui—they seem to have no Objection to White People settling there, but say that If their Brothers the Six Nations come there, they are so Numerous they will overrun their hunting grounds, and oblige them to retire to New and distant grounds not so good or convenient to them—these objections however may easily be removed by a purchase of such part of their Country as your Excellency may think necessary for the use of the Mohawks and others who may wish to Establish themselves on that Side of the Lake—I should imagine a purchase of the Lands Including the Islands from the Bay of Kenty downwards, and Including the Crown Lands, would be sufficient to Answer every purpose both for Loyalists and Indians.

"I beg leave to request that as the Officers and Men of my Regiment were the foremost in opposing His Majestys Enemies and the first that joined his Forces in this Province, they may be Indulged with the first choice of Lands, should any be granted to them they have had reason to expect from the Proclamation Issued at the Commencement of the War."...

Substance Requisitions by Captain Brant

Substance of Captain Brant's wishes respecting a settlement of the Mohawk & others of the Six Nation Indians upon the Grand River &ca.

That His Excellency the Commander in Chief should give the Superintendant & Inspector General of Indian Affairs Instructions and impower Lieut. Col. Butler to purchase from the Messessagué or Proprietors a Tract of Land consisting of about six miles on each side of the Grand River called Oswego running from the River La Tranche into Lake Erie, for the use of the Mohawks and such of the Six Nations as are inclined to join them in that Settlement. Col. Butler is fully acquainted with the views & Inclinations of Capt. Brant & the Mohawks respecting this Settlement and only waits the General's approbation to make the Purchase. The sooner this can be done the better, as they would remove this Spring, Time enough to plant Corn &ca.—And Capt. Brant would propose that some of his Party be sent off upon this Business to Col. Butler as soon as he returns to Montreal.

The above mentioned Limits are only meant for the Indians of the Six Nations who may settle there, but a more considerable Tract of Land may at the same Time be purchased on very reasonable Terms whereon to settle Loyalists or for any future Purpose.

As the Losses which the Mohawk Nation have sustained in their Settlements & Property by the Rebellion are very considerable, and have so impoverished them as to prevent their Settling upon fresh Ground with any Vigour unless assisted by Government, They Request that His Excellency will be pleased to indemnify their said Losses, which have been faithfully ascertained and amount to near

Sixteen Thousand Pounds New York Currency, or if any Delay should be necessary in this Business that he will in the mean time grant some part thereof for the
aforesaid Purpose, to be distributed amongst them where assistance is most necessary in proportion to the Losses which have been sustained. The Nation has
pressed Capt. Brant to be very solicitous upon this subject with the General. He
therefore cannot help being anxious for its success, having lost their whole substance and being deprived of every means of subsisting except by hunting;—They
further request that until their Settlements shall be in some forwardness, the
Commander in Chief will assist them with a reasonable Quantity of Provisions.

Capt. Brant in this application does not by any means wish that Partiality
should be shown to the Mohawks, he speaks in the behalf of the Six Nations in
General and altho' the Losses of the other Nations have been infinitely less considerable than those of the Mohawks, he is equally solicitous that they should be
considered, which, from his own knowledge & the Conversations he has had with
Sir John Johnson & Col. Butler, he thinks may be done to their satisfaction by an
Ample supply of Cloathing & he wishes this to be done before the Meeting with
the American Commissioners shall take Place, as well to Content the Indians, as
for Partial Measures.

From Sir John Johnson to General Haldimand

Montreal 11th March, 1784.

Sir

Captain Brant and David[1] have desired me to Acquaint your Excellency that
their business at this time is to propose a Settlement of the Mohawks and others
on the Grand River about twenty Miles from the head of Lake Ontario, their
Reasons are Politick and no doubt good—the Mohawks[2] here are determined to
Abide by their first resolution of Settling About the Bay of Kenty, the Chiefs John
and Isaac preferring the Rule of a few to the Risk of losing their Consequence
among the whole.

I Returned from Point Maligne last Monday Evening too late to Write by
Post, or I would have Informed your Excellency that the Morning after I arrived
at the Surveyors Camp Opposite St. Regis, being Sunday, I was Waited upon by
a great Number of the Chiefs and Warriors of that Village who had Watched my
Arrival. After the usual Ceremony they began by Approving of my endeavours to
re-establish those unfortunate People who had followed my Example and Shared
my fate in the Service of our King & Country, at the same time they said they
thought it would be unjust in their father to take away from them, who had acted

---

[1] David Hill, an interpreter, possibly a member of the Six Nations
[2] The Lower Mohawks led by Captain John and other chiefs

by our desire, in the same cause, the lands they had always looked upon as theirs, to make up the losses he had been the cause of, to others, without being consulted or our intentions even made known to them—they hoped, as I was appointed for the management of their Affairs, that I would not see any injustice done them, and that I would represent their Claim to your Excellency, which is from the River au Raisin Six Leagues in depth to a Creek a little above the Long Saut, they say their Deeds or papers for this tract was burnt in their Church when it was consumed, and that they were promised by my father to have it confirmed to them, that Colonel Claus knows their Claim, and that the Canadians and others always conceiving it to be their Right, paid them considerable Sums of Money for liberty to Cut Timber thereon—I told them I thought your Excellency would not have sent us up to those lands, were you not well assured they were the property of the Crown, for if they had a grant of them, it must have been Recorded and Consequently known to you—I asked them in case your Excellency should be inclined to think they had some Right to those Lands, and Wished to Indulge them, whether they would not be Willing to relinquish their Claim to two or three Leagues in Depth from the before mentioned River to the Long Saut for a Reasonable Compensation, they said it was a matter of Weight, and Merited serious consideration and that they would Assemble the whole of their People, and send me an Answer as soon as possible, in the meantime the People might Hutt themselves...

From General Haldimand to Sir John Johnson

Head Quarters Quebec 15th March 1784.

Sir

I have been favoured with your letter of the 11th Instant by Captn Brant & David with whom I have fully conversed upon the subject of the settlement they so much wish to form on the Grand River above the Head of Lake Ontario. After examining the situation of the Country upon the Map, and considering the Reasons which incline Joseph to this measure I am clearly of opinion that an accomplishment of it is much to be desired. I have communicated my ideas upon it to Joseph, and have promised Him every encouragement in my Power towards the success of it. He tells me that Colo. Butler is persuaded he can purchase the Right of the Land from the Messessagues for a very trifling consideration. You have therefore my authority to instruct him upon that subject whenever it shall be thought best, after the necessary steps for carrying the matter into execution shall be decided upon with Joseph & his adherents in this Plan—He informs me that altho' the Mohawks here, have not at first entered into his ideas, they will soon perceive the advantage of extending themselves into so fine a Country, forming a communication with the Delawares and other Indians who are settled there and strengthning themselves by the Emigration of some of the six nations who it seems are not inclined to remove to the Bay of *Quinte*. I nevertheless intend to reserve that spot for such of the Indians who may wish at present, or on some future day to settle there.

[E. A. Cruikshank, The Settlement of the United Empire Loyalists
(Champlain Society, 1966), pp. 4, 32-34]

Report of the Merchants of Montreal, 1787

To the honorable committee of council on commercial affairs and police:

The Establishment of a Chamber of Commerce duly incorporated
Observation.

However beneficial to Trade & Commerce institutions of this nature be considered, yet we are of opinion that the same would prove ineffectual & inexpedient at this time considering the connection that subsists more or less among the Trading people of this place.

Holding Terms and the Abolition of Circuits

From the frequency of holding Courts, and from the mixture of French and English Laws, great delays, procrastinations, and incertitude are experienced in the decision of suits to remedy which we are of opinion, that Terms should be established; Four in the year to sit from day to day for fourteen days each term, which would be sufficient and prove more eligible for the dispatch of business, than those continual Courts.

The present Establishment of Appeals in Commercial causes
Observation.

The same uncertainty that has hitherto prevailed in the Courts of justice, has made its way into the Court of Appeals, probably through the disadvantage it has long labor'd under, for want of a Gentleman bred to the science of the Law, presiding or sitting in it to point out to the other Members, the errors in the proceedings if any, and to explain the Law; indeed without any imputation on the Judges it is much to be lamented, that regular bred professional Men do not preside in all the Courts of Justice in the Province, to the want of which we may impute the great delays in the decisions of suits...

The Establishment of a Court of Chancery
Observation.

A Court of Chancery would be a very desirable object if it could be so constituted as to grant relief under the rigour of legal decisions with convenient dispatch and on moderate fees.

On a Register of all Deeds
Observation.

Frauds having been committed by Debtors mortgaging their Lands to different Creditors, also much inconvenience arisen to Purchasers of Lands who have no effectual means of discovering incumberances on them. There being likewise a considerable degree of obscurity in most transactions with regard to real property: We offer as a means of better ascertaining the Rights of Proprietors and Creditors, and avoiding Lawsuits.—That there be erected at Montreal an Office for the registering all Deeds in future which affect real property within the District.—That the Fees of such Office be moderate as possible.—That no such Deeds be valid in future unless passed by a Notary and so registered.— Considering the illiterate state of the Bulk of the Inhabitants,—That it shall be incumbent under a high penalty on the Notary who may pass any such Deed, to have the same registered in the proper office, and this within a short limited time, and before he delivers any Copy to the party.

On a Bankrupt Law
Observation.

A Bankrupt Law and equitable rules for the distribution of the property of persons failing in Trade, is become essentially necessary for the security of the fair Trader and for the prevention of those Frauds there is too much reason to believe are daily practised. We are therefore of opinion that such Law should ascertain what act of a Merchant amounts to an Act of Bankruptcy & should compel the insolvent Debtor, in that situation to a surrender of his Books, papers, and effects, on Oath for the benefit of all his Creditors, and to answer such questions to his Trustees or Creditors as they may put to him relating to his business. In which Law, the Rights of the Wives and Children of all persons concerned in Trade or Commerce to the real or personal Estate of such Bankrupt should be ascertained. A Distinction should be made in the Treatment of a fraudulent, & unfortunate Bankrupt; The former should be punished exemplarily, yet not cruely, least the end be defeated; and the latter entitled to a discharge, provided three fourths of his Creditors both in number & value consent.

The contradictions in the Judgements of Law on this subject mark the strongest injury to the commercial Interest, therefore require a speedy & effective remedy.

Police
The building a Goal [jail] in the District of Montreal

There can be little doubt, that many objects of police will be best provided for, by means of incorporating the Town of Montreal by Charter, But there are some, which as they concern the District at large, require to be more particularly adverted to.

The want of a proper Goal for this District has long been complained of and at divers times has been represented, by different Grand Juries, as well at the Courts of Oyer & Terminer, as at the inferior Courts of Quarter Sessions, but hitherto no remedy has been applied. The House which at present serves for a Goal consists of four very small Rooms in which are frequently confined promiscuously persons of different sexes and for very different degrees of crimes; The unfortunate Debtor cannot have a Room to himself, nor can the Malefactor when preparing for another World be accommodated with a place of retirement to deprecate the wrath of the offended Deity. The insufficiency of the goal in point of security occasions a Guard of Soldiers to be kept in the lower part of it, and even with that precaution many atrocious Offenders have escaped, insomuch that the Sheriff of the District has refused to confine Debtors, unless the Prosecutor agreed to take upon himself the risk of an escape.

The situation of this insufficient Goal heightens, the sufferings of those persons whom the Law dooms to imprisonment, offends every passenger in the warm season and is a Nuisance to the Neighbourhood, being without those conveniences requisite to carry off the Filth accumulated by want of them.

We propose as the means of obtaining a proper Goal, that an Assessment be laid on the District, for the purpose of raising a fund adequate to the building of the same, if the present Legislature is competent thereto.

Whether or not we should apply for a Charter incorporating a select number of Citizens, on some good and approved Plan, with powers to make Bye Laws, decide civil and criminal causes under certain restrictions, whether under the stile and Title of Recorder, Mayor, Alderman & Common Council of the City & County of Quebec, and the Precincts and Liberties thereof or under any other denomination.
And a like Charter for the City of Montreal
Observation.

The bad state of the Police in this Town calls loudly for reform, and tho' Government in its wisdom, have attended thereto by the appointment of an Inspector of Police; yet we are sorry to observe that the appointment has in no wise proven adequate to the intent. And by experience we find, that the exertions of the Magistrates are not sufficient to remedy the evil complained of, We therefore beg leave to point out as the only Remedy that can be applied with effect, the incorporating by Charter a select number of the Citizens of Montreal on a good and approved plan, with such powers and Privileges, as are usually granted to Corporations; for the purpose of police only. And we further beg leave to request, that in case the Honorable Council should approve of this mode, and Government incline to grant the same. That it be recommended to His Excellency Lord Dorchester to bestow on the Corporation such Lots of Ground and Houses, the property of the Crown within the Town and Suburbs of Montreal as Government have not present use for, in order to the same being applied, towards the erecting Schools, workhouses, and other Establishments of Public utility.

That a Regulation is necessary to prevent a greater Number of Licences being granted for the sale of Liquors than are necessary for the use of the Town & Country
Observation

The many complaints arising from the great number of disorderly public Houses call the attention of the Legislature: There is infinitely too many of them both in Town & Country; they are the bane of Industry, and only tend to debauchery & Riot, it is much to be wished that a fewer number of Licenses were granted, and those to persons of good Character only.

A Regulation to prevent the erection in future of Wooden Buildings or Fences within the City of Montréal
Observation

As the Legislature has carefully attended, by a wise Law, to prevent the dreadful accidents that might happen by fire in the Towns of this Province, we must beg leave to offer an Amendment that would be of real service, to prevent the Spreading of fire in this Town, that is by enacting that no wooden fence or building of Wood of what description soever, be erected in the Town of Montréal in future under a severe Penalty.

The establishing of Schools and Seminaries, for the Education of Youth from those funds now unemployed, as well in England as in this Province, and particularly a respectable College in this City, with able Professors, and erecting Free Schools at convenient distances throughout this extensive Province, for the purpose of opening and enlarging the human mind, conciliating the affections of all His Majesty's Subjects and having a tendency to render this a happy & flourishing Province
Observation

There remains for us to advert to a subject which we consider as the surest and best means of obtaining a chearful and dutiful obedience to the Laws, and Government, from Subjects in general, and that is by establishing throughout the Province at proper distances, Public Schools for the Instruction of Youth. We hardly know of a single School in any Country part of the District for teaching Boys, and it is to the zeal of the few Sisters of the Congregation, that we are indebted for all the little which is taught to Girls throughout the Country. The Captains of Militia who are frequently called upon to enforce Laws and Orders, are so illiterate, that not one in three can write or even read, the consequence is confusion and disorder, and frequent suits and Complaints between them and the Militiamen. It is not for us to point out the best plan for Establishing those Schools, but having understood that all the Estates which the Jesuits possess in this Country were granted to them for the purposes of Establishing proper Seminaries of Learning and that those Estates are likely to revert to the Crown, we humbly conceive that they could in no way be better employed than in that for which they were originally intended and granted. There may be further some unappropriated Funds in England for similar purposes, now that the States of America formerly Colonies of Great Britain are separated from her Dominion, which we would recommend to be applied for through the proper Channel.

Upon the whole of the Observations which we have humbly offered, may be collected the utter impossibility of promoting the welfare of this Province as a British Colony under the present System of Government. This consideration we submit to the Honorable Committee of Council, and refer them to the Petition we had the Honor to transmit to His Majesty and both Houses of Parliament two years ago, for granting a House of Assembly to His Majesty's faithful subjects of this Province, a copy of which accompanies this Report.

(signed)

Jacob Jordan	P. Bouthillier
James McGill	Richd Dobie
P^{re} Guy	Th. Perinault
Benjⁿ Frobisher	John McKindlay
M^{le} Blondeau	James Walker
A. Auldjo	Thomas McCord

Montreal 23rd January 1787

[Adam Shortt and Arthur G. Doughty, eds., Documents Relating to the Constitutional History of Canada, 1759-1791 *Volume I, Part 2 (Ottawa: 1918), pp. 915-920]*

Memoirs of the Life of Boston King, a Black Preacher, Written by Himself, During His Residence at Kingswood School [in London, England]

It is by no means an agreeable talk to write an account of my Life, yet my gratitude to Almighty God, who considered my affliction, and looked upon me in my low estate, who delivered me from the hand of the oppressor, and established my goings, impels me to acknowledge his goodness: And the importunity of many respectable friends, whom I highly esteem, have induced me to set down, as they occurred to my memory, a few of the most striking incidents, I have met with in my pilgrimage. I am well aware of my inability for such an undertaking, having only a slight acquaintance with the language in which I write, and being obliged to snatch a few hours, now and then, from pursuits, which to me, perhaps, are more profitable. However, such as it is, I present it to the Friends of Religion and Humanity, hoping that it will be of some use to mankind.

I was born in the Province of South Carolina, 28 miles from Charles-Town.

My father was stolen away from Africa when he was young. I have reason to believe that he lived in the fear and love of God. He attended to that true Light which lighteth every man that cometh into the world. He lost no opportunity of hearing the Gospel, and never omitted praying with his family every night. He likewise read to them, and to as many as were inclined to hear. On the Lord's-Day he rose very early, and met his family: After which he worked in the field till about three in the afternoon, and then went into the woods and read till sun-set: The slaves being obliged to work on the Lord's-Day to procure such things as were not allowed by their masters. He was beloved by his master, and had the charge of the Plantation as a driver for many years. In his old age he was employed as a mill-cutter. Those who knew him, say, that they never heard him swear an oath, but on the contrary, he reproved all who spoke improper words in his hearing. To the utmost of his power he endeavoured to make his family happy, and his death was a great loss to us all. My mother was employed chiefly in attending upon those that were sick, having some knowledge of the virtue of herbs, which she learned from the Indians. She likewise had the care of making the people's clothes, and on these accounts was indulged with many privileges which the rest of the slaves were not.

When I was six years old I waited in the house upon my master. In my 9th year I was put to mind the cattle. Here I learnt from my comrades the horrible sin of Swearing and Cursing. When 12 years old, it pleased God to alarm me by a remarkable dream. At mid-day, when the cattle went under the shade of the trees, I dreamt that the world was on fire, and that I saw the supreme Judge descend on his great white Throne! I saw millions of millions of souls; some of whom ascended up to heaven; while others were rejected, and fell into the greatest confusion and despair. This dream made such an impression upon my mind that I refrained from swearing and bad company, and from that time acknowledged that there was a God; but how to serve God I knew not... My master being apprehensive that Charles-Town was in danger on account of the war [American Revolution], removed into the country, about 38 miles off. Here we built a large house for Mr. Waters, during which time the English took Charles-Town. Having obtained leave one day to see my parents, who lived about 12 miles off, and it being late before I could go, I was obliged to borrow one of Mr. Waters's horses; but a servant of my master's, took the horse from me to go a little journey, and stayed two or three days longer than he ought. This involved me in the greatest perplexity, and I expected the severest punishment, because the gentleman to whom the horse belonged was a very bad man, and knew not how to shew mercy. To escape his cruelty, I determined to go to Charles-Town, and throw myself into the hands of the English. They received me readily, and I began to feel the happiness of liberty, of which I knew nothing before, altho' I was most grieved at first, to be obliged to leave my friends, and reside among strangers...

. . .

Soon after I went to Charles-Town, and entered on board a man of war. As we were going to Chesepeak-bay, we were at the taking of a rich prize. We stayed in the bay two days, and then sailed for New-York, where I went on shore. Here I endeavoured to follow my trade, but for want of tools was obliged to relinquish it, and enter into service. But the wages were so low that I was not able to keep myself in clothes, so that I was under the necessity of leaving my master and going to another. I stayed with him four months, but he never paid me, and I was obliged to leave him also, and work about the town until I was married...

Being permitted to walk about when my work was done, I used to go to the ferry, and observed, that when it was low water the people waded across the river; tho' at the same time I saw there were guards posted at the place to prevent the escape of prisoners and slaves. As I was at prayer one Sunday evening, I thought the Lord heard me, and would mercifully deliver me. Therefore putting my confidence in him, about one o'clock in the morning I went down to the river side, and found the guards were either asleep or in the tavern. I instantly entered into the river, but when I was a little distance from the opposite shore, I heard the sentinels disputing among themselves: One said, "I am sure I saw a man cross the river." Another replied, "There is no such thing." It seems they were afraid to fire at me, or make an alarm, lest they should be punished for their negligence. When I had got a little distance from the shore, I fell down upon my knees and thanked God for this deliverance. I travelled till about five in the morning, and then concealed my self till seven o'clock at night, when I proceeded forward, thro' bushes and marshes, near the road, for fear of being discovered. When I came to the river, opposite Staten-Island, I found a boat; and altho' it was very near a whaleboat, yet I ventured into it, and cutting the ropes, got safe over. The commanding officer, when informed of my case, gave me a passport, and I proceeded to New-York.

When I arrived at New-York, my friends rejoiced to see me once more restored to liberty, and joined me in praising the Lord for his mercy and goodness. But notwithstanding this great deliverance, and the promises I had made to serve God, yet my good resolutions soon vanished away like the morning dew: The love of this world extinguished my good desires, and stole away my heart from God, so that I rested in a mere form of religion for near three years. About which time, [in 1783,] the horrors and devastation of war happily terminated, and peace was restored between America and Great Britain, which diffused universal joy among all parties, except us, who had escaped from slavery, and taken refuge in the English army; for a report, prevailed at New-York, that all the slaves, in number 2000, were to be delivered up to their masters, altho' some of them had been three or four years among the English. This dreadful rumour filled us all with inexpressible anguish and terror, especially when we saw our masters coming from Virginia, North-Carolina, and other parts, and seizing upon their slaves in the streets of New-York, or even dragging them out of their beds. Many of the slaves had very cruel masters, so that the thoughts of returning home with them embittered life to us. For some days we lost our appetite for food, and sleep departed from our eyes. The English had compassion upon us in the day of distress, and issued out a proclamation, importing, that all slaves should be free, who had taken refuge in the British lines, and claimed the sanction and privileges of the Proclamation respecting the security and protection of Negroes. In consequence of this, each of us received a certificate from a commanding officer at New-York, which dispelled all our fears and filled us with joy and gratitude. Soon after, ships were fitted out, and furnished with every necessity for conveying us to Nova Scotia. We arrived at Burchtown [Shelburne] in the month of August, where we all safely landed. Every family had a lot of land, and we exerted all our strength in order to build comfortable huts before the cold weather set in...

. . .

In the year 1785, I began to exhort both in families and prayer-meetings, and the Lord graciously afforded me his assisting presence... I laboured in Burchtown and Shelwin [four] years, and the word was blessed to the conversion of many, most of who continued stedfast in the good way to the heavenly kingdom...

About this time the country was visited with dreadful famine, which not only prevailed at Burchtown, but likewise at Chebucto, Annapolis, Digby, and other places. Many of the poor people were compelled to sell their best gowns for five pounds of flour, in order to support life. When they had parted with all their clothes, even to their blankets, several of them fell down dead in the streets, thro' hunger. Some killed and eat their dogs and cats; and poverty and distress prevailed on every side; so that to my great grief I was obliged to leave Burchtown, because I could get no employment...

The circumstances of the white inhabitants were likewise very distressing, owing to their great imprudence in building large houses, and striving to excel one another in this piece of vanity. When their money was almost expended, they began to build small fishing vessels; but alas, it was too late to repair their error. Had they been wise enough at first to turn their attention to the fishery, instead of fine houses, the place would soon have been in a flourishing condition; whereas it was reduced in a short time to a heap of ruins, and its inhabitants were compelled to flee to other parts of the continent for sustenance...

[George Elliot Clarke, Fire on the Water: An Anthology of Black Nova Scotia Writing, *Vol. 1 (Nova Scotia:Pottersfield Press, 1991), pp. 49-56]*

Petition of Coloured People at Preston,
23 February 1841

To His Excellency
Lord Viscount Falkland
Lieut. Governor of Nova Scotia

We the undersigned Inhabitants of the Township of Preston, beg leave respectfully to approach your Excellency with a statement of the hardships of our Situation, and to request your Excellency's aid to remove the disabilities under which we labour.

Petitioners are Refugees,[1] brought from the plantations of the southern States, during the American War or their decendants, being placed by Government upon ten acre lots, of poor land, many of them including swamps and likewise entirely barren & unproductive, and none of them sufficient to yield subsistence for a family however skillfull and industrious, they have dragged on a miserable existence but few, if any of them, rising above the level of hopeless poverty. But few white men in this country seldom make a living upon ten acres even of good land, and petitioners believe that any number of them similarly placed to themselves in a strange country, and beneath a rigorous climate, after being recently relieved from the associations and pressure of slavery and the heat of a southern sun, would have for many years presented the same spectacle that the coloured people of Preston have exhibited.

The Object of the Petition is twofold:

1st. To humbly pray your Excellency to allow grants to pass confirming our titles to the lands we occupy, that those of us who wish to sell and remove to better locations or follow other employments may dispose of our lands and improvements to those who remain. At present, holding [land] under Tickets of Location, we cannot sell to advantage, we are tied to the land without being able to live upon it, or even vote upon it, without being at every Election questioned, brow beaten, and sworn.

2nd. Our humble prayer is, that your Excellency will cause some larger and better lots of land to be laid off, and assigned to those of us, who are willing to remove upon such terms of settlement as will enable us to acquire a freehold by patient industry and frugality and your Petitioners as is duty bound will every pray.

[Signed by William Dair Sr., Samuel Carter, and about 105 others.]

[George Elliot Clarke, Fire on the Water: An Anthology of Black Nova Scotia Writing. Vol. 1 *(Nova Scotia: Pottersfield Press, 1991), p. 57]*

---

[1] The Black Refugees were African-Americans who fought for the British in the War of 1812 in exchange for land and liberty in British North America (now Canada). They arrived in Nova Scotia in 1815, and few received the land grants they were promised.

Petition of Richard Pierpoint, Upper Canada, Former Member of the Colored Corps, to the Colonial Government, 1821

Your Excellency's Petitioner is a Native of Bondon in Africa; that at the age of sixteen years he was made a Prisoner and sold as a slave; that he was conveyed to America about the year 1769; and sold to a British officer; that he served his Majesty during the American Revolutionary War in the Corps called Butler's Rangers; and again during the late American War in a Corps of Color raised on the Niagara Frontier.

That Your Excellency's Petitioner is now old and without property; that he finds it difficult to obtain a livelihood by his labor; that he is above all things desirous to return to his native country: he wishes it may be by affording him the means to proceed to England and from thence to a Settlement near the Gambia or Senegal Rivers, from whence he could return to Bondon.

*[Michael Power and Nancy Butler, Slavery and Freedom in Niagara
(Niagara Historical Society, 1993), p. 44]*

A Loyalist Family in Quebec, 1789

. . . The night following that which we pass'd at Captin D's, we reach'd the house of an old servant of Mrs Powell's; the children were delighted to see her and I was well pleased with an opportunity of observing a new scene of domestic life. Nancy, it seems, had married a disbanded soldier who had a small lot of land where they immediately went to live and cultivated it with so much success that in a few years they were offer'd, in exchange, a Farm twice its Size to which they were just removed, and were obliged to live sometime in a temporary log house which consisted of only one room, in which was a very neat Bed where a lovely infant of 3 months old lay crowing and laughing by itself. A large Loom on one side, on the other all the necessary utensils for a family, everything perfectly clean. Nancy went to the door and brought in two more fine children and presented them to her old mistress. We asked her if she was happy, she said, "yes, perfectly so;" she work'd hard, but it was for herself and the children. Her husband took care of the Farm and she of the family, and at their leisure hours she wove Cloth, and he made and mended shoes for their neighbors for which they were well paid, and every year they expected to do better and better...

*[Beth Light and Alison Prentice, eds., Pioneer and Gentlewomen of British
North America, 1713-1867 (Toronto: New Hogtown Press, 1980),
pp. 117-118]*

1. Do the documents in this section demonstrate the effects the Revolution had on a number of different groups? If so, in what ways? How might the authorship of these documents affect their contents and points of view?

2. What considerations were involved in the Mohawk Loyalists' negotiations with the Colonial Office for war losses' compensation?

3. What kinds of changes to the fabric of Quebec society did the Montreal merchants desire?

4. It has been argued that Loyalist women in Ontario suffered a great deal from their experiences as refugees. What do Byles' letters and Powell's observations tell us about women's experiences of the Revolution and the importance of family?

5. Compare and contrast the experiences of black Loyalists with those of other Loyalists.

J. M. Bumsted. *Land, Settlement and Politics on 18th-Century Prince Edward Island* (Montreal and Kingston: McGill-Queen's University Press, 1987)

Margaret Conrad, ed. *They Planted Well: New England Planters in Maritime Canada* (Fredericton: Acadiensis Press, 1988)

R. Cole Harris and Geoffrey J. Matthews, eds., *Historical Atlas of Canada: Volume I: From the Beginning to 1800* (Toronto: University of Toronto Press, 1987). See Plate 68 "Eastern Canada in 1800," and Plate 69 "Native Canada, ca. 1820."

R. Louis Gentilcore and Geoffrey Matthews, eds. *Historical Atlas of Canada Volume II.: The Land Transformed 1800-1891* (Toronto: University of Toronto Press, 1993). See Plate 7 , "The Coming of the Loyalists."

Isabel Thompson Kelsay. *Joseph Brant, 1743-1807: Man of Two Worlds* (Syracuse: Syracuse University Press, 1984)

Neil MacKinnon. *This Unfriendly Soil: The Loyalist Experience in Nova Scotia, 1783-1791* (Montreal and Kingston: McGill-Queen's University Press, 1986)

Janice Potter-Mackinnon *While the Women Only Wept: Loyalist Refugee Women in Eastern Ontario* (Montreal and Kingston: McGill-Queen's University Press, 1993)

Ouellet, Fernand *Lower Canada, 1790-1840: Social Change and Nationalism* (Toronto: McClelland and Stewart, 1980)

L. E. F. Upton, *Micmacs and Colonists: Indian-White Relations in the Maritimes, 1713-1867* (Vancouver: University of British Columbia Press, 1979)

James W. St. Germaine Walker. *The Black Loyalists: The Search for a Promised Land in Nova Scotia and Sierra Leone, 1783-1870* (Toronto: University of Toronto Press, rev. ed. 1993)

The War of 1812— Imperial Politics and Colonial Realities

The causes of the War of 1812 were part of a larger imperial power struggle among England, France, and the United States, and at first had little to do with many colonists' daily concerns. Nevertheless, the war directly impinged on the lives of the inhabitants of British North America, particularly those of Lower and Upper Canada where much of the armed conflict took place. The colonists' reluctance to join or remain in the militia was a continual source of concern to the imperial government and military.

The colonial government issued a number of proclamations aimed at rallying civilian support for the war but for many of the farmers who were militia members, the problems of bringing in harvests and tending to their farms often outweighed the threat of American invasion. Yet in the Western District, the Niagara peninsula, York, and Kingston in Upper Canada, and in the Lake Champlain district in Lower Canada, the presence of enemy troops was more than a fantasy of government propaganda. Fighting spread throughout the provinces, American and British troops occupied various areas, and towns and farms were burned or plundered by the Americans.

The war also saw the involvement of Natives as military allies of the British. Many historians consider the war to signal the end of the First Nations' role as allies of the imperial government as, after it, Native peoples began to move onto reserves, losing their military and political centrality to British colonial rule. Yet, First Nations were initially cautious about supporting Britain, a hesitation recognized by British military officials. When Natives joined forces with British troops, it was often for reasons such as concerns about American continental expansion and appropriation of Native lands (as in the case of the Shawnee leader Tecumseh). Their alliance with the British, though, proved to be critically important to the latter's success in a number of engagements, such as the Battle of Detroit, or at Beaverdams.

Support for the war came from elites in the Canadas and the Atlantic colonies. The Lower Canadian assembly and the Catholic Church upheld Britain's involvement by authorizing and supporting conscription to the British side and decrying American republicanism. But some colonists felt a greater affiliation with the United States, particularly in areas of Upper Canada where ties with American family members and friends were still strong, and they demonstrated this bond by moving back across the border. The war left its mark in a number of ways. Elites in all the colonies profited financially or politically, since the war enabled groups such as the 'Chateau Clique' in Lower Canada and the 'Family Compact' in Upper Canada to consolidate their hold on state power. Other Canadians also profited, either by supplying the military or by selling consumer goods at higher prices. However, those who did not make their living in trade suffered economically from the war; they petitioned the colonial government for restitution for crops damaged or requisitioned and property taken or destroyed.

In the Atlantic colonies, which had seen important naval battles fought off their shores but which had not been invaded by land, the wartime influx of sailors into Halifax, Saint John, and St. John's created a temporary widespread boom. The war also precipitated the migration into Nova Scotia and New Brunswick of two thousand blacks fleeing slavery. While blacks in Halifax were seen at first as cheap labour and as such were welcomed, after the War the colonial government resettled them on poor land in the Hammond's Plains and Preston districts outside the city.

Perhaps one of the longest-lasting effects of the war, particularly in the Canadas, was the place it came to occupy in Canadian mythology. Like the coming of the Loyalists, the War of 1812 was cited as proof of the inhabitants' loyalty to Britain. It was also seen by many prominent Anglo-Celtic, middle-class Ontarians as a critical stage in the formation of the Canadian nation, providing a cast of heroes (Sir Isaac Brock, Tecumseh, Laura Secord, and Charles-Michel de Salaberry) who gave drama and romance to the myth.

Section A
Propaganda, Patriotism, and Reality

This section examines, first, the rhetoric of the propaganda that was deployed by both colonial officials, such as Upper Canada's military governor Isaac Brock, and self-proclaimed loyal colonists. Such writings were intended to promote patriotic sentiments among colonists and warn them of the supposed consequences of a successful American invasion.

These documents are followed by descriptions of the militia in Lower Canada and New Brunswick. They have been taken from the reminiscences of Dr. William Dunlop, a British doctor and future promoter of emigration to Upper Canada, and from the journals of Lieutenant-Colonel William Gubbins, a senior British officer who served in New Brunswick from 1811 to 1813. Gubbins' duties included the inspection of the colonial militia to which all males between the ages of 16 and 60 belonged.

A Manly and Prompt Resistance: A Colonist Warns of the Threat of Invasion

One of two things must happen, they [the Americans] are either stopt in their career by a manly and prompt resistance on our part, or they are allowed to proceed in their career of conquest. If the inhabitants of this province are true to themselves, and act with any degree of spirit and unanimity, or, if they are not greatly degenerated from what their ancestors were, the wantonness and rapacity of the American democrats will meet with a chastisement they little calculate upon. If the Canadians are loyal, they will be organized and trained to arms, in their own defence and, supported by the well-known courage and discipline of the British army; they will form an unpenetrable barrier, and prove the safeguard and shield of this country...

The corrupt and venal political speculators in the United States, preach to their deluded adherents the advantages that would result from an attack upon our possessions...

We have real liberty, grounded upon the most wise and equitable laws, we have property, either transmitted to us by our ancestors, or acquired by our own industry, arising out of the happy connexion subsisting between us and parent state—We have the characteristic feelings and attachments arising out of national associations, and virtuous habits—We have a clergy noted for the morality of their lives, and the lessons of virtue their example daily inculcates. The husbandman cultivates his farm with the comfortable assurance, that what he sows will reap...

Look at what is generally called the war faction, or democratic part of the American population — the heads of that party are the avowed patrons of slavery, and dealers in human blood, a traffic which has a natural tendency to eradicate from their minds every feeling of humanity...

No man talks lightly of war who knows anything about the matter, we may therefore conclude that those who have set up the war-whoop, on the other side of the line, have yet the trade to learn. While I deprecate war, and above all others, this most unnatural war, and the disgraceful and corrupt motives which have led to it, a war waged in cooperation with a bloody Despot, who has wantonly trampled upon the liberties of Europe, and deluged every country around him with the blood of its inhabitants. And that the American people should enlist under the banners of this fell destroyer of the human race, is a deplorable and striking example of human depravity... there can be no doubt whatever but the Canadian population will cheerfully come forward, and maintain the warlike character of their ancestors. The regular force we have already in the provinces is greater, and more efficient than all the United States army, and we can raise militia as fast as they can, and, as they are to be the aggressors, we shall remain quietly at home, while they must take a long journey to come to us... [regarding possibility of defeat] If the Canadians are, from faction or cowardice so dastardly as to suffer their country to be over-run, they will have time enough for repentance...

I say nothing of the liberties that may be taken with the weaker and unprotected sex by the unlicensed Banditti that may compose this army. I present merely an out-line, and leave it to the feelings of every husband and father to fill up the picture... [but] Our provident government has placed at our head an officer of great experience, and military talents, and one who cannot fail to inspire confidence, as he has not only merited, but obtained success, in all the vicissitudes of an active military life. Our troops have a confidence grounded upon the national glory, which they have no fear of tarnishing, and are longing for an opportunity of giving the democrats a lesson.

[Anonymous letter to the editor, Quebec Mercury *(republished in the* Kingston Gazette, *28 January 1811)]*

Proclamation by Isaac Brock

The unprovoked declaration of War, by the United States of America, against the United Kingdom of Great Britain and Ireland and its dependencies, has been followed by the actual invasion of the Province in a remote frontier of the Western District by a detachment of the armed force of US. The officer commanding the detachment, has thought proper to invite His Majesty's subjects, not merely to a quick and [?] submission, but insults them with a call to seek voluntarily the protection of his Government. Without condescending to repeat the illiberal epithets bellowed in this appeal of the American commander to the people of Upper

Canada... every Inhabitant of the Province is desired to seek the confabulation of such indecent slander in the review of his most particular circumstances where in the Canadian subject who can truly affirm to himself that he has been injured by the Government in his person, his liberty or his property [?] Where is to be found in any part of the world, a growth so rapid in wealth and prosperity as the Colony exhibits. Settled not 30 years by a band of Veterans exiled from their former possessions on account of their loyalty, not a descendant of these brave people is to be found who under the fatherly liberality of their Sovereign, has not acquired a property and means of enjoyment superior to what were possessed by their ancestors. This unequalled prosperity could not have been attained by the utmost liberality of the government or the persevering industry of the people had not the massive power of the mother country, secured to its colonists a safe access to every market where the produce of their labor was in demand.

The unavoidable and immediate consequence of a separation from Great Britain must be the loss of this inestimable advantage, and what is offered you in exchange? to become a territory of the United States and share with them that exclusion from the Ocean which the policy of their present Government enforces —you are not even flattered with a participation of their vaunted independence, and it is but too obvious that once exchanged from the powerful protection of the United Kingdom you would be rendered up to the dominion of France, from which the Provinces of Canada were wrested by the arms of Great Britain, at a great expense of blood and treasure from no other motive but to relieve her ungrateful children from the oppression of a cruel neighbor: this restitution of Canada to the Empire of France was the stipulated reward for the aid afforded to the revolted Colonies, now the United States; the debt is still due, and there can be no doubt but the pledge has been renewed as a consideration for Commercial advantages, or rather for an expected relaxation in the Tyranny of France over the Commercial world. Are you prepared, Inhabitants of Upper Canada, to become willing subjects or rather slaves of the Despot who rules Europe with a rod of Iron? If not, arise in a Body, exert your energies, co-operate cordially with the King's regular forces to expel the invader, and do not give cause to your children when groaning under the oppression of a foreign ruler [?] to reproach you with having too easily parted with the richest inheritance of the Earth, a participation in the name, character and freedom of Britains.

The same spirit of justice, which will make every reasonable allowance for the unsuccessful efforts of Zeal and Loyalty, will not fail to punish the defalcation of principle; every Canadian Freeholder is by deliberate choice bound by the most solemn oaths to defend the Monarchy as well as his own property; to shrink from the Engagement is a treason not to be forgiven; let no man suppose that if in the unexpected struggle his Majesty's Arms should be compelled to yield to an overwhelming force that the Province will be eventually abandoned... the endeared relations of its first settlers, the intrinsic value of its Commerce and the pretensions of its powerful rival to repossess the Canadian, are pledges that no peace will be established between the United States and Great Britain and Ireland; of which the refutations of these Provinces does not make the most prominent conditions.

Be not dismayed at the unjustifiable threat of the commander of the enemies forces, to refuse quarter should an Indian appear in the ranks. —The brave bands of natives which inhabit this Colony were, like his Majesty's subjects punished for their zeal and fidelity by the loss of their possessions in the late colonies, and rewarded by his Majesty with lands of superior value; the faith of the British Government has never yet been violated; they feel that the soil they inherit is to them and their posterity protected... By what new principle are they to be prevented from defending their property? If their warfare, from being different from that of the white people, is more terror to the enemy, let him retract his steps—they fear him not—and cannot expect to find women and children in an invading army; but they are men, and have equal rights with all other men to defend themselves and their property when invaded, more especially when they have in the enemies camp a ferocious and mortal using the same warfare which the American Commander appears to reprobate.

This inconsistent and unjustifiable threat of refusing quarter for such a cause as being found with a brother farmer [?] in defence of invaded rights, must be exercised with the certain assurance of retaliations not only in the limited operations of war in this part of the King's Dominion, but in every quarter of the Globe, for the national character of Britain is not less distinguished for humanity than direct retributive justice, which will consider the execution of the inhuman threat as deliberate murder, for which every subject of the offending power must make expiation.

Isaac Brock
Maj. Gen and President
Head Quarters, Fort George
22nd July 1812
By order of his Honor the President
L B Glegg, Capt A.D.C.
GOD SAVE THE KING

[Kingston Gazette, 28 July 1812]

The Lower Canadian Militia, Dr. William Dunlop, Montreal, April 1813

The news had arrived that the long threatened invasion had at last taken place, and every available man was hurrying to meet it. We came up with several regiment of militia on their line of march. They had all a serviceable effective appearance—had been pretty well drilled, and their arms being direct from the tower, were in perfectly good order, nor had they the mobbish appearance that such a levy in any other country would have had. Their capots and trowsers of homespun stuff, and their blue *tuques* [night caps] were all of the same cut and color, which gave them an air of uniformity that added much to their military look, for I have always remarked that a body of men's appearance in battalion, depends much less on the fashion of their individual dress and appointments, than on the whole being in strict uniformity.

They marched merrily along to the music of their voyageur songs, and as they perceived our uniform as we came up, they set up the Indian War-whoop, followed by a shout of *Vive le Roi* along the whole line. Such a body of men in such a temper, and with so perfect a use of their arms as all of them possessed, if posted on such ground as would preclude the possibility of regular troops out-manoeuvering them (and such positions are not hard to find in Canada), must have been a rather formidable body to have attacked. Finding that the enemy were between us and our regiment [the Connaught Rangers] proceeding to join would been out of the question. The Colonel therefore requested that we might be attached to the militia on the advance. The Commander-in-Chief finding that the old gentleman had a perfect knowledge of the French language, gave him command of a large brigade of militia, and, like other men who rise to greatness, his friends and followers shared his good fortune, for a subaltern of our regiment who had come out in another ship and joined us at Montreal, was appointed as his Brigade Major; and I was exalted to the dignity of Principal Medical Officer to his command, and we proceeded to Lachine, the head-quarters of the advance, and where it had been determined to make the stand, in order to cover Montreal, the great commercial emporium of the Canadas, and which, moreover, was the avowed object of the American attack.

Our force here presented rather a motley appearance; besides a small number of the line consisting chiefly of detachments, there was a considerable body of sailors and marines; the former made tolerable Artillery men, and the latter had, I would say, even a more serviceable appearance than an equal body of the line, average it throughout the army.

[Recollections of the American War, 1812-14 (Toronto: Historical Publishing, 1905)]

Colonel Gubbins' Tour, 1813

Journal of a Tour Performed in the Summer of 1813 Along the Coast of New Brunswick Bounded by the Gulf of St. Lawrence, Together with Some Accounts of the Settlements on the Miramichi River

In consequence of war having been declared against Great Britain by the government of the United States, it was judged expedient in the summer of 1813 that the country bordered on the west by the Gulf of St. Lawrence should be visited by me during that season, in order that the militia of those parts of the province of New Brunswick might be placed on as efficient a footing as possible consistent with the small means at the disposal of the executive, and directions were given me at the same time to make a report of the state of that extensive district, generally speaking, for that part of the country was not very perfectly known.

In the tour which I accomplished in the year 1811 I adverted to everything that appeared to me mark-worthy on my route from Fredericton as far as the settlements on the Memramcook and to Mr. Botsford's at West Cock. I need not here therefore re-tread that ground.

July 13th

I continued my journey on horseback through lands and roads similar to those traversed the day before, and was escorted by some of the officers of the militia. We arrived at the Chebuctouch at 1 p.m. from whence the road was not considered practicable, and as the militia of this neighbourhood had already set out the place of general assembly with the best of their boats, I was a good deal perplexed how to get on. After some enquiry a batteau was procured which had just been completed by one of the farmers for agricultural purposes. He had never launched it, and it was the first he had built. I was therefore not much surprised to find when put into the water that it would only be kept upright by being half filled with balast. In this craft, as the wind was fair, I had a temporary mast affixed and with a quilt for a sail; we took our departure at about 2 p.m. for Richibucto, distant 28 miles...

At length, after great exertions and some hair breadth escapes, at about midnight we reached the place of rendezvous, and were hospitably received by Captain Powell and his lady, persons of much respectability and most comfortably established.

The formation of a settlement by the English at the mouth of the Richibucto took place about ten years before I visited it. The great quantities of salmon, herrings, and other fish that are to be found in the Richibucto river, and on the shoals in its vicinity, induced Messers. Pagan's and Co. of St. Johns, New Brunswick, to erect buildings necessary for undertaking an extensive fishery, which has been carried into effect on a liberal scale, and has amply answered their expectations. Their success has since attracted other speculators to the place, and the lumber trade and the consequent encouragement to agricultural pursuits give this infant colony a cheerful and promising appearance.

July 15th

The 2nd Battalion of the Northumberland militia were assembled for inspection at 9 o'clock. They were almost entirely composed of persons of French extraction, unacquainted with the English language, and possessing no apparent military qualification but the desire of being instructed. Their attention on this occasion and their usual civility and decency could not but be marked by me, but their behaviour towards their parents and friends as well as towards their superiors and even strangers is particularly conspicuous when contrasted with the ignorant self-sufficiency of the commonality of English extraction.

By a clause in the Treaty of Peace of Utrecht the forefathers of these people were declared to be exempt from bearing arms against France. They were however instigated by the emissaries of that power to commit various predatory acts against our infant settlements in Nova Scotia, but they were subdued by our forces under Lieutenant Colonel Monkton, who succeeded also in reducing Fort Beausejour (now Fort Cumberland) and the other posts that had been fortified by that enemy in New Brunswick.

Until that period, anno 1755, these people had been allowed to remain neutral, but their bad faith was then punished by the sequestration of their lands, and by the banishment of the ringleaders to our more southern provinces. So attached were these exiles to their native land, that many afterwards returned from Virginia. Those who were not expatriated, as they could not get grants of land, they retired to the remote parts of this country, then an unexplored wilderness, where they for almost an age cultivated sufficient land for their maintenance, unknowing and unknown.

At the close of the American Revolutionary War, many very large grants of land were accorded to officers of our army and to the refugees from the revolted provinces, in which were often included the improved farms which had with infinite labour been brought into cultivation from the morass or forest by the French fugitives, the forefathers of the actual occupiers of the soil. Had these poor people been acquainted with the laws of Great Britain, they would have known that the quiet possession of those farms for such a number of years constituted to persons born within our Dominion a title to property as valid as the most formal patent, but they had never heard of our laws and looked upon themselves but as vassals of oppressors and conquerers, and they resigned their possessions without an effort to the English claimants, who in most cases found it in their interest to allow them to retain such small tracts as were sufficient for their immediate support.

These French settlers are bad farmers and have so little enterprise or industry that they content themselves with the absolute necessaries of life whilst the comforts are easily within their reach. As for their loyalty to the British Government, when contending with the United States we need be under no apprehension, for there appears to exist a hatred, resembling a natural antipathy, between the bigotted French and the irreligious or fanatical Bostonians (as the Americans are called by them).

With the Roman Catholic clergy in our interest the fidelity of these people might be relied upon in any war. The Papal Bishop of Quebec had made a tour through most of the settlements the year before I visited them, and by his exhortations had inspired the people with such enthusiasm in our cause that on the last days of exercise, when a certain number of men were to be drafted from the militia for permanent service, the young Frenchmen turned out as volunteers without a ballot, and this sentiment was general amongst them from Fort Cumberland to the head of the Bay of Chaleur. It must have required all the zeal of the Bishop to have enabled so corpulent a man as himself to endure the fatigues and privations to which he must have been liable in the course of this tedious and arduous journey. His excellency crossed the portage between the Memramcook and Shediac, which I had found so bad, upon a sledge, which was dragged through the morass by oxen, and he coasted the shore of the Gulf of St. Lawrence in Indian canoes.

The winter previous to my making this tour, I wrote officially to the commanding officer of the militia on the coast of the Bay of Chaleur to enquire whether, as the province was threatened with an attack, any part of population in his district could be reckoned upon for the defence of the frontier. Two hundred of these Frenchmen, headed by their major, brought their reply to headquarters, having without the aid of government passed through a wilderness of nearly 300 miles to get to Fredericton...

Prince Edward's Island can be seen from this coast, and the Indians not infrequently venture across in their canoes. The aborigines, it has been always observed, degenerate in proportion as they come on contact with Europeans, for as population and agriculture extend, game diminishes, and the Indian, having no longer the powerful stimulus of the chase to rouse him to exertion, he becomes inert, slothful and dependent. These vices, aggravated by the propensity of the race to the immoderate use of spirituous liquors, tend to reduce them to a state in many cases disgraceful to human nature.

The Michilimackinac [Mi'kmaq] tribe that I found in the vicinity of Richibucto maintain themselves principally by fishing and are in a much superior condition to any that I had before met with. Their Chief is a man of good talents and possesses unusual influence. When the weather prevented the men from going to sea, they were in the habit of cutting lumber for the merchants, by which means some of them had realized property, and they cultivated Indian corn and potatoes with success. It is mentioned as a remarkable instance of the superior state of this tribe, that a law suit having been gained against one of them, wherein he had been cast with costs and damages, he had paid them. The Indians of our colonies are Roman Catholics, very superstitious and often devout, and they are visited frequently by clergymen of that persuasion to whom districts are assigned by the Bishop of Quebec. By a contrivance of these missionaries a kind of hieroglyphic writing has been composed in which such few Indians as express a desire for education are enabled to read certain prayers and to make memorandums for their own satisfaction, and at the same time continue in ignorance of the contents of the Bible. The Chief of Richibucto shewed me a book of his own writing in this description of character, and he appeared proud of the mystery in which his notes were enveloped.

The wigwams, arms, canoes and dress of these people were of much better manufacture than [was] usual with the other tribes I had before seen, and it was a pleasing sight to observe their little fleet of canoes, sailing to the beach, heavily laden with salmon, cod, lobsters, oysters, etc.

The idea had been suggested of arming a body of these people to be employed as light troops, but it was abandoned, and I think wisely, for such a measure would have certainly been followed by a retaliatory one on the part of the enemy, and the lives and property of the inhabitants of both frontiers would have been placed at the mercy of savages without promoting the general object of the war. As guides they can at all times make themselves of important use. They ascertain their course through the woods in fine weather by the sun and when that is not visible the top branches of the hemlock tree, which always point to the south, is in this part of America their only resource. The Indians have often told me that, where this tree does not abound, they are as liable to lose themselves as we should be without a compass.

July the 23rd, 24th and 25th

On each of these days I exercised the militia, and had the satisfaction to observe that they improved by my instructions, and they showed great zeal and loyalty. One company of Scotchmen were completed in military appointments by their Captain Mr. McKenzie. The officers of this corps were generally of a superior order to those of the rest of the province, being mostly young merchants from England or Nova Scotia. This battalion, consisting of about 600 men, constituted the mass of British subjects by whose labour the timber shipped from this river was supplied but, their numbers being entirely inadequate to the increased demand for lumber of late years, a great many Americans had, notwithstanding the war, been allowed to come into the country and engage in the profitable business of cutting timber. This of course tended to keep down the price of the article and gave our settlers great umbrage, but the evil was unavoidable at that time when the northern ports of Europe were shut against us. There is no part of our dominions to which emigrants would be a greater acquisition than the quarter of North America of which I am now speaking.

July 26th

I took leave of my kind host and proceeded to Beauberes Island where there is a large mercantile establishment. Here is also the remains of a stone chapel built by the French in former days. On the part of our government no attention whatsoever has been paid to the religious or other instruction of the inhabitants, there being no Protestant clergyman resident either on this river or on any part of the coast from the Restigouche river to Nova Scotia, a tract of more than three hundred miles. The New Lights and other fanatics however are very active, and their efforts will in future probably entirely prevent the introduction of our national religion into these parts. In the medical line the inhabitants are if possible still worse off than in the ecclesiastical, for fellows the most unprincipled, as well as ignorant, practice the science with the greatest assurance, and thus commit murders with impunity. One of them to my knowledge prescribes Cayenne pepper in large boluses as a specific for the cure of pulmonic complaints, and another in a surgical case mistaking the fractured bone of the knee joint for proud flesh tried to burn it off with lunar caustic, a piece of which the Assistant-Surgeon of the 102nd Regiment found inserted in the wound.

July 30th

I proceeded homewards by a pleasant road leading through a number of thriving farms and by two o'clock in the afternoon I reached my home at Springhill, four miles from Fredericton, from which I had been absent six weeks.

A State of the Arms in Possession of Militia of New Brunswick 1811 Inspection

| | Pikes | English Arms | | | Dutch Arms | | | Ramrods | Bayonets | Scabbards | Pouches & Bells | Total Good English & Dutch Arms in Possession |
		Good	Repairable	Bad	Good	Repairable	Bad					
1st York County		10	10	10	111	60	4	191	191	191	191	121
2nd York County		36	"	11	48	"	2	95	92	85	61	84
Sunbury County		41	"	"	182	"	"	223	223	223	223	223
Queens County		30	"	95	"	"	"	74	30	26	20	30
1st Kings County		76	"	5	102	27	"	205	205	205	205	178
2nd Kings County		20	"	14	206	19	"	245	245	245	245	226
1st Northumberland County	"	"	"	"	"	"	"	"	"	"	"	"
2nd Northumberland County	"	"	"	"	"	"	"	"	"	"	"	"
3rd Northumberland County	"	"	"	"	"	"	"	"	"	"	"	"
Saint John County	15	267	37	7	46	3	28	353	353	322	330	313
1st Westmorland County	"	"	"	"	"	"	"	"	"	"	"	"
2nd Westmorland County	"	17	"	18	144	12	27	173	173	173	173	161
1st Charlotte County	"	80	11	10	229	4	18	324	324	324	324	309
2nd Charlotte County	"	10	"	8	18	2	6	28	28	28	28	28
Total	15	507	58	178	1086	125	85	1911	1864	1822	1800	1673

NB The Return from Northumberland does not state the Quality or Condition of the Arms in possession the Number Stated is 122.

The State of the Arms of the 1st Battn of Westmorland Could not be ascertained. Several of the Companies residing more than 200 miles from the parade, the others not having timely Warning did not in General attend the Battn. Received in 1795. Thirty Six Stand of English Arms & in 1808 One hundred & Eighty Six Stand of Dutch Arms all with appointments leaving a Total to be accounted for 222.

Colonel Wetmore of the Saint John Militia States that their [sic] are two Field pieces Brass Six pounders with Side Arms & Appointments Complete attached to the Battn Under his Command

J. Gubbins
Lt. Col. I.F.O.

[Howard R. Temperley, ed., Lieutenant Colonel Joseph Gubbins' New Brunswick Journals of 1811 and 1813 (Heritage Publishing, King's Landing Foundation, 1980), pp. 63, 72-77, 85-89]

Section B
Waging War

During the war the military leadership was well aware that they needed to maintain the loyalty of their First Nations allies and accordingly they assured them publicly of the Crown's support for Native peoples. Newspaper editors also attempted to ensure that non-Native colonists supported the war; in the case of Lower Canada, the account of the battle of Châteauguay was intended to reassure the civilian population that the militia had won a tremendous victory. However, as the reports from Lower and Upper Canada suggest, both the militia and the regular troops encountered their share of problems.

General Orders Affecting the Awarding of Presents to Indian Warriors, 7 August 1813

It being desireable that every proper means should be resorted to, to uphold and promote the power and influence of the principal leaders of the Indian Warriors, His Excellency the Commander of the Forces directs that those Officers of the Indian Department who do not accompany the Indian Warriors into the Field of Battle, but whose Duties have been confined to the care and distribution of Presents, shall no longer exercise their discretion in alloting Articles or Presents to the Indian Warriors but be guided in their Distribution by such tokens or Certificates of fidelity and bravery as are produced by them from the Officers or Chiefs of Renown who witnessed their gallant conduct before the Enemy—And should a General Officer in Command of a Division to which Indian Warriors are attached deem it advantageous to His Majesty's Service to place a proportion of the presents in the Indian Store at the disposal of an Officer or Chief of Renown, enjoying his confidence and possessed of influence over the Warriors, to enable him to reward his Warriors according to their respective merit, he is herby authorized to do so and the Officer of the Indian Department is to comply with his Requisition...

General John Vincent's[1] Speech to the Six Nations, 22 October 1813

Brothers—I have requested Colonel Claus to call the Chiefs and Warriors of the six Nations together, to inform them, that if my Government had decided to withdraw the Troops from this part of the Country, they should have had timely notice of that intention—From existing circumstances, I had some reason to suppose, that an attack might have been meditated by the Enemy upon both my flanks, and to defeat such an attempt, I judged it expedient to change my Situation from the four Mile Creek to Burlington where my force is more concentrated and I indulged a hope, that being in the neighbourhood of the Six Nations, I might have relied on their prompt assistance until joined by the Western Indians—

Brothers I will not conceal from you my surprise and disappointment, in having failed when making an appeal to your friendship—Having requested Colonel Claus to send a party consisting of only thirty or forty of the Six Nations to join the Troops under Colonel Harvey[2] at Stoney Creek, I had much reason to feel mortified on being informed that the Chiefs could not persuade that number to go out until their families were placed in a situation of security—

Brothers—it was painful to me to find this refusal persisted in, and I felt the more hurt from thinking the Six Nations did me the injustice to believe that I was capable of neglecting the security of their families, when on the contrary, I was endeavouring to promote it by every means in my power—

Brothers I have always spoken to you with frankness and truth, and I think it friendly to inform you in time, that if some exertion is not used by you to cooperate with the Kings Troops, I must be under the necessity of retiring to a stronger

---

[1]   John Vincent (1765-1848) was the British commandant at Fort George when it was evacuated under enemy attack in the spring of 1813. Troops under his general command were successful a short time later in turning back the pursuing Americans at Stoney Creek.

[2]   John Harvey (1778-1852), Deputy Adjutant-General of the Forces in Canada during the War of 1812, served brilliantly during the hostilities. He was Lieutenant Governor of Nova Scotia from 1846 to 1852.

Position—But on the Contrary if you are determined to come forward and hold me fast by the hand and unite your aid with that of the Western Indians I am confident that no American Army will venture to insult you or your families—

Brothers I will finish my speech by repeating my words to Colonel Claus and declare openly to you, that it is my decided determination to be governed in my future conduct and liberality towards the Six Nations and their families, by the support that is afforded me by the Chiefs and Warriors in carrying on the Kings Service.

[Charles M. Johnston, ed., The Valley of the Six Nations *(Champlain Society, 1964) pp. 206-207; P.A.C., Indian Affairs, Records and Correspondence of the Deputy Superintendent General, XXVIII, pp. 212-14]*

Creating Military Myths? The Battle of Châteauguay

The affair near the lines, at the River Châteauguay, is the first in which any considerable number of the natives of this Province have been engaged with the Americans since the war. In this case, the whole of our force, with a very few exceptions, from the commander downwards, were Canadians. The General Orders issued on this subject, shew that the result has been such as was expected from the former character of the people, and the zeal which they have repeatedly showen for the defence of their country. We are informed, upon authority which we deem unexceptionable, that the enemy lost about 100 men killed in this affair while we lost only five. This, together with the repulse of enemy, is incontestable proof of good officers and good soldiers. A few experiments of this kind, will probably convince the Americans that their project of conquering this Province is premature.

[Quebec Gazette, 4 November 1813]

Paying the Officers, Lower Canada, 1813
Charles-Michel de Salaberry to Freer, Montreal, 27 December 1813 on Recruitment Problems

The great expense to which officers of the Voltigeurs [militia] are exposed when employed on the recruting [sic] service (if not for recruting Commissions) by reason of [there] being no distrubution [sic] of the enlisting money allowed to the recruit a proportion of which should cover the recruting officers expense when a recruit deserts previous to his having been passed at the Head Quarters of the Regiment. So much loss has been sustained for want of due provision on this head that officers are averse to being sent on that Service.

Paying the Men [1]

The condition of penury in which I left you at my departure, always present in my mind, made me heap a thousand curses on the day when I enlisted in the Voltigeurs, and tormented me to the point of making me ill. Arriving in Kingston, I hastened to set the affairs of my Company in order and pay whatever I owed it, to have you draw the balance of this money remaining to me and thus give myself a little peace of mind. But alas, the necessary costs of a long journey, the continual demands and needs of my Company, made me more and more fearful with each day of being unfit to set a single penny aside for you... Seeing the difficulty our Captains were in to provide their Companies with the articles they lacked and that the reason arose from our want of money, our good Major made application to Govr Sheaffe, and he had us each advanced £25 reckoning from the next pay.

The Treatment of Voltigeurs in Upper Canada [2]

You know that a subscription has been taken to relieve the wives of those who lost their lives for the country's defence in Upper Canada, and that the greater part of the amount subscribed come from the in habitants of Lower Canada. Well, we had two men killed at Sackett's Harbour who left two widows and some children. Our Major has made application gain to the committee appointed to take care of this business, and the reply he received is that the Voltigeurs were not included in the public's generosity and are thus unworthy to share in the same benefits as the other corps. What a ghastly policy! What shame for the citizens of Upper Canada...

["Canadian Heritage," PAC, MG24, B3, Vol. 1, 1613 file, p. 208, F.–C.
Truteau to L.–J. Papineau, Cross Roads, Four Mile Creek, 2 Sept. 1813.
Taken from Michelle Guitard, The Militia of the Battle of the Châteauguay:
A Social History (Ottawa. Environment Canada/Parks Canada, 1983),
p. 67, endnote 66]

A Female of Improper Character

Several instances of irregularity and misconduct of the light company of the 89th Regiment having come to the knowledge of the Commander of the Forces, he attributes it to a want of zeal and due attention on the part of the captain, who has,

[1] Captain Jacques Viger, May 1813, responding to de Salaberry's demand that officers pay their company and be reimbursed when their men were paid. Viger was already owed over £50 by the army.
[2] Toussaint Casimir Truteau, complaining about treatment given Voltigeurs who were fighting in Upper Canada.

in breach of the General Orders of the Army and in violation of all regard to decency and decorum, incumbered the brigade of boats by bringing up under his protection a female of improper character. His Excellency cannot consider Captain Basden a fit officer to be entrusted with the charge of a select company in the advanced light corps, and therefore directs that Lieut.-Colonel Morrison will immediately appoint a captain to proceed to York to relieve that officer in the command of the light company of the 89th Regiment.

> *[E. Cruikshank,* A Documentary History of the Campaign on the Niagara Frontier in 1814. *'General Order, E. Baynes, Adjutant-General, Kingston, 14 July 1813' (Lundy's Lane Historical Society, n.p.d.), pp. 235-236]*

Section C
The Effects of War

This last section of documents examines the effects of war on both military participants and various civilians in New Brunswick and Upper Canada. The Winslow family letters were written by members of an elite New Brunswick family, whose sons and brothers were in the military. The excerpts from the Winslow correspondence are followed by extracts from the Report of the Loyal and Patriotic Society of Upper Canada, an organization formed by prominent members of York society and designed to promote loyalty to the British cause. Offering assistance to the needy families of militia members and those civilians who had suffered because of their loyalty was an important part of the Society's work.

This Hateful American War
Judge Edward Winslow to Edward Winslow, Jr.

Kingsclear, 13th June, 1811.

My very dear Son,—I indulge the hope that this letter will find you in England, well and happy. This anticipation keeps me cheerful under many perplexities. Our separation is indispensibly necessary and my anxieties are natural, and cannot be alleviated by any other means than by confirmation under your own hand. In you my son, my principal hopes are centred—any accident happening to you would render the remaining days of my life—insupportable. What I have suffered on account of your two elder brothers is known only to the Searcher of Hearts & myself. Wentworth is now a Lieutenant in His Majesty's 41st reg't of foot—(one of the best regiments in the King's service). He is under good patronage and station'd at Montreal, where I presume he will be contented and comfortable. He is a good officer, of very prepossessing address, and with a large allowance of humour and vivacity—uncommonly well made and handsome. The garrison of Newfoundland is confined and affords no other amusement but drinking & gambling. He will now have more inviting pursuits, and I flatter myself that in real service he will be distinguished. My [American] countrymen, I believe, mean to put us all to the test very soon in these colonies. I say soon, because I conceive it impossible that the British Government can longer endure the insolent equivocation & provoking threats of these Americans, who are but just peeping from their shell and scarcely deserve the name of a nation...

If they have any expectation that their political parent Great Britain will persevere in treating them as 'froward children,' with tenderness & affection on the present occasion—I trust they will find their mistake. This delicate sentiment has too long deluded our Government. Mama must be a ridiculous old fool indeed if she suffers these dear little ones to spit in her face, & knock her down. I think it will be more likely that such base ingratitude will excite her indignation and induce her to bestow upon 'em the chastisement which they so richly deserve...

I know not in what manner a war would affect us. An invasion of this province would be a bad speculation—they certainly would get a few hard knocks, and I cannot exactly discern what else they'd be likely to acquire. The old Acadians, as well as the Canadians, are undoubtedly disaffected, but they are contemptible and unenterprising, and, moreover, I do not discover any advantage that could result to America from the possession of any of these Colonies.

Our province (to use an American expression) is 'progressing,' but I fear unless more conciliatory measures are adopted [by Great Britain], and the original compact and constitution be more gravely & carefully attended to, there will be a great abatement of that zeal & alacrity which has always distinguished the inhabitants of N.B.

Our metropolis is wonderfully increased and is really a very beautiful town, our shoe makers are all turned merchants and appear to have made their fortunes. Slason, Sewell & E. Sloot have erected fine houses & are importers of goods. Mark Needham has bought Wm. Hazen's house for £700, & Grosvenor, the Messman, has built a complete house & is a very good man. A genteel house is also built by James Berton & all the street round about Capt. Sproule's is filled up. From Blair's corner the street is continued to the wind-mill, and the lots will soon be built upon...

Ed. Winslow.

Penelope Winslow to Edward Winslow, Jr.

20th November, 1812.

Do not my dearest Edward attribute my long silence to any falling off of my affection; this indeed is not the case. I'll do you the justice to say that as yet we have had no reason to complain of you. We had two epistles from you while at Madeira.

This hateful American war has frightened us not a little—this province has not as yet suffered by it, but there is terrible work in Upper Canada. Poor Wentworth is in the midst of it. He is with General Sheaffe at present.

I know of no great changes in our domestic concerns since I wrote you last, except the marriage of your cousin Lucy to an Assistant Surgeon of this regiment (Doctor Woodforde) which took place last week. He is a very fine young man only three and twenty years old. You will recollect that there must be some disparity in their years, which was the only objection to the match. It was a very sudden affair and has excited a few illnatured remarks. The number of spinsters in our circle is reduced pretty low and Fredericton is more stupid than ever... I have been a great invalid this year and was sent to St. John this summer for the benefit of my health and I assure you the jaunt had a very salutary effect. You have of course long ere this received our letters of acknowledgement and thanks for the things you sent us in the Spring. Indeed my dear brother I'm afraid your good will has induced you to be more bountiful than you could well afford. Your donation of muslin was most acceptable, and has made us fine, for some time at least. Every article you procured for us was exactly what we wished and wanted, but you did not pay my figure a proper compliment in the size of the gown and pelise. They were about an inch too large in the waist, and more than two inches too short in the skirt. I am much reduced in bulk since you saw me. The Judge has been afflicted with frequent attacks of the gout and violent pains in his head of late. The gout is not so violent as it used to be but returns much oftener.

Your friend Jenkins [the hero of the Battle of Ogdensburg, February 22, 1813] is a Captain in the Glengarry regiment, and fighting in Canada. We have lost our neighbors Garden and Lee—they both died this summer. Charles Lee is employed in the Commissariat and is certainly going to marry Sally Odell.

&c., &c.,
Penelope.

Penelope Winslow to Edward Winslow, Jr.

7th April, 1813.

It's almost an age, my dearest brother, since I wrote you last and much longer since we have heard from you...

Hannah has written you several times lately, but my father is so incessantly tormented with a head ache and dizziness, that it's almost torture for him to touch a pen. He has had less of the gout this winter than usual, but he has had a great deal to distress him, and has been much out of spirits for a long time. Murray has again left us. We did all we could for him. The Judge gave him much more money that he could afford, and about a week since he commenced a journey to Canada in hopes of obtaining some employment on the Lakes. God only knows what will become of him.

The 104th have at last left Fredericton for the field of action, and ere this are in Canada. Poor Jenkins has been fighting most gallantly. He is Captain of Grenadiers in the Glengarry regiment, and by his exertions an important Fort has been taken. He has received universal and unbounded applause, but you will think my dear Edward that he has paid very dearly for it when I tell you that he has lost one arm and the other is most severely wounded. After receiving these horrid wounds, he continued to encourage his men until he fainted from loss of blood.

I hate to make such a dismal letter of this, but must tell you my dear brother the present unhappy situation of poor Miller's family. Within one short week Anne and Leah were taken from them by a fever which a few days since attacked dear little George and the Doctors have pronounced that he cannot survive more than a day longer. When you recollect that out of six such sweet children as Mary [Mrs. Miller, Penelope's sister] had, only Winslow remains, you will wonder how the unfortunate mother can support existence; indeed she is almost stupified with grief...

You have heard I presume that your cousin Lucy is married to a young surgeon of the 104th (Woodforde). He has gone with the others to Canada and she is to follow him in the Spring. He is a fine promising young man. Bradshaw Rainsford has again turned a soldier and is recruiting for General Coffin's regiment. Allen has a company in it. I rather think it will be some time before they compleat it, as the 104th drained the Country pretty well...

Your ever affect'e Sister,
Penelope.

George Heriot to Judge Edward Winslow

Quebec, 23d. June, 1813.

Dear Sir,—Since the capture of Niagara by the Yankees they have received a complete drubbing from General Vincent, against whom they had advanced with 3,500 men to attack his position at the head of Lake Ontario. He anticipated their design and promptly advancing on them in the night defeated them and put them to the route. They fled for several miles; as far as 'forty mile creek,' so called from its being that distance from the town of Niagara where they re-established their camp; but Sir James Yeo having crossed the Lake with his squadron from York, dislodged them by the shot from his guns and captured several of their Boats. A report had spread itself among the enemy, that General Proctor had arrived from Amherstburg with a reinforcement accompanied by the Great Warrior Tecumseth. This circumstance created a panic which pervaded the whole of Lewis's army and they scampered off with astonishing rapidity. They abandoned Fort Erie and Chipawa and were said to be crossing from Fort George to their own territory as fast as they could embark. Of the affair at Sacket's Harbor the less that it said the better.

Generals Vincent and Proctor have unquestionably shared the whole of the laurels of Upper Canada between them ever since the death of the brave and gallant Sir Isaac Brock...

I enclose the General Orders &c, respecting the affair of General Vincent, and remain, Dear Sir,

Your most obedient humble servant,
Geo. Heriot.

E.G. Lutwyche to Judge Edward Winslow

July 30, 1813.

My dear Winslow,—Altho' I have written you so recently I could not let my young friend Chip depart empty handed, and hope this will find you in renovated health and spirits... Chipman will tell you everything about Phillimore place, and therefore I shall proceed to give you the news; but first I must advert to what is passing and most interesting to you.

Gen'l Prescott's dispatches are cheering, and from the Generalship and bravery of the British American Army, we entertain sanguine expectations that the Americans will be compleatly foiled in all their attempts on Canada, which is their primary object. They appear to be totally deficient in military skill or in courage, as all their defeats have been marked with disgrace...

[W.O. Raymond, ed., The Winslow Papers (New Brunswick Historical Society, 1901), pp. 669-670, 676-679]

Report of the Loyal and Patriotic Society of Upper Canada

The Honble. Mr. Justice Campbell
The Revd Doctor J. Strachan
Alexander Wood, Esqr. Secretary

Resolved Upon the application of John Puller, private in Captain Ridout's Company, of the York militia, representing the distress of his family, consisting of a wife and three children, 8, 5 and 1 year old, who all depend upon his labour for support, having no land. The Committee finding that he has been four months in garrison, direct that the sum of two pounds be paid for immediate relief, and two dollars per week, whilst he continued on duty, and no rations allowed to his family.

Resolved That in consequence of the death of Hannah Smith, since the allowance of ten shillings per week was ordered, for the support of her family, that the same sum be given weekly to the person who has the charge of her children.

Ordered that four pounds, an account of Stationary, for printing, be paid by the Treasurer.

Signed, Thomas Scott,
Chairman.

Alexander Wood
Secretary.
York

In the different conflic's during the severe weather in October, November, December, and January, the services of the militia have been duly appreciated by the Generals and Officers commanding, who saw them with exultation, resisting the several invasions of the Province with veteran intrepidity, nor do they hesitate to acknowledge, that by their gallant assistance, united with the small body of regular forces at their disposal, they have been enabled to take or destroy every enemy who has had the temerity to pass the borders.

But such meritorious efforts were not made without the most precious sacrifices, for while the militia, during six months, were thus bravely repelling an invading foe, many of their families were left in the greatest distress; called to arms, their agricultural pursuits were suspended, they were unable to reap their harvests, and consequently their farms produced little or nothing to comfort them through the inclemency of a long winter.

To consider the means of relieving their more pressing distress, and of preventing as far as possibly their recurrence in future, a general meeting of the inhabitants of the town of York, was convened.

When the following resolutions were unanimously agreed upon...

The Subscription of the Town of York amounted in a few days to eight hundred and seventy five pounds, five shillings, provincial currency, dollars at five shillings each, to be paid annually during the war; and that of Kingston to upwards of four hundred pounds. The Society have also received many liberal donations from persons not wishing to become members.

The Society knowing the warm interest which Lieutenant Governor Gore takes in the welfare of the Province, resolved to apply through him to the British public for assistance, and to furnish His Excellency with the views of the Institution; the following appeal was adopted and transmitted.

An Appeal to the British Public

The defenceless situation of the Province of Upper Canada, on the sudden and totally unexpected declaration of war against Great Britain, by the United States of America, instead of dispiriting its brave inhabitants, animated them with the most determined courage. Consisting chiefly of Loyalists driven from their native homes, during the American rebellion, they beheld with indignation their old enemy envying them, their new habitations won from the wilderness, and again thirsting for their blood. Proud of their country, their loyalty burst forth in all its ancient splendor; they volunteered their services with acclamation, hastened to join the very small number of his Majesty's troops, at the several points of attack, and exhibited a degree of valour and fortitude, worthy of the British name. All rejoiced in the opportunity thus given them, of shewing their ardour in defence of the Province, and their determination to cling to that gallant and illustrious nation which combats for the rights and liberties of the world, and of which they have the happiness to form a part.

Theirs was not the enthusiasm of the moment. It still burns with unabated vigor, and not only enables a raw militia to suffer with patience the greatest privations, or face death with astonishing intrepidity, but also to emulate veteran soldiers in deeds of honor and glory. Many, though exempted by age from military duty, scorn to claim the privilege, and it is not uncommon to see men of seventy leaving their homes, and demanding arms to meet the enemy on the lines. Others too feeble to bear arms themselves, are seen leading their sons to the military posts, and so strong is the spirit of patriotism among the people, that it infects the greater number of those who have recently come to settle for the Province, from the United States, and makes them efficient soldiers. Indeed this noble spirit which animates all our inhabitants, is most affecting, and can only be inspired by the justice of our cause.

This however being far short of the sums necessary for the purposes of the Institution, the Directors are induced to appeal to the known humanity and benevolence of a British Public, for such further assistance as they many be pleased to afford them on this important occasion.

Subscriptions will be received by _____, and William Halton, Esqr.., Private Secretary to the Lieutenant Governor, No. 4, Beaumont Street, Portland Place, to whom, or to his Assigns, the said _____ Bankers are hereby authorized to pay over all subscriptions to be remitted to the Receiver General of Upper Canada.

Signed Thomas Scott
President

At a meeting of the Committee of Directors of the *Loyal and Patriotic Society,* holden at the house of the Secretary, on the 17th day of May, 1813.

Present
The Honble. Mr. Justice Campbell, Chairman
Committee
The Revd. Dr. Strachan
Wm. Chewett, Esqr.
Wm. Allan, Esqr.

D. Cameron, Esqr.
Doctor Baldwin
John Small, Esqr.
D'Arcy Boulton, Esqr.
Peter Robinson, Esqr.
Thos. Ridout, Esqr.
Alexander Wood, Esqr. Sec'y.

Resolved   That the sum of twenty five pounds, Halifax, be given as a donation to Mrs. Dettor, whose husband was unfortunately killed in action on the 27th April, one half to be paid immediately, and the other half on the 1st of July next.

Resolved. That the sum of twenty five pounds, Halifax, be given as a donation to Mrs. Murray, whose husband was unfortunately killed in action on the 27th April, one half to be paid immediately, and the other half on the 1st of July next.

Resolved   That the sum of twenty five pounds, Halifax, be paid into the hands of Duncan Cameron, Esq. to be laid out by him on the natural children of the late Donald McLean, Esqr. who fell bravely on the 27th April, this sum being thought sufficient for their existence, till their relations are advertised of their situation.

The above liberal sums have been ordered by the Society, on account of the great necessity of the above cares from the largeness of the families left unprotected.

Resolved   That sixty-five dollars be given to Mary Grass, widow of George Grass, a private in the 1st regiment of Lincoln Militia, who was wounded on the 27th May last, in opposing the enemy when they landed near Fort George, and died on the 29th following, of his wounds; he left a wife and two children, and one born since his death, on the 14th October last, left no estate to support his family, he having rented lands of others; his family are in great distress.

Resolved   That Polly Spareback, widow, of the Township of Niagara, who lived at the 4 mile creek, on the cross roads, and whose crop of grain was last summer destroyed by the troops and Indians, being encamped on her farm, reducing her, and her two children to want, as stated by the report, 'this person does not appear to be in a situation to require the aid of this Society, being under the protection of her family, who appear to the Society to be able to support her.'

The foregoing list of applicants, with their situation and circumstances, is certified and signed by Ts. Ball, J.P. dated Niagara, 3rd February, 1814.

Signed,
Thomas Scott,
President

Alexander Wood,
Secretary

Resolved   That fifty dollars be paid to Mrs. Powers, wife of Lieutenant Powers, a prisoner with the enemy. Mrs. Powers was plundered while she continued in Niagara, and is at present without comfortable means of subsistence.

Resolved   That twenty five dollars each be paid to Saml. Cox, Hugh Freel, and James Freel, who lost all their grain, and have to purchase every necessary of life.

Resolved   That one hundred dollars each be paid to Mrs. Clench, and Mrs. Stewart, the former having a large family, and her husband a prisoner with the enemy, the latter widow of Alexander Stewart, late a Barrister at Law. Mrs. Stewart's house was burnt by the enemy.

Resolved   That one hundred dollars be paid to Mrs. Jones, widow of Captain Jones, who died a prisoner in the hands of the enemy; her house was burnt by the enemy, and she is left destitute with one sickly child.

Resolved   That twenty dollars be paid to widow Howell, whose house was burnt by the enemy, and she is poor and destitute.

Resolved   That one hundred dollars be paid to Mrs. Buttler, widow of Thomas Buttler; her house was burnt by the enemy, and most of her furniture. She is left with a large family, without support.

1815

Month	Day	Names	District No.	
April	24	To Mrs. Isa Hill	Niagara 55	£50.0.0.

This lady had an excellent property in the town of Niagara, or Newark, consisting of two houses, one of which she inhabited. Being a widow with her daughter, and was induced to remain after the retreat of General Vincent on 27th May. For some time, she was treated with some consideration by the American officers. Being a lady of cultivated understanding and agreeable manners, having seen much of the world; but at length matters changed, and she found it necessary to depart and leave almost all her property behind, especially as General Boyd assured her positively that they had orders to burn the town, in case of being forced to retreat (which was most cruelly accordingly done in December) she resided some time in the neighbourhood of York, and having determined to proceed to Jamaica; when the Society ordered to assist in carrying her there.

[Report of the Loyal and Patriotic Society of Upper Canada, Montreal: Wm. Gray, 1817]

QUESTIONS

1. What do these documents tell us about the colonial authorities' concerns, both before and during the war? Contrast both Upper Canadian and American government responses.

2. How did Upper Canadian civilians respond to the threat and to the realities of war?

3. What do these documents suggest about the role of Native peoples in the War of 1812?

4. The Loyal and Patriotic Society, founded in York during the war by members of the colony's elite, took it upon itself to reward loyal service. What kinds of concerns do these records of its activities indicate?

5. What do these documents tell us about gender ideals and gender roles in colonial society?

READINGS

Jane Errington, *The Lion, the Eagle, and Upper Canada: a Developing Colonial Ideology* (Montreal and Kingston: McGill-Queen's University Press, 1987). See chapter 4, "The Steady Decline to War."

R. Louis Gentilcore and Geoffrey Matthews, eds. *Historical Atlas of Canada Volume I: The Land Transformed 1800-1891* (Toronto: University of Toronto Press, 1993) Plate 22, "Invasion Repulsed, 1812-1814."

Michelle Guitard, *The Militia of the Battle of the Châteauguay: A Social History* (National Historic Parks and Sites Branch, Parks Canada, 1983)

W.S. McNutt, *New Brunswick. A History: 1784-1867* (Toronto: Macmillan, 1963). See chapter 7, "The Prosperity of War, 1808-1815."

Cecilia Morgan, "'Of Slender Frame and Delicate Appearance: The Placing of Laura Secord in the Narratives of Canadian Loyalist History," in *Journal of the Canadian Historical Association* 5 (1994): 195-212

——————————, *Public Men and Virtuous Women: The Gendered Languages of Religion and Politics in Upper Canada, 1791-1850* (Toronto: University of Toronto Press, 1996). See chapter 1,"That Manly and Cheerful Spirit": Patriotism, Loyalty, and Gender."

George Sheppard, *Plunder, Profit, and Paroles: A Social History of the War of 1812 in Upper Canada* (Montreal and Kingston: McGill-Queen's University Press, 1994)

G.F. Stanley, "The Indians in the War of 1812," in J.R. Miller, ed., *Sweet Promises: A Reader on Indian-White Relations in Canada* (Toronto: University of Toronto Press, 1991), pp. 105-124

David A. Sutherland, "1810-1820s: War and Peace," in Phillip A. Buckner and John G. Reid, eds., *The Atlantic Region to Confederation: A History* (Toronto: University of Toronto Press, 1994)

Victor J. H. Suthren, *The Battle of Châteauguay* (National Historic Sites Service, National and Historic Parks Branch, Dept of Indian Affairs and Northern Development, Ottawa 1974)

Wesley Turner, *The War of 1812: The War That Both Sides Won* (Toronto: Dundurn, 1990)

Morris Zaslow, ed., *The Defended Border: Upper Canada and the War of 1812* (Toronto: Macmillan, 1964)

Resource Economies and Mercantilism

Most of the economies of the British North American colonies were structured around certain primary resources such as fish, fur, lumber, and wheat, much of which was produced for export to international markets. Some of these products had a longer history than others; the fur trade, for example, had been ongoing for at least 200 years, and the fisheries and fishing interests had dominated Newfoundland's economic and political structures since the seventeenth century. But from 1790 to 1815, the fisheries expanded, employing more workers and requiring new ships. Lumber and grain took on an even larger economic role in the colonies, aided by such British legislation as the Corn Laws and timber regulations that gave preferential treatment to colonial grain and lumber. New Brunswick's economy in particular was heavily dependent on timber; by 1827, it comprised two-thirds of the colony's exports. Both in Lower Canada's St. Lawrence Valley and in southern Upper Canada, wheat dominated crop production, although by the 1820s Lower Canadian wheat farmers experienced what some historians have dubbed an 'agricultural crisis.' By the 1840s, Upper Canadian wheat production began to decline as land became scarce.

International markets and imperial attitudes toward the colonies affected economic conditions. By the 1840s, British support for free trade and that country's desire that the colonies should become more financially independent led to the end of the Corn Laws. The Napoleonic Wars of 1793 to 1815 also affected markets, merchants, producers, and consumers in British North America. At times, these international conflicts created increased demand, such as when the port and garrison towns of Halifax, Quebec, and Kingston experienced temporary booms because of an increase in the numbers of soldiers and sailors present. But at other times, wars unsettled economies through looting and the destruction of property (whether by privateers or occupying armies) and the disruption of international trade and internal economic patterns.

After the Napoleonic Wars, British North America saw a major influx of British immigrants; post-war unemployment, as well as shifts in agricultural and industrial production in Britain, changed the imperial government's attitude toward immigration. While the British government had no overarching policy of settlement for its American colonies, by 1845 there were almost 1 million Canadians of British origin—as opposed to 110 000 in 1791. Some came as part of assisted immigration and resettlement schemes, sponsored by government, private landholders, and land companies; others were brought over by recruiters but had to cope with settlement on their own. Still more came on their own, hoping to find new opportunities either independently or with the help of friends and family. The new arrivals were producers and consumers, labourers and capitalists, and thus to some might represent economic growth and prosperity—but the impact on those already resident in the colonies was far from uniform. The Native peoples, for example, were faced with demands both for farmland and the right to extract minerals and conduct logging on Native lands.

Another important aspect of the colonial economy was the unwaged work of women and children within families—whether on farms, in the fishery, or in artisan and merchant households. This work has proved more difficult to evaluate by traditional quantitative methods such as calculations of exports or wage rates. However, a number of historians have used other ways to demonstrate the centrality of women's contributions to household-based production. The social relations which governed women's work within the household were invariably—at least formally—those of inequality, since married women outside Lower Canada could not generally own the results of their efforts, and daughters were unlikely to benefit financially from their work as did their brothers.

Paternalism also governed many of the relations between employers and workers in the colonies. Legislation such as Upper Canada's 1847 *Master and Servant Act* allowed employers to prosecute employees who were insubordinate or left their place of employment. Although legal reforms did in time replace paternalistic ideologies with competitive individualism, the changes still offered greater protection for employers. While many craft unions did not emerge until later in the nineteenth century, from the French régime on, certain groups of workers in Lower Canada, Nova Scotia, and Upper Canada combined to protest rates of pay and hours of work.

By the mid-nineteenth century, the construction of railroads and trains, as well as canals and ships, was providing employment to large crews and skilled workers. The financing for these enterprises came from the colonial government, private investments, and the imperial state. The first colonial bank was the Bank of Montreal (1817); the Bank of Upper Canada was founded in 1822. These institutions spread across the colonies in the following decades and offered credit to both merchants and the state. As well, farmers and merchants set up mills—sawmills, grist-mills, and grain mills—to process the raw materials of farm and bush. By the 1860s, factories were being established in cities such as Montreal, St John, Toronto, and Hamilton, manufacturing iron goods, clothing, footwear, tobacco, and foods.

Section A
Shaping the Colonial Economy

This first section of documents covers a range of economic activities—from the problems of buying and selling goods in the Canadas in the late eighteenth century, to reports on the state of agriculture in Lower Canada in the 1820s and 1830s, to the community excitement stirred up in 1860s Lunenburg County, Nova Scotia, by the discovery of gold. These accounts were written by merchants and politicians, men with either business (such as Upper Canadian merchant Richard Cartwright) or political interests in the colonial economies. The material spans more than half a century, and demonstrates how colonial economies were shaped by factors such as climate, geography, and human activity.

Merchants and Trade in the Canadas, 1793
Richard Cartwright to Messrs T[odd] McGill & Co.

Kingston, 16th Sept[r], 1793

I addressed you on the 10th & 12th Curr[t] by Boats of the NW, Comp[y] and was yesterday favoured with yours of the 2nd—I am surprised and disappointed at the Account you give me of the Flour sent to Quebec—I did not know that Flour could be pack[d] too close, but took it for granted that the closer it was packed the better, but I will gladly receive any Instruction on this Subject, as it is my Inclination as well as Interest to have the Business done to Perfection.—Care was always taken to have it cooled for some Time before it was boulted.—I hope it will be sold without much Loss.

With Respect to the Pot Ash, though I would prefer a Sale of it in the Country, yet I am by no Means so much bent upon it as to let it go at an Undervalue, and will therefore leave it to yourselves to act as you shall think best In looking over the Acc^t Sales of last Season for that Article I find only 76 Casks accounted for. There were 77 sent you, and the missing one seems to be N° 78 a Bbl cont^g 332^{lbs} gross.—

I shall want about 12 Bbls granada Rum under Mark H.M. & about 20 of same Quality for myself, also a Puncheon of best Carrot Tobacco, a couple Hhds of your Teneriff [canary wine] & the same Quantity of your bencuarto Wine & a Chest of Bohea [China] Tea, but these Articles being intended for the Winter Supply may come at your Leisure.

Lieu^t Parrots Half Pay Vouchers now wait on you accompanied by those of Lt Church How I came to leave the former out of my Respects of 29th Ult^o I cannot account for.

The Articles in your six Boats under Morrisseau & Anels & Auge have been received apparently in good Order & conformably to Bills of Lading except in the N^o of 1 Cask I 4/# A which is marked in Boat 68 or 63 but should be 53—There being no Packs or Pot Ash here they will take their Lading below for which I have given them Directions conformably to the Tenor of your Letter from La Chine.—

By Morrisseau I send you a Bundle cont^g four Hangers [swords] which are very old Shopkeepers & totally unsaleable here.—I request you will have them sold at Quebec or otherwise disposed of for what they will fetch.—

You will please receive for me from Auge & Anel 5/6 for Bread.

Cartwright to Robert Hamilton

Kingston, 23rd Sept, 1793

I have now before me your Favour of 5th, 12th & 13th Inst. and am sorry to find that Mr Beasly has been so shamefully inaccurate in Bill Lading of 28th Augst. The Powder & the 7 Boxes A.S.R. were found minuted in the rough Dft of his shipping Account, though he had omitted them in copying off the Bill Lading from it.—I am well aware that the Articles included in that Bill of Lading did not look well, and on receiving them from the Boats I fully stated every Circumstance to Messrs T. McGill & Co. I opened every Bale, and sometimes went so far as to look into a Trunk or Box that appeared suspicious, and I had every thing that had been wetted hung out to dry & have had the Canadians whole Days at this Business but except in one or two instances I found no real damage had been sustained. Having thus done every thing that depended on me, and stated it fully to the House below, I do not think it necessary to address the Gentlemen of Detroit on the Subject.—With respect to the Cause I must frankly declare that I consider it as more owing to the uncommon Badness of the Weather than to any gross

Neglect on the Part of the Men, or Insufficiency in the Oil Cloths; and as an Instance of this I have to mention that I have not found so many Packages wetted in any Batteau that I have received this Season, as in one principally loaded for Mr Thibault, and in which he came Passenger himself.—

I should be sorry if my Letter to Mr Beasly has miscarried as it contains his Packing Invoice without which he must be greatly embarrassed in opening his Goods, however I shall send a Duplicate at all Events.—

With Regard to Shingles, Boards & Plank sometimes carried by Richardson on Deck, or over his Quarters, the Case stands thus.—While I was at Niagara I saw some Shingles on his Deck. He told me they were some he had engaged for with Mr Crooks & asked if I meant to charge him Freight for them.—My Reply was that as they did not appear to interfere with his Lading I did not think them an Object.—For the Boards he has never said any thing to me on the Subject; as they are only carried slung at his Quarter. I knew he would not take them unless they were to be a perquisite of his own; and they being for Messrs Geo. Forsyth & Co, I was silent on the Subject, lest they should think hard of my Interference. But notwithstanding all this, he openly claimed the Right of carrying goods in his Cabbin for his own Benefit.—Hence I cut him short & told him in the most positive manner that not a Package of Merchandise should go in any Part of the Vessel without paying Freight to the Owners.—If, as I suspect, the Charges he has made for goods carried in his Cabbin are extra & over & above the usual Freight, it is a Piece of infamous Extortion that few but himself would be guilty of; but if this should not be the Case, and no Freight hath been paid for them on Account of the Vessel, it shall most certainly be charged ag^st him at the close of the Navigation; till then it may be prudent to dissemble and as Business progresses it is necessary to deal with this Gentleman a little in his own Way.—Would you believe that he has given me Notice to provide another master for the *Lady Dorchester*, under the Pretense that he has been ill used in not being allowed to have his Choice of the two Vessels.—The Capt of the New One was particularly engaged to command her before he left London.—Though in Mr. Richardson we shall lose a very able & active Seaman, he has made himself so universally abnoxious that I shall not be very sorry to get rid of him.—

You rightly suppose that the Peas ND are at M^r McDonells own Risque & that I am no further concerned in them than to replace them with others of better Quality.—I shall in my next let you know what he says about them.—I have already mentioned that M^r McLean did not like to ship the Flour for Mr Bells Rent without some Directions from your Place.—Perhaps a Line from Mr Farquharson might suffice.—We have little Prospect of Aid from any of the Government Vessels; the Order for one of them has been since qualified with an Exception, if Government Stores & Provisions do not interfere, and these are now pouring in pretty plentifully.—

[*Richard A. Preston, ed.,* Kingston Before the War of 1812 *(Champlain Society, 1964), pp. 197-199]*

The Agricultural Crisis and Lower Canada

John Neilson, Seventh
Report on Crown Lands, 1824

From 1793, but particularly from about 1800, to the close of the late war in Europe, the progress of the settlements in the seigneuries was very great; where the lands were good, and were obtained at little expense, and on something approaching to the old terms, they were readily taken up, settled upon, and the roads laid out and made at the common expense, according to law. The distant journeys, delays and expenses and difficulties in obtaining Procèsverbaux, both before and after homologation, were a general subject of complaint; the high prices of agricultural produce, occasioned by the war in Europe, enabled the settlers to bear all, and overcome all obstacles in making the roads. Since the close of the war, the progress of the settlements has been yearly diminishing; the decline in the prices of agricultural produce, the obstacle of unusually high rents and new and onerous conditions of the grant, and absolute refusal to concede on the part of many of the seigneurs, with the expenses and difficulties of laying out roads as before mentioned, are more than they can bear.

C.-E. Casgrain, Rivière-Ouelle, to John Neilson, 1 January 1839

We are here in state of alarming poverty. The needs are such that I fear we will not be able to provide sufficient for the winter for all the poor who grieve us and sear our souls with their stories of hardship. The harvest has been so poor that a good half of the habitants will not have enough for themselves. Most of these are in debt and without [further] credit. The rest are little better in consequence of debts contracted in hope of good harvests which have been lacking for several years. It is a sad state of affairs partly the fault of the people themselves who have unwisely indulged in expenses beyond their means and conditions due to the excessive eagerness of merchants to make them advances and long-term credits which have brought if not ruin, at least great penury to many. To all I preach reform as much as I can to make them understand the necessity of denying themselves any object of luxury and of obtaining everything with the produce of their land and animals without turning to the merchants.

[Fernand Ouellet, Lower Canada, 1791-1840: Social Change and Nationalism (Toronto: Oxford University Press, 1980), pp. 142, 279]

Gold Mining in Lunenburg County, Nova Scotia

Friday June 28 1861

The Gold fever is now raging nearly over the whole Province. This County is not exempt from the mania, at the 'Gold River' a few miles above the bridge, beautiful and rich specimens of Gold have been found in small quantities...

Thursday July 18

This forenoon a large party, male and female, embarked on board the packet "Friend" and sailed for the gold region at the "Ovens," My daughter Eliza and myself made two of the party which consisted of about 70 persons; at about half past 1 O'clock we were all safely landed on the gold coast, and after partaking of a luncheon, which was prepared by the Ladies and enjoyed in the bush, the party scattered to different parts of the gold fields; the sight there was truly amusing and something surprising to see the busy aspect of the place; some were digging into the bowels of the earth with pick axe and shovel, others were hammering the quartz to powder, while others were blasting the tremendous rocks, all in search of the precious metal; several rough tents are erected, one for the purpose of supplying the diggers with sundries to feed the inner man, and conducted by Joseph Metzler of this town. I was much pleased with my visit to the diggings although there has been as yet only small quantities of gold found, yet I have no hesitation in saying a 'good time' will dawn on Lunenburg by the discovery of these gold diggings, provided skill, industry, and capital be employed to develop its riches.

Friday August [?] 1861

Within these few days past the diggers at the "Ovens" have discovered Gold amongst the sand on the Sea Shores. A young lady while amusing herself on the shore picked from the sand about two or three dollars worth without any exertion.

Thursday Aug 8 1861

The Town this evening was crammed with strangers bound for the Gold diggings at the "Ovens;" boarding houses and Hotels were full to overflowing, numbers were obliged to pitch their Tents on the Common.

Saturday August 10

This afternoon the Steamer "Neptune" arrived at the "Ovens" gold diggings with 75 passengers; the packet also arrived from Halifax with 104 passengers. This evening hundreds of strange faces may have been seen travelling through the streets.

Tuesday September 3 1861

Yesterday the gold excitement at the "Ovens" was raised to a high degree, by a Nugget of Gold having been dug up by a man named Crowel from his claim on the beach; this is the first nugget that has been taken; it was brought to town and exhibited; crowds gathered to see the wonder of the day;... being about one eighth part of an inch in thickness and valued at twenty-six dollars; several persons offered as high as forty dollars for it, they intending to retain it as a specimen.

Tuesday November 26th 1861

A tragic scene took place this forenoon at the "Ovens" gold diggings. Some persons had been amusing themselves firing at a Target with a revolver pistol which contained five charges; Mr. Traunweiser of this place had the pistol in his hand, and supposing that all the charges had been fired out, called out to a friend of his, a Mr. James McDonald, who was coming along the road, to clear the way or he would fire at him; to which McDonald immediately replied "fire away." Traunweiser pulled the trigger, and to the consternation of all around, McDonald fell dead, the bullet having entered his head near the eye; the report of the pistol and the immediate death of McDonald caused quite a sensation among the bystanders; neither Traunweiser or any of the party had the least idea of another charge being in the pistol. Both parties were very respectable persons, and connected with the gold diggings. McDonald was from Pictou, where he has left a widow and other relatives to mourn their loss. McDonald's remains were brought over to this town, from the gold diggings, this evening.

May 1862 [n.d.]

Emigrants are arriving daily to the "Ovens" gold fields. To day two vessels discharged the Cargoes freight there; they were from the United States and brought a large number of passengers. Buildings are being put up in that locality in large numbers, and the Ovens, which heretofore was only a barren desolate place is fast becoming a town.

[C.B. Fergusson, ed., The Diary of Adolphus Gaetz *(Public Archives of Nova Scotia, 1965), pp. 63-68]*

Section B
Working Together

The following documents cover types of economic activity—agriculture and fishing—in which husbands and wives, parents and children, worked together in what historians have described as a 'family enterprise.' The authors acknowledge the importance of such family labour, particularly women's work. Some of the writers were outsiders to the community being observed (for example, Johan Schrøder, a Norwegian writer who toured the Canadas in 1863 to report on the conditions of Norwegian settlements). Others, such as the journalist who penned an account of the Niagara Fair, were members of that community.

Johan Schrøder's Report on James Ward's Farm, Eastern Townships, Lower Canada, 1863

Ward took us through large areas of gentle sloping hardwood land with first-class soil, and he claimed that a property of one hundred acres, most of it cultivated and the rest cleared for forest, could not be had for less than $3,000, or $30 an acre. Of this sum, however, $10 an acre would be for buildings and fences. In addition, each lot should include fifty acres of forest, including about four hundred sugar maples with an annual yield of two to two and a half pounds of sugar from each tree. He had not found that tapping caused damage to the trees; he had been tapping for at least ten years.

The accounts for his farm, worth $3,000, with one hundred acres cultivated land and forty-six acres of forest and sugar maple, was as follows:

Expenses	
Annual interest on $3,000	$180.00
Taxes	$ 20.00
Hired labour:	
Two adult labourers at $125 each	$250.00
Two maids at $50 each	$100.00
One boy	$ 60.00
Farm equipment:	
Interest on estimated value at $125	$ 15.00
Annual depreciation and repairs	$ 50.00
Household expenses:	
Food and drink for the help mentioned above and	
for a family of five based on average market	
prices over the last three years, for ten persons at	
$50 per person	$500.00
Horses:	
500 bushels of oats, two tons of hay, and	
pasture at $5 per horse, for two horses	$ 75.00
Sugar shed and equipment for the sugar harvest:	
interest on $120	$ 7.00
Depreciation	$ 7.00
Sum	$1,306.00

Income

Sugar:

        from 400 trees at 2 1/2 pounds per tree = 1,000
        pounds at $7 per 100 pounds $ 70.00

Fodder:

        hay from 30 acres = 45 tons, which gives a
        return of $6 per ton when used through the
        winter for cattle and sheep $270.00
        straw and greens of root crops, which gives a
        return of $3 per acre as fodder $ 90.00

Seed:

        27 acres of a variety of grains, which, on the
        basis of a good oats harvest, gives 40 bushels
        per acre at 1 shilling & 9 pence per bushel =
        $14 per acre, amounting to $378.00

Potatoes:

        1 1/2 acres, 200 bushels per acre at 25 cents
        a bushel $ 75.00

Turnips:

        1 1/2 acres, 500 bushels per acre, which gives
        a return of $10 per bushel as fodder $ 75.00

Pasture:

        40 acres of meadows and 46 acres of forest land
        in six months for 50 sheep, 10 cows, 10 heifers,
        equals the profits on the winter fodder $360.00

(The total value of fodder for the full year, $720.00, for the farm's
        livestock can be broken down as follows:

From 2 horses, approx.	$ 20.00
wool and lambs of 5 sheep	$200.00
butter from 10 cows	$200.00
10 heifers at $20 each	$200.00
milk	$100.00
Sum	$720.00

Pork:

        annual product of garbage $ 50.00

Forest:

        The value of the forest would be impaired if
        used for anything but fences and firewood.
        Moreover, lumber is hardly marketable $000.00

Sum $1,368.00

The net profit of a farm of one hundred acres cultivated land and forty-six acres forest amounts to $62 if all help is hired and the farmer is merely a supervisor. I believe that these accounts come fairly close to the truth, even though I am aware that some will object to the small net profit I have arrived at.

It should be brought to mind, however, that the main income of the farmer class of all countries is derived from the labour of the farmer and his family. Consequently, when the farmer, his wife, and his children do the work instead of hiring help, it should be possible to save $235 in wages and $150 in food. If this is added to the net profit of the farm, the total will be $447. So gentleman farming is as unprofitable in Canada as in Norway, but the farmer who works his own farm can own his own land in a shorter time and for less money than in the latter country. Ward estimates that the work that he and his family did on the farm was worth about $300 a year.

[Orm Overland, ed., Johan Schrøder's Travels in Canada, 1863 *(Montreal-Kingston: McGill-Queen's University Press, 1989), pp. 90-92]*

The County Fair

We would here venture to make a remark or two on a department of our annual exhibition which always excites a good deal of interest, among the Ladies especially. We mean the department devoted particularly to articles of female taste and industry. It appears to us that this department might be extended so as to embrace many articles of female industry of a plainer description than those which are now entitled... Our exhibitions in this department look rather too exclusively to articles of mere ornament and luxury... The present regulations throw this department of our fair too exclusively into the hands of those ladies who have had the good fortune to receive a fashionable and genteel education. Now it does not detract one from the merits of hundreds of industrious and really accomplished country lasses to say that they have not had an opportunity of being initiated into those pretty arts of boarding school education alluded to. They possess generally a valuable compensation for this defect in a superior knowledge of things really useful. In the arts of plain needle work, knitting, spinning, plaiting straw, making straw hats, and in short, in the thousand and one daily avocations of an industrious girl, they exhibit a grace and acuteness which is as worthy of receiving notice at Fairs as the mere ornamental but less useful labours we are in the habit of inspecting there.

That articles of utility are not more generally exhibited in this department, is partly on account of their being no premium set down for them, partly we fear, on account of a mistaken idea, that more value is attached to matters of mere ornament, than to things of use. But we venture to say that the young lady who bravely ventured to exhibit a superior fine shirt in the midst of the crowd of innumerable creations of fancy at the late exhibition received as warm an approbation from the Judges as any exhibiting there. It was an innovation to be sure, but one which we hope to see followed by many imitations at our future fairs. The girl whose spinning wheel can turn off the finest yarn, or whose nimble fingers can knit the best stockings, ought to have a place at our exhibitions as well as those who crotchet... Make room then at another exhibition for a large increase in the ladies department!

[Niagara Mail, *31 October 1855*]

The Corduroy Road Between York and Burlington, 1830, J.P. Cockburn. *[Photograph courtesy of the Royal Ontario Museum Canadiana Collections © ROM]*

Fishing and Women's Work in Newfoundland
Labrador, 1838

Were the females of Labrador accustomed to no other labor than the mere cooking of food for their families, they would have a large portion of their time to spend in idle employments. But they engage in the hard and laborious toils of fishing with as much zeal and activity as the males. When the salmon and trout fishing commences, the women and children employ themselves assiduously in the sport, and are often out night and day while the season of this fishery lasts. At the fish stands, while the cod fishery is in the full tide of operation, the women are seen among the most constant and dextrous in dressing the fish, thrown up by the fishermen. Some of these females will dress two or three thousand fish in a single day. . .

[*Ephraim W. Tucker,* Five Months in Labrador and Newfoundland During the Summer of 1838 *(Concord, 1839), pp. 119-120]*

Labrador, 1855

And here I notice the fact that the number of females is quite disproportionate to that of the sterner sex, as may be gleaned from the last mentioned Report, which shows that in 1852 there were 364 men settled on the coast and but 62 females. This is of course detrimental to the prosperity of the place, and should be remedied by emigration or otherwise. Any plan which would alter the existing state of things must confer a boon on the country, because the more the coast is settled the better are its natural resources developed, and the miseries suffered by shipwrecked mariners, proportionately diminished. The fisherman's wants are few, and he can easily support a wife; moreover she could assist him in his calling as much as one of his own sex, and it often happens that the larger a fisherman's family becomes, the better are his prospects...

[Noel H. Bowen, "The Social Condition of the Coast of Labrador," Literary and Historical Society of Quebec, Report (1855), p. 334]

Section C
Employers and Employees

Labour relations in the pre-Confederation period involved many struggles between employers and employees over issues such as rates of pay, hours of work, the types of work performed, and employees' behaviour on the job. Such tensions between workers and their employers were not unique to industrial settings. Whether in the western fur trade, in shipping along the St. Lawrence and Atlantic coasts, or in mid-nineteenth century Ontario's railroad companies, employers attempted to impose various kinds of regulations and controls over their workers. The documents in this section suggest how employees reacted to their employers' efforts.

An Unruly Workforce in the Fur Trade
From the Athabasca Journal of George Simpson, Hudson's Bay Governor, 1821

In the Foregoing pages I have endeavoured to give your Honors an idea of the present general state of the Companys Establishments in Athabasca, and for particulars must take the liberty of referring you to my Journal and the Reports of the Gentlemen in charge of the Districts. I shall now do myself the honor of submitting a few observations which may throw some additional light on the affairs of this hitherto unfortunate Department and if the suggestions I am about to make are acted upon, I feel satisfied that our opponents cannot prolong the contest beyond an other year, when the Trade will not only repay the heavy losses sustained, but realize very handsome profits...

Physical power is all that is required, an additional levy of One Hundred Men and Officers independent of those expected from Canada this Summer are necessary to establish the whole of the Country: the advance of money to bring these Men into the Interior I am aware is considerable, but the enormous profits on goods sold to the Canadians would reduce the Wages, which is the grand item of expenditure to at least one third of the nominal amount. Hitherto we have been compelled to pay a great proportion thereof in hard cash, because we have not had Goods to supply them; even at the Depot they are discontented because they cannot get finery at several hundred p Cent profit, Cape Madaira at a Guinea p Bottle and various other articles at any price required. At Fort Wedderburn where we had Forty Four Men this Season at from 1000 to 2000 livers Wages we could have paid 3/4ths thereof in Spirits at 60 livers p pint or £18 Stg. p Gallon, which is the price I have this year charged, and the people are dissatisfied and unhappy that we have not been enabled to indulge them at those prices.

It has been held out to the people year after year, that large Brigades of Men were coming from Canada, but finding that these statements were incorrect, they know that we are dependent on their Services and exact such terms as they think proper; subordination is at an end, a common Voyageur does not hesitate to disobey the orders given to him or to call his Master a 'Sacra Crapp' knowing that the offence must be overlooked when his contract expires, and when he is asked to renew his engagement he not only insists on having all fines struck off his account but his Wages advanced about one third in some cases more. It is dangerous to attempt beating these fellows into good discipline as they may take it into their heads to return the compliment knowing that the other Fort offers an asylum for them: heavy fines is the only thing to bring them to a sense of their duty and these we cannot attempt to impose until a sufficient number of men are provided to enable us to dispense with the services of the most troublesome. The North West Coy. I believe have even more trouble with their people than we have, but they are altogether a superior class of Men, Stout active fellows in every respect qualified for the laborious Duties they have to perform, whereas the Compys. Agents in Canada appear to select the most miserable wretches the country produces for this Service, out of 38 or 40 fresh hands brought in last Summer there are not 10 real good Voyageurs...

I regret to say that generally speaking, there is a great dearth of talent among the officers of this Department, particularly the subordinate ones, some of whom are become spoiled by Opposition, and knowing that their Services are absolutely required take the most shameful advantages: Many of these fellows can hardly sign their own Names, have Salys. from £50 to £175 p annum and when required to do their duty, if unpleasant, threaten to 'go free' or in other words join the North West Coy.; I shall endeavour to purge the Country of a few of them, and have no doubt but they will be made examples of when the Govr. in Chief as [sic] acquainted with their conduct. A few Young Men of tolerable Education, and moderate expectations on Five Year contracts, are much required; they can in Scotland be engaged at from £30 to £50 and would in a very short time do the duty of some fellows now in the employ at double and treble those Salys.; in all we require about Twelve Young Men of 18 to 20 Years of Age; they cannot get into the interior the year they arrive at York, as the Brigade takes its departure before the Ships come into the Bay, I would therefore recommend that they are sent out with Bands of Indians the first Winter, which will innure them to the privations incident to the Country, give them a knowledge of the Cree Language which is understood throughout the Department, familiarise them to the habits and customs of the Natives and teach them the Rudiments of the Fur Trade; their future advancement will of course depend on their conduct and ability; Annexed I beg to hand a List of the Officers under my charge with a few remarks as to their character and abilities.

[E.E. Rich, Simpson's Athabasca Journal *(Champlain Society), pp. 397-398]*

Owen Rowlands' Log, 1860

Master of the **John Davies***, Quebec, 1860*

9 June 7 pm. James McCauley, seaman, and John Brown carpenter, went on shore in the boat. Went away from the boat without leave.

10 June They came on board at 9 am

13 June 7 pm. James Stanley, cook went on shore without leave

14 June All day—Stanley drunk and off duty, hired a substitute @ 10s.0d. per day.

15 June 10 am. Stanley went on shore without leave. Got drunk and returned but on going on shore was stopped by me, but still insisted on going ashore. Also refused to do my orders. I ordered the police boat to come to take him in charge. He went on shore before the boat arrived.

16 June John Flaherty went on shore without leave and did not turn to his duty. Laborer employed in his room @ 10s. per day. Stanley came on board after being absent without leave 22 hours. I sent for the police boat and gave him in charge. Stanley tried by the judge and ordered on board the ship to do his duty.

16 June 6 am. John Flaherty, Edward Lynch, Charles Kelly, Laurence Ryan and James Bresham refused to do their duty and went on shore without leave. Laborers hired in their place. The above came on board—called them into the cabin. Read the entry to them. They replied that they did not want their discharge and asked me to allow them to go to their duty.

17 June Stanley went on shore without leave, returned beastly drunk and on account of having divine services on board, I told the chief officer to set his room door and not allow him to come out until he was sober. After the service was over, I saw him going forward. Said to me, he should make me sweat before he was done with me. Hired a substitute in his place...

26 June Francis Cameron off duty drunk—hired a laborer in his place @ 7s.6d. per day.

27 June at 8 am I went down into the hold, I found James McCauley quarrelling with Mr. Knowles, the stevedore. I ordered him on deck, he said that he would not go. I called him on one side and asked what was the matter with him and why disobey my orders. He told me that I was working him up by sending him to attend the pitch pott for the carpenter. (The reason that I did send him to that light duty was because he was sick and off duty yesterday morning). I told him so and ordered him on deck again. He would not go, but wanted to fight me, I put my hand on his shoulder and told him not to make so much noise but to go on deck to his duty, whilst my face was turned from him he struck me in the right eye, my feet slipped between the beam fillings and he fell himself on top of me repeatedly striking at me and scratching my face with his nails, until some of the men took him off me. 10 minutes after the first assault he (after coming up on the upper deck) took up a work stave and struck me a very severe blow right over the left kidney. I took a warrant and had the man apprehended.

28 June The body of John Flaherty was picked up and identified by the crew.

29 June The body was buried, part of the crew being in attendance, the expense of the funeral being £3.3s.0d.

30 June 7 am. Thomas Jones, 2nd mate being drunk when the crew was ordered to duty by the chief officer, I went and spoke to him when he began to abuse me. I asked him to go on board. He said that he would go when he liked. (8 am) I asked him to come to the cabin and ordered him to his room. He then began to abuse and threaten to strike me. Also attempted to do it twice. I then put him under arrest and ordered the police boat away and told him that he might resume his duty and furthermore I gave him particular orders not to go on shore. (At 9 am) Thomas Jones went on shore without leave and remained until about 7 pm when he came on board. I ordered him into the cabin and told him to take his clothes &c out of the cabin. He refused to do so, and used high language. I ordered the steward to shut the cabin windows to prevent the noise from being heard in ships alongside and ordered him out of the cabin into the cuddy. He refused to go, but [I] took hold of him by the right shoulder, I then shoved him out towards the door. He then struck me. I then called for help, when the chief mate came down he ran ashore. About midnight he returned on board. I sent for the police and gave him in charge for drunkenness and absence without leave.

2 July 10 am I appeared in court against Thomas Jones, 2nd officer—case adjourned.

2 July noon James McCauley was brought on board by a police officer. He resumed his duty.

3 July James McCauley, James Bresham, Edward Lynch, Laurence Ryan, Charles Kelly, Robert Cooper deserted the ship taking their effects with them. I shall also remark that the above-named seamen have been constantly absenting themselves parts of each day since we commenced to take in cargo and sometimes all day.

4 July Joseph Walker and James Stanley (cook) deserted the ship taking their effects, the same remark as the above is applicable to these two men. Owen Ellis drunk and off duty—Laborer hired @ 7.6d. I discharged the case against Thomas Jones 2nd mate on the ground of him paying all expenses.

[Judith Fingard, Jack in Port: Sailortowns of Eastern Canada *(Toronto: University of Toronto Press, 1982), pp. 103-106]*

No Rudeness or Incivility to Passengers

Each person is to devote himself exclusively to the Company's service, attending during the regulated hours of the day and residing wherever he may be required

He is to obey promptly all instructions he may receive from persons placed in authority over him and conform to all regulations of the Company.

He will be liable to criminal punishment for disobediences or negligence of an order, and dismissal for misconduct, incompetency, using improper language, cursing or swearing while on duty.

He is not on any occasion to receive a fee or reward from any person without the sanction of the Company.

No instance of intoxication will be overlooked; and besides dismissal, the offender shall be deemed guilty of misdemeanour.

Any case of rudeness or incivility to passengers will meet with instant dismissal.

Every person must appear on duty clean and neat.

No person is allowed under any circumstances to absent himself from duty, without the permission of his superior officer, except in case of illness, and then notice is to be immediately sent to his immediate superior officer.

No person is to quit the Company's service without fourteen days previous notice; and in case he leaves without such notice, all pay then due will be forfeited.

The Company reserves the right to deduct from the pay such sums as may be awarded for neglect of duty as fines and for rent due to the Company.

Should any person think himself aggrieved he may memorialize the Board, but the memorial must be sent through the head of his department.

[Rule Book, Grand Trunk Railroad, 1857]

Toronto Rolling Mills, William Armstrong, 1864. *[Metro Toronto Library, John Ross Robertson Collection, (T10914)]*

QUESTIONS

1. What do these documents tell us about the importance of seasonal fluctuations to resource economies?

2. The documents in this section were written by a variety of authors (merchants and politicians from the Canadas and Nova Scotia, a travel writer from Norway, a journalist, a Hudson's Bay factor, a ship's captain, and a railroad company), and concern different places, and different forms of economic production. They also span a period of 75 years. In what ways do the authors reflect their specific interests and preoccupations? Are there any common themes and concerns that they share?

3. How did the unpaid labour of women and children and the household economy in general affect colonial economies?

4. How did colonial employers, whether the Hudson's Bay Company, the Grand Trunk Railroad, or an individual ship's captain, attempt to regulate and discipline their workforces?

5. What effects might the extraction of primary resources have upon local communities, as suggested in Adolphus Gaetz's description of the Lunenburg gold-rush?

READINGS

Marjorie Griffin Cohen, *Women's Work, Markets, and Economic Developments in Nineteenth-Century Ontario* (Toronto: University of Toronto Press, 1988)

Paul Craven, ed., *Labouring Lives: Work and Workers in Nineteenth-Century Ontario* (Toronto: University of Toronto Press, 1995)

Paul Craven and Tom Traves, "Canadian Railways as Manufacturers, 1850-1880," in *Historical Papers* (1983), pp. 254-281

Judith Fingard, *Jack in Port: Sailortowns of Eastern Canada* (Toronto: University of Toronto Press, 1982)

R. Louis Gentilcore and Geoffrey Matthews, eds., *Historical Atlas of Canada Volume II: The Land Transformed, 1800-1891* (Toronto: University of Toronto Press, 1993). See Plates 11-16 in "Expanding Economies," Plate 25, "Emergence of a Transportation System, 1837-1852," and Plate 26, "The Railway Age, 1854-1891."

Allan Greer, *Peasant, Lord, and Merchant: Rural Society in Three Quebec Parishes, 1740-1840* (Toronto: University of Toronto Press, 1985)

Douglas McCalla, *Planting the Province: The Economic History of Upper Canada, 1784-1870* (Toronto: University of Toronto Press, 1993)

John McCallum, *Unequal Beginnings: Agricu* *Economic Development in Quebec and Ontario* *1870* (Toronto: University of Toronto Press, 1980)

Françoise Noel, *The Christie Seigneuries: Estate Management and Settlement in the Upper Richelieu Valley, 1760-1854* (Montreal and Kingston: McGill-Queen's University Press, 1992)

Fernand Ouellet, *Economic and Social History of Quebec* (Toronto: McClelland and Stewart, 1981)

Eric Sager, *Seafaring Labour: The Merchant Marine in Atlantic Canada* (Montreal and Kingston: McGill-Queen's University Press, 1989)

Bruce Wilson, *The Enterprises of Robert Hamilton: A Study of Wealth and Influence in Upper Canada 1791-1841* (Ottawa: Carleton University Press, 1983)

Graeme Wynn, *Timber Colony: A Historical Geography of Early Nineteenth Century New Brunswick* (Toronto: University of Toronto Press, 1981)

Brian Young, *In Its Corporate Capacity: The Seminary Of Montreal as a Business Institution, 1816-1876* (Montreal and Kingston: McGill-Queen's University Press, 1986)

Colonial Community Formation

The colonies of British North America were not all alike. They were shaped by their own regional economies, political concerns, and different kinds of religious, ethnic, and racial groupings. However, between the coming of the Loyalists and Confederation we can see that there were some commonalities—the formation of a number of voluntary societies, the development of reform movements, both political and social, and the creation, albeit slowly and unevenly, of colonial middle classes. Community formation was not a smooth and peaceful process; it was marked by struggle and tension. Often, the development of one kind of community came at the expense of another, particularly where Native peoples were concerned.

After the War of 1812, a number of voluntary associations spread across the Maritimes and the Canadas. Some of these groups had their roots in developments prior to the War, particularly in Lower Canada and the Maritimes which had larger populations and a more developed social infrastructure than Upper Canada. But the influx of British immigrants after 1815, who either brought with them a commitment to voluntary organizations or provided a constituency for various philanthropic efforts (such as the Irish famine), helped provide the ideological and demographic impetus for the development of a number of associations.

Some of these, such as the agricultural societies of Upper Canada that discussed and promoted ways of improving farm production, were focused on self-improvement. Benevolent and charitable groups were aimed at alleviating social distress among the poor, often simultaneously trying to reform the latters' moral and socio-economic practices. Other groups were focused on specific issues and social 'problems,'—for example, the temperance movement that spread across British North America from the 1830s, or the Loyal and Patriotic Society of Upper Canada, formed during the War of 1812 to recognize loyal service and compensate those who had suffered losses because of their fidelity to Britain. While the abolition of slavery was never as widespread a concern or as prolific a movement as it was south of the border, it still attracted attention by mid-century. In Ontario, a number of anti-slavery associations were formed and the abolitionist activist Mary Anne Shadd Carey published her newspaper, *Provincial Freeman*, in the 1850s. Although influenced by local conditions and concerns, many of these organizations were also part of international movements through which the middle classes of Britain and America helped define themselves.

Religion, particularly Protestant evangelicalism, played an important role in shaping colonial communities. While religious organizations were of course present in the colonies prior to the Loyalists, they spread more rapidly in Upper Canada and the Maritimes from the 1790s on, and became both more numerous and varied after 1815. Religious bodies could be a focal point for either political conflicts (the separation of church and state, and denominational influences in colonial education) or they could help provide community cohesion, supplying both spiritual nurture and a forum for a community's social life (bazaars, teas, socials, and other gatherings). A number of churches also attempted to regulate their members' conduct—sexual practices, alcohol consumption, and other forms of behaviour came under the churches' scrutiny. In Lower Canada, the Catholic Church provided a central unit of local organization through the parish; as well, much of the colony's social welfare and education was supplied by religious orders, particularly nuns.

Religious institutions and their beliefs and practices were not immune to dominant groups' assumptions about hierarchy and order. However, many of the evangelical churches opened up avenues for leadership to those traditionally consigned to subordinate positions—women, the young, and working-class men. Religious beliefs, coupled with the colonial impetus to assimilate Native peoples into European ways of life, also fuelled missionary work throughout the colonies. Denominations ranging from the Methodists to the Roman Catholics sent missionaries, male and female, to live and work in aboriginal communities, attempting to convert Native peoples by holding services and setting up schools for training in agricultural and domestic employment. The missionaries were assisted in their work by various missionary societies who raised money for them and by Native converts who hoped to reshape First Nations' societies into agriculturally based communities.

Not all attempts at community building were strictly 'middle-class.' Some voluntary societies crossed boundaries of class, gender, race, ethnicity, and religion (although their leaders were invariably middle-class, Protestant, Anglo-Celtic men). Jews, blacks, and Irish Catholics, all of whom were outside or on the margins of the developing middle classes, also formed their own communities and founded societies designed to respond to their members' health, social welfare, and education needs. While there were fewer working-class organizations in this period than in the late nineteenth century, friendly and benevolent societies attempted to offer a bulwark against the seasonal downturns, illness, accidents, and death that so often devastated working families. Other men's organizations, ranging from fire companies to professional organizations formed by lawyers and doctors, were also founded during this period.

Section A
The Impact of Religion

Religion played an important role in shaping colonial communities. The first document in this section comes from the records of the Church of Jebogue, Yarmouth, Nova Scotia, in the 1760s; it demonstrates the different kinds of conduct that the congregation sought to control, and the reaction of those who came under censure. Document two is an extract from the published recollections of Kah-ge-ga-gah-bowh, or George Copway, an Ojibwa man who became a Methodist minister. In his writings, Copway reflects on the effects of his own conversion to Christianity, as well as recording his impressions of other Native communities to which he travelled as a missionary.

The Church Covenant Solemnly Made and Entered into by the Church of Jebogue in Yarmouth, December ye 18, AD. 1767

First. We do each one of us in particular, unfeignedly resign up our selves, and our Seed, to the Lord Jehovah, Father, Son, and Holy Ghost; receiving Jesus Christ as very God and very Man, and the only Mediator between God and Man, as our Lord and Saviour, thereby given of God to each one of us in particular, and revealed to each of us by the Holy Spirit of Promise; relying upon the free Grace of God for all the Benefits of the New Covenant, purchased by Christ for us; and to submit ourselves to the Word and Spirit of God.

Secondly. And we do acknowledge our selves indispensably bound, and will make it our great Care, to hold fast the Doctrines of Faith and good Manners, contained in the Scriptures of Truth; and that we will attend to all those Duties that are therein required for the Increase of our Faith, and Growth in Holiness, and of maintaining a good Conscience; namely, Gospel Preaching, mutual Exhortation, and the Ordinances of Prayer, Baptism, and the Lords Supper, and Singing of Psalms and Hymns.

Thirdly. And as God is the Author of Order, Unity and Peace, we do solemnly promise, that by the Assistance of God's Holy Spirit, we will labour mutually to watch over one another, which Christ hath enjoined, according to our respective Places: that is, Love without Dissimulation, in real Expressions thereof as Occasion serves; in daily frequent Exhortations to Duty; Admonition in Case of Sin and Failing; praying for one another and sympathizing with one another in Afflictions, and prosperous Enjoyments; and using all possible Means to promote the Welfare of each other.

Fourthly. We do submit our selves to the Discipline of Christ in this Church, which is as followeth; First. That supreme and lordly Power over all the Churches upon Earth, doth belong only to Christ, who is King and Head of the Church, and hath the Government on his Shoulders, and hath all Power given to him, both in Heaven and Earth, and exercised by him, (1) In calling the Church out of the World into holy Fellowship with himself, (2) in instituting the Ordinances of his Worship, and appointing his Ministers and Officers for the Dispensing them: (3) For giving Laws for ordering all our Ways, and Way of his House and Worship: (4) In giving Life to his own Institutions, and his People through them: (5) In protecting and delivering his Church against and from all his and their Enemies. Secondly, The Power granted by Christ unto the Body of the Church and Brotherhood, is a Prerogative or Privilege which the Church exerciseth, (1) In admitting their own Members; (2) In choosing their own Officers and ordaining them in Case of real Necessity, and where a Scripture Presbytery cannot be obtained: (3) In removing them from their Office, and also from their Fellowship in Case of Scandal, or any Thing that by the Rule of the Scriptures, renders them unfit therefor: (4) In supporting the Gospel Ministry, Ordinances, and the Poor of the Church, without using the civil Sword, or coercive Means to force Men thereto: Which Discipline we desire may ever take Place; and that Worship of God in all the Parts thereof, may ever be kept in the Power and Spirituallity thereof among us.

Fifthly. We do also promise that, by the Grace of God, we will oppose all Sin and Error wherever they appear, both in our selves and others, as far as in us lies; namely, All foolish Talking and Jesting, and Wantoness: All vain Disputing about Words and things that gender Strife, and doth not edify to more Godliness: Also vain Companykeeping and spending Time idly, at Taverns and Tippling-Houses, or elsewhere: Evil Whispering or Backbiting of any Person; also carnal and unnecessary Discourse about worldly Things, especially on the Sabbath Day: Unnecessary forsaking the Assembling of our selves together in private convenient Conferences, and also on the Sabbath Day: And all other Sins whatsoever, both of Omission and Commission.

Sixthly. We will teach all under our Care, as far as in us lieth, to know God, to fear him, and to live in his Ways. And now as a farther Testimony of our Faith and Covenant, we not only call God, Angels and Men to Witness, but subscribe and sign the same with our Hands. Amen.

MALES	FEMALES
John Frost	Phebe Rogers
Moses Scott	Lucretia Ring
John Crawley	Sarah Scott
James Robbins	Hannah Ellis
Ebenezer Ellis	Susanna Crawley
George Ring	Ruth Robbins
Cornelius Rogers	Temperance Ritchardson
Thomas Rogers	Mercy Ricker
Jonathan Scott	Anna Hobbs
Prince Godfrey	Mercy Abbot
Daniel Crocker	Miriam Frost
Ephraim Cook	Lydia Frost
Timothy Redding	Sarah Allin
Jeremiah Frost	Desire Nickerson

Mr. Prince Godfrey and Mrs. Temperance Ritchardson Admonished for Loose Behaviour

May the 16, 1773. This Day, the Church of Jebogue in Yarmouth, after divine Worship, chose Deacon Daniel Crocker and Deacon James Robbins, to assist the Pastor in admonishing Mr. Prince Godfrey and Mrs. Temperance Ritchardson, two Members of the Church, for their loose Behaviour, viz. Dancing and Frolicking with loose Company.

This Committee together with the Pastor, proceeded on the Work for which they were chosen and appointed by the Church; and succeeded so far in the Work, after some Difficulty, as to influence the Persons admonished to make some Reflections upon their Conduct and Behaviour, and seek the Removal of the Offence, by confessing and promising Amendment. Their Reflections which they made and presented to the Church, in writing, here next follows.

To the First Church of Christ in Yarmouth

Yarmouth, May ye 18, 1773.

Whereas we, the Subscribers, have lately grieved the Members of this Church, by our unbecoming Conduct and Behaviour, in join-ing with loose Company in Dancing and carnal Merriment; We do humbly and unfeignedly acknowledge our Fault herein, to God, and this Church, in that we have dishonoured God and our Profession, and given Occasion for others to speak reproachfully of the Ways of God, and of his professed People. And we do humbly ask your forgiveness, and your Prayers to God for us that he would forgive us what we have done to his Dishonour and the Dishonour of Religion: And we do unfeignedly promise before God and this Church, that, through divine Assistance, we will shun the like Evil, of which we are now convinced and do make Acknowledgement: And for Time to come we will endeavour to shun and avoid whatsoever exposes us to commit Sin.

Temperance Ritchardson her X mark
Prince Godfrey

The above being publickly read before the Church, the Church accepted of it; and forgave and restored the Persons to former Communion.

Question. Why was the Persons above named so publickly reproved by the Church, for the Instance of Frolicking and Dancing, seeing these Things are prac-tised by professors of Christianity in almost all Places, without being censured in a publick Manner by the Churches to which such Professors belong?

Answer 1. The Members of this Church looked upon the Practice of Frolicking and wanton Dancing, as being sinful both in its Nature and Tendency, being detected and forbidden in the Word of God.

Answer 2. The Church in their solemn Covenant had bound themselves to oppose this Sin. Under the fifth Head of their Covenant are these words, "We do promise that, by the Grace of God ye will oppose all Sin and Error wherever they appear, both in ourselves and others, as far as in us lies All foolish Talking and Jesting and Wantonness: Also vain Company-keeping and spending Time idly, at Taverns and Tippling-Houses, or else where." This the Church had sworn to at their entering into Covenant.

Answer 3. The Church being now in its Infancy, and just beginning to act as a Church, and according to the Constitution which they had agreed to; it was looked upon a particular and important Season to testify against the Sin of Frolicking and carnal wanton Company-keeping, not only by the preaching of the Word, but also by the Discipline and Censures of ye Church; that this ruinous Practise might be suppressed in the Church, as an Example to the Present Generation, and those that may come after: And as these Persons were the first in this Church who were convicted of wanton Dancing and Frolicking since the Church was gathered, they were made the first Examples of publick Reproof and Church Censure...

Recollections of a Forest Life: or, the Life and Travels of Kah-ge-ga-gah-bowh, or, George Copway, Chief of the Ojibway Nation

Chapter VIII

While he lives,
To know no bliss but that which virtue gives;
And when he dies to leave a lofty name,
A light, a land-mark on the cliffs of fame.—*M.*

Here comes the sunshine of my life. The first ray of light flashed in my soul, and, strange as it may appear, it remained. In the summer following my mother's death (1830), I felt that *I was converted.* The following are the circumstances connected with my conversion:—My father and I attended a camp meeting near the town of Colbourne. On our way from Rice Lake to the meeting, my father held me by the hand, as I accompanied him through the woods. Several times he prayed with me, and encouraged me to seek religion at this camp meeting. We had to walk thirty miles under a hot sun, in order to reach the place of destination. Multitudes of Indians, and a large concourse of whites from various places, were on the ground when we arrived. In the evening, one of the white preachers (Wright, I believe, was his name) spoke; his text was, "For the great day of His wrath is come, and who shall be able to stand?" He spoke in English, and as he closed each sentence, an Indian preacher gave its interpretation. He spoke of the plain and good road to heaven; of the characters that were walking in it; he then spoke of the bad place, the judgment, and the coming of a Saviour. I now began to feel as if I was a sinner before God. Never had I felt so before; I was deeply distressed, and knew not the cause. I resolved to go and prostrate myself at the mourner's bench, as soon as an opportunity offered. We were now invited to approach. I went to the bench and knelt down by the roots of a large tree. But how could I pray? I did not understand how to pray; and besides, I thought that the Great Spirit was *too great* to listen to the words of a poor Indian boy. What added to my misery was, that it had rained in torrents about three quarters of an hour, and I was soaking wet. The thunder was appalling, and the lightning terrific. I then tried again to pray, but I was not able. I did not know what words to use. My father then prayed with and for me. Many were praising God, all around me. The storm now ceased, but nearly all the lights had been extinguished by the rain. I still groaned and agonised over my sins. I was so agitated and alarmed that I knew not which way to turn in order to get relief, and while kneeling down with the rest I found relief, as though a stream had been let loose from the skies to my heart. Joy succeeded this knowledge, and, were I to live long, I never can forget the feelings with which I rose and spoke the following first English words—"*Glory to Jesus.*" I looked around for my father, and saw him. I told him that I had found "Jesus."

He embraced me and kissed me; I threw myself into his arms. I felt as strong and happy, yet as humble as a poor Indian boy saved by grace. During that night I did not sleep. The next morning, my cousin, George Shawney, and myself, went out into the woods to sing and pray. As I looked at the trees, the hills, and the valleys, O how beautiful they all appeared! I looked upon them, as it were, with new eyes and new thoughts. Amidst the smiles of creation, the birds sang sweetly, as they flew from tree to tree. We sang

"Jesus, the name that charms our fears."

O how sweet the recollections of that day! "Jesus, all the day long, was my joy and my song." Several hundreds were converted during this meeting. Many of the Indians were reluctant to leave the camp ground when the meeting was broken up. When we reached our homes at Rice Lake, everything seemed to me as if it wore a different aspect; everything was clothed with beauty. Before this, I had only begun to spell and read. I now resumed my studies with a new and different relish. Often, when alone, I prayed that God would help me to qualify myself to teach others how to read the word of God; this circumstance I had not told to any one. On Sabbath mornings I read a chapter in the New Testament, which had been translated for my father, before we went to meeting...

I joined my father's class meeting, and as often as possible I attended school during the period of two years. In June, 1834, our white missionary, Daniel McMullen, received a letter from the Rev. Wm. Case, in which it was stated that a letter had been sent to him by the Rev. John Clark, who was then the superintendent of the mission on Lake Superior. The superintendent requested that two native preachers and two native teachers should be sent to him. John Johnson and I were told that we were to accompany Brothers John Taunchey and Caubage to Lake Superior, to aid Brother Clark.

Brother Caubage and my cousin Johnson took their departure. John Taunchey hesitated about going, because I was undecided, and my father felt unwilling at first to let me go.

One day I determined to leave the village so as to avoid going to Lake Superior; I hunted along the river Trent, hoping that John Taunchey would be gone before my return; I felt very unwilling to go. I was absent over two weeks; they were the longest two weeks I had ever experienced. Yet the whole time I felt dissatisfied; something seemed to whisper to me, "George, go home, and go to Lake Superior with your uncle John Taunchey." I returned to the village. The first person I saw informed me that my uncle was waiting for me, and that my father had left it to me to decide whether to go or stay. Here I was; the missionaries came, and said, "George, your father has left it with you to go or stay. It is your duty to go; John is waiting, and to-day you must conclude." Our school-mistress, Miss Pinney, came and reasoned with me. I recollected, too, that I had prayed that God might prepare me to be useful to my brethren; and now, that I had some good reason to think that my prayers had been heard, and still to refuse to go, would perhaps be acting in opposition to the indications of God. I wept and prayed; but

O! that night of struggle! I could not sleep. In the morning, I said to my father, "I have concluded to go; prepare me for my journey." That morning we were prepared; and on the 16th of July, 1834, about noon, we were on the shore. The canoe was ready; many of the Indians prayed with us on the beach. After shaking hands with my father and the rest, we bid farewell to all we loved so tenderly. We went on board the steam-boat "Great Britain," at Cobourg, and arrived at Toronto the next day. On the 20th July, we left in the stage for Holland Landing; here we remained two days, for the want of a conveyance to the Snake Island mission. At this island we tarried the whole of the Sabbath with the Indians, and had some glorious meetings. They conveyed us to the Narrows mission. In crossing from Narrows to Cold Water mission, we were obliged to carry our trunks on our backs. About 11 o'clock we met two runaway horses on the road to Narrows. We caught them, tied our trunks on their backs, and led them back to Cold Water. Thus we were relieved of our heavy loads.

On Wednesday, the 26th July, we went from Cold Water mission to Pane-ta-wa-go-shene, where we saw a great number of Ojibways from Lake Superior, Ottowas, Menomenese, &c. Here we fell in with John Sunday, Frazer, and others, who were engaged in instructing the Indians in this vicinity...

Chapter IX

The clouds may drop down titles and estates,
Wealth may seek us, but wisdom must be sought.—*Y.*

I now began to feel the responsibility resting upon me. The thought of assuming the station of a teacher of the Indians, with so few capabilities, was enough to discourage more gifted men than myself. Frequently did I enter the woods and pour out my soul to God, in agony and tears. I trembled at what was before me, and said, "who is able for these things?" But a still small voice would answer, "My grace is sufficient for thee." Soothing words indeed, especially to an unlearned and feeble Red man—a mere worm of the dust.

Having provided everything necessary for our journey, and a residence of eight months at the Ke-wa-we-non mission, we started in company with Rev. Mr. Chandler, uncle John Taunchey, and the traders who intended to winter on the shores of Lake Superior and do business with the Ojibways. We were more than three weeks on our journey—three hundred and fifty miles. At one place, we were weather-bound for one week. Our French companions were the most wicked of men. They would gnash their teeth at each other, curse, swear, and fight among themselves. The boat, oars, the winds, water, the teachers, &c., did not escape their execrations. I thought now that I understood what *hell* was, in a very clear manner. My very hairs would seem to stand, while I would be obliged to listen to their oaths, when they gave vent to their malevolence and passions. They would fight like beasts over their cooking utensils, and even while their food was in their mouths. I will just say here that I have often seen them eat boiled corn, with tallow for butter.

On our road, we saw the celebrated Pictured Rocks, Sand Banks, and Grand Island. On a point of the latter place we encamped. Every Sabbath I devoted about an hour in sighing and crying after *home*. "What good can *I do*, when I reach the place of labour?" was a question that often occurred to my mind. Still we were going farther and farther from home. We were obliged, too, to do our own cooking, washing, and mending.

At last, in September, we arrived at the Aunce Bay. Here, our house was no better than a wigwam; and yet we had to occupy it as a dwelling, a school-house, a meeting-house, and a council-room.

We commenced labouring among our poor people, and those that had been Christianised were exceedingly glad to see us. Brothers Sunday and Frazer had already been among them more than a year. We began to build quite late in the fall, and although we removed a house from the other side of the bay, yet we experienced much inconvenience. We visited the Indians daily, for the purpose of conversing and praying with them. There were about thirty, who had, for more than a year, professed to experience a change of heart. As my uncle was experienced in conversing with the unconverted, I endeavoured to pursue his course in this respect. Each day we took a different direction in visiting the unconverted. We would sing, read the Scriptures, and then pray with them. Sometimes they would be impudent, and even abusive, but this did not discourage us, or deter us from our duty. By persevering, we soon discovered that the Lord was about to bless our efforts. While my uncle was visiting some four or five wigwams, I was visiting as many others—their wigwams being near us. Our influence, with God's blessing, was now felt among them. Singing and praying were their constant employments; and some of them seemed to know nothing else but the enjoyment of the truth of the Gospel, and that God can and does "forgive sin." They became the happiest of beings; their very souls were like an escaped bird, whose glad wings had saved it from danger and death...

On Sabbath evening, every converted Indian would try to induce his relatives to embrace religion, and pray in the wigwams of their unconverted relatives. These happy scenes often made me forget home.

Many of the unconverted were very revengeful; but we let them expend their vengeance on the air. One of them, *Kah-be-wah-be-ko-kay,—i.e.* Spear Maker,—threatened to tomahawk us, if we should come to his wigwam "with the white man's religion;" for, said he, "already some of my family are very sick and crazy." Notwithstanding this threat, we commenced our visits, and with no other weapon than a little calico bag containing our Testament and Hymn Book. Whenever he saw us near his wigwam (we were obliged to pass near his, in visiting other wigwams), he would run out, and grumble and growl like a bear escaping from its den for life. In this way we continued our visits, and had opportunities to converse with the family, which resulted in the conversion of all his children. In the month of February, he himself came to us, and pleaded earnestly for our forgiveness. He had gone out to hunt the marten, with his youngest daughter, who was about ten years old. While her father was preparing a marten trap, or dead-fall, as it is sometimes called, the daughter slipped behind a tree, knelt in the snow, and prayed for her father. The Lord heard her prayer. The old man "felt sick in his heart," and everything he looked at appeared to frown upon him, and to bid him "go to the missionaries, and they will tell you how you can be cured." He returned home three days earlier than he had intended. Just after day-dawn, we heard a number of Indians praying. John Southwind came in and said to us, "*Ke-ge-ke-wa-ye-wah, Kak-be-wah-be-koo-bay ke-che-ah-koo-sey*," i.e. "Your friend *Spear Maker* is very sick; he wishes you to call at his wigwam and pray with him." This was good news indeed! We went at once, and prayed with him. He could not speak, but sat sobbing and sighing over the fire. We conversed with him, and then left him; but before breakfast he entered our house with his large medicine sack, containing little gods of almost every description. He stood before us, and said, "*Ah bay, ah was ah yah mook*,"—"Here, take this." He cast the bag, or sack, down upon the floor, and wept and sobbed bitterly, saying, "I have done all I could against you, but you have been my friends. I want you to pray for me, and to burn these gods, or throw them where I can never see them." Shortly after this interview, he obtained religion, and became truly happy in the Lord...

During this spring, Brother Clark our superintendent, arrived from Sault St. Marie, with Brother William Herkimer and family, and my cousin Johnson. These were to take our places in the mission. We had now an excellent quarterly meeting. Brother Clark preached a sensible and warm sermon; my cousin interpreted it. It was a blessed time; over twenty were baptised before the services began. There was a circumstance which rendered the occasion peculiarly interesting; an old Indian woman of about eighty years came crawling to the meeting, for she was unable to walk; her name was Anna. The year before, she had travelled three hundred and fifty miles in a canoe, to be baptised by Brother Clark. She now lived about two miles from our mission, and on the Sabbath was brought to meeting in a canoe. But on this Sabbath the wind was so high that no canoe could be launched. In the morning, after the others had left, she started for meeting, and crawled over logs, through creeks, and other difficult places near the edges of rocks. Old Anna made her appearance in the house, to the astonishment as well as to the delight of all. She seated herself in front of the preacher, and listened attentively to the words of eternal life. She united with others in praising God for his mercy and goodness, especially to herself. She spoke of the day in which she was in darkness; but now she knew, by experience, that the Lord had forgiven her sins. She cared not for the *water, mud*, or *precipices*, if she could only crawl or creep to meeting, for she felt well rewarded, because the Lord blessed her. She did not, like some, fear to soil her clothes, neither was she a *fair-day visitor* of meeting. Before her conversion she was a celebrated conjuror, and a dread to the nation; every one was afraid to incur her displeasure. The last time I saw her was in 1842, and she was still confiding in the Lord.

[Kah-ge-ga-gah-bowh/George Copway, Recollections of a Forest Life or, the Life and Travels of Kah-ge-ga-gah-bowh, or, George Copway, Chief of the Ojibway Nation (London: C. Gilpin, 1851, reprinted by Canadian House, 1970), Chapters Eight and Nine, pp. 66-83]

Section B
Helping and Hindering

The following documents examine a number of themes in colonial community formation. The regulations of Quebec's Female Compassionate Society point to the need for colonial poor relief, particularly for women giving birth, while the excerpt from the diary of Adolphus Gaetz, a merchant in Lunenburg, Nova Scotia, discusses community fund-raising for a young blind woman. The address of Upper Canadian reformer John Rolph and the poem that follows it demonstrate how temperance advocates tried to build support for their cause. The final document, taken from Shadd Carey's *Provincial Freeman*, and possibly written by her, shows how different communities might clash over issues such as the representation of one community by another.

Report, Female Compassionate Society of Quebec, Quebec City, Lower Canada, 1822

Regulations
Of the FEMALE COMPASSIONATE SOCIETY, established for the relief of poor married women in their confinement:

I. The Society shall consist of a Patroness, a Lady President, and twelve Directresses, a Secretary, Treasurer and Storekeepers—Six of the Directresses shall be Canadian and six English Ladies; one of each shall take the office of Acting Directress on the first Tuesday in every second month—A general meeting of the Directresses shall be held quarterly, and a Committee consisting of five, (of whom the Lady President shall be one) shall meet the first Tuesday in every month.

II. No person shall be admitted to the benefit of the charity without a recommendation to the Acting Directress, signed by two Subscribers, or a Certificate from a resident Clergyman of the Protestant or Catholic Church.

III. The Articles of cloathing and nourishment shall be issued by the Storekeeper, on a Ticket from the Acting Directress, and the cloathing shall be returned to them within thirty days. On the Storekeeper's Certificate of their being complete and properly washed, a gratuity of half a dollar, or a suit of baby linen shall be given to the poor woman, at the discretion of the Acting Directress. If not returned within the time or not in proper order, the gratuity shall be forfeited, and the woman excluded from future relief. The allowance shall consist of

Half a pound of Tea,
Two pounds of Oatmeal,
Two pounds of Rice or Barley,
Two pounds of Sugar,
Six pounds of Beef,
Two loaves of Bread,
Two pounds of Soap,
Three suits of Baby Linen,
Two changes of Linen for the woman.

Medicine, Wine, Nutmegs, Wood and Bedding to be added at the discretion of the Acting Directresses.

IV. Medical aid will be afforded in all cases of necessity.

V. The Secretary shall enter in a book a list of the persons relieved, by whom recommended; the Acting Directress's report and the proceedings of the Committee.—Any resolves passed at a meeting shall be read to the Directress before the meeting is closed. No permanent rules shall be made but at the quarterly meeting.

VI. The Treasurer shall produce her books to the Committee the first Tuesday in every month—shall make all necessary purchases on order from the Secretary, and report them when made.

VII. It shall be the duty of Visitors to require that persons relieved, who have children of a suitable age, shall send them to their respective Churches on Sunday, and, if in their power, regularly to School. With the consent of the parents, the infants shall be vaccinated...

[Female Compassionate Society of Quebec (Quebec, 1822), pp. 14-15.
Bibliothèque de la ville de Montréal, Salle Gagnon]

View of Main Street, Yarmouth, Looking North, 1829, Sarah Bond Farish. *[Yarmouth County Museum, Yarmouth, Nova Scotia]*

The French Cathedral and Market, 1830, J.P. Cockburn. *[National Archives of Canada C2670]*

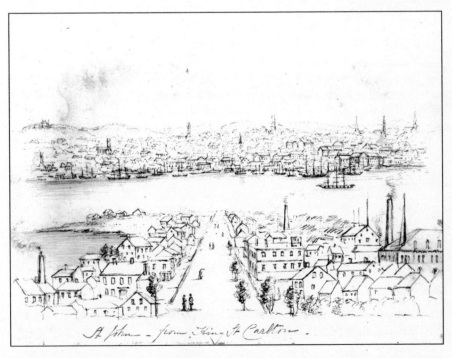

St. John (New Brunswick)—From King St. Carlton, c. 1865, Maria Frances Ann Miller. *[Nova Scotia Museum]*

Raising Money for Miss Bolman, Lunenburg, 1856

Tuesday December 11 1855

It being proposed to have a Concert for the benefit of Jane Bolman, a poor blind Girl, daughter of the late Dr. Bolman, a meeting for that purpose was held this evening, at Mrs. George Oxner's house, when several young ladies, and Gentlemen volunteered their services, accordingly several pieces of music, Sacred, and Secular, were practised.

Tuesday Jan 1 1856

This year commenced with a mild day. This evening the Concert got up for Miss Jane Bolman (the blind Girl), went off exceedingly well. Doors were to be open at 7 o'clock, but long before that time the Street leading to the "Temperance Hall," was thronged with people; it became necessary therefore to open the doors before the time appointed. Upwards of 350 persons were congregated in the Hall, and the proceeds amounted to £18.7.0., which after deducting expenses, left a balance of £16.6.3, which was handed over to Miss Bolman. The performers were,—

W.B. Lawson, bass singer.
Jasper Metzler, do.
Wm. Townshind, Clarionett.
A. Gaetz, do.
James Dowling, Bass Viol.
Wm. Smith, do., and bass singer.
Miss Jane Bolman, piano Forte, and Guitar
Miss Cossman, piano Forte.
Miss Frye; Miss Metzler, Miss Rebecca Oxner; Miss Dorothy Mooney; Mrs. Wm. Smith; Mrs . Daurey (formerly Miss Metzler); Mrs. Nichs. Zwicker.

The following were the pieces performed:-

1. Anthem from luke 2 chap. There were shepherds, etc.
2. He doeth all things well. Solo by Miss Bolman.
2. Sanctus, by Fallon.
4. Mortals Awake (Christmas piece).
5. The Little Shroud. Solo by Miss Bolman.
6. Haec Dies, by Webbe.
7. Great is the Lord.

Part 2nd

1. Home sweet Home, with Variations. piano solo by Miss Bolman.
2. The mountain Maid's Invitation.

3. Billy Grimes, Guitar accompaniment by Miss Bolman
4. Lily Bell
5. They welcome me again, Solo, by Miss Bolman.
6. Mary of the Wild Moor.
7. Give me a Cot. Solo by Miss Bolman.
8. The Grave of Napoleon.
9. The little Maid. Guitar accompaniment by Miss Bolman.
10. God save the Queen.

[C.B. Fergusson, ed., The Diary of Adolphus Gaetz *(Public Archives of
Nova Scotia, 1965), pp. 20-22]*

John Rolph's Address to the York Young Men's Temperance Society

It was thought, indeed, that the elder society in this Town had become a little *tor-pid*, and deficient in that ceaseless activity, which is the natural attribute of the noble spirit *of doing good*. Generous emulation properly belongs to youth; and attracted by the excellence of the work which their fathers had begun, the young men embarked in this enterprise of philanthropy. It is honorable that they wear their laurels meekly: and their seniors be assured, will derive the purest pleasure from this night's display of the zeal which they have happily kindled in youthful minds, and introduced into a field of moral exertion that promises in the end to yield a glorious harvest. It seems a delightful characteristic of the age in which we live, that not only all *classes* but that all ages should be taught to think, and act a part in the great Theatre of moral and religious duty, and prepare the world for regenerating changes which perhaps the youngest amongst us may even live to see...

Temperance Societies began without the aid of the Law or the patronage of the great. A few farmers and mechanics, lamenting the excesses which were humiliating and demoralizing a wide range of society, combined in the bold project of suppressing them by the power of persuasion and the influence of example... The vendor of spirits is a cold-blooded calculator... And only brighten his eye with a piece of shining silver, and he will deal out glass after glass, standing with pernicious aspect behind his well-paled retreat, he looks like a spider in his corner, which has spread his net to catch the first thoughtless beings that may chance to flitter by; and then, having got them into his toil, he assiduously infuses into them for their destruction the very venom of his decorated bar room.

[Christian Guardian, 18 September 1833]

The Benefits of Temperance

More of good than we can tell,
More to buy with, more to sell,
More of comfort, less of care,
More to eat and more to wear,
Happier homes with faces bright,
All our burdens rendered light,
Conscience clear, minds much stronger,
Debts much shorter, purses longer,
Hopes that drive away all sorrow,
And something laid up for tomorrow.

[Kingston Chronicle 20 July 1842]

Negro Songs

A correspondent, writing from Brantford, is justly incensed that a mistress in one of the public schools of that town should permit the children under her charge to sing Negro songs. The *national music*, as it is styled in the States, may do there; but it is a disgrace to Canadians and a direct insult to the coloured tax-payers who help to support such schools. It is well understood that such music tends to reconcile Americans to the "institution" of slavery; and its introduction into the public schools in this country cannot have an elevating tendency. The introduction of the Bible into the public schools is a certain bone of discord, but Yankee Negro Songs excite no fears for the morals of the young. Where are the Christians of Brantford, or what is the quality of their religion?

[n.a., possibly Mary Ann Shadd Carey, Provincial Freeman, 14 April 1855]

Portrait of Mary Ann Shadd Carey. *[National Archives of Canada, C29977]*

1. What concerns with regard to such issues as race, class, gender, and religion in colonial society do these documents reflect?

2. How did the formation of communities affect individuals? What do these documents suggest about the roles of both self-improvement and external moral regulation in colonial societies?

3. Contrast the role of religious beliefs and practices in the Yarmouth congregation with that of the Native Methodist converts discussed by Kah-ge-ga-gah-bowh, George Copway.

4. What kinds of community and individual needs do these documents suggest were being met by voluntary groups? How might the groups' own beliefs and social standings have influenced their actions?

5. What roles did colonial men and women play in the formation of communities? Did these roles differ because of gender?

READINGS

T.W. Acheson, *Saint John: The Making of an Urban Colonial Community* (Toronto: University of Toronto Press, 1985)

Donald Harmon Akenson, *The Irish in Ontario: A Study in Rural History* (Montreal and Kingston: McGill-Queen's University Press, 1984)

Marta Danylewcyz, *Taking the Veil: An Alternative to Marriage, Motherhood, and Spinsterhood in Quebec, 1840-1920* (Toronto: McClelland and Stewart, 1987)

David Gagan, *Hopeful Travellers: Families, Land, and Social Change in Mid-Victorian Peel County, Canada West* (Toronto: University of Toronto Press, 1981)

R.D. Gidney and W. P. J. Millar, *Professional Gentlemen: the Professions in Nineteenth-Century Ontario* (Toronto: University of Toronto Press, 1990)

Sheldon J. Godfrey and Judith C. Godfrey, *Search Out the Land: The Jews and the Growth of Equality in British Colonial America, 1740-1867* (Montreal and Kingston: McGill-Queen's University Press, 1996)

Janet Guildford and Suzanne Morton, eds., *Separate Spheres: Women's Worlds in the Nineteenth-Century Maritimes* (Fredericton: Acadiensis Press, 1994)

John Webster Grant, *Profusion of Spires: Religion in Nineteenth-Century Ontario* (Toronto: University of Toronto Press, 1988)

J.I. Little, *Crofters and Habitants: Settler Society, Economy and Culture in a Quebec Township, 1848-1881* (Montreal: McGill-Queen's University Press, 1991)

Marianne McLean, *The People of Glengarry: Highlanders*

in Transition, 1745-1820 (Montreal and Kingston: McGill-Queen's University Press, 1991)

Jan Noel, *Canada Dry: Temperance Crusades Before Confederation* (Toronto: University of Toronto Press, 1995)

George Rawlyk, *Ravished by the Spirit: Religious Revivals, Baptists, and Henry Alline* (Montreal and Kingston: McGill-Queen's University Press, 1984)

Peter S. Schmalz, *The Ojibwa of Southern Ontario* (Toronto: University of Toronto Press, 1991). See Chapters 5-8.

Donald Smith, *Sacred Feathers: The Reverend Peter Jones (Kahkeqaquonaby) and the Mississauga Indians* (Toronto: University of Toronto Press, 1987)

Alan P. Stouffer, *The Law of Nature and the Love of God: Antislavery in Ontario 1833-1877* (Montreal and Kingston: McGill-Queen's University Press, 1991)

William Westfall, *Two Worlds: The Protestant Culture of Nineteenth-Century Ontario* (Montreal and Kingston: McGill-Queen's University Press, 1989)

Shirley J. Yee, "Gender Ideology and Black Women as Community-Builders in Ontario, 1850-1870," in *Canadian Historical Review* LXXV, 1 (March 1994), pp. 53-73

Elite and Popular Culture in British North America

Canadian historians, often reluctant to include cultural developments in their narratives of 'the nation,' have tended to focus on political developments, economic structures and processes, and social formation. For those eager to find expressions of national cultural forms, the colonial period has frequently seemed devoid of true 'Canadian content,' since so much cultural expression came from outside the colonies, principally from Britain and America. But culture need not be defined as just artifacts such as literature, painting, photography, architecture, and clothing. It can be found in different kinds of leisure activities, in sporting events and in local fairs, and in popular institutions such as the local tavern; in these settings we can examine how colonists voiced their common interests and their differences.

After the American Revolution and on into the nineteenth century, British North Americans were both consumers and producers of a number of cultural forms. Novels, nonfiction prose, poetry, painting, serialized forms of fiction in the colonial press, theatre, and music all circulated in the Canadas and the Maritimes. The growth of the colonial press during this time was itself a major cultural and political development. That the audience for these works was primarily found in cities and larger towns is not surprising, although colonists' letters and diaries tell us that printed material, particularly newspapers and periodicals, reached the small communities and farms of literate settlers. Much of this material had come from the northeastern United States and Britain, and was part of this era's proliferation of published material for middle-class audiences. By mid-century touring theatrical companies from the U.S. and Britain also were able to perform in theatres in Toronto, Halifax, Montreal, and Saint John.

British North Americans, though, also began to produce their own written work. Loyalists in the Maritimes had penned essays, poetry, and sermons about their ordeals, and in 1824 the first novel by a 'Canadian-born' writer, Julia Hart of Fredericton, was published in Kingston. By the

1850s, accounts of life in Upper Canada and the Maritimes had appeared, written by Susanna Moodie, Catherine Parr Traill, T. C. Haliburton, and Joseph Howe. The colonies' past became of great interest to writers such as François-Xavier Garneau, Robert Christie, John Richardson, Calvin Hatheway, and John Stewart who wrote histories of the Canadas and the Maritimes. In addition to these better-known writers, there were many others, some anonymous, who published fiction, prose, poetry, and songs in the colonial press, much of this work focusing on 'Canadian' themes and content. In 1824, the Quebec Literary and Historical Society was formed, and its success inspired like-minded individuals to found the Historical Society of Upper Canada in 1861, although as a provincial organization the latter group was short-lived. The Instituts Canadiens, organized during the 1840s, also provided a forum for discussions and debates through their libraries and meeting rooms.

Print culture, of course, required a certain degree of literacy. It has always been difficult to ascertain literacy rates in British North America, but it seems that literacy was fairly high—at least so far as the ability to read and write at a basic level was concerned. And, even for those who could not read themselves, the practice of reading newspapers, pamphlets, and broadsides aloud in the home, at the workplace, and in other social settings such as taverns was quite common. In Upper Canada, the work of evangelical churches in founding Sunday Schools helped spread literacy among those who had little time and few resources to attend schools during the week. Egerton Ryerson's education reforms of the 1840s began to standardize Upper Canadian schools, replacing what had been a more eclectic body of educational institutions with a provincially-regulated system devoted to teaching moral discipline and self-control. In Lower Canada, where the Catholic Church began reasserting its power after the Rebellion of 1837-1838, educational legislation in the 1840s recognized the existing reality of two distinct patterns of schooling based on religious and ethnic differences and children from Catholic families attended schools run by religious teaching orders.

For many working-class children in all the colonies, however, full-time education was not the dominant childhood experience; instead, work (either waged or not) in order to contribute to the family's survival was usually a priority. Boys in more prosperous families could be sent to the grammar schools or Lower Canada's classical colleges, while their sisters might attend ladies' academies. It was not uncommon for wealthy colonists, such as the Cartwright family of Kingston, to send their children to the United States or overseas to be educated. During the colonial period a number of universities and colleges, often with religious affiliations, were founded;

King's College opened in Windsor, Nova Scotia (Church of England); Victoria College started in Cobourg (Methodist); Queen's College was established in Kingston (Presbyterian); and, in Canada East, McGill, Université Laval, and Bishops all began at this time.

Much of colonial cultural life was provided by amateur talent. Military officers in garrison towns, for example, often performed amateur theatricals; middle-class colonists frequently amused each other in their parlours with plays, songs, and tableaux, or reading aloud sessions. To be sure, a few painters, such as William Berczy and Joseph Légaré, have left us with portraits of elite patrons as well as scenes of colonial life. But they generally found it difficult, if not impossible, to earn their livings from their art. In 1856, William Notman opened his photography studio in Montreal, a commercial and artistic venture that proved highly successful.

Early landscape painting in British North America was more often done by amateurs, either visitors or 'gentlewomen' immigrants who had been given some training in sketching and painting. Unfortunately they tended to be more interested in reproducing an idealized vision of an English landscape than in depicting the countryside and people of British North America. The work of portrait painter Paul Kane, who travelled extensively throughout the Northwest during the 1840s–1850s and painted the area's Native population as well as pastoral and romantic scenes of the Canadas and the Maritimes, evoked great interest and enthusiasm among middle-class Canadians.

Colonists were spectators and participants in various types of popular culture, including tavern sociability, county fairs and agricultural exhibits, sporting events (cricket, lacrosse, and hockey), popular music (bands, church choirs, or missionaries' concerts with Native children singing), and storytelling and singing. For many British North Americans, political life provided much entertainment, whether it was listening to speeches at election time, watching parades, attending (or reading about) banquets to mark events such as the arrival of a new lieutenant-governor, or celebrating Queen Victoria's birthday. Material forms of culture—carving, architecture, embroidery, and quilting—reflected the diversity of colonists' racial and ethnic backgrounds. Needlework had for some time been the hallmark of an accomplished 'lady,' but for many women it was also an indispensable skill in contributing to the family economy. They produced items such as quilts; the potholders, penwipers, and antimacassars sold at church bazaars; or the banners embroidered by elite women and presented to military regiments or to fire companies.

Section A
The State's Influence

This section suggests the various ways in which the colonial state engaged in regulating and shaping colonial culture. The state might be involved in a number of ways, such as the inspection of teachers or the licensing of tavernkeepers and setting up rules for their establishments. The last document, an excerpt from the diary of Adolphus Gaetz, a Lunenburg, Nova Scotia merchant, suggests how particular political events, such as the arrival of the province's Governor, gave colonial subjects a reason for public celebrations.

Regulating Schools: A School Inspector's Report: John Gregory, New Brunswick, 13 August 1844

Teacher's Return
To be delivered to the Inspectors of Schools

County	Parish	District Name
Northumberland	Newcastle	Duglastown

Teacher's Name	Sex	Age	Married or Single	Date of Licence for Present School
Ann Stewart	female	32	Widow	15 June 1843

Average Number of Scholars in Daily Attendance	School Hours
Summer 20 Winter 21	Summer 20 Winter 21

Boys	Girls	Boys	Girls
	18		21

Books and Apparatus used in the School - Being a female School there are few Apparatees needed.

Branches of Education Taught - Reading Writing Plain and ornamental Needle work with lessons in knitting

Inspector's Return

1. Teacher's Name?   Ann Stewart

   Religious Profession of the Teacher,   Teacher and Children
   and of the majority of the Children?   Presbyterian

   How long in charge of School?   35 months

2. Contribution for the support of the   5s6 to 10 per quarter from
   Teacher beyond the Government   each scholar of the valued at
   allowance, and how paid?   £10 *perann*

3. Names of the Trustees of Schools for   Revd. William Henderson
   the Parish?   Christopher Milhart Alex.
                                                             Goodfellow

4. School House
   Public or Private Property, and by whom   By Teacher
   provided?

   Dimensions? $12 \times 10 \times 8$

   Has the Teacher any other accommodations   Lives in the same House
   connected with the School?

   Suitableness of Furniture, or Destitution of   Benches
   what may be essentially necessary?

5. Number of Children present on the Day   18 Girls
   of Inspection, distinguishing Boys and Girls?

6. Are the Children supplied with Books   By their friends but not
   including Bibles and Testaments, and in   sufficiently
   what manner?

7. Has Scriptural instruction been imparted,   Willison's "Mother's
   and with reference to any and what   Cathechisms"
   particular forms?

8. What Branches of Industry, if any, are   Needlework
   taught, distinguishing Boys and Girls?

9. What methods of discipline are resorted to; and, if any, what modes of correction and punishment for disobedience or misconduct, and whether
   rewards are given?

   Admonition and slight corporal punishment. No rewards.

10. The nature and extent of the Instruction given to the Children - the method in which imparted, orally or otherwise?

> Some of the children in this School could read tolerably well but it is doubtful whether they were taught by this Teacher. - She may be competent to give oral instructions in the arts of 'plain and ornamental needlework with lessons in knitting' but she's incompetent to teach spelling, reading, writing or Arithmetic. Her Autograph Return may be referred to in corroboration of the facts elicited at the inspection of the School. She was passed by the Board of Education under peculiar circumstances and with the view to the wants of the female children of the neighbourhood in which her School is established.

[Beth Light and Alison Prentice, eds., Pioneer and Gentlewomen of British North America, 1713-1867 *(Toronto: New Hogtown Press, 1980), pp. 75-78]*

Neptune Inn, Quebec, 1830, James Cockburn. *[National Archives of Canada, C012707]*

Regulating Taverns

Jane Oliver's Licence, 5 April 1787

Province of Quebec   Guy Lord Dorchester
Captain-General and Governor in Chief,
in and Over the Province of Quebec, &c. &c

To all whom these Presents may concern:

This licence is granted to Jane Oliver of the Parish of Quebec in the District of Quebec, to utter and sell Wine, Brandy, Rum, or any other Spirituous Liquors by Retail to be drunk out of her house. This licence to be in Force until the Fifth day of April, one Thousand Seven Hundred and Eighty Eight Provided that she the said Jane Oliver shall observe all such Rules and Regulations as are or shall be made in this Behalf.

5 April 1787   Dorchester

Regulating Innkeepers, Upper Canada, 1818

Regulations

To be observed by the Innkeepers, in the District of New Castle, made at a General Session of the Peace for the said District, on Monday the 28th December 1818, in pursuance of the Statute in that case made and Provided. -

1st That no wines or Spirituous liquors shall be sold to any Inhabitant or Inhabitants of the respective Town or Townships for when such Inn is Licensed on the Sabbath Day, Travellers of all description excepted -

2nd That no wines of Spirituous liquors shall be sold to any person or persons after Ten O'Clock at night - Travellers excepted.

3rd That Gaming shall not be allowed on any occasion -

4th That no Innkeeper shall have less than Three decent Beds in his House for the accomodation of Travellers Solely.

5th That no profane Swearing, or immodest or disloyal songs or Tales should be allowed on any pretence, and if an offender prove refractory, the Innkeeper shall take down his name and give information thereof to the nearest Justice of the Peace.

6th That every Innkeeper is to take particular notice, that the clause in a Provincial Statute respecting a Commodious yard be strictly complied with.

7th That every Innkeeper shall at all times provide proper attendance, particularly for Travellers Horses, Baggage &c -

By order of the Court
D. M. G. Rogers
Chs. J Jefrious

[Edwin C. Guillet, ed., The Valley of the Trent (Champlain Society, 1957)]

A Visit from the Governor

Monday August 9 1858 This forenoon the weather looked dull and threatening rain; notwithstanding the threatening aspects of the weather, long before 11 O'clock persons may have been seen moving through the streets dressed in their best 'bib and tucker', and soon after a general rising appeared to be taking place over the whole town. Soon after 11 O'clock a number of the principal inhabitants assembled at the house of the Customs (John Heckman Esqr.) for the purpose of proceeding to the wharf and receiving his Excellency in due form. The wharves were well sprinkled with persons of all sorts and sizes male and female, all anxiously awaiting to have a peep at the Governor. About 12 O'clock a boat was seen leaving the Steamer with a flag flying over the stern; - it was the Governor; on his landing he was welcomed by all the Gentlemen who had assembled there for that purpose; at the same moment that the Governor stepped on the wharf the first gun boomed from the Blockhouse hill, which firing continued until 19 rounds were disposed of; meanwhile his Excellency and his Lady, escorted by Ladies and Gentlemen of the town, proceeded towards the Court House; having arrived there, the Address from the inhabitants of this town was read by the Revd. H. L. Owen Minister of the Episcopal Church, and a suitable reply made by his Excellency. After preliminaries were gone through in the Court house, his Excellency and Lady, followed by Ladies and Gents., visited the Episcopal and Lutheran Churches, after which these distinguished visitors were escorted to the house of John Creighton Esq. (Queen's Counsel). After the Levee in the Courthouse, it was announced that the Countess would hold a Drawing Room at the residence of Mr. Creighton at 1 O'clock, accordingly at that hour numbers of town Ladies were to be seen moving towards the place appointed and were graciously received by her Ladyship. After the Drawing Room, the Earl and Countess accompanied by the Revd. Mr. Owen, the Sheriff (Mr Kaulbach) and other gentlemen and Ladies, rode, in wagons, as far as Mahone Bay, after returning they partook of a lunch at Mr. Creighton's, and at 5 O'clock returned on board the Steamer. The Countess observing two newly built Gigs plying up and down the harbour, offered a Purse to the winner, provided these boats would run a race. It being agreed upon to accept the offer, her Ladyship named 6 O'clock as the hour for the race to take place. At the hour named the whole population were in commotion, crowds of persons, including the lame, halt and the blind, may have been seen steering towards the wharves. At nearly 7 O'clock every thing was in readiness, pop goes the signal gun and off went the Gigs, each man rowing as hard as he could; the great multitude assembled however were doomed to disappointment; the oarsmen had scarcely made twenty strokes when one of the boats became disabled and was obliged to return, the other boat proceeded leisurely on her course to the winning point, having run the distance required the purse was handed over to them, there being no other claimants. As this in reality was no race at all, in consequence of the disabled boat having to return, the prize was much smaller than it otherwise would have been. The purse contained 10 dollars; it would have contained 40 dollars had the mishap not taken place.

[C. B. Fergusson, ed., The Diary of Adolphus Gaetz *(Public Archives of Nova Scotia, 1965), p. 43]*

Section B
The Colonists' Pleasures

Colonists participated in cultural forms in different ways. Some, like Rhoda Anne Page, wrote for colonial periodicals and newspapers. Her short story, 'An Hour in the Ice,' has a Canadian setting and uses the images of a beautiful, yet treacherous, landscape; but Page also draws upon images of domesticity and wifely devotion that would have been familiar to her audience from their reading of American popular fiction. Other colonists might have been audiences for the touring companies that arrived in the colonies, such as the anonymous 'company of play-actors' who roused William Lyon Mackenzie's ire, or the Heron family whose touring theatre company was enthusiastically received in Toronto. Attempting to attract an audience for their product, the vendors of patent medicine described in the extract from Gaetz's diary used music—a very popular form of cultural expression among colonists—with commerce. And, as the pieces on theatre and the editorial on 'Baby Shows' suggest, the question of what kinds of culture were appropriate was eagerly debated by British North Americans.

Minuets of the Canadians, 1870, J.C. Stadler after a watertint by J.C. Heriot. *[National Archives of Canada, Documentary Art and Photography Division, C252]*

An Hour in the Ice, by Rhoda Anne Page (1826-1863)

Sleigh bells! who has not listened for their glad music, when friends or dear ones have been waited for? Who has not watched for them, perhaps hopefully, perhaps anxiously, perhaps in that agony of suspense which has made their first tone seem as if struck from the very heart? Surely, if the term 'joy bells' can ever be rightly applied, it must be to those blithesome heralds of friends approaching. The very house-dog knows his master's bells, and changes his warning bark as he recognises them, to one of joyous welcome.

One evening, the close of a March day—it matters not how long ago—that merry peal might have been heard approaching the shore of one of the fairest of these island-studded 'back lakes', which, if they cannot vie with the broad Huron and Ontario in grandeur, yield in beauty to none of their mighty rivals. The winter had been severe and protracted and the lake was still frozen over, but the ice had been for some days reckoned unsafe, and in the darkness which was now fast gathering over all things, to cross upon it seemed a perilous attempt.

The person who now appeared, however, driving rapidly towards the shore, looked like one who had braved such dangers many a time before. Every thing about him, from his own blanket coat and crimson sash, to the rough but powerful team he drove, and the shaggy, good-natured collier dog which lay at his feet in the sleigh, spoke the true back-woodsman—one of those hardy, fearless, much-enduring men, who seem made to be the pioneers of civilization, clearing away forests for others to plant cities in their room.

As the night, however, closed about him, it became evident that even to him the prospect of crossing the unsound ice in the darkness was far from welcome. 'It will be as dark as pitch', said he, half aloud, 'and the ice is rotten in a dozen places. Well, there's no help for it now, and I know the road blindfold. Once safe on the other side and I've done with the ice for this winter. I promised Mary this should be the last time.'

As the young teamster—for such he was—spoke, he urged his already tired horses to greater speed, for their hoofs were splashing in several inches of water, and the ice beneath was in a state which allowed no dallying by the way.

The moon had not risen, nor could she have given him any assistance if she had, for the sky was covered with thick black clouds, and not so much as a solitary star peeped forth through the gloom. Relying, however, on his own knowledge of the track, James Gray drove on fearlessly until he was convinced that he must be nearing a point where it became necessary to make a wide *detour*, to avoid a spot where the ice was both thin and unsound. Rising to his feet in the sleigh, he peered eagerly into the darkness, to ascertain, if possible, his exact position.

Well was it for him that he did so, as by that movement he freed his limbs from the encumbrance of sundry empty bags, horse cloths, &c., which, when not required for their legitimate uses, were gathered about him as defences from the raw night air.

Even as he stood gazing wistfully forward into the black night, not daring greatly to slacken his horses' speed where the foundation on which they stood was at best so precarious, the brittle ice yielded, cracked, and finally gave way with a fearful crash, breaking into a thousand fragments, upon which the frightened animals vainly struggled to regain their footing. There were a few terrible convulsive efforts, a wild snort of terror, and then horses and sleigh disappeared in the black chasm.

As he felt the sleigh sinking under him, Gray sprang out of it, with a strong, sudden bound; but the treacherous ice again broke under him; he clung to its edge with the grasp of a drowning man, but though it supported his weight in the water, it crumbled and gave way beneath him, as often as he attempted, by its aid, to extricate himself from his terrible position. He shouted for help till his voice failed him, but no man heard or answered to his call. Then, as he literally hung there between life and death, his thoughts turned, as those of all human beings in such sore straits must, to One whose ear is never closed, and he 'cried unto the Lord in his trouble'.

'God have mercy upon me!' broke from his whitened lips, as he clutched yet closer the jagged edges of the ice which his numbed fingers now could scarcely feel. At this instant something swam by him, and a struggling and panting sound told him that his poor dog was still near him, striving, like himself, to escape from the abyss into which they had been so suddenly plunged. Even in his own utmost need the brave man could still spare a thought for his faithful friend.

Releasing, for an instant, his hold by one hand, he seized the poor creature and flung him as far as possible upon the firmer ice. He heard him shake his shaggy coat, and then, after a brief pause, as if in doubt whether to remain and share his master's fate, set off at full speed in the direction of his home. A ray of hope flashed at once through the mind of the despairing man. He well knew that Watch's appearance, alone and dripping with water, would arouse the fears of the anxious wife who awaited his return; she would probably surmise the truth, and then he felt that nothing would be left undone that human power could do, to seek for, and if possible to save him. Minute succeeded minute—time, which, to him, seemed like eternity, passed by, and still he clung with that vice-like grip to his frail support. Through his half-maddened brain all the scenes of his early boyhood, of his young, vigorous manhood, passed in rapid review; but above all rose the image of that fair, fond young wife, as he had seen her that morning standing at his side, with her baby in her arms, and forcing him to repeat, again and again, the promise that this journey across the lake should be the last. The last! the words seemed to ring in his ears; and as his brain whirled and his senses swam in that unutterable agony, a voice of fiendish mockery seemed to shriek them out— for the last time! for the last time!

...

Meanwhile, in the neat, cheerful, humble home on the farther shore, sat the expectant wife, awaiting the coming of her husband, listening eagerly for the first sound of his well-known bells. It was Saturday evening, and the small log house wore its neatest aspect, to welcome the return at once of the Sabbath and of its master. Everything, including Mary herself and her boy, was as neat and pleasant to the eye as hands could make it; and a fair object she was, as, seated by the cradle of her child, she plied her knitting-needles busily, or now and then interrupted her occupation to raise her head and listen.

Suddenly she started up, as a scratching and whining noise at the door caught her ear. She threw the door wide open, and poor Watch sprang over the threshold, wet, panting, and alone. The moon was shining feebly now, and one glance showed Mary that her husband was not there—another at the dog's dripping coat told her that her fears were but too well realized. A dizzy sickness came over her. It passed in an instant, and she stood, pale indeed as death, but with every faculty aroused, every nerve strung, to meet the need of the moment. Time enough would there be for tears and wailings, should the worst prove true; at present she must act—not waste, in idle sorrow, moments as precious as years.

Half-way between Mary's cottage and the lake, stood the rude cabin of an honest Irishman, who, with his 'boys', two stalwart young men, had come, not long before, to reside in the neighborhood. In less than five minutes Mary was on her way thither; her infant wrapped up, clasped even more closely than usual to her bosom, as if she feared to lose what might now be her only earthly treasure.

Great was the astonishment of honest Tim Martin and his household when Mary Gray suddenly appeared in their midst, (none of them ever knew exactly how she came there, for she had entered without knock or call), and still greater was the sympathy of their kind hearts, when, in accents of forced calmness, she told her story, expressing her belief that something (she could not bring herself to speak more plainly) had befallen her husband, and imploring them to aid her in her search for him. Gladly would they have persuaded her to remain in the cabin with the good dame while they went forth upon the search; but Mary was inflexibly determined to share in it.

'Ye can be of no use, darlin', said the good-hearted fellow, when the simple preparations for starting were completed; 'ye're better here by far; you, too, that slip about upon the ice like a cat in walnut shells.'

'I shall stand as firm to-night as any of you', said Mary, as she gave her child to Mrs. Martin and stepped out of the cabin. 'It's no use talking, Mr. Martin; do you think I can sit here when James is perhaps—' She could not finish the sentence, but she was understood.

With rapid steps the little party set off, followed by the dog, which, however, they lost sight of soon after they left the shore. Mary kept her promise of standing firm upon the slippery surface of the lake, for a far deeper fear had banished all timidity for herself, and it would scarcely have been felt had her path been through burning coals. Long and carefully did they search, narrowly examining every crack and fissure in the ice where it seemed at all possible that the catastrophe they dreaded but would not name might have taken place. At length one of the young men, who was a little in advance of the rest, suddenly started back with an exclamation of surprise, and lifting the lantern he carried shewed them a yawning gulf but a few feet from where they stood.

'There was no hole here this morning', he whispered to his brother; but low as was the tone in which he had spoken, it struck like a knell upon the wife's ear. With a sudden mad impulse, she sprang towards the chasm, but was instantly stopped by a strong but kindly hand. 'Ah! thin, the crathur', said the kind Irishman; 'sure ye wouldn't think of it. Think of the boy at home, jewel; why should ye lave him too?' Mary felt all that these words were meant to imply; but the sinful impulse was checked, and burying her face in her hands, tears—hot, burning tears—came to relieve her breaking heart.

Suddenly a low whine caught the ear of one of the young Irishmen, and at the same instant a faint gleam of moonlight showed him the dog at a little distance, standing at the edge of the chasm and looking fixedly downwards, apparently at the black waters below. With a mute sign to the others to keep Mary back, he crept cautiously round towards the faithful animal, and there, still clinging with that desperate, straining grasp to the rough edge, he saw James Gray, speechless, motionless, and evidently almost gone.

The lost was found, but his extrication was still not easy. The ice under the brave youth's feet cracked and strained, as, creeping as near to the edge as temerity itself could dare to go, he threw round the half lifeless body the knotted rope with which he had come provided.

A few minutes more and the now rejoicing little party were on their homeward way, bearing in their arms the rescued one, while Mary walked beside, now audibly blessing her kind true-hearted friends—now, in the silent depths of her heart, offering up thanksgivings to Him who had thus given her back her husband from the very gates of death.

My simple tale is told. James Gray is now a thriving farmer, with more gray than dark hairs upon his head. Mary has become a grave but gentle matron, with many fair young faces smiling round her, but neither has ever forgotten that awful night; and still when winter comes round again and the frozen lake lies glittering in the sunbeams, 'a sea of glass like unto crystal', do the thoughts of both travel backwards—hers to that agonizing search, and his to the untold, unspeakable sensation of that fearful Hour in the Ice.

[Maple Leaf (Montreal, 1853), Vol. 2, pp. 130-136]

Indian Wigwam in Lower Canada, 1847, Cornelius Krieghoff. Oil on canvas. *[McCord Museum of Canadian History, M19893/Musée D'Histoire Canadienne]*

Chief Maun-gua-daus, also known as George Henry c. 1847. *[National Archives of Canada, 125840]*

Two Views of the Theatre, Upper Canada

A Company of play-actors have been wiling the villagers of Niagara out of their money and time - we hope they may not come here (Queenston) and wish them no good luck if they do come.

[Colonial Advocate, 7 October 1824]

Little Agnes...really deserves a bumper...since we owe her so much for the merriment which has nightly sent so many home with cheerful hearts to happy slumbers...she is a genius of wonderful precocity, power and versatility, who excites more wonder the oftener she is seen...Fanny is a charming lively actress, always natural and 'at home,' possessed of a great gift in a voice of strength and sweetness...The powers of Miss Heron are truly astonishing. It seems impossible to imagine that the placid, unassuming, interesting girl can be so suddenly transformed into a 'bold' dashing man, and still more to see her come forth a perfect personification of a gay, rattling Irishman. Her 'Dr O'Toole' and 'Paddy Rafferty' are perfection itself...for there is a free, frank truthfulness in her delineation, that sets the real character alive before you—not an actor of an assumed part, but a reality—the man himself.

[Montreal Gazette, 18 July 1851]

A Concert for Patent Medicines, Nova Scotia

Monday July 17 1871 Open Air Concert! A new way of vending patent Medicines!!!. On Friday last a party of Men, consisting of four, arrived in town for the purpose of selling a Medicine called 'Kings instant Relief.' The method adopted by them for the sale of the article is novel and something quite new in these parts. They advertized an 'Open Air Concert' at a given hour in the Evening. At the time appointed they had their travelling waggon placed on one of the Streets most frequented, lighted with Torchlights; from the waggon, which served as their Stage, they sung a number of Comic and sentimental Songs, accompanied by a couple of Guitars; the Music attracted quite a crowd of listeners; after singing, the Chief of the party dilated on the Wonderful properties of the Medicine, the number of cures it had made, the instant relief it gave, etc. etc. The plausible stories of wonderful cures made by taking this Medicine, inwardly, and using it outwardly, induced many of the afflicted to make a purchase at the price of fifty Cents a bottle. Some of the buyers pronounce it a good article while others decry it as a thorough hum-bug; be this as it may, it is certain they have sold a very large quantity and up to the hour of their departure, which took place this afternoon, buyers were continually running for it.

[C.B. Fergusson, ed., The Diary of Adolphus Gaetz
(Public Archives of Nova Scotia, 1965)]

Baby Shows

We do not remember when the first Baby Show was got up, but we remember very well where. This bright notion originated like many other such things, in the United States. At the time we paid little heed to it. It appeared to be simply an abnormality. But by and bye other similar exhibitions were announced, which made many giggle, and a few indignant. We took our stand among the latter class, and we maintain our stand among them still. There is a propriety too in our now saying so, for the evil is spreading. We had hoped it would be confined to the land of the birth, and that the good sense, and decorum and morality of worthy Americans would speedily frown it down. It has not been so, however, and now the folly has crossed the Atlantic...

The Highland Society of Scotland inaugurated exhibitions of live stock. Then came the Royal Agricultural Society of England. Then the Royal Agricultural Improvement Society of Ireland. And so it was all right. Cattle might be improved; it was for the good of trade that they should be; therefore all classes encouraged every attempt to produce a better set of beasts. More than this, however, was not contemplated. No one supposed that the human animal was to be viewed and dealt with in the same way. But times change. This is a progressive age. Now we have 'Baby Shows.' The next thing we shall hear of will be an Association formed on the model for those already named, with special application to the human race. A 'Baby Show' is just such an organization in embryo. But this is a degradation for which Canada is not quite prepared. The United States and England have found men and women coarse enough to embark on it. Canada is yet undefiled by such abominations, and we hope ever will be.

'Baby Shows' are silly things. Imagine a man going into a crowded room, to stand there like a fool, with the poor infant in his arms! - Could any MAN do such a thing? Did any MAN ever do such a thing? We have no doubt that persons of the masculine gender have so acted, but we do not believe that any human being with the attributes of a MAN, ever so behaved himself. No MAN could do so. And what shall we say of the woman who have done so? How silly! How utterly unworthy of a wise mother is such conduct!... Standing there, simpering to every simpleton that gapes at her, with her poor insulted tricked out infant in her arms! Alas!...if such follies are to be continued or tolerated in the nineteenth century!

'Baby Shows' are indecent. A farmer intends showing a pig at the Exhibition in Cobourg. Months before, he pens it. Daily he cleans and beds it. Carefully and regularly he feeds it, selecting for the brute what will soon make it fattest. He gives his whole soul to inducing obesity. He weighs it often. He often pokes its ribs. It thrives. He puts it in a cart, goes to Cobourg, and there, before all the world, shows the fruit of his labours, and gets a prize. This is all right and proper and the pig and the man are glorified. In like manner, two individuals of the human species, male and female, wish to exhibit their offspring. They accordingly treat it like any other animal. Daily it lards over, until it lies helpless and stupefied in its mother's arms. In this condition, gorged and addled, it is carried to the Baby Show. There the parents take their place in a row of other parents, each pair of whom has its own animal to show. Is this decent? We spurn from our presences and despise the man who could act so. But we ask the woman, is this a mother's act? Does this comport with female gentleness, refinement, moral beauty? Is it thus that the child whom God gave you is by you to be mocked like the beasts which perish?

'Baby Shows' are immoral, grossly, and disgustingly, and unutterably immoral; but here we stop. In the States, the sentiment of the good is against them. In Britain, many of the Manchester public have expressed themselves disgusted. In Canada such things will never be enacted; and we hope, will never be attempted.

[The Daily Globe, *22 October 1855*]

Horse Race Among the Blackfoot Indians, Paul Kane, 1810–1871. *[National Gallery of Canada, Ottawa, 692-1]*

Mi'kmaq Beaded Box, 19th Century. *[McCord Museum of Canadian History, M196/ Musée D'Histoire Canadienne]*

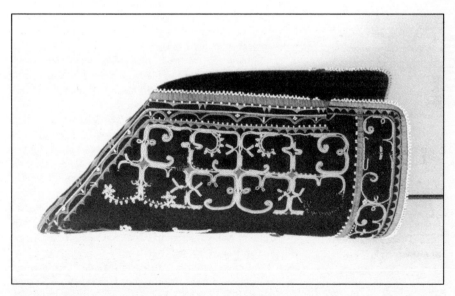

Woman's Peaked Cap, Mi'kmaq, 19th Century. *[McCord Museum of Canadian History, M8371.8/Musée D'Histoire Canadienne]*

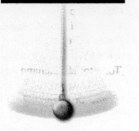

QUESTIONS

1. What types of cultural activities do these documents suggest colonists enjoyed? Can we see clear divisions between 'elite' and 'popular' culture?

2. What assumptions about female students' needs can be seen in the Inspector's report of Ann Stewart's school?

3. What do the paintings and photograph of Native peoples convey, as compared to the Mi'kmaq artifacts?

4. How can these documents help us to understand colonial identities and attitudes towards forms of cultural expression?

5. Analyze the role of the colonial state (local, provincial, and imperial) in shaping colonial culture.

READINGS

Colin Coates, "'Like the Thames towards Putney': The Appropriation of Landscape in Lower Canada," in *Canadian Historical Review* LXXIV, 3 (September 1993), pp. 317-343

Bruce Curtis, *Building the Educational State: Canada West, 1836-1871* (London: Althouse Press, 1988)

Nadia Fahmy-Eid et Micheline Dumont, *Maîtresses de maison, maîtresses d'école: Femmes, famille et éducation dans l'histoire du Québec* (Montréal: Boréal Express, 1983)

Chad Gaffield, *Language, Schooling, and Cultural Conflict: The Origins of the French-Language Controversy in Ontario* (Montreal and Kingston: McGill-Queen's University Press, 1988)

R. D. Gidney and W. P. J. Millar, *Inventing Secondary Education: The Rise of the High School in Nineteenth-Century Ontario* (McGill-Queen's University Press, 1990)

Herbert Halpert and G.M. Story, *Christmas Mumming in Newfoundland: Essays in Anthropology, Folklore, and History* (Toronto: University of Toronto Press, 1990)

Susan E. Houston and Alison Prentice, *Schooling and Scholars in Nineteenth-Century Ontario* (Toronto: University of Toronto Press, 1988)

Bonnie Huskins, 'From *Haute Cuisine* to Ox Roasts: Public Feasting and the Negotiation of Class in mid-19th-Century Saint John and Halifax,' in *Labour/Le Travail* 37 (Spring 1996), pp. 9-36

Carl T. Klinck, *Literary History of Canada: Canadian Literature in English* (Toronto: University of Toronto Press, 1976)

Patricia Jasen, *Wild Things: Nature, Culture, and Tourism in Ontario 1790-1914* (Toronto: University of Toronto Press, 1995)

Peter DeLottinville, 'Joe Beef of Montreal: Working Class Culture and the Tavern, 1869-1889,' in *Labour/Le Travail* 8/9 (Autumn/Spring 1981-82), pp. 9-40.

Mari Lu Macdonald, *Literature and Society in the Canadas 1817-1850* (Lewiston: Edwin Mellen Press, 1992)

Alan Metcalfe, *Canada Learns to Play: The Emergence of Organized Sport 1807-1911* (Toronto: McClelland and Stewart, 1987)

Ann Saddlemyer, *Early Stages: Theatre in Ontario 1800-1914* (Toronto: University of Toronto Press, 1990)

M. Brook Taylor, *Promoters, Patriots and Partisans: Historiography in Nineteenth-Century Canada* (Toronto: University of Toronto Press, 1989)

Suzanne Zeller, *Inventing Canada: Early Victorian Science and the Idea of a Transcontinental Nation* (Toronto: University of Toronto Press, 1987)

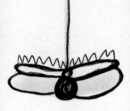

Political Unrest in the 1820s and 1830s— The Rebellion and Durham's Report

Colonial politics had never been peaceful before the War of 1812, and that did not change after the war ended. Postwar, various colonial elites consolidated their power; oligarchies, whether the 'Family Compact' in Upper Canada, the 'System' in Nova Scotia and New Brunswick, or the 'Cabal' in Prince Edward Island, maintained a close relationship with their respective lieutenant-governors, the nominal heads of colonial government who were also responsible to the imperial power. In this way, these elite groups dominated not only political issues but also the distribution of patronage appointments—a major component of colonial political life, as well as a major source of contention.

None of the political unrest and discontent in this period should be seen as completely local in origin. While local issues, such as land tenure and tenants' rights on Prince Edward Island, or the intransigence of individual lieutenant-governors in Upper Canada, gave shape to the specific direction of political protest, the 1770s to the mid-nineteenth century was a period of intense political upheaval in Britain, the United States, and France. It was also a time of revolt and rebellion in other British colonies— Ireland in 1798-99, India in 1857, and Jamaica in 1865. Although it would be misleading to characterize all British North America's political turmoil as a mass movement for 'popular democracy,' political reformers such as Louis-Joseph Papineau, Joseph Howe, William Lyon Mackenzie, and Robert Baldwin must be seen in the context of wider international calls for reform and representative government.

In Lower and Upper Canada, discontent over the colonial government's treatment of the elected assembly took place among concerns about procuring land for new farming families and tensions between more-established colonists and those who had arrived in the 1820s and 1830s. Seigneurial tenure was relevant to Lower Canadian reformers, who formed the *patriote* party in the 1820s; it was not an important issue for their coun-parts in Upper Canada. However, reformers in both provinces shared a umber of ideological concerns, such as the need for representative gov- ernment. Many of these men were also from middle-class backgrounds.

In Lower Canada, matters came to a head in early 1837 when the con- flict between elected and appointed members of the legislature brought nor- mal administrative matters to a halt; one of the most serious consequences of this impasse was the lack of funds to carry out routine affairs of state. In Upper Canada, proceedings appeared calmer since Reformers' defeat in the very violent elections of 1836. However, the extremely vocal Mackenzie expressed mounting despair about the possibility of obtaining justice from Britain, and moved closer to an affinity with American republicanism. Previously Mackenzie and more moderate reformers such as Baldwin had asked that colonial elites stop 'perverting' the operation of British parlia- mentary procedures and principles. Once the Colonial Office moved more troops into Lower Canada, the *patriotes* began organizing local-level com- mittees and rallies; they were soon joined by Upper Canadians, declaring their solidarity. As more and more troops were moved into Lower Canada and fighting broke out, Upper Canadians grasped the opportunity to attempt seizing Toronto, and another uprising broke out in the Western District of Upper Canada.

In the wake of the imperial government's suppression of the Rebellion, many fled to the United States where some continued to oppose Britain with border raids. In Lower Canada, the government declared mar- tial law, suspended *habeas corpus*, and conducted mass arrests. Upper Canada saw the execution of two rebel prisoners, Samuel Lount and Thomas Matthews, the arrest of many others, and the transportation of some to Australia. Related to all of these events was the post-Rebellion expansion of the British North American state during the 1840s, as well as Lord Durham's report and the unification of the Canadas; Lower Canada became Canada East, and Upper Canada was now Canada West.

While the Atlantic colonies did not experience armed rebellion, they witnessed their own degrees of political unrest. The Newfoundland House of Assembly, established in 1832, was the site of a number of conflicts and stormy, indeed violent, elections, marked by religious, regional, political, and economic discords; by 1842 Britain had amalgamated the Assembly and exec- utive councils in order to impose both calm and imperial control. In 1830s Prince Edward Island, the 'escheat' movement fought for an end to the system of land grants by the Crown. This practice had created absentee landlords and a large group of dissatisfied tenants. Upon being rebuffed by Britain, members of the escheat movement then called for responsible government, a demand that led to the enfranchisement of a larger group of male voters.

Timber rights and revenues were a major source of conflict in New Brunswick where, like their counterparts in the Canadas and Nova Scotia, reformers opposed patronage appointments to government offices. In many of the colonies, the reform press (*Le Canadien* in Lower Canada, the *Colonial Advocate* in Upper Canada, and the *Novascotian* in Halifax) played a critically important role in generating attacks on administrations and helping to mobilize reform sentiment. The vast majority of these debates over reform, however, were generated by middle-class, Euro-Canadian men. Although some women participated in the various movements at the local level and were affected by the events of 1837-38, the reform leadership was overwhelmingly male and saw 'democratic' politics as being the domain of literate, property-owning, primarily Anglo-Celtic, men.

Section A
Reform and Its Aftermath

This opening section deals, first, with the colonists' dissatisfaction with their government in the Canadas. 'Instructions to the Agents' outlines the concerns of reformers such as Louis-Joseph Papineau, who, with a number of other, like-minded men, wrote to reformers who were travelling to England to petition the British government for the redress of their grievances against the colonial administration. The next document is Upper Canadian reformer William Lyon Mackenzie's draft constitution—plans for a new government run by the colonists without British supervision. The final two documents examine the aftermath of the Rebellion. The list of some of the *patriotes* transported to Australia in 1840 gives us clues about these men's socio-economic backgrounds (they were also, with two exceptions, Roman Catholics). The letter from the Canada East politician Marcus Child, who represented the province's Eastern Townships in the legislature, suggests how turbulent colonial politics were even after the government's suppression of the Rebellion.

Instructions to the Agents, 6 Feburary 1828

The Committee of Montreal is convinced that:

The agents of the province, unanimously chosen by a deputation of most influential people brought together from all parts of the province, will satisfy its expectation, whether or not they receive instructions as to the manner in which they must fulfil the honourable mission entrusted to them.

The intention of the Committee of Montreal in offering the agents the following instructions is not so much to prescribe what they will have to do as to express the full confidence of the Committee in their enlightened patriotism by leaving to their discretion the choice to act conformably to the wishes of the said Committee or to deviate from them as the welfare of the country at the service of which they have been for so many years and to which they are still devoting themselves on this occasion, will seem to require.

Once in England, they will ascertain, more easily than could be done here the views of His Majesty's ministers, whom they will beg to punish the oppressive acts which we have suffered under the present provincial administration and to give us some new and necessary securities against the repetition of such acts under future administrations.

Our constitution has been modelled on the constitution of the mother-country. It must have been administered, almost invariably, in disagreement with its spirit and its principles as, a condition which would be impossible in England, the Executive here has constantly been able to treat public opinion with scorn; to ignore the demands of the people; to refuse a great number of most useful bills, adopted by the representative body; to become with impunity the slanderous accuser of the representatives of the country; to waste revenues and to apply them, for many consecutive years, without legal appropriation; to compose the Legislative Council and Courts of men so subject to the Executive that the name is the only distinction between the different bodies and, in reality there is only one power under different forms. The result of such a striking error is that this unfortunate country has been governed in the midst of dissensions such as England would experience if we could imagine there a King with the influence of his Executive Council only and without the medium of the House of Lords, trying to govern and, for more than thirty years, being always in minority in a House of Commons which would have with the nation as much weight and influence as the House of Commons actually has. From an order of things so contrary to the rights of the British subjects would result an irrepressible hate between two parties; the party of the courtiers holding itself only with the help of a host of bribed outsiders, and that of the nation, suffering to the point of slavery or being forced to fight. What would be the most absurd fiction for England is too real in its colony. Consequently, the great majority of the inhabitants is convinced that a change of the actual composition of the Legislative Council is essential. To have the Governor in Chief recalled and deservedly punished would not prevent the return of the excesses he committed if the same men were allowed to set the same traps for his successors.

The most serious of the numerous complaints exposed in the request of the district of Quebec and in the one from the districts of Montreal and Three Rivers, also in the resolutions adopted in the different counties, is the radical defect in the composition of that body (the Legislative Council) where the Executive calls whoever appears to them suitable, without any qualifications being required as security against subjection or bribes on the part of legislators so appointed for life. The agents will bring to light the good reasons we have for complaining in this regard. They will set forth the necessity of naming in the Council new men, worthy of the esteem of both the Government and the public and who, thanks to their principles and land holdings should be interested in the security of the one and the progress of the other. All other remedies would only be palliatives against evils which would revive at the first opportunity...

We consider our Constitutional Act the most solemn and sacred pact that the Imperial Parliament could have given us to guarantee the preservation of our rights. It is an agreement to which the Parliament is only one of three interested parties. The inhabitants of Lower Canada, numbering to-day more than five hundred thousand and redoubling their number every second decade, and those of Upper Canada whose population is to-day nearly two hundred thousand and which has redoubled every decade, are equally parties to this agreement. Their safety is troubled and public faith violated if one of the parties to the agreement injures the interests or changes the condition of either of the two others without her knowing it or against her will. Consequently, any proposal or attempt to replace this act by another one must be opposed with unrelenting firmness by the agents who will maintain that any changes not provided for nor contained in the Constitutional Act itself can be legalized only by the free assent of the people of the two provinces, self-expressed or voiced by their representatives.

If however, the agents were of the opinion that some changes proposed in Parliament are evidently in the interest of the country, while insisting that such measures be adopted only with the assent of the province, they will, without fail, commend all liberal ideas which would tend to secure, for the continental colonies of America, a greater degree of freedom than is so far enjoyed and a greater influence in their local government, such as is called for by the rapid increase of the population, the equal distribution of property amongst the inhabitants and the proximity of the United States of America which we should have no cause to envy.

Any request to unite the Legislatures of the two provinces, heretofore refused with indignation by the inhabitant and now proposed by the governor and the weak faction surrounding him, must be rejected and denounced as a crime on the part of a person sent to administer the laws and constitution of our country as they are enacted and established, who has the indecency to declare openly that for a long time and unknown to us he has begged the Government of the Empire to make changes which we do not want.

All idea of division of the province of Lower Canada, under the pretext of providing Upper Canada with a port of entry, or under any other pretext, must be rejected as a shameful spoliation of the rights attached to private properties which, for the Canadians, would become insecure or rather, surely destroyed and encroached upon, if a certain number were placed under the government of a province whose great majority of legislators, administrators and judges, would ignore every principle of French civil laws under which the properties have been acquired, transferred and administered in Lower Canada. It would be like compulsorily separating children of the same family to whom had been guaranteed, on the strength of capitulations, treaties and the acts of 74 and 91, the right to keep perpetuate and defend together their religion, laws, customs and property, are exposed to suffer by this project of iniquitous subdivision of Canada, heretofore divided in two provinces, in the avowed plan which afforded strict justice maintaining for the subjects of French origin in Lower Canada their laws and their private privileges, as long as they would be attached to them, and for the subjects of British origin, their laws and private privileges, in another province, Upper Canada...

The agents will form lasting connections with some printing firm, where they will have published, as they think fit, their observations to the English public on the state of the province; that practice will be maintained after their return to Canada by sending extracts of provincial papers to be reprinted. They will inform the Committee of the measures to be taken and of the sums necessary to put into effect this useful project.

Montreal, February 6th, 1828.

Frs Ant. LaRocque, V.P.
Louis Roy Portelance, V.P.
F.A. Quesnel
L.J. Papineau
R. Kimber
Jocelyn Waller
H. Heney
Daniel Tracey
J.B. LeBourdais
J. Berthelot
J. Raizenne
Frs. Ricord
Simon Valois
P. Ritchot
A.V. Morin
A. Jobin
L.M. Viger

[Neilson Papers, Vol. 6, pp. 53-60]

William Lyon Mackenzie's Draft Constitution, 15 November 1837

To the Convention of Farmers, Mechanics, Labourers, and other Inhabitants of Toronto, met at the Royal Oak Hotel, to consider of and take measures for effectually maintaining in this colony, a free constitution and democratic form of government.

The Committee appointed to report a popular Constitution, with guards suitable for this Province, in case the British system of government shall be positively denied us, respectfully submit the following draft:

WHEREAS the solemn covenant made with the people of Upper and Lower Canada, and recorded in the Statute Book of the United Kingdom of Great Britain and Ireland as the 31st Chapter of the Acts passed in the 31st year of the reign of King George III., hath been continually violated by the British Government, and our rights usurped; *And Whereas* our humble petitions, addresses, and protests and remonstrances against this injurious interference have been made in vain— WE, the people of the State of Upper Canada, acknowledging with gratitude the grace and beneficence of GOD, in permitting us to make choice of our form of Government, and in order to establish justice, ensure domestic tranquility, provide for the common defence, promote the general welfare, and secure the blessings of civil and religious liberty to ourselves and our posterity, do establish this Constitution:

1. The legislature shall make no law respecting the establishment of religion, or for the encouragement or the prohibition of any religious denomination.

2. It is ordained and declared that the free exercise and enjoyment of religious profession and worship, without discrimination or preference, shall forever hereafter be allowed within this State to all mankind.

3. The whole of the public lands within the limits of this State, including the lands attempted, by a pretended sale, to be vested in certain adventurers called the Canada Company (except so much of them as may have been disposed of to actual settlers now resident the State), and all the lands called Crown reserves, clergy reserves and rectories, and also the school lands, and the lands pretended to be appropriated to the uses of the University of King's College, are declared to be the property of the State, and at the disposal of the Legislature, for the public service thereof. The proceeds of one million of acres of the most valuable public lands shall be specially appropriated to the support of Common or Township Schools.

4. No Minister of the Gospel, clergyman, ecclesiastic, bishop or priest of any religious denomination whatsoever, shall, at any time hereafter, under any pretence or description whatever, be eligible to, or capable of holding a seat in the senate or house of assembly, or any civil or military office within this state.

5. In all laws made, or to be made, every person shall be bound alike—neither shall any tenure, estate, charter, degree, birth, or place, confer any exemption from the ordinary course of legal proceedings and responsibilities where unto others are subjected.

6. No hereditary emoluments, privileges, or honours, shall ever be granted by the people of this State.

7. There shall neither be slavery nor involuntary servitude in this State, otherwise than for the punishment of crimes whereof the party shall have been duly convicted. People of Colour, who have come into this State, with the design of becoming permanent inhabitants thereof, *and are now residents therein,* shall be entitled to all the rights of native Canadians, upon taking an oath or affirmation to support the constitution.

8. The people have a right to bear arms for the defence of themselves and the State.

9. No man shall be impressed or forcibly constrained to serve in time of war, because money, the sinews of war, being always at the disposal of the Legislature, they can never want numbers of men apt enough to engage in any just cause.

10. The military shall be kept under strict subordination to the civil power. No soldier shall, in time of peace, be quartered in any house without the consent of the owner, nor in time of war, but in a manner to be prescribed by law.

11. The Governor, with the advice and consent of the Senate, shall choose all militia officers above the rank of Captain. The people shall elect their own officers of the rank of Captain, and under it.

12. The people have a right to assemble together in a peaceable manner, to consult for their common good, to instruct their representatives in the legislature, and to apply to the legislature for redress of grievances.

13. The printing presses shall be open and free to those who may wish to examine the proceedings of any branch of the government, or the conduct of any public officer; and no law shall ever restrain the right thereof.

14. The trial by Jury shall remain for ever inviolate.

15. Treason against the State shall consist only in levying war against it, or adhering to its enemies, giving them aid and comfort. No person shall be convicted of Treason unless on the testimony of two witnesses to the same overt act, or on confession in open court...

16. The real estate of persons dying without making a will shall not descend to the eldest son to the exclusion of his brethern, but be equally divided among the children, male and female.

16a. The laws of Entail shall be forever abrogated.

17. There shall be no lotteries in this State. Lottery tickets shall not be sold therein, whether foreign or domestic.

18. No power of suspending the operation of the laws shall be exercised except by the authority of the Legislature.

19. The people shall be secure in their persons, papers and possessions, from all unwarrantable searches and seizures; general warrants, whereby an officer may be commanded to search suspected places, without probable evidence of the fact committed, or to seize any person or persons not named, whose offences are not particularly described, and without oath or affirmation, are dangerous to liberty, and shall not be granted.

20. Private property ought, and will ever be held inviolate, but always subservient to the public welfare, provided a compensation in money be first made to the owner. Such compensation shall never be less in amount than the actual value of the property.

21. *And Whereas* frauds have been often practised towards the Indians within the limits of this State, it is hereby ordained, that no purchases or contracts for the sale of lands made since the _____ day of _____ in the year _____, or which may hereafter be made with the Indians within the limits of this State, shall be binding on the Indians and valid, unless made under the authority of the legislature.

22. The legislative authority of this State shall be vested in a General Assembly, which shall consist of a Senate and House of Assembly, both to be elected by the People...

29. In order to promote the freedom, peace, and quiet of elections, and to secure, in the most ample manner possible, the independence of the poorer classes of the electors, it is declared that all elections by the People, which shall take place after the first session of the legislature of this State, shall be by ballot, except for such town officers as may by law be directed to be otherwise chosen...

43. No member of the legislature, who has taken his seat as such, shall receive any civil appointment from the governor and senate, or from the legislature, during the term for which he shall have been elected.

44. The assent of the Governor, and of three fourths of the members elected to each branch of the legislature, shall be requisite to authorize the passage of every bill appropriating the public monies or property for local or private purposes, or for creating, continuing, altering, or renewing any body politic or corporate; and the yeas and nays shall be entered on the Journals at the time of taking the vote on the final passage of any bill.

45. The members of the legislature shall receive for their services a compensation to be ascertained by law and paid out of the public treasury.

46. Members of the General Assembly shall, in all cases, except treason, felony, and breach of the peace, be privileged from arrest during their continuance as

such members; and for any speech of debate in either House, they shall not be questioned in any other place.

47. No Judge of any Court of law or equity, Secretary of State, Attorney General, Register of Deeds, Clerk of any Court of Record, Collector of Customs or Excise Revenue, Postmaster of Sheriff, shall be eligible as a candidate for, or have a seat in, the General Assembly...

58. The Executive power shall be vested in a Governor. He shall hold his office for three years. No person shall be eligible to that office who shall not have attained the age of thirty years.

59. The Governor shall be elected by the People at the times and places of choosing members of the legislature...

61. The Governor shall have power to grant reprieves and pardon, after conviction, for all offences, except in cases of impeachment.

62. The Governor shall nominate by message, in writing, and, with the consent of the Senate, shall appoint the Secretary of State, Comptroller, Receiver General, Auditor General, Attorney General, Surveyor General, Postmaster General, and also all judicial officers, except Justices of the Peace and Commissioners of the Courts of Request, or Local Courts.

63. The Judicial Power of the State, both as to matters of law and equity, shall be vested in a Supreme Court, the members of which shall hold office during good behaviour, in District or County Courts, in Justices of the Peace, in Courts of Request, and in such other Courts as the Legislature may from time to time establish...

66. A competent number of Justices of the Peace and Commissioners of the Courts of Request shall be elected by the people, for a period of three years, within their respective cities and townships...

69. The Governor and all other Civil Officers under this State, shall be liable to impeachment for any misdemeanor in office...

80. No religious test shall ever be required as a qualification to any office or public trust under this State.

[Constitution, *15 November 1837*]

Execution of Lount and Matthews. *[National Archives of Canada, C1242]*

Patriotes Transported to Australia, 25 February 1840

Name	Age	Reads & Writes	Neither Reads nor Writes	Married	Single	Children	Occupation
Allay, Michel	38		x	x		one boy	joiner
Bechard, Théodore	49		x	x		2 boys, 8 girls	farmer, veterinarian
Bergevin, Charles	53		x	x		7 boys	farmer
Bigonesse, François	49		x	x		3 boys, 4 girls	farmer
Bouc, Guillaume	48	x		x		2 boys, 5 girls	clerk
Bourbonnais, Désiré	20		x		x		blacksmith
Bourdon, Louis	23	x		x		1 boy 1 girl	farmer, merchant's clerk
Bousquet, J B	44	x			x		farmer, miller
Buisson, Constant	30	x		x		3 girls	blacksmith
Chevrefils, Gabriel	43		x	x		1 boy 5 girls	farmer
Coupal, Antoine	50		x	x		2 boys, 10 girls	farmer
Defaillette, Louis	48		x	x		4 boys, 4 girls	farmer
Ducharme, Leon	23	x			x		merchant's clerk
Dumouchelle, Joseph	47		x	x		3 boys, 1 girl	farmer
Dumouchelle, Louis	42		x	x		2 boys, 4 girls	farmer
Dussault, Louis Guérin	37	x		x		3 boys, 1 girl	merchant
Gagnon, David	29		x	x		2 girls	joiner & carpenter
Goyette, Jacques	49		x	x		2 boys, 1 girl	mason & farmer
Goyette, Joseph	29	x		x		2 boys, 1 girl	carpenter
Guertin, François	44	x			x		carpenter & joiner
Guimond, Joseph			x	x		1 boy 2 girls	carpenter & farmer
Hebert, Joseph-David	49		x	x		3 boys, 2 girls	farmer
Hebert, Joseph Jacques	42		x		x		farmer
Huot, Charles	53	x			x		notary public
Laberge, Jean	36		x	x		4 boys, 2 girls	farmer
Lanctot, Hyppolite	23	x		x		2 boys	notary public
Langlois, Etienne	26		x		x		farmer
Languedoc, Etienne	22		x		x		farmer
Lavoie, Pierre	49		x	x		8 boys, 1 girl	farmer
Leblanc, David Drossin	36	x		x		5 boys, 1 girl	farmer
Leblanc, Hubert Drossin	32	x		x		2 boys, 2 girls	farmer
Lepailleure, François Macervie	33	x		x		2 boys	house painter
Longtin, Jacques	59		x	x		4 boys, 8 girls	farmer
Longtin, Moyse	21		x		x		farmer
Marceau, Joseph	34	x		x		2 boys, 1 girl	farmer & weaver
Morin, Achille	25	x			x		clerk
Morin, Pierre Hector	54	x		x		3 boys	mariner
Mott, Benjamin	43	x		x		2 boys, 3 girls	farmer
Newcombe, Samuel	65	x		x		3 boys, 2 girls	surgeon
Papineau, André	40		x	x		3 boys, 4 girls	blacksmith
Pare, Joseph	48	x		x			farmer
Pinsonnault, Louis	40		x	x		2 girls	farmer
Pinsonnault, Paschal	27		x		x		farmer
Pinsonnault, René	48		x	x		3 boys, 4 girls	farmer
Prevost, François-Xavier	30	x		x		2 boys, 1 girl	innkeeper
Prieur, François-Xavier	24	x			x		merchant

Name	Age	Reads & Writes	Neither Reads nor Writes	Married	Single	Children	Occupation
Robert, Théophile	25		x		x		farmer
Rochon, Jérémie	36	x		x		5 girls	wheelwright
Rochon, Edouard Pascal	39	x		x		1 boy	carriagemaker, painter
Rochon, Toussaint	30	x		x		2 girls	carriagemaker, painter
Roy, Basile	42		x	x		6 boys	farmer
Roy, Charles	52		x	x		5 boys, 3 girls	farmer
Roy, Joseph	24		x	x		1 girl	labourer
Thibert, Jean-Louis	52		x	x		2 boys, 1 girl	farm labourer
Thibert, Jean-Marie	38		x	x		2 boys, 2 girls	farm labourer
Touchette, François-Xavier	32	x		x		1 boy 3 girls	blacksmith & farmer
Trudelle, Jean Baptiste	34		x	x		4 boys,1 girl	farmer & joiner
Turcot, Louis	36	x		x		5 boys, 1 girl	farmer

[Information taken from Stanley B. Ryerson, Unequal Union: Confederation and the Roots of Conflict in the Canadas, 1815-1873 *(Progress Books, 1973)]*

Politics in the United Canadas, 1840s

Marcus to Lydia Child, 7 November 1843

Kingston 7th Nov 43

My Dear wife

This morning snow is falling and is already 4 inches deep but not cold—and very calm—last night we went thro. in committee with the Judicature Bill for Lower Canada—And should have reported it, but for two things, one of which is the police clause the other the fees to Lawyers—I am willing to allow them a fair compensation for their services but I think their fees have been too high, and should be reduced—On Thursday, it will come on again and I have the consent of the Honel mover of the Bill—to reduce the atty's fees—twenty-five percent— Yesterday the Legislative Council met and adjourned for the want of a speaker also—Marney was returned from the Co. of Hastings—with a great multitude of his supporters and they escorted him to the very door of the House, and then set up such a yelling, that it was hardly possible to hear what was going on in our House, however, I perceived the noise growing less and less strong, and after some little time, it ceased entirely—and truly glad was I to get rid of the noise and confusion and brutal violence of upper Canada Toryism—I am disgusted with the coarse and ill bred habits of their people, and were we, in Lower Canada, to be compelled to adopt them, by the union; I would, for one, say let us immediately separate—We, Anglo Saxons of Lower Canada are not sensible how much our manners are affected by being in contact with the polished politeness of our French fellow subjects, and yet, being contrasted with them we appear less so, than when put in contrast, with the habits of our own race, in Upper Canada and the United States.—These remarks may be better understood by you if the noise & rude conduct of the scene in front of our door, could have been witnessed by you, last night—I am disposed to let them go to heaven their own way; and that they may all get there, is my fervent prayer.—Our list of Orders is long and we shall now be working closely and I see no good reason why we should not be thro. by the 15 Dec.r next—I am inclined to get leave of absence just before the close of navigation and come home. I am quite well and enjoy myself well I have had many compliments for my views on the subject of Emigration—The debate, as I expected, is going the rounds of all the papers in upper Canada, and it is quite likely that it will be published in most of the papers in Lower Canada—and also in the United Kingdom...

Your Husband
Marcus Child.

[J.I. Little, ed., The Child Letters: Public and Private Life in a
Canadian Merchant–Politician's Family, 1841-1845
(Montreal-Kingston: McGill-Queen's University Press, 1992), pp. 97-98]

Section B
The Effects upon Women

In this section of documents, we look at the different experiences of women in the political unrest of the 1830s, and their reactions to these events. Some women, such as Amelia Harris and Jane Ellice, sided with the government, in part because of their family backgrounds. Harris was from a Loyalist family and was a member of elite society in London, Ontario; Ellice was married to a colonial official whose father, Edward Ellice, was a merchant-banker, politician, and proprietor of the seigneury, Beauharnois, where Jane and her husband were taken captive by the *patriotes*.

The writings left by Eugenie Saint-Germaine Cardinal and Maria Wait suggest a contrasting perspective—that of women who husbands fought for the reform cause. Cardinal's petition to Lady Colborne, wife of Sir John, governor of Lower Canada at this time, was unsuccessful. Her husband, Joseph, was hanged the next day. Wait's letter to Sydenham was part of her campaign to have her husband, Benjamin, returned to Canada from Australia, where he had been transported for his part in the Upper Canadian rebellion. The couple were reunited shortly after, when Wait escaped.

Our Kitchen Is Turned into a Guard Room

Amelia Harris to Henry Becher, London, 14 December 1837

...after you left information was sent here yesterday that the Rebels are assembling in Oakland about 9 miles this side of the Grand River today the London Militia were called out & they have marched for St. Thomas...there was a meeting of the Radicals that is all the leaders in the middle of the night preceding our news of their defeat at Toronto. Mr Harris urged & entreated to have them arrested but his answer oh no we must remain quiet, we must not irritate them...had I been a man and clothed with any authority they should all have been lodged in the cells to keep them out of harms way on Saturday night when the news came the Rebels were defeated Col. H—said dont Hurrah do not Hurrah, it will excite them but I am happy to say it was not in his power to suppress the true British feeling...last Sunday during the hours of Service the children & myself were employed in running Bullets I was rather abashed when Mrs Cronyn came in & caught me at it but she displayed a pair of Bullet Moles [moulds] she had just borrowed & was going home to employ her self in the same way we have been several times notified that Mr Harris was to be shot & our house burned Mrs Cronyn was notified that her house would be Burned as it was church property but she need not be alarmed as her & the children would be allowed to walk out—very civil...our kitchen is turned into a guard room and it appears to me it is not the same world we where living in when you left us I hope god will protect my husband & restore him safe to us how happy shall I be to see you all together again enjoying the blessings of home & peace...

[Colin Read and Ronald J. Stagg, eds., The Rebellion of 1837 in Upper Canada *(Ottawa: Carleton University Press, 1985), pp. 321-323]*

Is It in This Way You Punish?

Eugenie Saint-Germaine's Petition to Lady Colborne

20 December, 1838, Chateauguay, Lower Canada
To Lady Colborne,
My Lady,

You are wife and you are a mother! A wife, a mother, under the stress of hopelessness, forgetting the rules of etiquette, which separate her from you falls at your feet, trembling with fear and a broken heart, to ask you for the life of her beloved husband and the father of her five children! The death sentence is already signed! The fatal hour approaches!

Tomorrow, alas! Tomorrow! God! O God! I have no strength left to face such a horrid end. I would be stronger if another life did not depend on mine. But my miserable child will never see daylight! He will die with his mother under the gallows where his father, who deserves a better destiny, will have perished. O God! Is it in this way that you punish? No, No forgive me that blasphemy. Only men have recourse to such vengeances. Only men kill the innocent with the guilty...guilty...What am I saying? And my husband, of what was he pronounced guilty? The most that one could say is that a bit of excitement, a weakness perhaps, led to his ruin...By character very timid, mixing little in society, — not enjoying life except amidst his family who adore him—he took no part in the trouble which preceded the final scenes of disaster. It was in his house that he was surprised by a sudden and unexpected movement. He did not make victims, on the contrary, he himself is a victim. That is his only crime, and for that crime, (if it is one), hasn't he already atoned? Hasn't he already suffered too much? And during the time of his imprisonment in his solitary prison, neglected by all, we, your humble petitioner and her children, haven't we suffered sufficiently for him? Formerly, happy with him, although in a humble condition, were we not banished from our home by the torch and brutality of an incendiary? Were we not stripped of everything, even our clothes? Weren't we obliged to live on bread provided by the goodness of God, and given to us by charitable persons, who for the love of God, take pleasure to distribute it to those who are in need. And you, My lady, what heavenly treasure has not been placed in your hands? Have you not been given an immense influence over the heart and the spirit which today governs our destiny? Act like those charitable individuals of whom I have spoken, use this treasure for your eternal advantage, for that of the husband who you cherish and for your children who are your glory and happiness. Oh! humanity is certainly not banished from this land by vengeance, humanity must have taken refuge in the hearts of women, without a doubt, in the hearts of mothers, such as yours. Humanity will speak from your lips—it will be persuasive, eloquent, irresistible —it will stop the sword of death, ready to slay all the victims, it will bring joy to the hearts of all the wretched who dread tomorrow's dawn, it will be heard even in heaven and will be written to your credit in the book of life.

I have the honor to be

My lady

Your, very humble and afflicted servant

Eugenie Saint-Germain, wife of Joseph-Narcisse-Cardinal.

[*Beth Light and Alison Prentice, eds.,* Pioneer and Gentlewomen of British North America, 1713-1867 *(Toronto: New Hogtown Press, 1980), pp. 165-166]*

Maria Wait, on Behalf of Her Husband, Benjamin, and Other Transportees, to Governor Sydenham

18 September 1840

I can assure you, sir, you need be apprehensive of no violent outbursts of feeling, or what is commonly termed a *scene*; and which gentlemen are generally (perhaps properly) fearful of, when approached by females, in supplication, on subjects especially of the painful nature of the one which brings me to your Excellency for mercy; but two years and a half of mental agony, have so inured me to suffering and trial, that feeling has almost ceased to flow in its natural channel.

[Benjamin Wait, Letter's from Van Dieman's Land *(1841)]*

An English Gentlewoman and the *Patriotes*
Excerpts from Jane Ellice's Diary

Sunday, 4 November 1838

It's an odd thing that last night when we went to bed both Tina & I said we thought something was going to happen. Twice I awoke Edward, because we heard the dogs barking & the *Turkeys* making a noise. About 1 o'clock a messenger came saying there was a disturbance at *Châteauguai* & several British farmers had fled from the Canadian rebels. E. E. had hardly come to bed again, when we thought we heard a *hallo*. He opened the window & listened, but all was still, & just as he was getting into bed a *yell* like the *Indian war cry* burst close to the house & guns fired at the same moment; struck the house on all sides, breaking the windows &c. Edward jumped *into* his clothes & drag'd Tina and I *en chemise*, without shoes or stockings, down stairs and put us thro' a trap door into the cellar. The house was surrounded on all sides; Edward & Mr. Brown taken prisoners, and were carried off we knew not where, leaving Tina & I alone, *en chemise*, in the middle of a group of the most *'Robespierre'* looking ruffians, all armed with guns, long knives & pikes, without a single creature to advise us, every respectable person in the village being taken prisoner. What a day we passed, sitting hand in hand, in the midst of a heap of confusion, comforting each other & praying for protection to Him who orders all things well. But it was a severe trial. The ruffian looking men coming in every now & then, quite drunk. In the evening the Priest came to see us & we got leave to come to his house. What a wretched day, & yet how much worse might it have been. Poor Edward, how miserable he must be about us...

Tuesday, 6 November 1838

We begin to wonder what we are to do for provisions, every thing in the shape of food having been taken from the *Seigneury* house. I had an audience with one of the rebel Capts. who gave me a written permission allowing me to kill some of *my own sheep* & cattle & to get some milk from some of my 25 *cows*, now in possession of the enemy. The ground is covered with snow & blowing a gale so that we knew no Vessel could come to our assistance. They examined the baggage of all the prisoners & Mr. Masson opened and read all their letters, most of which were private but *some* were about military affairs. He translated the contents for the benefit of the *Capts.* They took no money from any one however. One of the Guards at our bed room door today was a horrid looking man with a villainous expression that made me *creep*. How is all this to end? If Edward was with us I should be much more easy...

Friday 9 November 1838

Another day of watching & wondering, & we may put out our eyes & imagine what we like, but all to no purpose. The Guards have taken it into their heads to be doubly severe for a variety (of reasons) & would neither open our shutters or allow us to get milk or any other thing else from the house — the *Wreck* as I call it. However we did at last get the shutters open...

Indeed a prisoner's life is not an agreeable one. Besides our prison is so crowded—62 people—some of them insufferably *dirty* , and squalling children in abundance, all *spoilt* and some of them sick...The Curé is as kind as possible. What spoilt children there are in the world. Mrs. Usher, with all her scolding, has as good a specimen of a spoilt child in her *'Mary Jane, my child'* as one could wish to see. And as to Mrs. Brown's *Annette*, were it not for Georgine with her bandaged eye, the little monkey would be quite unmanageable, but this ugly look-ing eye inspires her with a little wholesome terror. She is a quick, clever child and knows how to manage her Mama. She amused me often when I felt much more inclined to cry than to laugh.

Monday, 12 November 1838

Saw the funeral of the poor soldier who was buried with military honours, all the wild Glengarry men following & and the bagpipes playing a Lament, a mournful, touching sight. Walked thro' the village which nearly made me cry, & thro' the Seigniory house which nearly made me sick. Such destruction & devastation I never imagined. Picked up some of the bullets which might have shot us the other night...Yesterday Edward returned safe and sound and I feel like a different person. All last night he laid on his Buffalo [skin] to be beside our Stretcher telling us of his adventures & narrow escapes. Those treacherous *Captains* who told [me] he was quite comfortable & in want of nothing! They did not tell me that all long week he was shut up in a very small room with other people, where every ray of light & breath of air was excluded, so that they did not know night from day. He never took off his clothes and was obliged to sleep on the floor. He was badly fed, until the nuns taking compassion upon the poor prisoners sent them up a number of little things, which however the rebels cut up into the smallest pieces in case any written paper should have been inserted. Sometimes too they were very insolent, coming up to him: "Vous êtes un chien Anglais, mais moi je suis français. *Allons*, ne parlez pas, vous étes trop *béte* pour savoir parler." He heard the order given that if any of the prisoners approached the shutters they were instantly to be fired at, and the guards kept their fingers on the locks of the guns to be ready to fire as desired...On Saturday, they were marched off on their way to Napierville, where their greatest force was assembled. They were all tied, hand & foot in pairs, and thrown like sheep in a cart, but upon one old man begging he might drive Edward in his Cart and his promising not to make his escape, he was untied...When they were in the wood talking of battle & murder and how they could do the most mischief, an unfortunate pigeon flew past, upon which they all set off full cry in pursuit of it, every one as *eager* in the chase as if they had nothing else to think of. The Canadians are certainly very like the french in many ways...They then took the prisoners further into the bush as fast as they could until they came to a small clearing and a shanty where they found some more of the rebel army. Edward and all the other prisoners, at that moment, felt convinced that they could only have been brought to that lonely place for one purpose—to be shot. The rebels then consulted amongst themselves what was to be done with the prisoners, as they must for the present fly from the troops. Some few asked Edward if he would promise (were he released) that they should not be punished by the Govt. Edward answered that if he did promise such a thing, the Govt. would not regard it in the least, and *that* they might know very well. One old villain then harangued them upon the necessity of putting him to death, and a most brutal, violent speech. Many others joined him. They then commenced fighting amongst themselves. Fortunately Edward persuaded one of their principal leaders to listen to reason & convinced him that it would be more for his interest to let him go than to put him to death. He then used his influence, and in the confusion that ensued, the Prisoners made their escape, & tho' quite unacquainted with the country, by following the course of the river, they contrived to find their way thro' the snow, cold & rain and about the middle of the night arrived in *La Prairie,* where a small detachment of Grenr. Guards were quartered...

Montreal, Wednesday, 14 November 1838

Georgine & all the servants & 'butin' have as yet none of them made their appearance. I hope they have not again been taken prisoners. Called upon Lady Colborne at the Govt. house, which had been made so comfortable for Lord Durham. She was very anxious to hear all that had befallen us during our imprisonment. Every one believed that Tina had been wounded & it was mentioned as a fact in every newspaper...*The Glengarries* boast is *'No fear of our being forgotten, for we've left a trail six miles broad all thro' the country,'* People are less afraid of the Indians than of the Glengarries. They seem to be a wild set of men —very like what one imagines *old* Highlanders in Scotland & equally difficult to manage. One of them who rowed us over to Lachine told me that the *houses they had spared in coming down the country, they would surely burn in going back.*

Montreal, Sunday 18 November 1838

E. not well enough to go to church, tho' I do not think he caught any *Hospital disease.* Tina & I walked there and were a quarter of an hour too late...News came of an engagement at Prescott. *40* of our men killed & one officer and the *Yankees* have got possession of a stone house & mill, wth. cannon.

> *[Patricia Godsell, ed., The Diary of Jane Ellice*
> *(Montreal: Oberon Press, 1975), pp. 130-152]*

QUESTIONS

1. What political ideologies can be found in the Committee of Montreal's Instructions and Mackenzie's Draft Constitution? Are there common beliefs shared by the authors of these documents? Are there any significant differences?

2. What does the quantitative information in the chart of transportees tell us about this group of men? What is missing from such information?

3. What does Marcus Child's letter to his wife tell us about the political situation in the Canadas after the Rebellion?

4. Compare the documents left by women whose lives were affected by the Rebellion. What differences, based on their social and political situations, emerge from these writings? Did they share any common ground?

5. Using Jane Ellice's diary, suggest the attitudes that British officials might have held toward French-Canadians during this period.

READINGS

Janet Ajzenstat, *The Political Thought of Lord Durham* (Montreal and Kingston: McGill-Queen's University Press, 1988)

Murray Beck, *Joseph Howe Volume I: Conservative Reformer, 1804-1848* (Montreal/Kingston: McGill-Queen's University Press, 1982)

Rusty Bitterman, "Women and the Escheat Movement: The Politics of Everyday Life on Prince Edward Island," in Janet Guildford and Suzanne Morton, eds., *Separate Spheres: Women's Worlds in the 19th-Century Maritimes* (Fredericton: Acadiensis Press, 1994)

Philip A. Buckner, *The Transition to Responsible Government: British Policy in British North America, 1815-1850* (Westport, Co.: Greenwood Press, 1985)

S.D. Clark, *Movements of Political Protest in Canada, 1640-1840* (Toronto: University of Toronto Press, 1959)

Jane Errington, *The Lion, the Eagle, and Upper Canada: A Developing Colonial Ideology* (Montreal/Kingston: McGill-Queen's University Press, 1987)

John Garner, *The Franchise in British North America, 1755-1867* (Toronto: University of Toronto Press, 1969)

Allan Greer, "1837-38: Rebellion Reconsidered," in *Canadian Historical Review* LXXVI, 1 (March 1994), pp. 1-18

——————. *The Patriots and the People: The Rebellion of 1837 in Rural Lower Canada* (Toronto: University of Toronto Press, 1993)

Gertrude Gunn, *The Political History of Newfoundland, 1832-1864* (Toronto: University of Toronto Press, 1964)

J.K. Johnson, *Becoming Prominent: Regional Leadership in Upper Canada, 1791-1841* (Montreal/Kingston: McGill-Queen's University Press, 1989)

A.B. McKillop and Paul Romney, eds., *God's Peculiar Peoples: Essays on Political Culture in Nineteenth-Century Canada* (Ottawa: Carleton University Press, 1993) (essays of S.F. Wise)

David Mills, *The Idea of Loyalty in Upper Canada 1785-1850* (Montreal/Kingston: McGill-Queen's University Press, 1988)

Cecilia Morgan, *Public Men and Virtuous Women: The Gendered Language of Religion and Politics in Upper Canada, 1791-1850* (Toronto: University of Toronto Press, 1996)

S.J.R. Noel, *Patrons, Clients, Brokers: Ontario Society and Politics, 1791-1896* (Toronto University of Toronto Press, 1990)

Fernand Ouellet, *Lower Canada, 1791-1840: Social Change and Nationalism* (Toronto: McClelland and Stewart, 1980)

Colin Read, *The Rising in Western Upper Canada, 1837-8: The Duncombe Report and After* (Toronto: University of Toronto Press, 1982)

Ian Ross Robertson, ed., *The Prince Edward Island Land Commission of 1860* (Fredericton: Acadiensis Press, 1988)

Gordon T. Stewart, *The Origins of Canadian Politics: A Comparative Approach* (Vancouver: University of British Columbia Press, 1986)

John Manning Ward, *Colonial Self-Government: The British Experience, 1759-1856* (Toronto: University of Toronto Press, 1976)

Brian Young, *George-Étienne Cartier: Montreal Bourgeois* (Montreal/Kingston: McGill-Queen's University Press, 1981)

The State in British North America—Law, Crime, and Popular Protest

Prior to the 1830s, colonial governments attempted to establish various administrative and regulatory bodies, especially in Lower Canada. Every colony had its courts, judiciary, and penal institutions, although their effectiveness in both enforcing the law and responding to community concerns varied widely from province to province, and region to region. But after the Rebellion, the state in British North America expanded its powers considerably, particularly in Upper Canada where it codified and regulated to a much greater extent areas such as local government, commerce, banking, and transportation.

The colonial state also broadened its abilities to regulate the conduct of individuals and communities by implementing initiatives such as the formation of the police in Lower Canada, and the standardization of primary education in Upper Canada. As well, the state helped create definitions of masculinity and femininity and the appropriate 'domains' for each gender, through legislative or administrative mechanisms—deliberately excluding women from the electoral franchise in the Canadas, for example. Such definitions were also shaped by ideologies of race and class. The state's 1851 definition of 'Indian' status was based on patrilineality, or descent through the male line, and this particular kind of gendered philosophy was continued in the Dominion government's 1869 decision that Native women who married non-Native men were no longer 'Indians.' And, as professional organizations in law and medicine—many of their members themselves participants in the state—sought to expand their powers to regulate entry, membership, and codes of conduct and practice, they too defined themselves as Anglo-Celtic 'gentlemen.'

One very obvious area of state expansion was the penal system. The opening of Kingston Penitentiary in 1835 was the clearest example of the state's desire not merely to punish, but also to reform the characters of those considered 'deviant.' A similar impulse saw the foundation of many other institutions in colonial cities and towns—insane asylums, Houses of Industry, hospitals, orphanages, and industrial schools. Such establishments were shaped by the desire of middle-class reformers to extend humanitarian aid, as well as to regulate and reshape moral character so that other groups in society might meet with the reformers' own standards of 'appropriate' behaviour—displaying thrift, industry, and sobriety. The family, reformers came to feel, lacked the resources to deal with some forms of deviant behaviour as well as a specialized institution aimed at specific moral problems could.

Whether colonial societies were more 'immoral' or more 'violent' than the home country is a question that is difficult to answer. Certainly, violence occurred in a number of places in British North America. From the beginning of European settlement, Native peoples were vulnerable to violence at the hands of white colonists; newly freed Blacks might be subjected to kidnap attempts (some successful) by those paid by white slaveholders to return them to slavery. Elections were often very violent; secret ballots were not used and rival factions used a number of tactics, from providing alcohol, to physical intimidation, on would-be voters at polling places. Taverns, while furnishing space for sharing news and community organizing, could also erupt into spontaneous outbursts of verbal and physical violence, as could workplaces such as the lumber camps of the Ottawa valley and the canals of the Niagara area. Violent behaviour was not confined to working-class men; upper- and middle-class men still used duelling as a means of settling political and social disputes. Although evangelical and other reform groups attempted to promote companionate marriages and more compassionate treatment of children by their parents, husbands and parents, particularly fathers, were still granted formal control over their wives' and children's persons.

What some might regard as violence, others saw as popular protest. Historians have pointed to the role that religious, class, and ethnic tensions played on the Welland canals, in the Shiners' wars in the Ottawa valley, and in New Brunswick Orange riots. In 1837, the British writer Anna Jameson witnessed the efforts of black Upper Canadians, armed with stakes and stones, to prevent escaped slave Solomon Moseby from being extradited from Niagara to his former master in Kentucky. Two of Moseby's defenders were killed by prison guards trying to stop the wagon in which he was being transported, while Moseby vanished into the crowd. Jameson sympathized with the crowd's intentions. Another gentlewoman writer, Susanna Moodie, saw in another form of community protest—the *charivari*—lawlessness and 'mob rule.' In Moodie's account of an Upper Canadian *chari-*

vari, the principal target, a black man who had married an Irish woman, was tormented until he died from exposure. *Charivari* was an older type of protest and means of enforcing community standards; its targets ranged from the inter-racial marriage of Moodie's experience to wife-beaters and, in Lower Canada, to unpopular political figures during the Rebellion.

Section A

Blacks, Natives, and the Law

In this section, we examine Blacks' and Natives' experiences with the law, crime, and violence in British North America during the early 1790s. These range from the arrest of an anonymous black woman, accused of infanticide, and described here by Liverpool merchant Simeon Perkins, to the murder of Chief Snake in Upper Canada and the arrest of two soldiers accused of the crime, to the kidnapping of Chloe Cooley, a black Upper Canadian.

The various authors of these documents do not tell us what became of the people involved—the soldiers accused of murdering Chief Snake or the woman accused of infanticide—and court records from this period are often sporadic and incomplete. We can wonder, though, what Perkins meant by the 'unforseen Difficulties' that might have proved embarrassing—could he have been alluding to the (possibly white) paternity of the woman's dead infant? And what might have become of Chloe Cooley?

She Carried It to the River, and Laid It in the Tides
Excerpts from Simeon Perkins's Diary, 1793

Liverpool, May 13, 1793
Sir

I wrote you the 29th of April on the Subject of the Black woman in Gaol, to which [I] beg leave to refer you, Since which she has appeared to [be] in distress of mind, and Some people were of [the] Opinion that she wished to Confess the Truth. Mr. Thomas, and myself this morning called, at the Gaol, & she said she wished to confess all the Truth, on which she was taken out, & examined by Mr.

Thomas, in my presence. She now Says that the Child that was found, was her Child, that She was delivered of it in her Chamber about a fortnight, as Near as she can tell before she was taken up; that there was not a person present when she was delivered, and that she did not perceive any signs of Life in it, after it was Born; that She carried it to the River, & laid it in the Tides, but not in ye water; that She did not do anything to Murder it. She appeared perfectly calm & I am included to think she did Speak the truth. I thought it my duty

to acquaint you of the Circumstance, and would wish His Excellency may, as Soon as convenient, determine in regard to Appointing a Court, but not to have the Judges residing here. — In haste I am, Sir,

> Yr. Most Obed. Serv.
> S.P.
> Sampson Salter Blowers, Esq.

● ●

Liverpool, May 17, 1793
Dear Sir

as to the Black Girl, I am sorry to find you are doubtful whether any one will come from Halifax. I must repeat my request, that the Judges to compose the whole Court, may not be appointed in this County. there is Strong prejudices in the minds of Some people. the girl is a Slave to Benajah Collins, Esq. Mr Johnstone is too old to act in Such a Capacity, and in Short, we have not Gentlemen in this County Suitable, or Competent for the purpose. I must therefore Earnestly Intreat his Excellency will be pleased to Send a Judge from Halifax. I wish there may be a fair, and Impartial Tryal, which is not So likely to be the case in Such a Small Settlement, and under Such Circumstances as this. unforseen Difficulties may arise in the Course of the Tryal which may Embarris the Court. the Jury may need to be Instructed in Some points that are beyond our capacity. for all these reasons, I most Sincerely pray that my request may be granted. I should be very sorry to refuse any service Government thought proper to appoint me, to, but in this case I shall be under the disagreeable Necessity of excusing my Self if Nominated, as I am conscious I cannot execute the Business with propriety, & Satisfaction to the publick, or to my Self.

> Simeon Perkins
> Honble. Sampson Salter Blowers, Esq.

[C.B. Fergusson, ed., The Diary of Simeon Perkins *(Champlain Society, 1978)]*

The Murder of Chief Snake, 1792

J. White[1] to Simcoe

Kingston, Upper Canada, July 3rd, 1792

An Inquisition having been taken on the 2d day of July upon the body of an Indian Chief named Snake, by John Howard Coroner of the District of Mecklenburgh [later Midland] in this Province, and this day presented to me; certifying that the said Snake was wilfully murdered in the evening of the 25th day of June last past by some person or persons to the Jurors then unknown. But which Inquisition upon the oaths of Jonathan Sills, John MacMahon, John Culbertson, Sampson Bagnet and James Simpson amongst others then and there sworn, strongly induces a suspicion that five persons therein mentioned of the names of—Walter, Thomas Picard—Mitchell—Nabbing and—Robertson or Robinson, Soldiers in his Majestys 26 Regiment are guilty of the said Murder.

As his Majesty's Attorney General for this Province I am to request that your Excellency will give such orders as may to your Excellency seem most proper, for the apprehension of the persons above mentioned that they may be bro't to Trial according to the due course of law.

Chief Justice William Osgoode[2] to Simcoe

Kingston July 27, 1792

The Soldiers supposed to be concerned in the homicide of the Indian arrived here early this Morning—They had been Examined before Mr Cartwright and two of them are fully committed for Tryal—As it is necessary that fifteen Days should intervene between the date of the precept to the Sheriff to Summon a Jury and the Return thereof, and as the precept ought to recite the Commission—I am to pray of Your Excellency to authenticate both my Commission as Chief Justice and also that for the Oyer and terminer of this District and to order them to be returned by the first Opportunity that the Seal of the Province may be affixed thereto.

Osgoode to Simcoe (Private)

Kingston, July 27, 1792

From what I have heard of the Evidence likely to be produced against the two Soldiers. It is probable that one or both may be convicted—I therefore wish to receive Your Excellencys Command respecting the Execution of their Sentence or the Respite thereof should it unfortunately become my unpleasing Duty to pro-

---

[1] John White, Attorney General for Upper Canada, 1791, member of the Legislative Assembly for Leeds and Frontenac, 1792

[2] William Osgoode (1754-1824), first Chief Justice of Upper Canada, a member of the Legislative Council and its Speaker. In 1794 he became the Chief Justice of Lower Canada.

nounce it.—Towards the Close of Your Instructions Your Excellency will find what Latitude is given to the Governor's Discretion in Cases of Conviction for a Murder. By Law in Crimes of this sort Execution must take place the day next but one to the Conviction.

I shall wait a reasonable time for the Return of the two Commissions but in Case of unusual Delay will issue the precept to the Sheriff presuming that they will arrive before the Expiration of the Fortnight—& always taking care to be in time to pay my Duty to You before the twelfth of September...

[Richard A. Preston, ed., Kingston Before the War of 1812 (Champlain Society, 1964), pp. 357-258]

The Kidnapping of Chloe Cooley

As told to Lieutenant-Governor John Graves Simcoe, Chief Justice William Osgoode, and Peter Russell at a meeting of the Executive Council of Upper Canada, March 1793.

Peter Martin a negro attended the Board for the purpose of informing them of violent outrage committed by one Fromond (William Vrooman), an Inhabitant of this Province, residing near Queenston on the person of Chloe Cooley, a negro girl in his service by binding her violently and forcibly transporting her across the river, and delivering her against her will to certain persons unknown, to prove the truth of his allegation he produced William Grisley. William Grisley an Inhabitant near Messissague point in this province says: that on Wednesday evening last he was at work at William Fromonds near Queenston, who in conversation with him told him he was going to sell his negro wench to some persons in the States, that in the evening he saw the said negro girl tied in a rope that afterwards a boat was brought and the said Fromond with his brother, and one Venevry forced the said negro girl into it, that he was desired to come into the boat which he did, but did not assist, or was otherwise concerned in carrying off the said negro girl, but that all others were, and carried the boat across the river, that the said negro girl was then taken and delivered to a man upon the bank of the river by Fromond that she screamed violently, and made resistance, but was tied in the same manner, as when the said William Grisley first saw her, and in that situation delivered to man; William Grisley further says that he saw a negro at a distance, he believes tied in the same manner, and has heard that many other persons mean to do the same by their Negroes.

[Michael Power and Nancy Butler, Slavery and Freedom in Niagara (Niagara Historical Society, 1993)]

Section B
Extra-Legal Justice

The following documents examine colonists' attempts to regulate community life through what historians have dubbed 'extra-legal' means of justice. The first tells us of *charivari* in Lower Canada, as seen through the eyes of a British emigrant. The next documents deal with the practice of duelling in Upper Canada. The final document in this section relates an incident involving the Irish Catholic labourers who built the Welland Canal.

As these documents demonstrate, colonists did not always agree on what was 'proper' behaviour and what was violent lawlessness. The colonial state reacted with varying degrees of severity to what it considered unacceptable, although members of the working class and immigrants were more likely to be treated harshly than gentlemen obeying the 'code of honour.'

A Source of Great Annoyance to Some, and of Amusement to Others

Edward Allen Talbot on the *Charivari*, Montreal, 1821

Another custom, which is called *charivari*, is frequently a source of great annoyance to some, and of amusement to others, of the Lower Canadians. When a young man marries a widow, or a young woman a widower, the surrounding inhabitants collect together, and, providing themselves with rams' horns, old kettles, tin trumpets, and a variety of other equally obstreperous instruments of war and music, proceed to the house of the newly-married couple, and demand the usual fee extorted on such occasions. The amount of the sum is always regulated by the wealth or poverty of the parties on whom it is levied; and if it not be immediately paid, their dwelling is closely blockaded, and a perpetual fire of scandal is kept up for several hours, under cover of an ancient usage. the unmusical band is all the while playing *the Cuckold's March*, and other offensive and appropriate airs. If the sum demanded is not produced on the first application, the same proceedings are renewed on the second and every subsequent night; until the besieged parties, tired of the din of war, capitulate or surrender.

The sum demanded on these occasions sometimes amounts to £100; and though the Magistrates frequently endeavour to put a stop to these lawless assemblies, their exertions seldom produce any good effect...

While I was in Montreal in the winter of 1821, a widow lady of considerable fortune was married to a young gentleman of the Commissariat Department; and a night or two after the celebration of their nuptials, £100 was demanded, in the way I have described, from the bridegroom, for the support of the 'Female Benevolent Society,' of which his lady was herself the patroness. The following is an account of the proceedings which took place on the occasion:

"The evening of the nuptials, and the succeeding one, were decorously suffered to pass tranquilly; but that of the third day brought before the mansion of the happy couple a large body of friends and acquaintances, assembled for the purpose of congratulation, merriment, and requiring the usual donation for the benefit of the poor. To surrender on the first summons, is neither customary, nor would be magnanimous: The party, therefore, invested the house in form, and, after a few hours' blockade, retired.— On the succeeding evening, operations were resumed, and the besiegers, considerably re-inforced, rendezvoused at the Old Market. Amongst them were 40 masqueraders, equipped as Turks, Persians, &c. exhibiting the usual proportion of nose grotesqueness of profile, but lamentably deficient in those demons and calibans whose longitude of tail and other comely decorations used formerly to have so happy the effect. After some time spent in arrangement, those personages, at the head of a dense column of about 500, commenced their march to the martial harmony of cow-horns and trumpets; made the tour of a part of the city, and returned into St. Paul-street. So far matters had gone on peaceably; but when they arrived opposite Mr. Wragg's hard-ware store, they were accosted by the deputy chief-constable, at the head of his myrmidons, who commanded them to retire—an order to which they only replied by an emphatic vociferation of the word 'stick!' Dismayed by this ominous monosyllable, the posse opened to the right and left, and the column passed sternly through. Thence it pursued its former route, and was moving down St. Francois Xavier-street, when lo! at the corner of the Canada Bank appeared the watch. Here the same command met with the same reply; but the guardians of the night, unable to brook the defiance, rushed in amongst the throng and were seizing several persons, when a most tremendous scuffle began; stick clashed with stick; wooden sabre encountered watchman's baton, in irreverent disregard of the G.R. marked on it; and knock-down blows were distributed with a liberality and skill truly Hibernian, while the narrow street echoed with the shouts of the combatants. Superior numbers, however, decided the contest; and the watch, after a courageous resistance of a few minutes, fled in disorder, some prudently to their homes, and the rest with more spirit to the watch-house. The victors pursued the latter to the gates of their fortress; and, learning that some of their comrades had been picked up by a party of constables who had hung on their flanks and rear, sent forward a flag of truce to demand their liberation; but the valiant garrison, hastily fortifying themselves, returned a refusal and prepared for desperate defence. At this moment, that obnoxious personage the chief constable, who had entered by a postern to encourage his troops unfortunately popping out his head to reconnôitre, was recognized: the besiegers uttered a dreadful yell of hostility; and the forlorn hope, bearing a piece of timber by way of battering-ram, assailed the gate, under cover of a shower of snow-balls, pieces of wood, and such other missiles as the spot afforded. Under the energy of the attack, the door was soon reduced to splinters; the defenders were chased into the yard in the rear; and luckily escaped from their pursuers, by jumping over a fence with extraordinary agility, communicated by the urgency of the occasion. The prisoners were triumphantly released, and the *chari-*

variers, after a few tours, dispersed.—The fourth day a special session of the Magistrates was held, and a proclamation issued, prohibiting a recurrence of the *charivari*, and inviting all well-disposed persons to unite with the municipality in its suppression, if attempted. This, nevertheless, did not prevent an assemblage much more numerous than on the proceeding evening; the party remained unmolested; but something serious might possibly have occurred, had not the bridegroom flung open a window and capitulated.—On the fifth day, £50 was in consequence presented to the Female Benevolent Society, thus adding another to those acts of beneficence and charity which the bride is in the daily habit of performing. The *charivari* principally consisted of mercantile and professional men; thought afterwards augmented by other persons, attracted by the novelty of the spectacle and a desire of amusement. Several individuals were afterwards apprehended.

> *[Edward Allen Talbot,* Five Years' Residence in the Canadas: Including a Tour Through Part of the United States of America *(London: Longman, Hurst, Rees, Orme, Brown and Green, 1824)]*

Refusing to Meet a Challenge to Duel

J.T. Williams, Justice of the Peace, Newcastle District, to Lieutenant-Governor Sir John Colborne

May 8, 1832

May it please your Excellency,

I did myself the honor on the 5th Inst to address your Excellency; since that date acts of aggression of greater publicity have here taken place, Mr. Bullock finding the most insulting language and opprobrious epithets could not induce me to violate the laws, has now exhibited Placards in every direction subscribed with his name denoucing me as a Poltroon and a Coward...as he did that human nature under such tortuous accusation could not refrain from the...insult by an appeal to Arms. Educated in the same school as your Excellency, imbibing the same principles of honor from a sister profession[1] the natural feelings of Man would be to repel the aspersion by mortal combat, and such I admit to your Excellency would have been my conduct at an earlier stage of my existence when surrounded by my Associates in Arms, but your Excellency, time with me has shed a dim lustre over these acts of violence—reflection has taught me to fear God rather than Man, that the Laws of Honor (so called) are in direct opposition to the Human and Divine Law, and that I might set to to appeal to them. It cannot fail to call forth your Excellency's just reprehension when it be considered by whom, and at what time this aggression is committed, by a Man sworn to maintain and preserve the Peace by your Excellency's commission[2]; at a time when Your Excellency issues a

---

[1] Williams had been a naval officer and commanded a vessel on Lake Ontario.

[2] Bullock, William's adversary, was also a J.P.

Royal proclamation commanding all Men to observe a General Fast, a day of humiliation and prayer supplicating Almighty God to (watch over) the impending danger over these Colonies; and shall I on that sacred day in direct violation of that Proclamation, and against the considers of my better judgment imbue my hands in a Brother's blood—God forbid.

[PAO, Upper Canada Sundries, 66902-3]

Conflict at the Welland Canal

On the 12th, instant the Steamer 'Admiral,' having on board a highly respectable party consisting of between five and six hundred 'Conservatives' from Toronto, and the steamer 'Eclipse,' from Hamilton, with a less number on board, passed up the Niagara to Queenston, where the passengers landed, and proceeded to the Falls either by the railroad or by vehicles of different descriptions provided for the purpose. It being determined that the laborers on the Welland Canal intended to leave their work for the purpose of attacking the 'Conservatives,' a detachment of the Royal Canadian Rifles, under the immediate command of Col. Elliot, left this post by the 'Transit' before the other boats passed up.

It had been ascertained the day previous what the intentions of the canal laborers were; and Mr. Merritt and their own priest exerted themselves to dissuade them, but all to no purpose. Some mischievous persons had told them that the Conservatives were Orangemen—that their pleasure excursion was nothing more or less than a procession in honor of the day—that Orange banners would be displayed, and that the Pope and O'Connell would be burned in effigy. It is hardly necessary to say that none of these things had been contemplated—but if they all had been even perpetrated—we do not see in what worse position a single laborer would have been placed.

Other mischievous persons, it is said, had told the 'Conservatives' that the Steamers would be attacked immediately after they reached Queenston; and it is added that they had prepared arms for the purpose of resisting aggression. If this was true, the arms remained on board.

Preparations were made by the local authorities for the prevention of breaches of the peace, and we are happy to say they proved sufficient to prevent bloodshed. The parties of Rifles stationed at St. Catharines, Thorold and Chippewa, were marched to the Falls, and Messrs. Merritt and Thorburn, M.P.'s; Colonel Delatre; Messrs. Gibson, T.O. Street, Turney and other Magistrates, were early in attendance and actively employed. On the arrival of the first car containing the 'conservatives' the inmates (chiefly ladies and children) were terrified at discovering a vast body of laborers, computed to number 200, drawn up in a line extending from the Ontario House downwards, and headed by a man in a blue coat with a drawn sword in his hand. A large portion of the laborers were armed with muskets and other fire arms; others carried pikes, pitchforks, &c., and the rest brandished shillelaghs.

One of the cars was pelted with stones, and we understand that more than one of the inmates, was severely bruised, and a good deal of insulting language was used towards the 'conservatives.' Col. Delatre read the riot act, and ordered the laborers to disperse, on pain of being charged by the military if they did not do so within a limited time. Fortunately, they did do so, and to the presence of the Riflemen and the firmness of the magistrates it is owing that a great effusion of blood was prevented.—The 'conservatives' dined at the Pavilion, and enjoyed themselves till towards evening, when they returned to Queenston and there embarked. We saw them at the wharf here where they stopped a few minutes, and certainly they seemed to form as respectable and well conducted a party as one could desire to see under the banner of conservatism. They left our wharf amid the cheers of numerous spectators, and reached their respective ports without accident. The 'Admiral' was excessively crowded, and the 'fair sex' and children seemed to form a majority of her passengers.

These canal laborers, and those who guided their movements, would have been much better employed in attending to their own proper duties, than in manifesting such a disposition as they proved themselves to be actuated by on the 12th July. Every one who was at the Falls was of the opinion that but for fear of the personal injuries they would themselves receive from the rifles of the military, they would have attacked the unarmed men, women, and children, composing the pleasure party; and the weapons they had provided themselves with showed what sort of attack was the one they meditated. It is inconceivable to us how a body of men can entertain such a feeling of deadly animosity towards their fellow creatures as these men evidently do; it seems so unnatural, as well as so opposite to all ideas that can possibly be formed of what duty to God and man demands, that we cannot comprehend it. There is the fact, however, notwithstanding its incomprehensibility.

From an account in the Hamilton *Gazette,* evidently written by an eye-witness, we copy the following particulars:—

> When the cars were about two miles from the Falls, they were stopped by these ruffians—about 100 knelt down on one knee and levelled their guns; one or two only fired, and the balls whistled by. They then threw stones; one boy was much hurt, and a gentleman of Toronto, who formerly lived in Hamilton, was severely struck on the side, and for a time could scarcely walk. When returning home at night, a man in a waggon was twice fired at; on the second fire, he leaped out and seized the ruffian; and as he was firing the pistol, knocked his arm in the air. I spoke to some of the men, and took one of their rifles; it was loaded, and had a cap on. Bills were placarded that O'Connell was to be burnt in effigy. A gentleman from Boston, who came across from the other side, observed to a lady that he had expected to see every thing peace-

able and quiet, but the most he had met were barbarians. The Riot Act, I believe, was read, and the soldiers having charged, the rioters finding they had no one to fight but defenceless men and women, or the armed soldiers, they at length returned by waggons to the Canal, and other places from which they had come, at distances of from five to thirty miles.

[The Niagara Chronicle, 17 July 1844]

Section C
Gender, Morality, and Public Order

This next section of documents looks at colonial societies' efforts to regulate gender relations through parental control of marriage, attempts to prevent women from adopting a masculine identity, and the control of prostitution by the state or voluntary societies. Many of the documents demonstrate the state's concern with gender, morality, and public order—for example, Mary Palmer, the woman who cross-dressed in Halifax, disturbed the peace as well as pretending to be a man, and was also dressed as a member of the military, which represented the power of the imperial government. The documents here, like those in previous sections, also suggest that colonists often contested middle-class and state definitions of appropriate gender roles and norms.

An Elopement in Bridgewater, Nova Scotia

Thursd. 11th Sept 1855

Married this evening about 9 o'clock, at Bridgewater, by the Revd. Henry Deblio, James B. Weddleton, formerly of Yarmouth, to Miss Caroline Jost, daughter of H.S. Jost of this place. This was an 'Elopement extraordinary.' The parties having been intimate with each other for about two years, the young gentleman at last resolved to lead the young lady to the Hymenial Altar; such however met with strong opposition from the father of the bride, and more particularly from her step-mother, who, like the generality of step-daughter, and which caused a deal of disagreement between them while living together. Things however were not to remain so, and the young folks, spite all opposition from father and step-mother, were determined to be united in the bonds of holy Matrimony. Accordingly, every thing being previously arranged, the young lady left her fathers house about 4 O'clock this afternoon, and walked about two miles from town, where her lover awaited her with a chaise and pair; as soon as she reached the carriage she jumped in and off they drove to the young man's residence at Bridgewater, where the marriage ceremony took place.

[C.B. Fergusson, ed., The Diary of Adolphus Gaetz (Public Archives of Nova Scotia, 1965), p. 35]

An Arrest for Cross-Dressing in Halifax, 1823

Police, Union Hall—The neighbourhood of this Office was crowded perhaps beyond all former occasions on Saturday, in consequence of the apprehension and examination of a lady, who had thought proper to dress herself in the clothes of a military gentleman, while he was asleep in bed, and to adopt the manner of those offensive characters by which the whole Metropolis is infested.

Mary Palmer, the woman who thus distinguished herself, has been some time on the town, and possesses a very fine figure and face, but both are of the masculine order.—She had in the course of her speculations in St. George's Fields, on Friday night, met with an officer in the army, who being a little 'far gone,' accompanied her to her lodgings, where he fell asleep in a very short time. As the hour at which he retired to bed did not suit Miss Palmer, she determined to leave him to himself for a while, and to join her companions in the Kent Road, where she had left them. She felt an inclination also to ascertain how far they would be likely to carry their jealousy towards each other, by going in the midst of them in the character of a dandy; and having observed that her military friend was not likely to cause any interruption to her plan, she rose from the bed, slipped on his trowsers, boots and spurs, shirt, waistcoat, coat, hat, and neckhandkerchief, and sailed out, thus equipped, in search of amusement. She was able to deceive her old companions, by whom she was surrounded and caressed. After having for some time caused a very strong feeling of animosity among the girls, to each of whom she pretended a sudden fondness, she suddenly started away from them, and called on the watchmen to clear the road of women of bad character, upon pain of being complained against before the Magistrate the next morning. The watchman, struck with the tone, and appearance of the person who gave the order, did not delay to execute it, and the Kent-road was soon in such a state, that a modest woman or a drunken man might walk there without danger. So far her sport was not calculated to do mischief, but she soon began to show her powers of imitation to perfection—every one who approached her came in for their share of abuse, which was composed of oaths and epithets that terrified even the guardians of the night. At length a sense of duty prevailed over their apprehensions; they seized her by the collar, and lodged her in the watch house. As soon as she entered the room in which the constable sat to receive the charge, she whispered to him that she was no man, and that officer, in astonishment, informed the watchman, who had just described the prowess of the gentleman over whom they had obtained a victory. She begged very hard to be permitted to depart, and promised never to offend again, but the constable would not listen to the request, and she was compelled in the morning to wait on the Magistrates in the dress in which she had been taken.

The defendant, before the Magistrates, prayed to be forgiven, declared that what she had done was done in frolic. She declared that she should never more disturb the peace in the character of man or woman.

The Magistrates, who were apprised that she was not known as an old offender, very sharply reprimanded her for the impropriety of her conduct; promised her, upon any future occasion of ill behaviour, to make an example of her and fined her 5s. after which they desired her to appear as quickly as possible in the dress of the sex to which she might have been an ornament instead of a disgrace.

The defendant appeared grateful for this lenity, and immediately drove home where the military gentleman, who had got tired of the bed was sitting up with part of her dress on his shoulders, and her cap on his head, in anxious expectation for her return.

[The Acadian Recorder, *18 June 1823*]

> *A Heroine Rewarded*
> The Legislature has granted the sum of £50 as a reward to Mrs. Becker for rescuing the crew of a Schooner, which was wrecked off Long Point last autumn. Little enough is £50, considering that this brave woman quite unaided, saved the lives of some six or seven individuals.

[Niagara Mail, *23 May 1855*]

A Disorderly House

A respectable female waited on the Police Magistrate yesterday morning, and informed him that a relative of hers, a young lad of about sixteen years of age, named John Maxwell, had been enticed into a house of ill fame on Duchess Street, by a set of dissolute women. His worship promptly despatched two officers to the house designated. When the officers entered the house, they found a number of women of all ages, some of them lying on the floor, others on bundles of rags, and a few of them intoxicated. The only articles found in the house were some boxes used as seats, an old bedstead, a bottle of whiskey, a looking-glass, and some potatoes. Seven of them were arrested and sent to prison for one month with hard labour.

[The Daily Globe, *3 March 1855*]

The Magdalene Asylum Annual Meeting

The Annual Meeting of the Toronto Magdalene Asylum was held in the Hall of the Mechanics' Institute on Friday evening. John Arnold, Esq., President of the Institute, in the chair. The attendance was not large but a number of Ladies and Gentleman most prominent in the perception of the Institute were present.

Rev. Mr. Reid opened the meeting with an appropriate prayer. Mr. James Lesslie then read the Second Annual Report of the Asylum

Report

In the early part of the year 1853 some individuals, deeply impressed with the wretched and hopeless condition of the female outcasts, who nightly are found wandering the streets of the city, suggested the adoption of these measures: their relief and recovery in society. The suggestion was favorably received, and means were employed to raise the requisite funds, and to organize a society of such friends of the cause as were deemed most likely to harmonize and become its efficient agents. The appeal to the benevolent of all denominations for aid was met in a spirit of generous liberality, and the institution was established, although on a very limited scale at first, until the probability of all usefulness should be tested by experience. During the first year of its existence, although the results were comparatively small, yet the measure of success which had attended the labors of the Society, and the magnitude of the objects to be attained, encouraged its Managers not only to prosecute the work in which they had engaged, but if possible to enlarge the institution and establish it open a permanent basis...

In reviewing the details of the institution for the year, or from January 1854, the Board and Committee have reason for gratitude to the bountiful giver of all good, that their labour has not wholly been in vain, and that encouraging evidence have been given that some have been relieved from suffering, some rescued from a life of infamy, some restored to their friends, and one, it is hoped, has been led to the Saviour, 'whose blood cleanses from all sin.'

During the period named, thirty individuals have been under the protection of the Society, whose ages have ranged from 15 to 40—the average being about 23 1/2 years. Of these, at lest three-fourths are victims of intemperance, two only have been found of sober habits, and one of these appears to have been led astray at the early age of 12 years. More than one-half the entire number could read, several could read and write, and a few are said to have had the advantages of parental instruction; and had been atten-dants at Sabbath School; but these are the exceptions, it is believed, to the early history the unhappy beings who have come under the influence of the Society.

The record kept by the matron of the institution shows that six have been sent into the service of respectable families and are doing well; four have been restored to their friends; three have been taken into the House of Industry; three or four, the number now remaining in the Asylum, are in a hopeful condition; and one has died in the Hospital under circumstances which induce the belief that there was 'hope in her death'—that she had, in the hour of her extremity, 'fled for refuge to lay hold on the hope set before her in the Chapel.' On the other hand eight have been discharged from the institution at their own request; two or three have been discharged for bad conduct...Amidst all those discouragements... there is abundant cause for gratitude that so much fruit has been reaped within so short a period—an amount which, though small, may be found upon examination to equal that of any similar insti-tution in large cities...

The industrial aspect of the Institution is also equally gratify-ing and encouraging, and proves in the most satisfactory the effi-ciency and fidelity with which the matron has discharged the duties of her onerous and important office. It appears that the total avails of work done at the New York Asylum, where sixty individ-uals had, during the year, been brought under its protection and care, was almost $128; while the avails of work during the same period in the Toronto Asylum, where only thirty individuals had been under its protection and care, exceeds $157. That is, the industrial proceeds of the latter, in proportion to the number of individuals, is more than double that of the former, and this is the more gratifying as several of the inmates had to be instructed in the ordinary branches of needle-work by the matron, after they had entered the Asylum. Steady, useful employment forms an important part of the remedial means employed by the Ladies' Committee for the recovery of the inmates, and in order to fit them for service at home or with others; and to encourage them in the formation of those habits of industry and economy which are essential to their welfare and happiness, a portion of the proceeds of the labour of such is wisely reserved for the use of the individual, but more especially when leaving the institution with consent.

The Board and Committee record with gratitude the important services which have been rendered to the institution by the various ministers of the Gospel, who have, in rotation, afforded religious instruction to the inmates every Lord's Day throughout the year. This, together with the daily reading of the Scriptures, morning and evening, and the religious instruction given by the weekly visitors, and matron, have succeeded, there is reason to believe, in awakening some to a sense of their sin and danger, and they seek to be delivered from the snares of vice in which they have been held.

One of the most important agencies connected with the Institution has been periodical visits of the Ladies to the Jail, which is steadily occupied by the unhappy victims sought to be rescued by this Society. It is from this agency, principally, that the asylum has been able to gather in the outcasts; and, while the visitors have to add their testimony to that of all others, as to the fearfully hardening influences of this institution on the hearts of the individuals, yet they also record with gratitude that their visits have been uniformly kindly received; while under the faithful and affectionate appeals of Christian love, the exhibition of the grace and mercy of God our Saviour as manifested in the Gospel many a weeping eye has given testimony; that the springs of sensibility had not wholly been dried up in that moral desert, and that that Gospel is adequate to their wants...

The importance of keeping open an Asylum for those outcasts from society, who cherish any desire to return to the paths of virtue on being discharged from prison, may be seen in the fact not only that they have generally neither home nor friends, but they are watched for by those monster criminals who keep houses of infamy and live by the ruin and death of women. The Christian community of Toronto are not sufficiently alive to the gigantic form which the vice of systematic licentiousness has assumed in the city. It is gratifying to learn that, through the commendable efforts of his Worship the Mayor active means have been adopted to search out these dens of infamy; to ascertain their number, and to check the moral dissolution they are spreading throughout society.

It is said that no less then ten houses of bad fame exist in this city and neighbourhood, and there is reason to believe that the most wicked artifices are being employed to supply them with victims. Many unsuspecting young females and particularly such as are strangers in search of situations or employment have, it is believed, been enticed into those haunts of vice, detained by force, and ruined... It appears, therefore, to be the duty of Christian philanthropists not only to stretch out the arm of benevolence to save those perishing victims...but to try to discover and remove the causes which lead to their ruin. Were those monster criminals who trade in the debasement, the sufferings, and the ruin of women to be assigned...to the Provincial Penitentiary for a period of some years, or during the term of their natural lives, instead of...the payment of a fine, or a brief imprisonment, the number of those houses of infamy would no doubt be greatly reduced. This proposal is therefore respectfully recommended to the...civic authorities.

...In closing the Report it is due to the managers and friends of the institution to refer to the great principle by which the Christian should be animated amidst arduous, self-denying labour, productive...of good...

Rev. Dr. Lett moved the adoption of the Report and that it be printed and circulated. Few could tell, he said, of the many temptations and snares, and miserable traps that are out for young females to draw them from the paths of virtue, but from the statements now and again met with in the New York papers, it appeared that the destruction of young females was as much a trade, as procuring the necessary corn and other commodities for the public market. He had been asked to move the adoption of the Report, and he did so with great satisfaction. He admired it exceedingly. It treats of a difficult subject with the greatest possible delicacy of feeling. The Dr. then alluded to the amount of vice and criminality practised by the juvenile portion of the community, and expressed a wish that the authorities might be appealed to to get the Jail put into such a condition as would admit of proper classification of prisoners, for when young people were put in with those hardened in wickedness, they came out much more depraved and ready for...greater deeds of villainy.

Mr. Bartt seconded the motion of adoption ... The motion was put and adopted...

Rev. Mr. Stewart moved...

'That the Society do not confine its efforts for reformation to one class, as heretofore, but that female prisoners, or others exposed to dangers shall receive shelter and relief until they can return to their friends or be able to provide for themselves, and that the name of the institution be therefore changed to 'The Industrial House of Refuge.'

Mr. Brett seconded the motion which was then put and carried.

Mr. Gee moved that the following be the Board of Managers for the current year:

Managing Board

Rev. A. Sansom
Rev. Dr. Burns
John F. Marling, Esq.
James Lesslie, Esq.
Treasurer—R.H. Brett, Esq.
Physician—Dr. Robinson
Secretary—James Lesslie, Esq.

John Arnold, Esq.
R.H. Brett, Esq.
G.W. Allan, Esq.
F. Badgley, Esq., M.D.

Ladies' Committee of Management

Mrs Arnold
Hon. Mrs De Blaquiere
Mrs McCutcheon
Mrs Wilson
Mrs J. Baldwin
Mrs Wickson
Mrs J.B. Richardson
Mrs Burns
Mrs L. Robinson
Mrs Freeland
Mrs Brett
Mrs Lesslie
Mrs James Shaw
Mrs Carr
Mrs W. Reid
Mrs Brrass

Mrs E. Baldwin
Mrs Dick
Mrs Clark
Miss Rankin
Mrs Dunlop
Mrs Blake
Mrs Mulholland
Mrs Badgley
Mrs Ross
Mrs Telfer
Mrs J.H. Robinson
Mrs. B. Gilmor
Mrs Thompson
Miss B. Rankin
Mrs Petkins

A letter from J.T. Kirby, Esq., was handed in containing a check for the sum of £15 from the Masonic Lodge for the objects of the institution.

The meeting was here closed with prayer by the Rev. Dr. Burns.

[The Daily Globe, *20 May 1855*]

The Burning of Parliament, 1849, Joseph Légaré. Oil on wood. *[McCord Museum of Canadian History, M11588/Musée D'Histoire Canadienne]*

1. Examine the types of crimes that many of these documents discuss. How did the British North American state deal with such behaviours?

2. What do these documents suggest about the encounters of Blacks and Natives with the colonial state?

3. Analyse the statements about duelling made by Williams. What does he tell us about gender ideologies and behaviour during this period?

4. Using Ruth Bleasdale's study of the Welland Canal (see Readings), suggest how we might evaluate the newspaper's condemnation of the canal workers.

5. What kinds of concerns about sexual behaviour in British North America do these documents suggest? Why were members of the colonial middle class so concerned about sexuality that they attempted to regulate sexual conduct?

READINGS

Constance Backhouse, *Petticoats and Prejudice: Women and Law in Nineteenth-Century Canada* (Toronto: Women's Press, 1991)

Blaine Baker, '"So Elegant a Web": Providential Order and the Rule of Secular Law in Early Nineteenth Century Upper Canada,' in *University of Toronto Law Journal* 38 (1988), pp. 184-205

Ruth Bleasdale 'Class Conflict on the Canals of Upper Canada in the 1840s,' in Michael S. Cross and Gregory S. Kealey, eds., *Pre-Industrial Canada, 1760-1849* (Toronto: McClelland and Stewart, 1982), pp. 100-138

Michael Cross, '"The Shiners' War: Social Violence in the Ottawa Valley in the 1830s," in *Canadian Historical Review* LII, 1 (1973), pp. 1-26

Judith Fingard, *The Dark Side of Life in Victorian Halifax* (Nova Scotia: Pottersfield Press, 1989)

——————————, 'The Poor in Winter: Seasonality and Society in Pre-Industrial Canada,' in Michael S. Cross and Gregory S. Kealey, eds., *Pre-Industrial Canada 1760-1849* (Toronto: McClelland and Stewart, 1982), pp. 62-78

David H. Flaherty, ed., *Essays in the History of Canadian Law,* Vols. 1 & 2 (Toronto: The Osgoode Society, 1981 and 1983)

Philip Girard and Jim Phillips, eds., *Essays in the History of Canadian Law,* Vol. III, *Nova Scotia* (Toronto: The Osgoode Society, 1990)

Allan Greer and Ian Radforth, eds., *Colonial Leviathan: State Formation in Mid-Nineteenth-Century Canada* (Toronto: University of Toronto Press, 1992)

Tina Loo, *Making Law, Order, and Authority in British Columbia, 1821-1871* (Toronto: University of Toronto Press, 1994)

Cecilia Morgan, '"In Search of the Phantom Misnamed Honour": Duelling in Upper Canada,' in *Canadian Historical Review* 76, 4 (December 1995), pp. 529-562

Bryan D. Palmer, 'Discordant Music: Charivaris and Whitecapping in Nineteenth-Century North America,' in *Labour/Le Travailleur* 3 (1978), pp. 5-62

Nicholas Rogers, 'Serving Toronto the Good: The Development of the City Police Force, 1834-84,' in Victor L. Russell, ed., *Forging a Consensus: Historical Essays on Toronto* (Toronto: University of Toronto Press, 1984), pp. 116-140

Paul Romney, *Mr Attorney: The Attorney General for Ontario in Court, Cabinet, and Legislature 1791-1899* (Toronto: The Osgoode Society, 1986)

——————, 'From the Types Riot to the Rebellion: Elite Ideology, Anti-legal Sentiment, Political Violence and the Rule of Law in Upper Canada,' in *Ontario History* 79 (1987)

Scott W. See, *Riots in New Brunswick: Orange Nativism and Social Violence in the 1840s* (Toronto: University of Toronto Press, 1993)

John C. Weaver, *Crimes, Constables and Courts: Order and Transgression in a Canadian City, 1816-1970* (Montreal and Kingston: McGill-Queen's University Press, 1995)

From Red River to the Pacific—The West, the North, and British North America

Patterns of white expansion and settlement and their effects on the Native population of north-western and western Canada were heavily influenced by the fortunes of the fur trade. The far north was an exception, however, for its climate and landscape were too forbidding for the majority of Europeans. Thus, the north's Inuit peoples were less influenced by European culture than southern aboriginals, and were able to maintain their society's structures and values for a much longer period of time. Inuit culture, shaped by the need to survive in a very harsh environment, was based on principles of community co-operation. As the few Europeans who ventured into the far north on expeditions such as Sir John Franklin's search for the Northwest passage discovered, the Inuit's knowledge of the area was essential to the Europeans' survival.

The founding of the North-West Company in 1783-1784 brought about more aggressive competition in the fur trade. More natives were drawn into it and some, such as the Ojibwa, became more dependent on the trade and were part of its westward movement. Other First Nations peoples of the plains were less dependent—at least in their initial contact with the trade—and, although they too moved west into southern Alberta and Montana, pushing the Shoshoni and Kutenai of the area across the Rockies, they were able to maintain a greater degree of cultural and economic autonomy.

The expansion of the trade westward also saw an increase in Métis communities, particularly at the Red River valley. Here, both French- and English-speaking Métis developed their own languages, dances, clothing, and decorative arts, and the distinctive 'Red River cart.' But the unique hierarchy of the fur trade—with its factors, traders, clerks and apprentices, *engagés* (postmaster, interpreter, voyageur, labourer)—left the Métis clustered at bottom.

Imperial decisions and international socio-economic changes also affected the fortunes of the west and of the Métis in particular, when the Red River settlement was established by Lord Selkirk in 1812 as an enclave for dispossessed Scottish Highlanders. The Métis distrusted the new arrangement, and their feelings were shared by North-West Company traders, who encouraged Métis actions against the settlement. The Hudson's Bay Company governor attempted to stop Métis hunting practices, and banned the export of pemmican supplies, a trade dominated by the Métis, from Assiniboia. Although a Métis attack on the colony forced the settlers to leave, they returned with military reinforcements and a new governor equally uninterested in Métis concerns. The fur-trade merger of 1821 and layoffs of company employees triggered the influx of more settlers into Red River, many of them Métis. The French-speaking Métis community in the valley developed a strong sense of identity, shaped by language, religion, and their Indian background. But, as more white settlers arrived in the colony, racist attitudes intensified and racist practices became more common. Métis and Native women, formerly an integral part of fur-trade society, particularly through intermarriage with white traders, were shunned by upper-class white women.

The First Nations of the Pacific northwest were a diverse group that spoke 34 distinct languages. Prior to contact with Europeans, they were economically self-sufficient. It is estimated that two-thirds of the Native population lived along the coast, with economies based on salmon and cedar. Different groups of non-Natives—Russians, Spanish, British, and Americans—arrived in the course of the eighteenth century, but the sea-otter fur trade with Britain and America was established after the landing of Captain James Cook's expedition in 1778. Non-Native traders were initially dependent on the Nuu'chah'nulth, or Haida, as Europeans called them, for their expertise. Native society did not appear to suffer from the maritime trade and the new material goods brought by Europeans.

After a decline in the coastal trade in the 1820s and the voyages of Alexander Mackenzie, the inland trade began to expand. By 1834, Fort Simpson had been established in the interior, and one group of Natives, the Tsimshian, moved their villages to the lower reaches of the Skeena river in order to participate in the inland fur trade. Increased contact with Europeans brought more long-lasting and detrimental consequences to Native society. Smallpox epidemics in particular were extremely damaging to coastal Native societies, which were based on inherited ranks and a clearly delineated kinship system.

The Hudson's Bay Company held a ten-year lease on Vancouver Island, although Britain named its governor and required the company to recruit British settlers over a five-year period. However, with British concern over American settlement in the Pacific northwest, and Canada West's dreams of annexation, colonization became an increasingly important issue. Hudson's Bay Company official James Douglas's purchases of Native land on Vancouver Island in the 1840s, the arrival of missionaries, and the beginning of coal mining were all indicative of fundamental changes in the region. Following the gold rush of 1858 along the Fraser river, and acting in support of Douglas who had been trying to control arrivals of miners from California, Britain cancelled its lease with the Hudson's Bay Company and declared the mainland a Crown colony with Douglas as governor.

The area's economy was divided among farming in the interior, lumbering and provisioning at Fort Victoria and Esquimalt, and coal mining at Nanaimo. The European population was dominated by adult males. This fact, along with the presence of prostitution, led Douglas to advertise for British working-class women to emigrate as domestics, with the hope that they would eventually marry British male settlers. Retired fur traders and their wives made a concerted effort at Fort Victoria to replicate 'British' society.

The earlier relations between Natives and whites—where whites depended on Native knowledge—changed. European-descended settlers generally had very low opinions of Natives, and conflict ensued when they tried to take Native land. Many Natives ended up as wage labourers in commercial fishing, the canneries, sailing, coal mining, lumbering, and farming. Chinese settlers, mostly men but also some women, arrived with the gold rush of 1858. They came mainly from California and Hong Kong, and worked as gold prospectors, importers, fishers, gardeners, and restaurant workers and entrepreneurs.

The nature of Manitoba's and British Columbia's entry into Confederation in 1868-1870 and 1871 were different. In Manitoba, negotiations took place between the Canadian and imperial governments and the Hudson's Bay Company, with informal input from white settlers in Red River. The sale of Rupert's Land to the British government (which then transferred it to Canada) was completed without consulting the area's Métis population. Their fears of being pushed aside by the new government were not without foundation, as road construction and surveys were undertaken, and Métis land, religion, and language appeared to be either appropriated or disregarded.

Métis hostility erupted in an uprising led by Louis Riel in 1869-1870, and the shooting of Orangeman Thomas Scott. These events were followed by negotiations between the government in Ottawa and Red River representatives. The result was the 1870 Manitoba Act, in which the province, defined as 100 square miles (25 900 hectares), entered Confederation. The Métis received 1.4 million acres (567 000 hectares) and the guarantee of bilingual services, although the way in which this acreage was set up did little to protect the Métis culture.

In British Columbia, matters were—at least ostensibly—more peaceful. The colony asked to be admitted to Confederation as a means of obtaining both responsible government and financial assistance in repaying its debts. After the legislature passed a motion calling for union, negotiations took place between the colonists' representatives and Canada, and its major concerns—a rail link, responsible government, debt relief, and other financial assistance—were met.

Section A

The Far North

The documents in this section present both Inuit and European perspectives on the far north, including a traditional Inuit song, as well as diary entries written by John Richardson and George Back, respectively surgeon and midshipman on John Franklin's northern expedition of 1819-1822. We know considerably more about the lives of Richardson and Back than we do about the men who might have written or sung 'My Breath'—indeed, it is virtually impossible to provide a precise date for the song's origin. Keep in mind also the fact that this song has been translated—but we should consider it as one of the different viewpoints available on life in the north. Similarly, aboriginal people's oral testimony can suggest how an event such as the arrival of Europeans into First Nations communities might have looked from an aboriginal point of view.

Inuit Traditional Song: 'My Breath'/ 'Orpingalik'

I will sing a song,
A song that is strong.
    Unaya - unaya.
Sick I have lain since autumn,
Helpless I lay, as were I
My own child.

Said, I would that my woman
Were away to another house
To a husband
Who can be her refuge,
Safe and secure as winter ice.
    Unaya - unaya.

Sad I would that my woman
Were gone to a better protector
Now that I lack strength
To rise from my couch.
    Unaya - unaya.

Dost thou know thyself?
So little thou knowest of thyself.
Feeble I lie here on my bench
And only my memories are strong!
    Unaya - unaya.

Beasts of the hunt! Big game!
Oft the fleeting quarry I chased!
Let me live it again and remember,
Forgetting my weakness.
    Unaya - unaya.

Let me recall the great white
Polar bear,
High up its black body,
Snout in the snow, it came!
He really believed
He alone was a male
And ran toward me.
    Unaya - unaya.

It threw me down
Again and again,
Then breathless departed
And lay down to rest,
Hid by a mound on a floe.
Heedless it was, and unknowing
That I was to be its fate.
Deluding itself
That he alone was a male,
And unthinking
That I too was a man!
      Unaya - unaya.

I shall ne'er forget that great blubber-beast
A fjord seal,
I killed from the sea ice
Early, long before dawn,
While my companions at home
Still lay like the dead,
Faint from failure and hunger,
Sleeping.
With meat and with swelling blubber
I returned so quickly
As if merely running over ice
To view a breathing hole there.
And yet it was
An old and cunning male seal.
But before he had even breathed
My harpoon head was fast
Mortally deep in his neck.

That was the manner of me then.
Now I lie feeble on my bench
Unable even a little blubber to get
For my wife's stone lamp.
The time, the time will not pass,
While dawn gives place to dawn
And spring is upon the village.
      Unaya - unaya.

But how long shall I lie here?
How long?
And how long must she go a-begging

For fat for her lamp,
For skins for clothing
And meat for a meal?
A helpless thing - a defenceless woman.
    Unaya - unaya.

Knowest thou thyself?
So little thou knowest of thyself?
While dawn gives place to dawn,
And spring is upon the village.
    Unaya - unaya.

[Daniel David Moses and Terry Goldie, eds., An Anthology of Canadian
Native Literature in English *(Toronto: Oxford University Press, 1992),
pp. 1-3]*

The Arrival of *Koblunas* to the Land of the *Netsilingmiut*

An Inuit Oral History of James Ross' Expedition to the Arctic, 1829

One day during the summer [Sept. 2, 1829] two men were fishing at *Ow-weet-tee-week* [the place where whales abound]. This is a river to the north [Agnew River] of Neithcille, and the Inuit would often go there to fish. When the men looked out to sea they could see a large black thing, not an animal, far out to sea. It was slowly being taken to the south by the ice. They had never seen such a thing before and were much alarmed, so they returned to the place where they lived and told the others. All agreed that this must be a white-man's *umiak* [ship or boat]. None of the seal-people had ever seen a *kobluna* [white man], but the wife of *Archnaluak*, who was named *Kakekagiu*, had heard many stories from her sister.

This sister of *Kakekagiu* had been at *Neyuning Eitdua* [Winter Island] and *Ogloolik* when the great *eshemuta* [Captain] Paree brought his two ships to the land of the *Arilingmuit* (1821-1823). The *koblunas* had spent two winters with the *Arvilingmuit* and had been very friendly. They had given the Inuit many fine presents of wood and iron. They were very rich in all of the things which the seal-people most lacked, and the people decided to visit the *kobluna umiak* when it came to rest in their country. The Great Spirit brought the white man to a very good place, quite near Sarfak where the Tunrit ruins are. This place was later called *Qavdlunarsiorfik* [the place where one meets white men], and after the white men departed the Inuit would go there to find iron and things which the *koblunas* left behind.

It was near the middle of winter [8 January 1830] and the people were living quite near this place when some men went out sealing. One of these was *Agliktuktoq* [he who is unclean], and he was hunting a little to the south of the others. His dog was straining to go faster and *Agliktuktoq* thought that it had scented a bear so he followed as quick as he could. What the dog had smelled was not a bear but some strange men who were walking near a strange kind of house with smoke coming out of it. Greatly frightened, *Agliktuktoq* hurried back to the village to tell the others of the thing that he had seen.

The people gathered in the dance house to discuss the matter and the *angeko* [shaman] gathered his charms and his white cloak of caribou belly hide. He took a large deerskin and pegged it to the west wall of the house, had all of the lamps extinguished, then crawled behind the hide to talk to the spirits. All of the spirits said that *Agliktuktoq* had seen the white men, and that these were friendly and would welcome a visit from the Inuit.

The next morning everyone went to the place where the house was. *Illictu* and his son *Toolooa* (who had lost his leg to a bear) were drawn on a *komotik* [sledge]. They found some footprints in the snow and were astonished to see their size and strange shape, and after a conference the people decided to proceed cautiously. Some said that the Great Spirit would destroy the people if they did not kill these strangers. The people hid behind some snow blocks and could see that the house was really a ship with a snow wall around it.

The hunter *Niungitsoq* [the good walker] was sent alone to see what the white men would do, but when the white men started to approach him, the other men, wishing to show that they were not afraid, came out from behind the snow. Two white men came forward and stopped. Then they shouted "*teyma teyma*" so the Inuits knew they were friends. The other white men came up and laid their weapons on the ice, and then the Inuit put down their knives and harpoons, and soon all were embracing and dancing together.

The white men took the people to their big ship and gave them each a piece of iron. Then the *eshemuta* asked for the hunter who had been seen the day before, and when *Agliktuktoq* was brought forward he took him into the big cabin and gave him an *ooloo* [woman's knife]. *Agliktuktoq* was a great hunter and was offended by being given such a thing, but he saw a hand saw which was hanging on a nail and mentioned that he would prefer that. But the *eshemuta* became angry and he took the *ooloo* back and chased *Agliktuktoq* out of the house empty handed.

[David C. Woodman ed., Unravelling the Franklin Mystery: Inuit Testimony (Montreal-Kingston: McGill-Queen's University Press, 1991), pp. 11-13]

Excerpts from Dr. John Richardson's Diary, 1821

Monday February 12 1821 Fort Enterprise

A party of six men was again dispatched to Fort Providence to bring up the remainder of the stores. Two hunters are to join them from Akaicho's band. Pierez St. Germain went to Akaicho now hunting to the southward and westward of the house.

On comparing the language of our two Eskimaux with a copy of St. John's gospel printed for the use of the Moravian missionary settlements on the Labrador coast, it appears that the Eskimaux who resort to Churchill speak a language essentially the same with those who frequent the Labrador coast. The Redknives too recognize the expression Teyma used by the Eskimaux when they accost strangers in a friendly manner, as similarly pronounced by Augustus and those of his race who frequent the mouth of the Coppermine River.

The tribe to which Augustus belongs, reside generally a little to the northward of Churchill. In the spring before the ice quits the shores they kill seal, but during winter they frequent the borders of the large lakes near the coast, where they obtain Rein-deer and Musk oxen. Augustus has never been farther north than Marble Island, but he says that Eskimaux from the Arctic sea come overland to trade with his tribe and that canoes can go to the country of the strangers by following the sea-coast. Some uncertainty exists however with respect to this northern sea and it may prove that he speaks of Chesterfield inlet which is nearly 200 miles deep.

The winter habitations of the Eskimaux who visit Churchill are built of snow, and judging from one constructed by Augustus today they are very comfortable dwellings. Having selected a spot on the river, where the snow was about two feet deep, and sufficiently compact, they commenced by tracing out a circle, twelve feet in diameter. The snow in the interior of the circle was next divided with a broad knife having a long handle, into slabs three feet long, six inches thick and two feet deep, being the thickness of the layer of snow. These slabs were tenacious enough to admit of being moved about without breaking, or even losing the sharpness of their angles, and they had a slight degree of curvature, corresponding with that of the circle from which they were cut. They were piled upon each other, exactly like courses of hewn stone, around the circle which was traced out, and care was taken to smooth the beds of the different courses with the knife and to cut them so as to give the wall a slight inclination. The dome was closed somewhat suddenly and flatly by cutting the upper slabs in a wedge-form instead of the more rectangular shape of those below. The roof was about eight feet high and the last aperture was shut up by a small conical piece. The whole was built from within and each slab was cut so that it retained its position without requiring support until another was placed beside it; the lightness of the slabs greatly facilitating the operation. When the building was covered in, a little loose snow was thrown over it, to close up every chink and a low door was cut through the walls with the knife. A bed-place was next formed and neatly faced with slabs of snow, which were covered with a thin layer of pine branches to prevent them from melting by the heat of the body. At each end of the bed a pillar of snow was erected to place a lamp upon, and lastly a porch was built before the door and a piece of clear ice was placed in an aperture cut in the wall for a window.

The purity of the material of which the house was framed, the elegance of its construction and the translucency of its wall, which transmitted a very pleasant light gave it an appearance far superior to a marble building and one might survey it with feelings somewhat akin to those produced by the contemplation of a Grecian temple reared by Phidias. Both are triumphs of art inimitable in their kinds.

Annexed there is a plan of a complete Eskimaux snow-house with kitchen and other apartments, copied from a sketch made by Augustus, with the names of the different places affixed. The only fire-place is in the kitchen, the heat of the lamp sufficing to keep the other apartments warm.

Monday October 29th 1821

When we entered Fort Enterprise, in the dusk of the evening, and had the melancholy satisfaction of embracing Mr. Franklin. No language that I can use, being adequate to convey a just idea of the wretchedness of the abode, in which we found our commanding officer. I shall not make the attempt, but merely mention, that the greatest part of the house had been pulled down for firewood, and that the only entire chamber which was left, was open to all the rigour of the season, the windows being but partially closed by a few loose boards. Peltier, Semandrè and Adam were Mr. Franklin's only companions, the others having left him to go in search of the Indians on the 21st instant. Of these Peltier alone was able to bring in firewood, Semandrè was scarcely able to stir from the fire side, and Adam was confined to bed. The noise that we made on entering the house, was first heard by Peltier and he rushed to the door in expectation of seeing the wished for Indians, but turned away in despair on beholding our ghastly countenances. He recovered however, in a short time, sufficiently to welcome us to this abode of misery, but the disappointment had evidently given him a great shock. The hollow and sepulchral sound of their voices, produced nearly as great horror in us, as our emaciated appearance did on them and I could not help requesting them more than once to assume a more cheerful tone. The partridge that Hepburn had killed was divided amongst the party and in return they supplied us with singed hide. Our spirits rose during this meal and we endeavoured to cheer them with the prospect of Hepburns being able to kill a deer and thus providing for their subsistence until the arrival of the Indians. Having finished supper and read the evening service we retired to bed in hopes that to morrow the chase might prove fortunate.

[C. Stuart Houston, ed., Arctic Ordeal: The Journal of John Richardson, Surgeon-Naturalist with Franklin, 1820-1822 (Montreal-Kingston: McGill-Queen's University Press, 1984), pp. 26-29, 159]

Excerpts from George Back's Journal, 1820

January 18, 1820, Cumberland House to Fort Carlton

It is not my business to enter into the mode in which the traders conduct matters—
it is sufficient for me to say that after some delay we left Cumberland House this
morning at 8h 30m AM and took our way through some woods which soon
brought us to the River Saskashawan intending to follow its course as far as
Carlton House—the next post of any consequences in that river. Our number consisted of Lieut Franklin and myself, our drivers with dogs and carioles, a third one
with provisions, and our own servant—besides a clerk and four more sledges
appurtaining [sic] to the company. Having harnessed our feet with snowshoes three
feet long—we took leave or our two friends with some of the gentlemen of both
establishments and pursued our route with eagerness and alacrity through the
recent fallen and yet unfrozen snow of the river—a man who sets out on a journey
in the middle of a North American winter the thermometer of 42 minus zero cannot be supposed to make much use of his pen—particularly as his nightly shelter
is the exposed but sublime canopy of the heavens—on the contrary he endeavours
by a quick step in the day, or drawing close by the fire at night to prevent some
parts of his person from being too nearly allied to the hostile elements around him.
The method of travelling is as follows. One man precedes the company and per-
forms an office which is termed beating a track—the rest follow successively—
each sledge taking its turn of advancing—the one relieved falling into the rear—
the people also adhering to the same plan with respect to the track—It is custom-
arily likewise to halt about noon to refresh both persons and dogs—We did not
make much distance, arising from the depth of the snow—and the river was
extremely serpentine—at sun set we fixed on the NE side of the banks—to pass
the night. Nothing is easier when surrounded by comforts than to speak with gai-
ety of spending a night in the woods and scarcely anything is more difficult when
in that situation than to unite one object within the pale of its relation. It may not
be improper or uninteresting to give a description of such a place—The Canadians
call it a hut or encampment—for what reason I know not—as there is no more a
comparison, than between an open space and well covered house. After selecting
a spot sufficiently large to admit the party—the men seperate to different employments, some with the snow shoe clearing the snow away—others felling large trees
for fuel—this one is employed lopping the branches off the pine—that, is laying
them along the ground for a bed—when these are ended the fire is kindled—not
the least cheering sight to the traveller—the men assemble, liberate their dogs, sus-
pend their traces &c on a tree and either dry their frozen shoes or busy themselves
in some requisite occupation til the hour of supper when they make a prodigious
meal, and having a blanket each, sleep soundly through the night. It must be
observed that the shoes worn in winter are very different from those in England.
They are after the manner of the Indians, made of the scraped and smoked skin of
the elk or deer—reaching above the ankle, and fastening with a foot or two of
thong—from the want of tanning—they are so soft and porous that the least mois-

ture will saturate them—two pair with blanket socks are generally worn with snow shoes—but in any other case, they are preferred to shoes of a different country—the foot has a free action and is not confined, consequently is less exposed to congealation. Every person who has tried snow shoes is aware that one can no more avoid being miserably chafed in the feet, than one can of falling into the water when the ice breaks underneath—They worked a quick reformation in men, for in a few days to my great surprise I had not a single corn on my feet which before were something annoying. Being novices in this mode of travelling one might naturally expect some advantage would be taken—but my suspicions never extended to the dogs. The kindness of the Governor had provided some little dainties for us—and at night our servant had very carefully placed them near my head under a bag without informing me. Now if you wish to avoid being frost bit it is absolutely necessary when once laid down under your blanket and buffalo skin that you do not move one jot, though you may ache in every joint, for if you do and should avoid the first, you are certain of trembling through the long hours of the night, without a glance of rest—Besides stories however true, lose nothing by telling—I had seen two people with stamped noses and chins—that was quite sufficient for me to determine, not to move the breadth of a hair one way or the other—but human nature is frail—a short time shows us how fallacious our determinations are, and sometimes informs us that in providing for the future we are too apt to neglect the present. Now our servant had placed these things near me for security or perhaps thinking if he took them under his protection, he must be necessarily disturbed, had decided the questioning my favour and went to rest—The dogs have the privilege of sleeping on you—because it is well known you would prefer that to the trouble of kicking them away—This was not only my case, but throughout the night there was nothing but a fighting and growling of dogs about my head and it was evident they were munching something—after endeavouring to recollect what it could be for the space of half an hour—a sudden thought whispered it was our fine meat balls—assuredly said I rather loud, the rascals are devouring our best of luxuries—are?—perhaps have—for much may be done by hungry dogs even in half an hour—It was time to do something—I felt at my nose—then at my chin—the smallness of the first put that out of the question—the second—aye the second—there is nothing invulnerable about that thought I—how then!—still wishing to put the matter off—why should I move, for certainly no one can possibly sleep with such a clatter—and after all t'is but to decide a doubt—a mere doubt—I had almost satisfied myself, when two of equal might—stamped so unmercifully on me in their scuffle that I could no longer withhold my rage—I started up—away went the thieves—When oh! unfortunate sight—the faint glimmer of the fire shewed me the empty sack—the subject of all my fears—quite gone—irretrievably lost—never in my life did I hold the canine species in such abhorrence—it was of no use—I wrapped myself up and meditated dire revenge.

October 30, 1820 Fort Enterprise to Fort Chipewayan

At 7h AM the 30th we set out in the expectation of gaining the Slave Lake by the evening—but our progress was again impeded by unfrozen places—so that the whole day was spent, in forcing our way through thick woods—among deep snow—which covered the swamps and deceived our footsteps—whilst innumerable pointed and loose rocks slid from under us and made our way both difficult and dangerous -once we were interrupted by a towering and almost perpendicular rock which not only added to our detension, but caused much anxiety for the safety of the women—who being heavily laden with skins—and one of them with a child—could not exert themselves with the activity that such a situation required—fortunately nothing serious occurred—at dark we put up—greatly disappointed at not having gained the lake. Weather cloudy with thick mist and snow—The Indians expected to have reached a bear's den—and to have made a hearty meal of the animal—it was the subject of conversation all day—but when we came to the spot—oh! misericorde—it had already passed the devouring jaws of some young hunters—who only left sufficient evidence that such a thing once existed—One however caught a fish which with the assistance of some weed scraped from the rocks—made us a tolerable super—it was not of the choicest kind, but sufficiently good for a hungry man—at night the hunters brought us a small quantity of pounded meat fat and a greater proportion of deer and Indian hair than either—this they had collected from the remnants of an old skin which had formerly been used for the purpose of carrying provisions in—and though it may not appear very enticing to a person in England it was thought a great luxury—after three days starvation in America—indeed had it not been for the precaution and generosity of the Indians—we must have gone without sustenance—till we reached the Fort—I forgot to mention that one of the Indians broke through the ice in the early part of the day—and escaped with a sound ducking.

[C. Stuart Houston, ed., Arctic Artist: The Journal and Paintings of George Back, Midshipman with Franklin, 1819-1822 (Montreal-Kingston: McGill-Queen's University Press, 1994), pp. 28-31]

Section B
Intermarriage, Mines, Farms...

The first three documents in this section examine Native-European relations in the fur trade through the lens of intermarriage between Native women and European men. The Bouchard-Fainiant marriage contract sets out the terms of their union; note its proviso that the marriage was to be 'solemnized according to the custom of civilized countries' as soon as possible. The entries from Hudson's Bay factor John Work's diary suggest how such unions might have turned out—at least from the perspective of the European man. The selections from James Douglas's letters, written from Fort Victoria in 1850-1851, touch upon a number of themes, such as the impact of the introduction of mining into the area and its effect on both Natives and non-Natives. Douglas's letters also document European attempts to establish farms, churches, and schools—in his words, 'improvement'—at Fort Victoria.

The Bouchard-Fainiant Marriage Contract, 1828

Contract of marriage drawn up and executed between Louis Bouchard of the parish of Maskinongé in the province of Lower Canada, party of the first part, and Charlotte Fainiant of Fort William in the province of Upper Canada with the consent of her parents, party of the second part.

The said Louis Bouchard willingly binds himself and promises faithfully in the presence of God and the church to protect, cherish, and support the said Charlotte Fainiant as his lawful wife, in sickness as in health, during the term of his natural life, and, on the first good opportunity, to have their marriage solemnized according to the custom of civilized countries, and, moreover, the said Louis Bouchard, in case the said Charlotte Fainiant survives him, willingly binds himself to transfer and bequeath for the exclusive use and benefit of the said Charlotte Fainiant and any children born of this marriage all the property—in cash, furniture or other goods—of which the said Louis Bouchard dies possessed, and in case the said Louis Bouchard dies without having fulfilled faithfully the articles and settlements mentioned above—to marry the said Charlotte Fainiant—he consents and willingly binds himself to bequeath and have paid to the said Charlotte Fainiant all the credit and cash that he now has or may have in the future in the hands of the honorable Hudson's Bay Company, and out of his wages the said Louis Bouchard consents to leave a tenth part in the hands of the Company each year he remains in their service for the express purpose of making a small provision for the benefit of his family in case of his accidental death

Drawn up and executed at Fort William, Lake Superior District, on the afternoon of October 18, 1828, and signed—except for Louis Bouchard who, having declared that he was unable to sign his name, made his ordinary mark after the document was completed.

Witnesses	His
Benj. McKenzie	Louis X Bouchard
Duncan Haggart	Mark

[NAC, H.B.Co. Records, B-231-z, Fort William Miscellaneous Items]

Excerpts from John Work's Diary

Columbia River 13th Decr. 1834

I must tell you the wife and the little ones are well, I have now here four fine little girls, had I them a little brushed up with education, and a little knowledge of the world, they would scarcely be known to be Indians. I must not forget to tell you that Miss Maria is now become a fine girl and well educated & I have no doubt will make an excellent wife, were Frank to remain in the country I would be happy to see him possessed of her...

1st Jany 1836

I had not my family with me last year and am obliged to leave them this year again and have parted with them more reluctantly and with more regret than ever on any former occasion, I might have taken them along but could not think of exposing them to the dangers and inconveniences of a winter voyage in such a country, indeed the coast altogether is no place for families, it is sufficient for myself to be exposed to the dangers from Shipwreck and the Savages treacherous Indians, This is a cursed country where one is obliged to separate from all that is dear to him in the world. I am heartily tired of it and shall certainly leave it as soon as my means admit which I trust will not be long... I am aware that my family being natives of this country would not be fit for society, but that gives me little concern, they are mine and I am bound to provide for them and shall do so, while they conduct themselves well, My old cronies would still call upon me and I want no more. I have four fine little girls here now the youngest a little more than a year old, the two eldest can read pretty well, for we have a school at Vancouver....I dare say you have heard that our friend Tod got married when home to a girl that had been out in R.R. some time, I fear he has been guilty of great imprudence, This is not a fit country for white women...

N.W. Coast America 10th Feby. 1838

The wife and two youngest children found me at Ft. Simpson on the last day of 1836 and since then has presented me with another fine little girl which I have named Mary. The Mother and these three were well when I left them a few days ago. The two eldest ones remained at Vancouver under the docters charge and are attending School and have made considerable progress they are now able to write to me... I am inclined to hang on for 3 or 4 years yet & get 12 or 1500£ more, I am aware that in the mean time I am missing the opportunity of having my children educated as they ought to be, but at the end of that period the eldest will not be over 15, and with what she may get in this country may still not be too old to improve, I have not seen her these two years, but every body tells me she is a fine girl of her age, indeed so far as looks go I need not be ashamed of any of my children in any country...

Fort Simpson 15th Feby. 1841

The good wife and little ones are well, on my return from Vancouver she had a fine boy to present me with, this makes six, five girls and a boy like most old fogies I am quite proud of the little fellow, I had given up hopes of having a boy, The two eldest girls are in the Willamet with the Missionaries. My friends tell me that they are improving, and well under the care of the people they are with, I have not seen them for more than two years nor has the mother seen them for more than four years. On account of my illness last fall I could not allow the mother to go and see them, but I intend sending her now.—The little wife and I get on very well, She is to me an affectionate partner simple and uninstructed as she is and takes good care of my children and myself. We enjoy as great a share of conjugal happiness as generally falls to the lot of married people...

6th Feby. 1844

I have my family all with me 6 girls & 1 boy They with the Mother are well. I am endeavouring to instruct them the best way I can, the five eldest read the scriptures pretty well and are making some progress in writing and Arithmetic, John is 4 1/2 years old and more mischievous than all his sisters put together. The youngest Catherine 20 Months old, running about, does not speak yet but noisy enough.—My friend the great responsibility of a parent is deeply impressed upon me, Neglecting the proper training of our children, as far as in our power will no doubt be visited with retribution both in this world and the World to come. The fear of their not being properly looked after during my absence has been in part the cause of my not having gone home before now.

Nisqually 10th Jany. 1846

When I left Fort Simpson end of Sept. Josette and the family were all well, we have now eight children, six girls and two boys, the three eldest girls as tall as their mother, John is a fine smart little fellow about 6 years old, Henry is about 20 months.—We are in woful want of a School, I am instructing them the best way I can and endeavouring to bring them up in fear of God, which I consider of far more importance than many other much thought of accomplishments...

Fort Victoria 14th March 1853

Myself and family are well during my absence I nearly lost my youngest child by an attack of Scarlet fever, but she is now recovered, during last Season I have enjoyed better health than for years back, but I am going down the hill fast nevertheless. The Good wife Wears well and is still strong and vigorous She desires to be Most Kindly remembered to you. Since I last wrote our two Married daughters have each had another child...

[Excerpts from the John Work papers, 1834-1844. Beth Light and Alison Prentice, eds., Pioneer and Gentlewomen of British North America, 1713-1867 (Toronto: New Hogtown Press, 1980), *pp. 129-130]*

Interior of a Clallam Winter Lodge, Vancouver Island, 1847, Paul Kane, 1870–1871.
[National Gallery of Canada, Ottawa, 692–3]

Colonization and Conflict on Vancouver Island: James Douglas, Fort Victoria Letters, 1850-1851

We have not been able to attempt much in the way of improvement this year at Fort Victoria, in consequence of the small force stationed here, which is barely sufficient to keep the present system in motion.

There is yet a great deal to do, before we get things in so complete or convenient a form, as is desirable for the transaction of business, but we shall go on improving our system and arrangements, as speedily as circumstances will permit. The severe winter of 1848/49 retarded the farm work so much, that it was late in Spring, before the seed could be put into the ground, and to that cause principally coupled with the injury sustained, by the Winter Wheat, we attribute the very short wheat Crop of this year. The Oats on the contrary were the finest ever grown on this farm, but owing to the late sowing, 20th May they ripened only in part. The pease have produced remarkably well, but the potato Crop has in a great measure failed, not only here, but in all other parts of the Country, and will be a scarce article this winter. I much regret that circumstance, as we could have sold, almost any quantity, to Vessels calling at this port.

We were more fortunate with the Salmon fisheries, which yielded over 500 Barrels, though we could not take one half of the fish brought in, by the Indians for Sale, had we been provided with Casks. I firmly believe from the quantity of fish taken, that 2,000 Barrels might have been cured.

A quarrel took place last Spring, between the Indians of this Post, and the Cawitchin Tribe, which nearly involved us, and disturbed the peace of the settlement. The immediate cause of difference was the murder, of a Young Cawitchin nephew of a principal Chief, by an Indian of this place. The Cawitchin Tribe took up the part of their Chief very warmly, and sent out War parties to avenge his cause.

These hovered about this place for several weeks, keeping us in a constant state of alarm, and not one of our labouring Indians, could be induced to leave the Fort, or attend to any out door occupation without an escort. On one occasion, a party of Cawitchins burst suddenly into the Saw Mill during the Night, but offered no violence to the people, and retired as soon as they discovered, that no Indians of the hostile Tribe were present.

On another occasion, they shot an unfortunate Indian lad, who was imployed at one of the Company's Daries about four miles from the Fort. The house was riddled with Balls, but fortunately none of our people were hurt. As it was thought necessary to take notice of that glaring insult, we sent out an armed party to scour the country in all directions. The Cawitchins were seen at a distance, and made quietly off to the woods, on discovering their persuers. This demonstration had the good effect of putting an end to this mischievous feud, which kept the Indians in a constant state of alarm.

The Cawitchins have been often at the Fort trading, since that time, and we have had no further cause to complain of their conduct.

Fort Victoria, 3 April 1850
Archibald Barclay Esqre
Secretary, H. Bay Compy
Sir

I had this honor on the 7th February and herewith transmit duplicate of that communication...

Chief Factor Work arrived here lately by canoe from Fort Rupert to consult about the affairs of that place, which are in great disorder. The Miners, with the exception of Mr. and Mrs. Muir and their youngest boy, left that place with their families for Calefornia, by the Bque. *England*; Walker the Blacksmith and six other men, recruits by the *Norman Morison*, whose names are enclosed, absconded at the same time. The other men on the establishment consisting of 11 of the *Norman Morison* recruits and a party of 11 Canadians influenced by their example, had struck for double pay and many other allowances inconsistent with the rules of the service. Another party of eight men left the Fort in presence of the Officers and made their way by canoe to this place. To check the spirit of insubordination in the bud, I mustered a party of one clerk Mr. H. Moffat and 12 men volunteers and others and despatched them to Fort Rupert with instructions to Mr. Blenkinsop the officer in charge to treat the mutineers as prisoners at large, and to feed them on bread and water, until they return to duty on the terms of their agreement. With that re-inforcement there will be a force of 18 men not concerned in the strike which will be sufficient to protect the Fort. The mining operations are completely suspended as Mr. Muir objects to shanking without the assistance of regular miners. The Indians however continue to bring in coal, which owing to increased numbers at work, they produce in larger quantities than last year. There were by last accounts about 700 tons in the coal yard near the Fort. These difficulties have in many respects a baneful effect on the service by impairing our influence with the natives and destroying the character of the service. These effects have been felt at Fort Rupert as I have received letters from Mr. Blenkinsop and Dr. Helmcken declaring their intention of leaving the service at the close of the present year, a circumstance which adds greatly to my own pressing anxieties.

Chief Factor Work left this place a few days ago by canoe on his return to Fort Rupert, and will see that the instructions to Mr. Blenkinsop are carried out to the letter.

Another object of Mr. Works visit to this place was to communicate intelligence of an important discovery lately made by the natives of Queen Charlotts Island, who have found Gold on the west coast of the Island, as far as we can gather from their reports, about Cape Henry Englefields Bay...

1851

A party of Natives from the Gold District, a weak tribe oppressed by all their neighbours visited Fort Simpson last autumn. They brought no Gold with them, but report it abundant, and that their people had considerable quantities of the ore in their possession and some large pieces of Gold in nearly a pure state which they would have brought to the Fort but were afraid of being plundered by their enemies on the way. It is evident from the specimens we have received that there is Gold in that Country, but whether it exists in large quantities, and the difficulties in the way of procuring it do not so certainly appear. By the Indian accounts it is found in viens, running horizontally, in a bed of White Quartz, which they compare to the spaces between their fingers and account for the circumstance of their not bringing it in larger quantities for sale, first by the dread of being plundered by their neighbours and secondly by the difficulty of breaking it out of the rock, without the aid of proper tools—which is obviously a very substantial reason.

They made an offer of their lands to the Company at a price to be agreed upon hereafter and begged hard that people might be sent immediately to form an establishment there. Pierre Legace who was sent, by Chief Factor Work last autumn, under the safe conduct of a party of Natives on a visit to Queen Charlottes Island, did not succeed in reaching the Gold District in consequence of the jealousy of two influential Chiefs who threw every possible difficulty in his way.

He however decided an important Geographical question that there is a clear passage from Skeddigats on the east, to Englefield Bay on the West Coast of the

Island, with, as he supposes, sufficient depth of Water for Ships. The indians report several other passages leading to the conclusion that it is a group rather than a single Island.

Fort Victoria, 16 April 1851
Archibald Barclay Esq.
Sir,

...We are now in the midst of seed time, having sown all the land formerly under cultivation, except that reserved for grass and hoe crop. The weather continuing favourable for field work we have about 100 Indians employed in clearing the Brush and trees and bringing new land into cultivation, a process involving much labour, though well repaid by the land reclaimed; which is generally speaking of better quality than the Prairie Soil. The labour is done by contract at a cost of 30/per acre. The quantity of Grain sown, up to this date, is 301 Bushels of Wheat, Oats, Pease and Barley—and we have land prepared for planting 400 Bushels of Potatoes.

Our operations at present embrace a wide range for our small force, consisting in all of 61 labouring servants including invalids, A party of ten hands are employed in erecting buildings on the Pugets Sound Reserve, at Esquimalt and breaking up land for cultivation. They have finished two dwelling houses ea. 40 x 22 ft., and have several smaller buildings in progress. Another party is similarly employed on the Fur Trade farm at Cadboro Bay where two dwelling Houses 40 x 20 ft. are finished and timber cut and squared for several smaller buildings. They have also 10,000 fence poles split and ready for carting to the spots required and ten acres of New land broken up.

Another building party is at work putting up buildings about the Fort, having a dwelling House, Bakery, and a Flour Mill in progress.

A dairy is established about four miles north of the Fort and another in its vicinity. Another party is employed dressing Barrel Staves, having a sufficient number nearly ready for 1,000 Barrels; as we propose salting Salmon for exportation on a large scale next Summer. The Blacksmiths are preparing Iron works for the Interior and the Baker equally busy in his department for the Ships and Fort consumption. The Indian department requires much time and attention; while the demands of the general business, Sale shops, stores, shipping and receiving cargoes, supplying the Outposts Accounts &c keeps every member of the establishment in *more* than *active* employment...

I have the honor to be Sir

Your Obedt. Servant

James Douglas

P.S. Duplicate of my letter of 10th Inst. is herewith forwarded   J.D.

Fort Victoria, 8 October 1851
Archibald Barclay Esqr
Sir

I have received a petition from the Settlers at Soke Inlet about 25 miles west of this place, praying to have a road opened by the sea coast to their settlement, as they are now put to a great expense for canoe hire for want of a good horse road. I think favourably of the object of their petition, and beg to recommend it to the favourable consideration of the Governor and Committee, as it will contribute greatly to the convenience of the inhabitants, and otherwise promote the interests of the Colony...

I will also take the liberty of calling the attention of the Governor and Committee to the subject of education by recommending the establishment, of one or two elementary schools in the colony to give a proper, moral, and religious training to the children of Settlers, who are at present growing up in ignorance, and the utter neglect of all their duties to God and to society.—That remarks applies with peculiar force to the children of Protestant Parents; the Roman Catholic families in this country, having had, until lately, a very able and zealous teacher in the Revd. Mr. Lempfritz, a French Priest of the Society des Oblats', who is now living with the Indians in the Cowetchin valley.

One School at Victoria and one at Esquimalt, will provide for the present wants of the settlement—A fixed salary of £50 a year to be paid by the Colony, with an annual payment by the Parents of a certain sum not to exceed thirty shillings, for each child, with a free house and garden, is the plan and amount of remuneration I would propose to the Committee.

In regard to the character of the Teachers I would venture to recommend a middle aged married couple, for each School, of strictly religious principles, and unblemished character, capable of giving a good sound English education, and nothing more; those Schools being intended for the children of the labouring and poorer classes; and children of promising talents, or whom their Parents may wish to educate further, may pursue their studies, and acquire the other branches of knowledge at the Company's school, conducted by the Revd. Mr. Staines.

I would also recommend that a good supply of School Books, from the Alphabet upwards, with slates and pencils, be sent out with the Teachers, as there are very few in this country.

The sum of £4,000 that I was directed by the Governor & Committee to pay on the demand of the late Governor Blanchard, for the purpose of building a Church, and making other improvements, was never called for, and no measures were taken by him to carry out these views, which I presume it is the wish of the Committee, that I should now take in hand; I will therefore give them my earliest attention.
I have the honor to be Sir
Your obt. Servt.
James Douglas

[Hartwell Bowsfield, ed., Fort Victoria Letters, 1846-1851 (Winnipeg: Hudson's Bay Record Society, 1979), pp. 62-172 (excerpts)]

Guy Tuttle's Residence Yale, British Columbia, c. 1870. *[Provincial Archives of British Columbia, 9760]*

'The Hurdies,' German Dancing Girls in the Cariboo Goldfields, c. 1868, Frederick Dally 1838-1914. *[Provincial Archives of British Columbia, 95344]*

Section C
The Red River, 1869–1870

The final documents in this topic examine the situation at Red River in 1869-1870. The formal List of Rights drawn up 1 December 1869, by the Provisional Governing Council of the Métis Nation sets out the Council's conditions for the entry of Rupert's Land into Confederation. Two different perspectives on the problems at Red River are seen in the letter to the editor of the *Daily Globe*, presenting 'loyal' natives' point of view, and in Riel's protest against Ontario's reaction to the Provisional Government's actions, reprinted here in translation from the original French.

Household of an Industrious Métis Farmer, c. 1822. *[National Archives of Canada, C001937]*

List of Rights, Created by the Provisional Governing Council of the Métis Nation, 1 December 1869

1. That the people have the right to elect their own Legislature.

2. That the Legislature have the power to pass all laws local to the Territory over the veto of the Executive by a two-thirds vote.

3. That no act of the Dominion Parliament (local to the Territory) be binding on the people until sanctioned by the Legislature of the Territory.

4. That all Sheriffs, Magistrates, Constables, School Commissioners, etc., be elected by the people.

5. A free Homestead and pre-emption Land Law.

6. That a portion of the public lands be appropriated to the benefit of Schools, the building of Bridges, Roads and Public Buildings.

7. That it be guaranteed to connect Winnipeg by Rail with the nearest line of Railroad, within a term of five years; the land grant to be subject to the Local Legislature.

8. That for the term of four years all Military, Civil, and Municipal expenses be paid out of the Dominion funds.

9. That the Military be composed of the inhabitants now existing in the Territory.

10. That the English and French languages be common in the Legislature and Courts, and that all Public Documents and Acts of the Legislature be published in both languages.

11. That the Judge of the Supreme Court speak the English and French languages.

12. That Treaties be concluded and ratified between the Dominion Government and the several tribes of Indians in the Territory to ensure peace on the frontier.

13. That we have a fair and full representation in the Canadian Parliament.

14. That all privileges, customs and usages existing at the time of the transfer be respected.

All the above articles have been severally discussed and adopted by the French and English Representatives without a dissenting voice, as the conditions upon which the people of Rupert's Land enter into Confederation.

The French Representative then proposed in order to secure the above rights, that a Delegation be appointed and sent to Pembina to see Mr. Macdougall and ask him if he could guarantee these rights by virtue of his commission; and if he could do so, that then the French people would join to a man to escort Mr. Macdougall into his Government seat. But on the contrary, if Mr. Macdougall could not guarantee such rights that the Delegation request him to remain where he is, or return 'till the rights be guaranteed by Act of the Canadian Parliament.

The English Representative refused to appoint Delegates to go to Pembina to consult with Mr. Macdougall, stating that they had no authority to do so from their constituents, upon which the Council was dissolved.

The meeting at which the above resolutions were signed was held at Fort Garry, on Wednesday, Dec. 1, 1869.

Winnipeg, December 4, 1869.

[*Charlebois,* The Life of Louis Riel]

Letter from a Red River Loyalist on the Rising of 15 February 1870

Red River Settlement
February 22, 1870

Sir—As an old settler, and one who has never swayed in his fealty to country or Queen, will you, Mr. Editor, permit me to occupy a brief space in your valuable columns with comments on the present aspect of affairs in unhappy Red River Settlement.

Before this reaches Toronto you will doubtless have heard of the bloodless fight of the 15th inst., of Riel's victory, and of the imprisonment of forty-eight more loyal men; but we, who constitute the majority, would like you to weigh the facts well before either branding us as cowards or believing that the Provisional Government is the choice of the people, expressed through their delegates. One fact, however, must speak for itself. Within three days after Riel's election, and James Ross, the renegade, had received the price of his allegiance in a Judgeship, eight hundred loyal men were under arms in the interests of Canada, and wild to oust the rebels from Fort Garry. Why then, you will ask, has the insurrection reached so formidable a point, if public sentiment is so averse to it? To explain I must digress. Fifteen years since, after a brief sojourn in Canada, when I returned to my birthplace, I soon discerned what time has but more fully impressed on my mind, that this Settlement is as completely priest-ridden as ever unfortunate Ireland was. Not the French alone, but all nations and creeds represented here, are to a great extent ruled by the clergy; and though I believe that power has not been abused, except in isolated instances, few of our simple credulous people dare exercise their own discretion in temporal matters, when opposed by their spiritual leaders.

Bishop Taché sowed the seeds of rebellion, and had it not been for priestly influence, aided by Hudson Bay Co.'s Pemican, it would have died a natural death long ago. On the other side, the Protestant clergy are for 'Peace, peace, when

---

[1]   Bishop Robert Machray, the Reverend John Black, and, probably, Archdeacons McLean and Cowley

there is no peace;' and to that cause, and that cause alone, must be attributed the failure of the English to make head against the French.

The Indian element is strong enough within us to make us fight like demons when once aroused; and when our noble little army had spontaneously gathered together at Kildonan, on the 14th February, if the Reverend quartette[1] had quietly studied their sermons, or in their closets offered a prayer for our success, instead of going through our ranks discouraging our men, we would ere this have had the proud satisfaction of seeing 'the flag that braved a thousand years' floating over Fort Garry, and not be disgraced by that symbol of Jesuitical Fenianism that now hangs from the flag staff. I will do them the justice to say their motives may have been good; but our sentiments are, too many peace overtures have been made already, and why is our blood more precious than that so freely asked time and again, in the contest for that liberty which every true Briton holds to be dearer than life? True, we are Indians, at best but half civilized; but we all feel an innate love for Great Britain; and three-fourths of our people, if left to themselves, would gladly welcome the representative of our Queen as our future ruler. And if such a policy is to be adopted, as not only to restore peace here, but to make it a home for Canadian emigrants, the first move should be to send an army large enough to show you are in earnest; make no compromise with such arch rebels as Riel and O'Donohoe; banish such knaves as Ross and Burns, who have sold themselves and their constituents, in the expectation that Canada will be glad to bid higher for their talents in the formation of the new Government, and burn the infamous 'Bill of Rights' (which never would have passed the Convention if it had not been that a refusal on the part of the English delegates was threatened with fearful vengeance towards the prisoners confined at Fort Garry). If such a course is adopted, Canada will find the inhabitants to a man fly to her Standard. Long ago we had enough of Hudson Bay Company's justice mumbled out by Judge Black. Annexation we will not consent to, and to much longer endure the oppression and tyranny under which we now groan would be even more than the clergy could exact. Riel talks of peace, but it is futile to expect him to disband his men while Governor McTavish, in his easy chair, looks on, in the vain hope of this glorious country again becoming the resort of fur bearing animals, and helps feed the flame the Jesuits have kindled to exterminate Protestantism...

I am glad to see the *Globe* is down on Howe for the sentiments expressed when here. McDougall may not have been the right man in the right place, but assuredly that was the wrong time to spread disloyalty. We can only hope with the first buds of spring to see our deliverance near at hand, and again I say adopt the policy that so soon ended the Abyssinian war, and Canada will be victorious. A handful of troops would be our ruin.

Is it known in Canada a great part of Riel's forces are American subjects, halfbreeds from Pembina and St. Joe? We have just heard one hundred and fifty mounted men are to-night to start for the Portage and subdue that loyal little Colony. —X.Y.Z.

[The Daily Globe, *28 March 1870*]

Protest of the Peoples of the North-West: A Proclamation Issued by Riel, 14 May 1870

The present state of excitement against us in certain parts of Canada: [amended to 'of certain Canadian parties against us'] gives us a fitting occasion to demonstrate the difference between their principles and ours. Is it true that so many Canadian newspapers and so many people who approve them exercise themselves against us simply and sincerely in the interest of the Confederation? Is it in the interest of England? If it is so, how is it that Snow, Dennis, McDougall, and so many other recipients of sympathy principally in Upper Canada, should have chosen ways so tortuous, and should have sought so deviously to deceive the people to throw them into an agitation as great as it is general? The men of Upper Canada, with whom we have avoided all sorts of frays during the last six months, have sought to divide us, to arouse us one against the other, to bring us to the horrible collision of a civil war! Has not civil war been proclaimed in our midst? And those who have dared to do so, have they not usurped, in an infamous manner, the name of Her Majesty? As many outsiders as we have been constrained, at different times, to make prisoners, have they not been generously set at liberty again, when we knew that they would hasten to do against us the evil that they are raising to-day in Upper Canada, perjuring themselves the while? And because one of those who through obstinacy continued to trouble the public peace, which they alone had put in jeopardy amongst us, and which we made so many efforts to keep in the North-West, has forced us to make an example of him by which others might learn, they wish to declare war on us, while Sir John A. Macdonald, the Prime Minister, is compelled in justice to say that Canada has no jurisdiction in the country. No, those people have not worked and are not working in the interest of England! They concern themselves with the Confederation only so far as they believe it necessary to the success of their plans, of which the aims are too personal and too exclusive to be just! These persons through a great lack of honesty and loyalty have thought to impose on us a supremacy altogether to be condemned, to achieve which these false British subjects have not wanted and do not wish to respect the rights of anyone in a British colony. They flattered themselves with the shameful hope of being able to combine their selfish projects with those of Imperial policy in British North America. There is one thing they have forgotten: the policy of a government having to concern itself with the general interests of society, without distinction of language, of origin, without distinction of religious belief, is always incompatible with the restricted views of individual interest, when the latter, in place of imposing itself on the former, is not entirely subordinate to it. They should have known it: the sole means of assuring the existence and extension of the Confederation is to place on the same equal and generous footing all the provinces of British North America. If it is true that the Hudson's Bay Company has neglected the political advancement of their country, the people themselves, as soon as they could, have had to act. They have formed a government, and this government which calls itself provisional does not wish that the North-West enter into Confederation until in this country all claims of civilized men shall have received a guarantee of being on the same noble footing of equality.

In the month of October last, when the first representatives of the people of Red River had first publicly assembled to take, in the name of their constituents, the title and function of 'Protectors of the rights the people,' they declared:—

1. That they were loyal subjects of Her Majesty the Queen of England.

2. That they were beholden to the Hudson's Bay Company for the well-being they had enjoyed under its government, whatever the nature of that government.

3. That the Hudson's Bay Company being about to lay down the government of the country they were ready to accept the change involved. But at the same time being settlers, having lived on the lands which they had assisted the Hudson's Bay Company to open up, the people of Red River, having acquired in that fashion indisputable rights in the country, proudly asserted those rights.

4. That the people of Red River having up to this time upheld and supported the government of the Hudson's Bay Company, under the Crown of England, Snow and Dennis have disregarded the law of nations in coming to carry out here public works in the name of an alien authority without paying the respect owing to the authority then existing in the country.

5. The Colony of Red River having always been subject to the Crown of England, having been developed in isolation, through all the hazards of its situation, these representatives declared in the name of their constituents, that they would do all in their power to have respected, on their behalf, all the privileges so liberally granted by the Crown of England to any English colony whatever.

These principles have been published in Canada in the month of November last. They are still as they were then the line of conduct of the Provisional Government. The English flag which floats over our heads displays fully to the eyes of the world its grand testimony in our favour. Filled with confidence in these principles which are our strength, we do not consider that they are loyal subjects of Her Majesty the Queen of England who have wished to make war on us up to now, and who would wish still to wage it on us, because of the way we have conducted ourselves under these resolutions. In order to ruin us, and raise themselves on our ruins, they have always held us to be barbarians. However, the magnitude of our great difficulties has never led us to call to our aid the dangerous element of the wild Indian tribes. On the contrary, while we have spared ourselves no effort to keep them quiet, these others have just sent across our country where their government has no jurisdiction, some agents for the criminal purpose of creating enemies for us among the Indians. But we hope that Providence will aid us to complete the pacification of the North-West; we hope that the authority of the Crown of England will assist the solution of the great complications which have been caused by a major political impudence.

Our cause is that of a British colony! Our cause is that of liberty! God and the world know how we have been outraged.

People whom progress and civilization fill with ambition border us on one side and on the other numerous wild tribes who live on the alert and in apprehension. The people of Red River is sprung from these two great divisions in order to serve both as intermediary. In effect we are bound to both by blood and by custom.

The Province of Ontario in arresting our delegates that the Federal Government had invited by three special commissions has just committed an act against which we protest in the name of all the peoples of the North-West. We denounce the opprobriousness of such a proceeding to all civilized people; we appeal to the law of nations which Upper Canada has always disregarded where we are concerned, which the Federal Government has not done itself the honour to uphold, but which we claim before God and before men in every way open to us and in every way which shall be open to us.

Louis Riel

President

Seat of the Provisional Government,

Fort Garry, May 14, 1870

[W. L. Morton, ed., Alexander Begg's Red River Journal, 1869-70 *(Champlain Society, 1958), pp. 524-527]*

QUESTIONS

1. What do documents such as the marriage contract between Louis Bouchard (a Hudson's Bay Company employee) and Charlotte Fainiant (a Native woman), tell us about gender and family relations in the fur trade? How might the structure of the fur trade have affected these relationships?

2. Discuss the relations between European-Canadians and Natives described in these documents. What do they tell us about Native perceptions of whites, and their reasons for continuing these relationships?

3. What were European-Canadians' motives and interests in western expansion?

4. Assess Douglas's behaviour in his colonial contexts. What were his motivations in governing?

5. What do the documents on Red River tell us of Métis conceptions of community and nation?

READINGS

Jean Barman, *The West Beyond the West: A History of British Columbia* (Toronto: University of Toronto Press, 1991). See Chapters 1-5.

Jennifer Brown, *Strangers in Blood: Fur Trade Families in Indian Country* (Vancouver: University of British Columbia Press, 1980)

Jennifer Brown, Robert Brightman, and George Nelson, *The Orders of the Dreamed: George Nelson on Cree and Northern Ojibwa Religion and Myth* (Winnipeg: University of Manitoba Press, 1988)

Ken S. Coates, *Best Left as Indians: Native-White Relations in the Yukon Territory, 1840-1973* (Montreal-Kingston: McGill-Queen's University Press, 1991)

Robin Fisher, *Contact and Conflict: Indian-European Relations in British Columbia, 1774-1890* (Vancouver: University of British Columbia Press, 1979)

Gerald Friesen, *The Canadian Prairies: A History* (Toronto: University of Toronto Press, 1987). See Chapters 2-7.

R. Louis Gentilcore and Geoffrey Matthews, eds., *Historical Atlas of Canada* Volume II, *The Land Transformed 1800-1891* (Toronto: University of Toronto Press, 1993). See Plates 2 & 3, 17-19, 21, 34-36.

James Gibson, *Otter Skins, Boston Ships and China Goods: The Maritime Fur Trade of the Northwest Coast, 1785-1841* (Montreal-Kingston: McGill-Queen's University Press, 1992)

R. Cole Harris and Geoffrey J. Matthews, eds., *Historical Atlas of Canada:* Volume I, *From the Beginning to 1800* (Toronto: University of Toronto Press, 1987). See Plates 57-67.

C. Stuart Houston, ed., *Arctic Artist: The Journal and Paintings of George Back, Midshipman with Franklin, 1819-1822* (Montreal-Kingston: McGill-Queen's University Press, 1994).

——————————————, *Arctic Ordeal: The Journal of John Richardson, Surgeon-Naturalist with Franklin, 1820-1822* (Montreal-Kingston: McGill-Queen's University Press, 1984)

Tina Loo, *Making Law, Order, and Authority in British Columbia, 1821-1871* (Toronto: University of Toronto Press, 1994)

Jacqueline Peterson and Jennifer S. H. Brown, eds., *The New Peoples: Being and Becoming Métis in North America* (Winnipeg: 1985)

Doug Owram, *Promise of Eden: The Canadian Expansionist Movement and the Idea of the West 1856-1900* (Toronto: University of Toronto Press, 1980). See Chapters 1-5.

Arthur J. Ray, *Indians in the Fur Trade: Their Role as Hunters, Trappers and Middlemen in the Lands Southwest of Hudson Bay, 1660-1870* (Toronto: University of Toronto Press, 1974)

Sylvia Van Kirk, *'Many Tender Ties': Women in Fur-Trade Society in Western Canada, 1670-1870* (Winnipeg: Dwyer, 1980)

David C. Woodman, *Unravelling the Franklin Mystery: Inuit Testimony* (Montreal and Kingston: McGill-Queen's University Press, 1991)

An 'Imagined Community'—The Canadas, the Atlantic Colonies, and Confederation

L ike the Rebellion of 1837-38, the formation of voluntary organizations, and institution-building in British North America, Confederation should be seen in the broad international context of the formation of nation-states during the nineteenth century. Historian Benedict Anderson has argued that nations are 'imagined communities,' brought into being through the efforts of the nineteenth-century middle classes who were firmly committed to industrial progress. They were convinced that the nation-state would be the most effective means of achieving their goals. Anderson has also pointed out that, through the medium of the press in particular, the middle class was able to see itself as being united in a way that would—in theory—rise above religious, ethnic, and regional differences; the nation would bring together men who had not and never would physically meet each other in a common 'national' identity.

The process was not a straightforward one in Canada or many other parts of the nineteenth-century world. In Canada, regional, ethnic, and religious distinctions clearly complicated the process of 'nation-building.' Relations of gender and race in the Confederation period have received far less attention than other issues until now, and such differences were often either ignored or papered over in attempts to create an apparently ascendant national identity.

In British North America, discussions about founding a nation took place during the late 1850s. (Before this time, the term 'Canadian' had been used in Upper Canada, and Lower Canadian reformers thought of themselves as 'Canadiens.') Much of the debate revolved around the need to counter the rapidly-expanding entity south of the border, as well as the need for economic union to continue the boom of the mid-1850s that had happened as a result of the Crimean War and the 1854 Reciprocity agreement in resource products between British North America and the United States. The middle-class men who promoted Confederation had placed their faith in state—and often their own—investments in railways, canals, and roads. They were convinced that closer economic ties would benefit both themselves and their fellow-colonists. There was no clear consensus on just how a Canadian 'nation' would relate to Britain: would it simply enjoy somewhat looser ties to the imperial power, or would it break away as a sovereign state that, while part of the empire, would no longer be subject to British rule? These were questions that continued to perplex Canadians into the twentieth century.

Other concerns surrounded Confederation, making the unification of the provinces far from inevitable. In the Canadas, the issue of representation by population was highly contentious by the start of the 1860s; Canada West's population doubled from 1841 to 1851, while that of Canada East grew more slowly. Responsible government was no longer an issue around which Reformers in both provinces could unite; the *rouges* in Canada East, and George Brown's Canada West Reformers were divided by different attitudes toward language, religion, and ethnicity. The latter group made 'rep by pop' a central part of their political platform, along with a desire to annex the North-West and see the Maritimes become a market for Upper Canadian manufactured goods. As well, colonists in the Canadas were divided over other issues such as education, funding for separate schools, and the financing of railways. The railway question was particularly contentious, and charges of political patronage and corruption concerning the Grand Trunk were rife.

In the Atlantic provinces, debates over Maritime union took place in Nova Scotia; this colony and New Brunswick were most interested in union. Like the Canadas, railway promotion and financing were central items on Nova Scotia's and New Brunswick's political agendas. Howe's promotion of the Intercolonial (Halifax to St. Lawrence) Railroad had by 1863 incurred large amounts of public debt. The completion of this railway has been seen as an enticement for the Maritimes to enter Confederation—it would move their goods into the continent's interior markets and, in return, the Maritimes would have easy access to products from the West. On Prince Edward Island, the problem of absentee landlords and tenants' rights was uppermost in politicians' minds. The province did not see a railroad until 1871, and subsequently had fewer internal financial difficulties. The Island did not join Confederation until 1873. While Newfoundland's Premier Hoyles expressed interest in Confederation, the province was not invited to the first Charlottetown conference in 1864. Although Newfoundland attended the second conference, Confederation was rejected by both the legislature and, in 1869, the Newfoundland electorate.

Britain, however, was eager that 'white settler' colonies take more responsibility for their own finances, particularly in the area of defence. The American Civil War and related Fenian raids had increased the need for British troops in British North America, especially since cash-strapped provincial legislatures were unable to provide adequate funding for their own militias. With the imperial power's urging, the premiers' meetings ended with their agreement to the British North America Act. The creation of this 'imagined community' was fraught with a number of tensions—the Maritimes suspicions' of the degree of centralization vested in the Canadas (provinces where government had broken down throughout the 1850s and which had also seen armed rebellion in the 1830s); the example of America, where federal union had broken down in a bloody civil war; and Canada East's *rouge* opposition to the prospect of being linguistically and culturally swamped by Canada West and the Maritimes.

Some historians have argued that the 'clinchers' that sold Confederation were economic and physical fears—the United States' revocation of the Reciprocity Treaty, and the threat posed by the Fenians. Whatever the case, Confederation appears to have been primarily an 'imagined community' created by elites—New Brunswick was the only province prior to 1867 to hold an election on the subject. Historians are faced with many absences and silences on the part of groups such as women in general, or First Nations, who were not asked to the Conferences, and who had been generally excluded from formal political decision making by 1867.

Section A
Politics and People

This first section of documents presents us with glimpses of, first, how definitions of the electorate were contested in the pre-Confederation period. Document one is a petition to the Lower Canadian House of Assembly that argued for women's right to vote. However, by the mid-century, women had been formally excluded from the franchise. Yet as the excerpts from Adolphus Gaetz's diary demonstrate, women still could be found at political gatherings, albeit as spectators and not formal participants.

Women's Suffrage, Petitions to the House of Assembly, Lower Canada, 4 December 1828

Upper Town of Quebec Election—Petition of Electors

A Petition of divers Electors of the Upper Town of *Quebec*, whose names are thereunto subscribed, was presented to the House by Mr. *Clouet*, and the same was received and read; setting forth: That in July One thousand eight hundred and twenty-seven, *William Fisher Scott* was appointed Returning Officer for the election of two Citizens to represent in Parliament the Upper Town of *Quebec*, and that on the seventh of August a Poll was opened for that purpose near the Bishop's Palace: That the Candidates were Messrs. *Joseph Remy Vallières de St. Réal*, *Andrew Stuart*, *George Vanfelson* and *Amable Berthelot:* That the Polling was continued to the fifteenth August, when Messrs. *Joseph Remy Vallières de St. Réal* and *Andrew Stuart* were returned as duty elected: That, however, on the fourteenth, Mrs. Widow *Laperrière* did tender to Mr. *Scott*, the aforesaid Returning Officer, her vote, under oath, which Mr. *Scott* did refuse to take and enregister, whereupon a protest against such refusal was served. That the Petitioners allege that the following conclusions are to be drawn from this refusal:

1. That Mr. *Scott* acted contrary to law; 2. That the election of Mr. *Stuart* is void. That the Petitioners saw with extreme concern and alarm this refusal to take a vote tendered under oath, in the terms of the law; and they allege that Mr. *Scott* had no discretion to exercise, that he was bound to follow the letter of the law, that he was not to sit as a judge of the law. That the Petitioners need hardly avert to the danger of such a power as Mr. *Scott* has exercised. They will not place their dearest right, their elective franchise, in the hands of any one man, but especially they will not place it in the hands of an officer appointed by the Executive, and whose opinions and feelings under almost every circumstances must endanger the free choice of the people, and thus strike at the root of their liberties. That the Petitioners, therefore, deem this refusal to take a vote offered in the terms of the law, a most dangerous precedent, contrary to law, and tending to subvert their rights and constitutional privileges. That the Petitioners represent on the second head, that, as the votes of the Widows were not taken, the return of Mr. *Stuart* is void, inasmuch as the free choice of all the electors was not made known. That the Petitioners may presume to trouble the House with the reasons which they deem conclusive as to the right of Widows to vote; neither in men nor women can the right to vote be a natural right: it is given by enactment. The only questions are, whether women could exercise that right well and advantageously for the State, and whether they are entitled to it. That the Petitioners have not learned that there exist any imperfections in the minds of women which place them lower than men in intellectual power, or which would make it more dangerous to entrust them with the exercise of the elective franchise than with the exercise of the numerous other rights which the law has already given them. That, in point of

fact, women duly qualified have hitherto been allowed to exercise the right in question. That the Petitioners conceive that women are fairly entitled to the right, if they can exercise it well. That property and not persons is the basis of representation in the English Government. That the qualifications required by the Election Laws sufficiently shew this. That the same principle is carried into our own constitution. That the paying certain taxes to the State is also a basis of representation; for it is a principal contended for by the best Statesmen of England, that there can be "no taxation without representation." That the duties to be performed to the State may also give a right to representation. That in respect of property, taxation and duties to the State, the Widow, duly qualified by our Election Laws, is in every essential respect similarly situated with the man: her property is taxed alike with that of the man: she certainly is not liable to Militia duties, nor is the man above forty-five: she is not called to serve on a jury, nor is a physician: she cannot be elected to the Assembly, nor can a Judge or Minister of the Gospel. It may be alleged that nature has only fitted her for domestic life, yet the English Constitution allows a woman to sit on the Throne, and one of its brightest ornaments has been a woman. That it would be impolitic and tyrannical to circumscribe her efforts in society, —to say that she shall not have the strongest interest in the fate of her country, and the security of her common rights: It is she who breathes into man with eloquent tenderness his earliest lessons of religion and of morals; and shall it be said that his country shall be forgotten, or that she shall mould his feelings while smarting under hateful laws. That the Petitioners allege that Widows exercise, generally, all the rights of men, are liable to most of the same duties towards the State, and can execute them as well. And they pray from the premises:

1. That the House declare Mr. *Scott*, the Returning Officer, guilty of malversation in office, and take measures to enforce the law in such case provided. 2. That the proceedings at the late Election for the Upper Town of *Quebec*, concluded on the fifteenth August One thousand eight hundred and twenty-seven, by the Return of Mr. *Stuart*, be declared void...

Mr. *Clouet* moved to resolve, seconded by Mr. *Labrie*, That the grounds and reasons of complaint set forth in the said Petition, if true, are sufficient to make void the election of the said *Andrew Stuart*, Esquire.

Ordered, That the consideration of the said motion be postponed till Tuesday next.

William Henry Election; Petition of Electors.

A petition of divers Electors of the Borough of *William Henry*. whose names are thereunto subscribed, was presented to the House by Mr. *Stuart*, and the same was received and read; setting forth: That on the twenty-fifth day of July in the year of our Lord One thousand eight hundred and twenty-seven, a Poll was legally opened by *Henry Crebassa*, Esquire, Returning Officer, for the Election of a Burgess to serve as the Representative of the said Borough of *William Henry*, in the Provincial Assembly; *James Stuart* and *Wolfred Nelson*, Esquires, having offered themselves as Candidates: That although the said *James Stuart* was afterwards elected by a majority of legal votes, yet an apparent and colourable majority in favour of the said *Wolfred Nelson*, to the exclusion of the said *James Stuart*, was obtained by the admission of unqualified persons to vote, by various corrupt, illegal, criminal and unwarrantable means and practices destructive of the right of Election in the persons legally qualified to be Electors, and subversive of the constitutional franchise, rights and privileges of the Petitioners and of the whole body of Electors: That the Petitioners, as well in consideration of the justice due to the person who has been the object of their choice, as from regard to their own rights which have been grossly violated, deem it to be their duty to resist and oppose the illegal Return of the said *Wolfred Nelson*, and having recourse to the House for their interference, pray leave succinctly to represent the principal facts and grounds on which the said Return is to be considered an undue Return, and as being null and void in law: That many votes were given in favour of the said *Wolfred Nelson*, by persons without any qualification whatever, and whose want of qualification was even apparent on their own statements; such persons having been induced to vote and even to take the oaths to entitle them to do so, by criminal solicitations, and by assurances pressed upon them, before the Returning Officer himself, that they would incur no harm from such conduct, and that they would be guaranteed and indemnified by the said *Wolfred Nelson* and his partisans against all consequences: That the votes of women, married, unmarried, and in a state of widowhood, were illegally received for the said *Wolfred Nelson*, although the illegality of such votes was strenuously urged by the said *James Stuart*, and notwithstanding the opposition made by him and by divers of the Electors to the admission of them: That in divers instances several persons were admitted to vote for the said *Wolfred Nelson* on one and the same alleged qualification; in others, persons under oath declared themselves proprietors of houses to which they had no right or title; in others, an arbitrary and untrue value, exceeding the real value, was assigned, even on oath, to property of which the value was not sufficient to confer a right of voting; and in almost all these cases an undue and improper influence by promises, by violence, and otherwise, was exercised over such persons even at the Poll, and in the presence and hearing of the Returning Officer, to stifle their scruples, and prevail on them to give their votes for the said *Wolfred Nelson*; nay, even to induce them to commit perjury by taking the Oath of qualification...

Mr. *Stuart* moved to resolve, seconded by Mr. *Solicitor General*, That the grounds and reasons of complaint set forth in the said Petition, if true, are sufficient to make void the Election of the said *Wolfred Nelson*, Esquire.

Ordered, That the consideration of the said motion be postponed till Saturday next.

[Journals of House of Assembly, Lower Canada, 1828-29, *pp. 81-84*]

Election-Time in Nova Scotia

Thursday Apr 28 1859

Electioneering excitement running high. The Candidates for Legislative honors are the following, viz.,—

Conservative: Henry S. Jost, of this town. Benjamin Zwicker, of Mahone Bay. Charles Lordly, of Chester

Radical: Henry Bailey, of this town. Henry Moseley, of Bridgewater. Benjamin Wier, of Halifax.

The struggle between the parties will be great. The Arch Demagogue Joe Howe, who has been hired by the Radical faction, has in conjunction with the radical candidates, been perambulating the County, holding their meetings at different places and endeavouring to persuade ignorant people that their party are all right, and that their opponents are all wrong.

Thursd. May 5 1859

This is "nomination Day," early in the morning the flags of both parties were to be seen floating from the different places in town. About 9 O'clock the Conservative party with Banners and music marched out to meet the party on their way from Bridgewater; soon the two parties met and marched into town in good order, displaying a large number of flags and banners and accompanied with a goodly number of musicians. The great Radical party soon followed, by their appearance was rather [?] considering the great preparations made by them for the occasion. At 11 O'clock the several candidates were nominated, after which each in turn made his speech which occupied the whole time until 4 O'clock when the Sheriff closed the meeting. Until about 5 O'clock in the afternoon the streets were thronged with people, after that hour they dispersed, and the town soon became quiet. A large number of persons of both sexes were assembled in town, the excitement was greater than on any former occasion.

[C.B. Fergusson, ed., The Diary of Adolphus Gaetz *(Public Archives of Nova Scotia, 1965), pp. 48-49]*

Section B
Politicians, the Press, and Confederation

The documents in this section look at the various positions taken by politicians and the press on the issue of Confederation. The first two selections depict reactions to the Charlottetown Conference that was held in September 1864, where it appeared to many onlookers that representatives from the Canadas were trying to woo—perhaps even seduce—Maritime delegates into support for Confederation. The next documents present Newfoundland newspaper writers' thoughts on the subject—some of these articles suggest that Confederation was seen as a solution to a desperate economic situation. Finally, there is a poem by a Nova Scotian writer who took the opposite point of view to union.

A Disapproving Observer at the Grand Ball, Charlottetown Conference, September 1864

A few days after the close of the circus, a great public "Ball and Supper" is announced; the evening of the day arrives; the proud and the gay, arrayed in fashion's gauds, flock to the scene where revelry presides...Pleasure panoplied in lustful smiles meets and embraces exuberant Joy...the fascinating dance goes merrily, and the libidinous waltz with its lascivious entwinements whiles in growing excitement; the swelling bosom and voluptuous eye tell the story of intemperate revel...In this scene, where intrigue schemes sin...our moralist mingles; here he rocks his piety to sleep, and cradles his morality in forgiveness; and the saint who could not tolerate satan in the circus, embraces the Prince of Darkness in the gilded scene of fashion's vices, and the reeking slough of debauchery.

[Ross's Weekly (Charlottetown), 15 September 1864]

A New Brunswick View

Reader you know as well as I,
How there 'mid scenes of revelry,
At festive boards, at midnight balls,
With dance and song, in lordly halls...
Where'er they turned, on every hand,
They met the Wizard with his wand,
He sparkl'd in the ruby wine,

He glitter'd in the dresses fine...
Yet there amid these scenes they laid
The cornerstone of what they said,
Would make of us a mighty nation,
And christen'd it, "Confederation."

> [Borderer *(Sackville, New Brunswick), 17 March 1865]*

The Newfoundland Press on Confederation

[If Confederation would sweep away] this serfdom...if it shall be the broom which will thoroughly purge this Augean stable—piled up with pauperism, nurtured, fostered, cherished pauperism—piled up too with dirty exclusiveness...then we say by all means let us have Confederation, or anything else that will promise relief.

> [Day-Book, *30 November 1864]*

If any one of the Provinces more than another should seek a change, it is this. We do not mean to assert that we should adopt a change blindly, but unlike our Sister Colonies, our circumstances—the condition of our Trade—the depressed state of our people, demand a change, even if Confederation had never been proposed...A state of things so injurious, so anomalous, and so baneful to the well-being of an integral part of a powerful state would command decisive measures, and the power and authority of the General Government would not be fruitless, though our local means have failed.

> [Newfoundlander, *5 January 1865]*

Small and isolated communities with sparsely scattered populations,—infantile in wealth, influence and position—have suddenly encased themselves in political habilments out of all proportions to the capacity of the body politic. And, like so many infants, with their parents' boots, hats, caps and coats on, they stagger about the world scarcely able to put one foot before the other...much to the amusement of the grown-up people who see themselves mimicked in the unfortunate struttings and strivings of the young folk.

> [St. John's Daily News, *1 December 1866]*

Nova Scotia's Opposition to Confederation

Shall we yield our independence—
Fling our dearest rights away?

Shall we link our fate with a bankrupt State,
 And our native land betray?...

From broad TOOWAUBSCOT's wave, that moans
 With restless ebb and flow—
From each and all, in trumpet-tones,
 Rings forth the anwer—No!

[Yarmouth Tribune, 4 January 1865]

Section C
The Confederation Debate

Debates on Confederation were held in Quebec in 1864 and 1865—the excerpts reprinted here represent various perspectives, both anti- and pro-Confederation. Prince Edward Island's representatives, Thomas Haviland and Edward Palmer, presented their concerns about the potentially damaging effects of Confederation on their province, as did Canada East's Antoine-Aimé Dorion, a leader of his province's opposition to the union. Much of the support for Confederation in the Canadas is summed up in the speeches made by Canada East's George-Etienne Cartier and Canada West's George Brown (who was also the owner of the *Daily Globe*). The last two documents in this section suggest how the press represented these debates to their colonial readers.

Confederation Debates of 1864 and 1865
19 October 1864

[on the issue of an increase in the number of Newfoundland's representatives]
Carried. Prince Edward Island alone voting nay.

Mr. Haviland—Prince Edward Island would rather be out of the Confederation than consent to this motion. We should have no status. Only five members out of 194 would give the Island no position.

Mr. Tilley—This is rather a singular ground of objection, for they have objected to the basis of representation by population. Now it was fully understood at Charlottetown that those who came to the Conference expected representation by population. Some difficulty might have arisen on those points but not on this.

Mr. Palmer—I am not inimical to the grand scheme of Confederation. I believe it will be productive of great benefits. But I take exception to the principle adopted by this resolution. Representation by population is not applicable when a certain number of Provinces are throwing their resources into one Confederation, and giving up their own self-government and individuality. When a colony surrenders that right, she should have something commensurate in the Confederation. The debt of Prince Edward Island is nothing. Our taxation is vastly below that of the other Provinces. Our trade and revenue are rapidly increasing. Why give up so great certainties for an uncertain benefit when we have only a feeble voice? Looking first at the Larger Provinces, Canada has secured to herself a greater number of representatives than she had before. It may be said that we may join with the other Maritime Provinces in any matters affecting our common interests, but even then our united strength would still be far below Canada's number of representatives. Not even two or three more members would induce me to give my assent to the scheme. I never understood that nay proposition at Charlottetown was to be binding as to representation by population. It was there made by those from Canada and I did not think it necessary to remark on it, as it was a mere suggestion then thrown out by Canada for consideration.

[G.P. Browne, Documents on the Confederation of British North America (Ottawa: Carleton Library, Carleton University Press, 1969), p. 108]

7 February 1865

George-Etienne Cartier:

I do not fear the rights of Lower Canada will any way be placed in peril by the project of Confederation, even though in a general legislature the French-Canadians will have a smaller number of representatives than all other nationalities combined. The resolutions show that, in the questions which will be submitted to the Federal parliament, there will be no more danger to the rights and privileges of the French Canadians than to those of the Scotch, English or Irish...While the American union had divided against itself, the Canadians, who have the advantage of seeing republicanism in operation for a period of eighty years, of perceiving its faults and vices, have been convinced that purely democratic institutions cannot assure the peace and prosperity of nations, and that we must unite under a federation so formed as to perpetuate the monarchical element...five different groups inhabiting five separate provinces have the same commercial interests, the same desire to live under the British Crown...If we unite we will from a political nationality independent of the national origin and religion of individuals. Some have regretted that we have a distinction of races, and have expressed the hope that, in time, this diversity will disappear. The idea of a fusion of the races in one is utopian; it is an impossibility. Distinctions of this character will always exist; diversity seems to be the order of the physical, moral, and political worlds. As to the objection that we cannot form a great nation because Lower Canada is chiefly French and Catholic, Upper Canada English and Protestant, and the Maritime Provinces mixed, it is completely futile...In our confederation there will be Catholics and Protestants, English, French, Irish and Scotch, and each by its efforts and success will add to the prosperity, the might, and to the glory of the new federation. We are of different races, not to wage war among ourselves, but to work together for our common welfare...

[on the church] *The True Witness*, a Catholic journal which opposes the project, is of the opinion that if it is adopted the French Canadians will be assimilated, whilst its confrère in violence, the Protestant *Witness*, assured us that it will be the Protestants who will suffer...Those of the clergy who are high in authority, as well as those in humbler positions, have declared for Confederation, not only because they see in it all possible security for the institutions they cherish, but also because their Protestant fellow countrymen, like themselves, are also guaranteed their rights. The clergy in general are opposed to all political dissension, and if they are favorable to the project, it is because they see in Confederation a solution to the difficulties which have so long existed...We know that the approbation of the Imperial Government is assured. If, therefore, Canada adopts these resolutions, as I have no doubt it will, and if the other British North American colonies follow its example, the Imperial Government will then be called upon to accord us a central government established on a broad and solid basis, and provincial governments under whose protection will be placed the persons, the properties, and the civil and religious rights of all classes of society.

[Mason Wade, The French Canadians, 1760-1967, Volume 1, 1760-1911
(Toronto: Macmillan of Canada, 1968), pp. 322-323]

Antoine-Aimé Dorion:

The people of Lower Canada are attached to their institutions in a manner that defies any attempt to change them in that way. They will not change their religious institutions, their laws and their language for any consideration whatsoever. A million of inhabitants may seem a small affair to a philosopher who sits down to write out a constitution. He may think that it would be better that there should be one religion, one language and one system of laws, and he goes to work to frame institutions that will bring all to that desirable state; but I can tell honorable gentlemen that the history of every country goes to show that not even by the power of the sword can such changes be accomplished...I know that there is an apprehension amongst the British population in Lower Canada that, even with the small power that the local government will possess, their rights will not be respected.

How, then, can it be expected that the French population can anticipate any more favorable result from the general government, when it is to possess such enormous powers over the destinies of their section of the country? Experience shows that majorities are always aggressive, and it cannot be otherwise in this instance.

[Later in the debates Dorion argued] I am opposed to this confederation in which the militia, the appointment of judges, the administration of justice, and our most important civil rights will be under the control of the general government, the majority of which will be hostile to Lower Canada, of a governor-general vested with the most ample powers, whilst the powers of the local government will be restricted first by the limit of the powers delegated to it, by the veto reserved to the central authority, and further by the concurrent jurisdiction of the general authority or government. Petitions with more 20,000 signatures attached by them have already been presented to this House against the scheme of confederation. Numerous public meetings have been held in nineteen counties in Lower Canada and one in the city of Montreal. Everywhere this scheme has been protested against and an appeal to the people demanded; and yet in defiance of the expressed opinion of our constituents we are about to give them a constitution, the effect of which will be to snatch from them what little influence they still enjoy under the existing law. We are about, on their behalf, to surrender all the rights and privileges which are dearest to them, and that without consulting them. It would be madness—it would be more, it would be [a] crime. On these grounds I shall oppose the scheme with all the power at my command, and insist that under any circumstances it shall be submitted to the people before its final adoption.

[Mason Wade, The French Canadians, 1760-1967, Volume 1, 1760-1911
(Toronto: Macmillan of Canada, 1968), pp. 325-327]

George Brown:

Look, sir, at the map of the continent of America, and mark that island [Newfoundland] commanding the mouth of the noble river that almost cuts our continent in twain. Well, sir, that island is equal in extent to the kingdom of Portugal. Cross the straits to the main land, and you touch the hospitable shores of Nova Scotia, a country as large as the kingdom of Greece. Then mark the sister Province of New Brunswick—equal in extent to Denmark and Switzerland combined. Pass up the river St. Lawrence to Lower Canada—a country as large as France. Pass on to Upper Canada—twenty thousand square miles larger than Great Britain and Ireland put together. Cross over the continent to the shores of the Pacific, and you are in British Columbia, the land of golden promise,—equal in extent to the Austrian Empire. I speak not now of the vast Indian Territories that lie between—greater in extent than the whole soil of Russia—and that will ere long, I trust, be opened up to civilization under the auspices of the British American Confederation. Well, sir, the bold scheme in your hands is nothing less than to gather all these countries into one—to organize them all under one government, with the protection of the British flag, and in heartiest sympathy and affection with our fellow-subjects in the land that gave us birth. Our scheme is to establish a government that will seek to turn the tide of European emigration into this northern half of the American continent—that will strive to develop its great natural resources—and that will endeavour to maintain liberty, and justice, and Christianity throughout the land...We imagine not that such a structure can be built in a month or in a year. What we propose now is but to lay the foundations of the structure—to set in motion the governmental machinery that will one day, we trust, extend from the Atlantic to the Pacific... I say that no man who has a true regard for the well-being of Canada, can give a vote against this scheme, unless he is prepared to offer, in amendment, some better remedy for the evils and injustice that have so long threatened the peace of our country...Mr, Speaker, there are two views in which this scheme may be regarded, namely, the existing evils it will remedy and the new advantages it will secure for us as a people. Let us begin by examining its remedial provisions. First, then, it applies a complete and satisfactory remedy to the injustice of the existing system of parliamentary representation. The people of Upper Canada have bitterly complained that though they numbered four hundred thousand souls more than the population of Lower Canada, and though they have contributed three or four pounds to the general revenue for every pound contributed by the sister province, yet the Lower Canadians send to Parliament as many representatives as they do. Now, sir, the measure in your hands brings this injustice to an end;—it sweeps away the line of demarcation between the two sections on all matters common to the whole province; it gives representation according to numbers wherever found in the House of Assembly; and it provides a simple and convenient system for readjusting the representation after each decennial census...But, Mr Speaker, the second feature of this scheme as a remedial measure is, that it removes, to a large extent, the injustice of which Upper Canada has complained in financial matters. We in Upper Canada have complained that though we paid into the public treasury more than three-fourths of the whole revenue, we had less control over the system of taxation and the expenditure of the public moneys than the people of Lower Canada. Well, sir, the scheme in your hand remedies that. The absurd line of separation between the provinces is swept away for general matters; we are to have seventeen additional members in the house that holds the purse; and the taxpayers of the country, wherever they reside will have their just share of influence over revenue and expenditure. We have also complained that immense sums of public money have been systematically taken from the public chest for local purposes of Lower Canada, in which the people of Upper Canada had no interest whatever, though compelled to contribute three-fourths of the cash. Well, sir, this scheme remedies that. All local matters are to be banished from the General Legislature; local governments are to have control over local affairs, and if our friends in Lower Canada choose to be extravagant, they will have to bear the burden of it themselves.

...But, Mr. Speaker, there is another great evil in our existing system that this scheme remedies; it secures to the people of each province full control over the administration of their own internal affairs. We in Upper Canada have complained that the minority of our representatives, the party defeated at the polls of Upper Canada, have been, year after year, kept in office by Lower Canada votes, and that all the local patronage of our section has been dispersed by those who did not possess the confidence of the people. Well, sir, this scheme remedies that. The local patronage will be under local control, and the wishes of the majority in each section will be carried out in all local matters...Mr. Speaker, I am in favour of a union of the British American Colonies, first, because it will raise us from the attitude of a number of inconsiderable colonies into a great and powerful people. The united population of Canada, Nova Scotia, New Brunswick, Newfoundland and Prince Edward Island, is at this moment very close on four millions of souls. Now, there are in Europe forty-eight Sovereign States, and out of that number there are only eleven having a greater population than these colonies united...I am persuaded that this union will inspire new confidence in our stability, and exercise the most beneficial influence on all our affairs. I believe it will raise the value of our public securities, that it will draw capital to our shores, and secure the prosecution of all legitimate enterprises...But secondly, Mr. Speaker, I go heartily for the union, because it will throw down the barriers of trade and give us the control of a market of four millions of people...If a Canadian goes now to Nova Scotia or New Brunswick, or if a citizen of these provinces comes here, it is like going to a foreign country. The customs officer meets you at the frontier, arrests your progress, and levies his imposts on your effects. But the proposal now before us is to throw down all barriers between the provinces— to make a citizen of one, citizen of the whole; the proposal is, that our farmers and manufacturers and mechanics shall carry their wares unquestioned into every village of the Maritime Provinces; and that they shall with equal freedom bring their fish, and their coal, and their West India produce to our three millions of inhabitants. The proposal is, that the law courts, and the schools, and the professional and industrial walks of life, throughout all the provinces, shall be thrown equally open to us all.

But, thirdly, Mr. Speaker, I am in favor of a union of the provinces because— and I call the attention of the honorable gentlemen opposite to it—because it will make us the third maritime state of the world. When this union is accomplished, but two countries in the world will be superior in maritime influence to British America—and those are Great Britain and the United States...But, in the fourth place, Mr. Speaker, I go for a union of the provinces, because it will give anew start to immigration into our country. It will bring us out anew prominently before the world—it will turn earnest attention to our resources, and bring to our shores a stream of immigration greater, and of a better class, than we ever had before...But, fifthly, Mr. Speaker, I am in favor of a union of these provinces, because it will enable us to meet, without alarm, the abrogation of the American Reciprocity Treaty, in case the United States should insist on its abolition. I do not believe that the American Government is so insane as to repeal that treaty. But it is always well to be prepared for contingencies—and I have no hesitation in saying that if they do repeal it, should union of British America go on, a fresh outlet for our commerce will be opened up to us quite as advantageous as the American trade has ever been...But, sixthly, Mr. Speaker, I am in favor of the union of the provinces, because, in the event of war, it will enable all the colonies to defend themselves better, and give more efficient aid to the Empire, than they could do separately...it must be admitted—and there is no use of closing our eyes to the fact—that this question of defence has been placed, within the last two years, in a totally different position from what it ever occupied before. The time has come—it matters not what political party may be in power in England—when Britain will insist on a reconsideration of the military relations which a great colony, such as Canada, ought to hold to the Empire. And I am free to admit that it is a fair and just demand...I have no belief that the Americans have the slightest thought of attacking us...But, Mr. Speaker, there is no better mode of warding off war when it is threatened, than to be prepared for it if it comes. The Americans are now a warlike people. They have large armies, a powerful navy, an unlimited supply of warlike munitions, and the carnage of war has to them been stript of its horrors. The American side of our lines already bristles with works of defence, and unless we are willing to live at the mercy of our neighbors, we, too, must put our country in a state of efficient preparation. War or no war—the necessity of placing these provinces in a thorough state of defence can no longer be postponed...Never, I venture to assert, was any great measure too thoroughly understood, and so cordially endorsed by the people of Canada, as this moment now under consideration. The British Government approves of it—the Legislative Council approves of it—this House almost unanimously approves of it—the press of all parties approves of it—and though the scheme has already been directly submitted to fifty out of the one hundred constituencies into which Canada is divided, only four candidates ventured to appear at the hustings in opposition to it—all of them in Lower Canada—and but two of them were elected. And yet, sir, we are to be told that we are stealing a march upon the country; that it is not understood by the people; and that we must dissolve the House upon it, at a vast cost to the exchequer, and at the risk of allowing political partisanship to dash the fruit from our hands at the very moment we are about to grasp it!...An appeal to the people of Canada on this measure simply means postponement of the question for a year—and who can tell how changed ere then maybe the circumstances surrounding us? Sir, the man who strives for the postponement of this measure on any ground, is doing what he can to kill it almost as effectually as if he voted against it.

[J.M. Bliss, ed., Canadian History in Documents, 1763-1966 (Toronto: McGraw-Hill Ryerson Press Co, 1966), pp. 113-119]

The Press and the Debates

The Confederation discussion is growing woefully stale; not a new idea is to be coined and honorable gentlemen are doomed to talk to the clock and empty benches of the Legislative Chambers...In truth the question of the Union of the Provinces...is worn threadbare, and no one cares to listen to vain repetitions, worse and worse, presented as each fresh speaker brings the dead carcass of a worn-out argument to fill up the leaden periods he is endeavoring to make acceptable to an unwilling and wearied audience.

[Morning Chronicle (Quebec), 6 March 1865]

The House was in an unmistakeably seedy condition, having, as it was positively decided, eaten the saloon keeper clean out, drunk him entirely dry, and got all the fitful naps of sleep that the benches along the passages could be made to yield. For who cared at one, two, three, and four in the morning, to sit in the House, to hear the stale talk of Mr. Ferguson, of South Simcoe, or to listen even to the polished and pointed sentences of Mr. Huntingdon? Men with the strongest constitutions for Parliamentary twaddle were sick of the debate, and the great bulk of the members were scattered about the building, with an up-all-night, get-tight-in-the-morning air, impatient for the sound of the division bell. It rang at last, at quarter past four, and the jaded representatives of the people swarmed in to the discharge of the most important duty of all their lives. (4:30 am, main motion agreed to)

[Stratford Beacon, *17 March 1865*]

Section D

Disagreement from Nova Scotia and New Brunswick

The following documents point to the amount of dissension over Confederation in New Brunswick and Nova Scotia. The first was written by William Annand, a leader of the Nova Scotia opposition, politician, and proprietor of the influential (and anti-Confederate) Halifax paper, *Morning Chronicle*. Annand is writing to A.J. Smith, premier of New Brunswick and an opponent of union. The second document, written by Nova Scotia premier and Confederate supporter Charles Tupper, is a letter to Lord Henry Carnarvon, the British Secretary of State for Colonies.

Nova Scotia and New Brunswick: Nays and Ayes

William Annand to A.J. Smith, 20 March 1866

Halifax

My dear Smith;—

I have felt very anxious since the meeting of your Parliament, as to how you would come out of the fight, and whether you would be able to hold your ground against the enemy. We have not yet heard the result of the want of confidence motion, but I was glad to see a telegram from a member of your Government on Saturday last that the Administration would be sustained, and that you were safe for the present as regards Confederation. I had made up my mind, previous to the receipt of the telegram, to visit Fredericton with the view of conferring with you, and taking such steps as might be thought advisable in the interests of both Provinces. Like yourself, I desire no political Union with Canada, because I feel that the Maritime Provinces, in any scheme that may be matured, must be seriously injured by a connexion with a colony which must necessarily exercise a preponderating influence over all the others. But if, either through the exertions of the British Government, or change of opinion, or want of pluck on the part of the people of the seaboard Provinces, it may be necessary to deal practically with the Union question, then I want to be in a position to make the best possible bargain under the circumstances for my own country.

Now, as long as you can rely upon your own people, there will be no necessity to move here. Large as is the Government following in our Assembly, upon the Confederation question, they are powerless, and will so continue as long as New Brunswick maintains her present attitude. But it is right you should know that, however universal the feeling in the country, the majority in the House is not [to] be relied on should your Province back down. I find a growing feeling among members in favor of union of some sort, and a proposition for a new Convention from our side of the House would be eagerly seized on by some of the government supporters. Now, if we are to have a Union, let it be one that has some more redeeming features than the Quebec Scheme...

My chief object in now writing is to learn if you have an idea of proposing a new Convention, because, if that policy is to prevail in the maritime provinces I would like to be in a position to take the initiative in our Assembly...Let me know at your earliest convenience what your views are, and if necessary, telegraph on receipt of this. If we are to have a Union we must take care that it is a fair one, and this can only be done by Nova Scotia and New Brunswick acting cordially together. *Trusting that there may be no change in the* POLITICAL CONDITION *of these two Provinces for many a day [to] come,*

> I am,
> Yours sincerely,
> W. Annand.

Charles Tupper to Lord Henry Carnarvon, 28 July 1866

Sir,

At a convention held at Quebec in Oct. 1864 a plan for the Union of the B.N.A. Provinces since known as the Quebec Scheme was agreed upon by the delegates representing Canada, Nova Scotia, New Brunswick and Newfoundland and P.E. Island. This project as you are well aware was cordially approved by the British Government and obtained the sanction of the Legislature of Canada where an address to the crown was passed in the session of 1865 asking Her Majesty to obtain an act of the Imperial Parliament to give it effect. In New Brunswick an appeal to the people resulted in the defeat of Mr. Tilley's Government and the return of a large majority of the Assembly in opposition to the Union of the Provinces. In Nova Scotia it was found that a majority of the Assembly could not be induced to sanction the scheme and an issue upon the question was avoided during the session of 1865...

In Nova Scotia, Mr. Howe has organized an active and formidable opposition to the union of the Lower Provinces with Canada and although Messrs. Archibald and McCully who have been the leaders of that opposition to the present government have cooperated with us most earnestly and are sustained by the uncommitted group of that party, yet the great body of the opposition will unite with Mr. Howe to defeat confederation and obtain power. On the other hand the Government have rendered themselves and many of their supporters extremely unpopular by carrying a measure providing for the support of education by direct taxation. Many of the Bankers and most wealthy merchants who formerly sustained us under the impression that confederation will injure their position have transferred their support to Mr. Howe. The financial position of Nova Scotia is in the most flourishing condition and the opponents of confederation excite the masses of the people by the assertion that their taxes will be increased to sustain the extravagance of a Canadian Government and to defend the long line of exposed Canadian frontier while the best interests of the Maritime Provinces will be sacrificed by a Government in whose Legislature their influence will be overborne by numbers. Just at the time when the friends of confederation were endeavouring to meet these arguments Mr. Galt has proposed a Bill largely increasing the expenditure and the people of Nova Scotia are deeply annoyed at finding that the fisheries of the Maritime Provinces have been sacrificed by the adoption of the Canadian policy to issue fishing licences to foreigners. Able agitators thus effectively armed with the means of inflaming the popular mind against Canada are obtaining numerously signed petitions to the Imperial Parliament against confederation and there can be no doubt that an appeal to the people would result in the reversal of the resolution of the Legislature in favor of the Union and the defeat of the measure for many years. Indeed so strong is the feeling excited against Canada on the question by the fisheries that I have reason to fear that any delay in consummating the Union may involve the members of the Legislature by whose votes a majority was obtained to sanction the Union memorializing Her Majesty in opposition to any action being taken thereon until it has been submitted to the people.

C. Tupper

[P.B. Waite, The Life and Times of Confederation, 1864-67 *(Toronto: University of Toronto Press, 1962), p. 227]*

Imagining the Community: Dominion Day in Lunenburg

Monday July 1 1867

Dominion Day! This first day of July, in the year of our Lord, 1867, is the Birth Day of the Dominion of Canada. Nova Scotia has entered to day into a new state of things, having now entered into partnership, for ever, with New Brunswick, and the Canadas. The booming of the Cannon early this morning announced the Birth of the New Dominion, and the ringing of the Church Bells proclaimed the gladness. Shortly before Sunrise this morning the Volunteer Artillery company mustered and marched to the Gallows Hill where they fired a salute of 21 guns amidst the ringing of the Church Bells. At 10 o'clock there was service in the Episcopal Church, which was crowded. As many Union Jacks as could be obtained, floated in the breeze from different buildings in this town. At Midday the Artillery again mustered and marched with the Band at their head to the square in front of the Academy, where the High Sheriff, Kaulbach, read the Queen's Proclamation, immediately after another salute of 50 Guns was fired, the Children of the Academy who had previously assembled on the ground, sang the Queen's Anthem in good style, after which three hearty Cheers were given for Queen Victoria, and three more for the New Dominion the band finishing off with God save the Queen. A large concourse of people were assembled. During the greater part of the day the Band discoursed good music through the Streets. A general Holiday was made, all shops and places of business were closed, and every body seemed to enjoy themselves. At sunset another salute of 21 guns was fired which ended the programme for the day, and all wished Peace, Happiness and Prosperity to the Dominion of Canada.

[C.B. Fergusson, ed., The Diary of Adolphus Gaetz *(Public Archives of Nova Scotia, 1965), p. 70]*

Heart's Content Bay: Newfoundland: Arrival of Transatlantic Cable, 1866, Robert Dudley. *[Photograph courtesy of the Royal Ontario Museum, Canadian Collections © ROM]*

MOTHER BRITANNIA.—" See ! Why, the dear child can stand alone ! "
UNCLE SAM.—" Of course he can ! Let go of him Granny ; if he falls I'll catch him ! "

Child Canada Takes Her First Step. *[National Library of Canada, C50336]*

QUESTIONS

1. What were the arguments both for and against women's voting in 1828?

2. What do the excerpts from Adolphus Gaetz's diary tell us about the significance of political events in colonial communities?

3. What do the Quebec conference debates help us to understand about the support and the opposition to Confederation?

4. Compare and contrast the rhetoric used in the conference debates with the language used in the colonial press reports.

5. What, according to Annand and Tupper, were Nova Scotia's and New Brunswick's objections to Confederation by 1866?

READINGS

Benedict Anderson, *Imagined Communities: Reflections on the Origin and Spread of Nationalism* (London: Verso, 1991)

Murray Beck, *Joseph Howe, Volume II: The Briton Becomes Canadian, 1848-1873* (Montreal and Kingston: McGill-Queen's University Press, 1983)

Francis W.P. Bolger, *Prince Edward Island and Confederation, 1863-1873* (St. Dunstan's University Press, 1964)

J.M.S. Careless, *Brown of the Globe, Vols I & II* (Toronto: University of Toronto Press, 1959)

————————, ed., *The Pre-Confederation Premiers: Ontario Government Leaders, 1841-1867* (Toronto: University of Toronto Press, 1980)

Donald G. Creighton, *The Road to Confederation: The Emergence of Canada, 1863-1867* (Toronto: Macmillan, 1964)

————————————, *John A. Macdonald, Vols. I & II* (Toronto: Macmillan, 1965)

Ged Martin, ed., *The Causes of Canadian Confederation* (Fredericton: Acadiensis Press, 1990)

Jacques Monet, *The Last Cannon Shot: A Study of French-Canadian Nationalism, 1837-1850* (Toronto: University of Toronto Press, 1969)

W. L. Morton, *The Critical Years: The Union of British North America, 1853-1873* (Toronto: McClelland and Stewart, 1964)

S.J.R. Noel, *Politics of Newfoundland* (Toronto: University of Toronto Press, 1971)

Kenneth Pryke, *Nova Scotia and Confederation: 1864-1874* (Toronto: University of Toronto Press, 1979)

George Rawlyk, *The Atlantic Provinces and the Problem of Confederation* (St. John's: Breakwater Press, 1980)

Ian Ross Robertson, ed., *The Prince Edward Island Land Commission of 1860* (Fredericton: Acadiensis Press, 1988)

A.I. Silver, *The French-Canadian Idea of Confederation, 1864-1900* (Toronto: University of Toronto Press, 1982)

P.B. Waite, *The Life and Times of Confederation, 1864-67* (Toronto: University of Toronto Press, 1962)